Chicago Board Options Exchange

LaSalle at Van Buren, Chicago, Illinois 60605
312 786-7760

D1213831

THE BUSINESS ONE IRWIN GUIDE TO THE FUTURES MARKETS

THE BUSINESS ONE IRWIN GUIDE TO THE FUTURES MARKETS

Stanley Kroll
Michael J. Paulenoff

with special contributions by
Thomas E. Aspray
Dawn Diorio
Joanne M. Hill
Larry Hite
Steve Nison
Donald W. Westfall

BUSINESS ONE IRWIN
Homewood, Illinois 60430

Other Books by Stanley Kroll

The Professional Commodity Trader
Cruising the Inland Waterways of Europe
Kroll on Futures Trading Strategy

© STANLEY KROLL and MICHAEL J. PAULENOFF, 1993

All rights reserved. No part of this publication may be
reproduced, stored in a retrieval system, or transmitted,
in any form or by any means, electronic, mechanical,
photocopying, recording, or otherwise, without the prior
written permission of the publisher.

This publication is designed to provide accurate and
authoritative information in regard to the subject matter
covered. It is sold with the understanding that neither the
author nor the publisher is engaged in rendering legal, accounting,
or other professional service. If legal advice or other expert
assistance is required, the services of a competent
professional person should be sought.

From a Declaration of Principles jointly adopted by a Committee
of the American Bar Association and a Committee of Publishers.

Sponsoring editor: Amy Hollands
Project editor: Gladys True
Production manager: Diane Palmer
Jacket designer: Sam Concialdi
Designer: Jeanne M. Rivera
Production services: Elm Street Publishing Services, Inc.
Compositor: Carlisle Communications, Ltd.
Typeface: 11/13 Century Schoolbook
Printer: Book Press, Inc.

Library of Congress Cataloging-in-Publication Data

Kroll, Stanley.
    The Business One Irwin guide to the futures markets / Stanley
Kroll, Michael J. Paulenoff ; with special contributions by Thomas
E. Aspray . . . [et al.].
        p.   cm.
    Includes bibliographical references (p.   ) and index.
    ISBN 1-55623-625-5
    1. Futures. 2. Futures market. I. Paulenoff, Michael J.
II. Business One Irwin. III. Title.
HG6024.A3K75   1993
332.64'5—dc20   92–9465

Printed in the United States of America
    2   3   4   5   6   7   8   9   0   BP   9   8   7   6   5   4   3

To Joyce and Susan

A Book of Verses underneath the Bough,
A Jug of Wine, a Loaf of Bread—and Thou
Beside me singing in the Wilderness . . .
    (Edward FitzGerald, "The Rubaiyat of Omar Khayyam")

PREFACE

After cumulatively working for more than 50 years on Wall Street in futures research, trading, and brokerage, we amassed a sizable reservoir of knowledge about what people need to do to prepare themselves for a rewarding trading experience in the futures markets. For this book we have put that experience to use to explore the most salient topics involved in futures trading—from a history of the "contract" to sophisticated and esoteric trading techniques—all or parts of which we believe must be understood to succeed in the trading and hedging areas.

Novices as well as experienced and professional traders will be able to rely on this volume as a resource and continually refer to it for assistance in the markets. We have consulted a number of specialists who describe in detail the latest techniques employed in their respective fields of expertise.

Features of this book include:

- An evaluation of fundamental and technical methods of price analysis.
- A survey of a relatively new charting technique known as candlestick charting.
- A detailed, four-chapter section devoted to the computer in technical analysis.
- An examination of program trading.
- A detailed coverage of options on futures, including examples.
- A chapter written by the managing director of one of the world's largest futures fund management companies, Mint Investment Management.
- An entire chapter that discusses hedging strategies.

We have sought to provide our audience with a comprehensive text on the subject of futures trading, and it is our hope that this book will fill a void that may exist in the available literature on the subject. This work is also directed toward financial institutions and those who manage or are responsible for hedging or options strategies.

In addition to appealing to speculative and trade interests, one audience to which this book directs particular attention includes university and graduate school students who are interested in the expanding role and impact of futures trading in markets in the United States and abroad.

Finally, we have tried to portray as candidly as possible the problems that face anyone who tries to "beat the futures markets." It is our intention to discourage those who, by fortune or disposition, are ill-suited to the hazards of futures trading. At the same time, we expect the strategic portions of the book to be particularly helpful to all who trade futures, whether speculators, producers, or hedgers.

Stanley Kroll
Michael J. Paulenoff

ACKNOWLEDGMENTS

I must confess that, in the spring of 1989, when Stanley Kroll asked me to coauthor a book about the futures market, I had no idea how much time and effort would be required to complete the manuscript. Three years, two children, two homes, and many sleepless nights later, I am elated that the project is completed. Most important of all, I am proud to be associated with the finished product.

I cannot thank Stanley Kroll enough for continually believing in me and providing encouragement along the way.

In a similar regard, I would like to thank our personal editor, Merrell Feuer, who painstakingly edited and organized the manuscript prior to the Business One Irwin deadline.

My love and appreciation go out to my wife, Susan, and my children, Eric and Jennifer, who put up with me waking at 4:00 A.M. three times a week to work on the book.

I must express my most sincere thanks to Tom Aspray, without whom an entire section of this book would not exist.

I would like to thank Don Westfall, analyst *extraordinaire* at Abel, Daft & Earley, economic consultants, for devoting his valuable time to writing chapters 4 and 13.

Special thanks go out to Joanne M. Hill, Ph.D., vice president, Equity Derivatives Research, Goldman Sachs & Co., and her co-author, Dawn Diorio, vice president of Paine Webber's Derivative Products Research Group, for masterfully explaining the complicated topic of program trading in chapter 26.

In addition, I would like to express my gratitude to Larry Hite, managing director of Mint Investment Management, for sharing with us his unique trading philosophy and success story in chapter 28.

So, too, does Steve Nison deserve thanks for adding a new dimension to the technical price analysis section with his fascinating study of candlestick charting.

On the subject of charting, I would like to thank the following firms for permitting us to use their price charts in the text: FutureSource, a division of Oster Communications; Computrac, a Telerate Company; Commodity Research Bureau, a Knight-Ridder Financial Publishing Group; and the Industrial Metals Futures Department of Paine Webber, Inc.

Gratitude goes out to Amy Hollands, acquisitions editor at Business One Irwin, for her patience and guidance in helping us to put this project together.

Finally, I would like to thank my business partner at MJ Capital, Jason Katz, Esq., for his constructive critique of much of my work, and David McNamara, vice president of fixed income at Paine Webber, and Joanne McQuillan, vice president of Aubrey G. Lanston & Co., for their help and humor along the way.

M.J.P.

ABOUT THE
CONTRIBUTING AUTHORS

Thomas E. Aspray is the president and research director of Aspray, Parsons and McClintock Asset Management Corp. As a former biochemist, he has applied many of his scientific research techniques to the financial markets. Several of his methods of computerized trading analysis are now employed by various other professional analysts. He is also the publisher of the APM Forex Service.

Dawn Diorio is vice president in the Derivative Products Research Group at Paine Webber, Inc. She is responsible for handling various requests for the derivative sales and trading desks as well as the Structured Products Group. Prior to working at Paine Webber, Dawn was an analyst at Kidder Peabody. She received a B.S. in finance from St. John's University.

Joanne M. Hill is vice president, Equity Derivatives Research, at Goldman Sachs & Co. Prior to this position, she was managing director in charge of Paine Webber's Derivative Products Research Group. Her academic background includes a Ph.D. and M.B.A. in finance and quantitative methods from Syracuse University, an M.A. in international affairs from George Washington University, and a B.A. in international service from American University.

Larry Hite is founder and managing director of Mint Investment Management. He received a B.S. in motion pictures and television from New York University. After years in the entertainment field, Larry entered the futures business in 1970. In 1981, he founded Mint, now one of the most successful commodity fund management firms in the world.

Steve Nison is chartered market technician, vice president, and director of research at Nikkhah Group at Refco, Inc., in New York. He has an M.B.A. in finance and investments from Baruch College and has been analyzing the futures markets for 17 years. Steve has spoken before many professional organizations, appeared on television, and authored a book titled *Japanese Candlestick Charting Techniques*.

Donald W. Westfall is a vice president of Abel, Daft & Earley, an economic consulting firm in Alexandria, Virginia, that advises agribusiness and trade association clients on grain, oilseed, and sweetener markets. Educated at Bowdoin College and Georgetown University, he joined Washington-based Schnittker Associates in 1977 as a sugar analyst. After a two-and-a-half-year tour as director of marketing for the Maine Department of Agriculture, he returned to the Washington area in 1984 and joined Abel, Daft & Earley.

CONTENTS

LIST OF TABLES AND FIGURES

SECTION 1

HISTORY AND DEVELOPMENT OF FUTURES MARKETS

CHAPTER 1

THE HISTORY OF FUTURES MARKETS

Once the exclusive province of farmers, the agriculture industry, and a few outside speculators, commodity futures trading has, in recent years, undergone a revolution—in product proliferation and expansion and public awareness and participation. In the last two decades, futures trading has evolved into a sophisticated business of risk management and into a fast-paced arena of speculation that has adapted to the needs of a rapidly changing and highly technological world.

It was not always this way. Prior to the 1970s, agricultural commodities were linked with organized commerce for some 50 centuries. Active regulated markets in commodities existed in China, Egypt, Arabia, and India 12 centuries before the coming of Christendom. Laws were enacted to assure food supplies and to prevent manipulation in the city-states of Greece, which were occasionally beset by famines. The specialization of markets for trade in a single commodity was accomplished in pre-Christian Rome. According to Baer and Saxon,

> In the heyday of Roman dominion and power by land and sea there were in Rome nineteen . . . trading markets called "fora vendalia" (sales markets), which specialized in the distribution of specific commodities, many of them brought from the far corners of the earth by caravan and galley.[1]

---

[1] J. B. Baer and O. G. Saxon, *Commodity Exchanges and Futures Trading (New York: Harper & Brothers, 1947)*, p. 4.

Modern futures markets are offshoots of medieval European seasonal festivals, the most important of which took place in the county of Champagne, in central France. Typically, the locale of these fairs was the principal production or distribution center for each particular commodity. Although initially established as annual events, many of these bazaars evolved into important year-round markets, incorporating such features of present-day futures markets as self-regulation of business conduct, guarantee of contract fulfillment, and mutual trust among merchants.

As the volume of goods traded on these interregional markets expanded, the merchants became increasingly sophisticated and began to concentrate on particular specialized facets of marketing. The history of commerce reveals an early recognition by businessmen of the risks involved in owning goods and a continuing attempt to either reduce or transfer these risks to others. It has been reported that the ancient Chinese and Romans formed syndicates to pool risks and share profits. But it was not until the 16th century that the pooling of risks, that of marine loss in northern Italian commercial centers, was actually documented. During the latter part of that century, a great commercial insurance dynasty was founded in the British coffeehouse of Edward Lloyd.

The Industrial Revolution, beginning in the late 18th century, witnessed an extensive replacement of hand labor by machinery for the production and processing of goods. The time required for conversion of raw material into finished products was telescoped, and the demand for commodities multiplied. To supply this growing demand, an enormous volume of commodities poured into the channels of world trade. For example, British imports of raw cotton soared from an estimated 11 million pounds in 1785 to approximately 588 million pounds in 1850.

THE BEGINNING OF TO-ARRIVE TRADING

The profits of the world's merchants swelled, but frequent market debacles marred their good fortune. It became increasingly urgent that some workable means be found to reduce the price risks inherent in ownership of commodities. Such efforts took place in both the cotton and the grain trades around the beginning of the 19th century.

Buyers of cotton and grain, particularly those European merchants who imported these commodities from the United States, were exposed to price risks of ownership from the time their agents bought the raw commodities in North America until the goods were received and ultimately sold on the Continent. Typically, this involved a high-risk period of several months. In order to reduce this interval, a number of European importers arranged for their purchasing agents to forward details and samples, via fast clipper ships, while the goods themselves were being shipped aboard slower cargo vessels. So aided, these merchants began selling their goods on a "to-arrive" basis, while the goods were still afloat. Such contracts were arranged for the to-arrive delivery of specified lots of wheat as early as 1821. Liverpool developed one of the earliest organized to-arrive markets. When the volume of trading expanded sufficiently to attract speculators and full-time brokers in "arrival" contracts, an outdoor trading place was established on an area adjoining the site of the present Liverpool Cotton Exchange Building.

In 1866, the first transatlantic cable came into service. A Liverpool cotton importer, John Rew, conceived of a way to limit price risks by arranging for his American correspondents to immediately report their purchases for him by cable. He then sold to-arrive contracts in equal quantities on the theory that, if prices declined, he could offset his "actuals" losses through a gain on the short to-arrive sale. Within a brief time, other importers imitated this practice, and there soon developed a thriving volume of trading in to-arrive contracts. This practice became known as **hedging,** a term still commonly used today.[2]

Discussing the development of modern futures trading in the cotton industry, Lamar Fleming of Anderson Clayton stated:

> Originally, the Liverpool "to-arrive" contracts named a specific vessel. As the usefulness developed of trading for deliveries more remote than those of a vessel currently loading or afloat, the original contract was revised to provide for sailing within a specified

---

[2] Hedging is discussed in detail in Section 7.

month. As the use became more general of steam cargo vessels, trading began in contracts for delivery in New York or in Liverpool in a specified month. Then the contracts came to be known as "futures" contracts instead of "to-arrive" contracts.

Use of futures contracts became so extensive that adequate contract forms and rules and provisions for adjudication of the differences and enforcement of contracts had to be worked out. In 1868 the New York Board of Cotton Brokers was organized, with a fixed set of rules and regulations for trading for future delivery. In 1870, 106 merchants and brokers organized the New York Cotton Exchange and rented trading rooms.[3]

TO-ARRIVE TRADING IN THE UNITED STATES

Coincidental with the introduction of to-arrive trading in Liverpool, grain trading evolved in the United States on a to-arrive-Chicago basis. In his book, Edward J. Dies vividly recalls the development of Chicago as the major grain center of the time:

> Like the finger of destiny, the historic pilgrimage of pioneers pointed ever Westward, straggling onward in unending lines. "Caravans of Faith" they were called as they joggled along Illinois and into Iowa. Theirs was a profound faith, the faith of the dreamer striking out for the land of his dreams.
>
> The acreage which the pioneers planted to grain continued widening each year. They shipped their grain to Chicago, then an ugly little town cuddled on the shore of the lake. Part of the money received in return was quickly converted into farm implements. These implements meant larger production. Subsequently, the stream of grain that poured into Chicago bulged the sides of the little town and made necessary almost constant expansion of marketing and storing facilities.[4]

In the early 1850s the volume of grain shipped into Chicago was so heavy that many streets became completely congested with

---

[3] Lamar Fleming, Jr., Chairman of the Board, Anderson Clayton and Company, in addressing a symposium sponsored by the New York Commodity Exchanges, in New York, November 7, 1961.

[4] Edward J. Dies, *The Wheat Pit (Chicago; Argyle Press, 1925), p. 10.*

produce-laden wagons. The existing cash markets were inadequate to handle the vast influx. With most merchants overstocked and banks unable to finance additional inventory expansion, farmers were forced to sell for whatever prices they could get. Prices of grain plummeted, and many farmers lost not only their grain but their teams and wagons as well.

To avoid the recurrence of such widespread distress selling, the more enterprising and farsighted grain producers began to offer contracts to deliver a specified quantity of grain at a designated place within a given number of days. This marked the introduction of to-arrive marketing in the United States and stimulated the development of the Board of Trade of the City of Chicago. The Chicago Board of Trade, as it is commonly called, was officially established in 1848, but it did not function as an organized futures exchange until 1865.

The development of trading in to-arrive contracts in the United States represented a major advance in the field of marketing, providing elements of flexibility not present in earlier cash markets. Forward sales could be made on the basis of samples, or even on description of goods by reputable merchants. Delivery time could be extended over a period of months, although actual title of ownership was transferred at the time that the to-arrive agreement was executed. Thus was introduced the concept of a negotiable title to goods, which could be traded back and forth many times prior to settlement via delivery. For example, in August 1856, during a period of rising prices and speculation occasioned by the Crimean War (1854–56), it was reported that a single parcel of 15,000 bushels of corn passed through 14 different hands during a two-day period, ultimately settling time contracts amounting to approximately 200,000 bushels.

The pattern of rising prices and speculation in commodity markets that developed during the Crimean War was duplicated on a much larger scale during and shortly after the Civil War. In this period of greatly expanded world commerce, weaknesses of the to-arrive system of marketing became evident. Through the to-arrive contract, the burden of price risk was successfully shifted from the commodities seller (the farmer and producer) to the buyer (the processor, manufacturer, and importer). This latter group was forced to seek higher profit margins as compensation for their additional price risks. However, marketing competition exerted pressure on profit margins as well as on the price spread between producer and consumer. Moreover, after assuming the risks of ownership, trade firms frequently found themselves unable to arrange sufficient bank loans on their unhedged inventory. This, in turn, inhibited the expansion and development of the commodities industry.

It was obvious that the risk of price fluctuation in ownership of commodities had to be transferred once more. But to whom? There existed, at that time, just a limited number of speculators willing to trade in to-arrive contracts. What the commodity markets needed was a much larger speculative following to provide the breadth and liquidity that was lacking.

To-arrive shipments varied in grade and quantity. Unfortunately, the to-arrive contract, the sole medium of commodity speculation, contained too many variable factors to attract sufficient nontrade speculative capital. A speculator not closely connected with a particular commodity could rarely determine in advance exactly what goods were involved in any given transaction. Prices were frequently established through secret "deals," with large operators enjoying price advantages over small traders. The nontrade speculator was unable to ascertain the price of his goods at any given time. In addition, terms of payment were subject to individual bargaining and, as such, varied.

The lack of an effective mechanism to enforce contract compliance was another serious weakness in to-arrive trading. A speculator had no guarantee that the other party to a transaction would fulfill his contractual obligation, particularly if a substantial settlement was involved. Also, there was no assurance that the goods, upon delivery, would be in acceptable condition and of the prescribed grade and quantity.

These impediments to the expansion of commodity markets were recognized. Specific measures were taken to improve both the exchanges and the contracts, and to encourage large-scale speculative participation. Thus, the modern futures contract and organized futures exchanges were developed, replacing the earlier to-arrive system of marketing.

CHANGES IN THE SYSTEM

During the past century, the futures contract and the operations of the commodity futures exchanges have been greatly refined. The basic elements of futures trading have been standardized to meet the requirements of both trade firms and speculators. With the exception of some financial futures such as stock indices, a futures contract specifies the quantity, the grades deliverable, and the delivery location. A standard contract grade is specified, with a schedule of premiums and discounts established to provide for delivery of other approved grades. In order to be eligible for delivery, the actual commodity must have been inspected to ensure that it meets the contract quality standards, and it must have been stored in an approved storage facility.

Trading may be conducted only during prescribed hours, on specified licensed exchange, and between exchange members. Prices must be established openly by public outcry through bids and offers, and payment in full must be made at the time of delivery.

Commission firms and commodity solicitors who handle customers' orders and who solicit business must be qualified and registered. Each major futures exchange operates in conjunction with a clearinghouse, which simplifies clearing and settlement of transactions and ensures contract compliance.

Those refinements set the stage for a new period of change in the arena of commodities. Nonagricultural raw materials like plywood and copper had already been added to the roster of traded commodities by 1970, when a period of dramatic destabilization—characterized by unprecedented inflation and high interest rates—created the need for a different breed of price-discovery and risk-management instruments. The first of those instruments to be adopted by the futures markets was money itself.

Modern currency values and a system of international payments were established during a meeting of industrialized Western nations held at Bretton Woods, New Hampshire, in 1944. At the core of that system was the U.S. dollar, valued then in terms of $35 per troy ounce of gold. Amid periodic modifications, the agreement functioned well for more than two decades. However, changing world economic and political conditions, and changes in perceptions of the value of the dollar, eventually rendered the system created at the agreement at Bretton Woods insufficient to satisfy the growing needs of the international trade community.

During the 1960s, the United States entered a period of aggressive spending for its "Great Society" social programs and for the Vietnam War. Efforts to finance those campaigns altered perceptions of the efficacy of the U.S. government, perceptions that eventually caused the first devaluation of the dollar, in 1971. Shortly afterward, signatories of the original Bretton Woods agreement decided to permit considerably greater fluctuations between foreign currencies.

Advocates of the futures markets quickly realized that the techniques of commodity trading could be applied to free-floating currency markets, largely because the potential for frequent fluctuations created identical needs for price determination and risk transfer. The International Monetary Market (IMM), opened in Chicago in 1972, created the first centralized market for currency futures trading. Included were contracts based on the currencies of the world's major industrialized nations, such as the British pound, the West German Deutsche mark, the Japanese yen, the Swiss franc, and the French franc. The popularity of these currencies rapidly spread among financial institutions that had never before seen the need or justification for futures trading. Foreign and domestic banks, foreign exchange brokers, corporations, and a variety of other institutional and public investors with foreign currency exposure helped push total annual volume in currency futures trading to nearly 28 million contracts by the end of 1991.

Concurrent with the end of dollar-based currency agreements, restrictions imposed in 1934 on private ownership of gold by U.S. citizens were reevaluated and ultimately lifted on December 31, 1974. Trading in gold futures commenced in December also and gained widespread acceptance among consumers and a large audience of speculators. Gold was the most actively traded nonagricultural futures contract by 1978, and remained so through 1981.

The successful creation of the currency futures paved the way for the development of a broad spectrum of nontraditional commodity instruments that came to be known as financial futures. If there had been any doubts about the applicability of "paper" instruments to futures trading, they were eliminated after 1972 by the experience of trading in the currency futures markets.

Just as international trade and foreign exchange risks created the need for currency futures, turmoil in international relations and political instability created the need for interest rate futures.

Energy prices, like interest rates, had never been particularly volatile before the Organization of Petroleum Exporting Countries (OPEC) imposed its embargo on oil shipments to the United States in 1973 and 1974. The impact could hardly have been more dramatic. Americans who were accustomed to gasoline prices of less than 50 cents per gallon watched prices double in a matter of months. Skyrocketing fuel costs were passed from manufacturers to consumers and end-product users, creating an inflationary spiral that permeated every sector of the country's economy.

The uncertainty inherent in the energy crisis of the early 1970s converted most business decisions into a guessing game based on assumptions about the rapidly escalating cost of raw materials as well as the cost of borrowed money. Raw material risks could be hedged on the futures markets; interest rates could not. Enter financial futures with a mechanism for refining financial management in a climate of economic uncertainty.

THE BIRTH OF FINANCIAL FUTURES

In 1975, the Chicago Board of Trade introduced the first interest rate instrument—a contract in Government National Mortgage Association futures (GNMAs). Two years later, with economic volatility showing no sign of easing, trading began in U.S. Treasury bond futures. That contract proved to be one of the most popular ever developed, taking the lead (in terms of volume traded) from the traditional front-runners, corn and soybeans, by mid-1981.

Inadvertently, the utility of the young financial futures industry was magnified beyond previously imagined proportions by actions taken by the Federal Reserve in 1979. Through its monetary implementation arm, the Fed Open Market Committee, and under the direction of its chairman, Paul Volcker, the Fed elected to make a direct attempt to control the money supply by targeting bank reserves rather than through curbs on the Fed funds rate.

An examination of interest rate fluctuations during 1979–80 illustrates the impact the Fed policy shift had on the cost of money. To begin with, the prime rate changed 29 times between July 1979 and May 1980. Treasury-note yields went from 10 percent just before the policy shift in October 1979, to just below 11 percent in November, down to 10 1/4 percent in December, up to 13 1/8 percent in February 1980, all the way down to 9 1/2 percent in June, and up once again to 15 3/4 percent in October before slipping back to 13 1/4 percent in mid-November 1980. Certificates of deposit (CDs) yielded 13 percent in January 1980, 18 percent in April, 8 percent in May, and 20 percent in mid-December.

Any financial institutions that did not yet consider the credit markets volatile enough to require hedging soon reassessed their thinking on the subject. In fact, with the acceptance of financial futures, a whole new group of participants ventured into futures trading. Any business, institution, or government agency whose affairs involved financing could find some measure of stability in interest rate hedges. Many of those customers were already involved in the cash markets on which these new contracts were based. Futures, however, offered the increased liquidity lent by speculative participation, which was lacking in the cash markets.

Futures trading volume continued to grow from less than 15 million contracts in 1971 to 263 million by the end of 1991. The futures industry matched the growth pace of the markets with efforts to design new financial contracts tailored to the needs of their new hedge customers.

In 1982, stock index futures and exchange-listed options attracted insurance companies and pension funds into futures trading despite regulatory uncertainties and the traditional disinterest of those industries. Hedging with stock index futures was considered within the bounds of the "prudent man" guidelines of institutional investing, which facilitated greater use of an instrument that promised to outstrip the growth of all other commodity sectors in its first year of operation. In 1983, combined volume of the Standard & Poor's (S&P) 500 and the New York Stock Exchange (NYSE) composite indices was approximately 719,000 contracts. Treasury-bond futures, which posted the largest gains among contracts in existence one year earlier, showed volume of 355,000 contracts.

Stock index futures also carried the potential for a ripple effect on futures trading as a whole. By 1989, the combined volume of contracts traded on the S&P 500, NYSE composite index, and the Major Market index had expanded to over 13 million. It was expected that equities investors attracted to futures for the first time by stock index contracts would take their newfound enthusiasm into other markets as well, breaking through the traditional reluctance of yet another group of new customers to trade futures.

Stock index futures contracts were blessed with an unusually fast start due to a long-awaited rally in underlying stock markets just after their introduction. Independent of that rally, rapid acceptance was predicted by industry observers who forecast that the marriage of leverage, liquidity, and profit potential from futures markets with the breadth and familiarity of stock markets would prove quite attractive to speculators. Traditional equities investors were already conversant with the underlying cash indices on which each contract was based. Furthermore, settlement in cash eliminated the common speculative fear of having to take delivery of, for example, a truckload of pork bellies. From the hedger's point of view, plans to introduce trading in subindices such as the New York Stock Exchange's transportation index promised to match hedging opportunities more closely to the needs of portfolio managers.

Exchange-listed options received a less enthusiastic reception. Customer confusion and lack of familiarity, as well as internal difficulties faced by brokerage houses attempting to juggle an unprecedented number of new financial products, impeded their immediate success. Lurking in the background was a long history of trading scandals and brokerage house failures that gave options trading a tarnished reputation.

One of the biggest options controversies involved an attempt by "Doc" Crawford to corner the Chicago wheat futures contract in 1933, which led to a ban on trading options on many agricultural commodities. Later cases involved the loss of $70 million in customer funds in 1973 and another $12 million in 1977. The following year, Congress turned aside efforts to expand options trading pending development of effective regulations.

By 1982, amid a new atmosphere of acceptance for innovative financial instruments, options remained an untapped medium for hedgers and speculators who were attracted to them because of limited liability. Since options carried the right—rather than the obligation—to buy or sell the underlying futures contract and limited the risk to just the initial investment, more conservative investors such as pension funds and smaller participants were expected to view them with special interest. COMEX (Commodity Exchange, Inc.) captured that feeling with a promotional slogan that referred to its gold options contract as "gold for the not so bold."

Under a three-year pilot program marked by strict controls, trading in options on exchange-listed futures was approved by the Commodity Futures Trading Commission (CFTC) in 1982. The CFTC, created by Congress in 1974, was, like the Securities and Exchange Commission (SEC), an independent federal board, charged with tightening the regulations of what had grown to be a $500 billion industry. Its options program was approved after five years of study and delay. An important factor in the timing of its decision was a plan by the SEC to proceed with an options program of its own.

Regulatory overlaps like the one involving options trading illustrate the blurred distinctions between equities and futures. The question of jurisdiction of options regulation led to extensive negotiations between then CFTC chairman Philip Johnson and then SEC chairman John Shad. The Johnson–Shad agreement gave the CFTC authority over all futures contracts, as well as options on futures. The SEC retained the power to regulate options on debt instruments. Governance of foreign currency trading was to be determined by the exchange on which those contracts were traded.

New products, their flexibility, and the speculative and institutional interest they generated brought legitimacy to futures trading on Wall Street. A 1975 SEC decision to deregulate stock commissions may have further fed the enthusiasm of large brokerage houses suddenly facing the prospect of intense competition for customer commission dollars. With the advent of more sophisticated contracts came a new era of professionalism. Some of the revenue realized by formerly overlooked commodity departments found its way back into their research divisions, where computers introduced extensive possibilities for price projections and deeper study of trading strategies. Mathematicians and economists became commonplace in departments dominated through the early years of the industry by unsophisticated traders.

For those with the inclination and the funds to speculate, but lacking the willingness or ability to make their own trading decisions, futures funds were formed. Virtually unknown in 1974, they attracted more than $500 million from investors by 1983 and $20 billion by the end of 1991.

Trading venues also became more varied. Link-ups between exchanges in New York, Chicago, and Singapore extended the trading day in compatible contracts to, for example, 15 hours in currency futures. During U.S. trading hours (between 8:20 A.M. and 3:00 P.M. Eastern Standard Time), speculators and hedgers could initiate new positions or protect existing ones; then between 7:15 P.M. and 4:05 A.M. Eastern Time they could "pass along" the orders from the close of the IMM in Chicago to the Singapore International Money Exchange (SIMEX). Contracts traded on the IMM can be offset with those on the SIMEX, and vice versa. Finally, traders and institutions with high net worth and strong credit lines can protect their positions overnight (24 hours a day, in fact) by trading in the "cash" currency and precious metals interbank markets. If need be, they can convert the cash positions into futures contracts during IMM and COMEX trading hours the following day.

As increasing amounts of money entered the futures markets in the late 1980s, and as volatility increased (partly due to the influence of overnight trading by Far East investors), 24-hour trading became vital to all market participants.

The proliferation of futures trading even extended the roles played by previously disinterested market participants. Once banks, savings and loan associations, and insurance companies overcame their reluctance to trade futures, they formed service

Interbank Trading: 24 Hours

desks to trade futures for themselves and their customers as part of a movement toward the creation of "financial supermarkets."

Certainly, the incentive to hedge and speculate did not diminish during the years after double-digit inflation and high interest rates. Risk management has been equally important in the disinflationary years since 1982, especially with respect to widespread use of stock index futures in institutional program trading.

The modern futures market has evolved into a complex mechanism that has created new dimensions of risk management for an interrelated political and financial world in constant change. The futures markets have gone far beyond the original goal of facilitating agricultural commodity hedges. They continue to provide the most basic functions while satisfying a multitude of modern needs in the business and financial community.

CHAPTER 2

THE COMMODITY FUTURES CONTRACT

How is it that the futures markets function so efficiently, providing an instant liquid market for both buyer and seller? The answer lies in the unique nature of the futures contract, and in the operation of the supporting institutions of the futures exchange and the clearinghouse.

ESSENTIALS OF THE FUTURES CONTRACT

A **futures contract** is a legal instrument that binds both the buyer (the holder of a "long" position) and the seller (the holder of a "short" position) to the fulfillment of certain obligations. The buyer, barring an offsetting transaction in which the long commitment is closed out (sold), must accept delivery of the cash commodity when tendered, sometime during the delivery month for the respective future. The seller, unless he has previously closed out (bought) his short position, must deliver the cash commodity sometime during the delivery month for the respective future. *Delivery is at the option of the holder of the short position* with respect to the date of delivery (at any time during the delivery period), the particular grade of the cash good, and the place of delivery (subject to limitations and conditions specified by the respective exchange).

A standard grade is established for each commodity future, which usually conforms to the most important grade of each commodity traded in the cash market (see Table 2.1). This standard grade is deliverable against the futures contract at "deliv-

TABLE 2.1
Standard Contract Grade (as of 1/91)

Commodity	Grades
Corn	No. 2 yellow corn
Cotton	U.S. upland cotton, strict low middling 1 1/16 inch
Treasury Bonds	Long-term U.S. Treasury bonds, not callable for at least 15 years
Gold	100 troy ounces, minimum 995 fineness
Sugar	Cane sugar growths of Argentina, Brazil, and other countries, delivered f.o.b. and stowed in bulk on receiver's vessel
Soybeans	No. 2 yellow soybeans

TABLE 2.2
Tenderable Grades of Soybean (as of 1/91)

Grade	Differential
No. 2 yellow soybeans (max. 14% moisture)	Contract price
No. 1 yellow soybeans (max. 13% moisture)	3¢/bu *over* contract price
No. 3 yellow soybeans (max. 14% moisture)	8¢/bu *under* contract price

ery price" (the price existing at the time of delivery), with cash settlement of the price difference from the original contract.

To promote a broad and equitable market, however, other grades of the cash commodity may be delivered at specified premiums to, or discounts from, "delivery price," as illustrated in Tables 2.2 and 2.3 with respect to soybeans and coffee.

Traditional, nonfinancial futures contracts have been standardized to ensure equity for both buyer and seller. Standardized items carry contract size, basic contract grade deliverable at contract (delivery) price, other tenderable grades plus their respective premiums and discounts, and approved "spot" depositories and delivery locations. Only the price at which the trade

TABLE 2.3
Tenderable Grades of Coffee (as of 1/91)

Grade	Differential
Arabica Coffees from: Brazil, Mexico, El Salvador, Guatemala, Costa Rica, Nicaragua, Kenya, Tanzania, Uganda, New Guinea	Basis (no premium)
Honduras	−1¢/lb (discount)
India	−3¢/lb (discount)
Peru	−4¢/lb (discount)
Ethiopia	−6¢/lb (discount)
Colombia	+2¢/lb (premium)

was executed, the delivery month, and the names of the buying and selling clearing firms distinguish the individual futures contracts.

Some financial futures contracts, such as Eurodollars and stock indices, use cash settlements instead of the traditional delivery procedures. Immediately after expiration of the futures contract (the day following the last trading day), the exchange offsets any remaining (open) futures positions by using a formula involving the underlying cash index (i.e., the S&P 500 cash index is used to offset the S&P futures). Instead of facilitating the delivery of a standardized "good" such as soybeans, the exchange calculates the differential between the final futures contract price and the underlying cash index price, and then facilitates the exchange of cash in the form of either a credit to or a debit from the respective client's futures account.

Commodity futures have a life span of between 9 and 23 months.

TRADING UNITS

Each futures exchange establishes a standard contract size, called a **unit of trading,** for each of its commodities. For example, a cocoa contract consists of 10 metric tons, a contract of silver consists of 5,000 troy ounces on New York's Commodity Exchange, and a contract of S&P 500 stock index futures consists of $500 times the value of the underlying S&P 500 cash stock index.

At times, an exchange will alter the size of one of its contracts if the change will better serve the interests of all parties. For example, in January 1988, the Chicago Mercantile Exchange (CME) enlarged its British pound contract from £25,000 to £62,500 to bring specifications into line with and make it competitive with the larger Deutsche mark, Swiss franc, and Japanese yen contracts traded on the IMM.

Maximum Daily Price Fluctuations

Some futures exchanges also specify maximum daily price limits on trading. No trade may be executed at more than a specified number of cents or points above or below the official close of the previous session or, in some markets, not more than a specified number of cents or points above the low or below the high for that day's trading session. Once the limit has been reached, trading may continue only at or within the prescribed limit. (See Table 2.4.)

Trading limits were established to lessen the possibility of particularly violent short-term price fluctuations by providing overnight "cooling off" periods. During these periods, when appropriate (and independently from the exchanges), commission houses often raise margins and/or issue overnight margin calls

TABLE 2.4
Maximum Price Fluctuations (advance or decline from previous close)

Trading Unit	Contract Size	Fluctuation
Copper	25,000 lb	Limits abolished in 1987
Pork Bellies	40,000 lb	2¢/lb = $800
British Pound	62,500 pound sterling	No limits
Bond Futures	$100,000 face value	3 points = 96/32
Wheat	5,000 bu	20¢/bu = $1,000
Coffee	37,500 lb	6¢/lb = $2,250

to protect themselves and their clients from adverse and extreme price movements. In the event of extreme price changes, the cash markets, which operate without any maximum price limits, and the London markets can serve as an escape or safety valve that enables traders to position themselves beneficially or extricate themselves from their futures contracts.

Some futures exchanges suspend trading limits for an expiring contract during all or part of the delivery period (approximately three weeks), allowing the nearest future to more accurately reflect the supply and demand conditions existing in the cash market.

TRADING MONTHS

Only certain months are traded in each future. Every exchange establishes the trading months for its contracts, choosing those months in which trade interests have the greatest need to hedge. Because this varies from one industry to another, there exists no uniformity in the active trading months of different commodities (see Table 2.5).

Futures trading in Chicago wheat, for example, is actively conducted in March, May, July, September, and December. July is the first month of the new crop of winter wheat, and the July future provides a hedging medium for purchases of cash wheat. The new crop of spring wheat comes to market around September and can be hedged in that delivery month. The December future facilitates hedging against grain stored during the three or four months that navigation is closed or hampered because of frozen Midwestern waterways. The March future represents the midpoint between heavy winter storage and heavy spring consumption and marketing, while the May future can reflect either old or new crop fundamentals, depending upon which is more dominant during a particular year.

Conducting trading in specific months also tends to concentrate the entire trading volume in a half dozen or so futures contracts, which results in a more broadly traded market. This captures the interest of both speculators and hedgers.

TABLE 2.5
Most Active Trading Months for Selected Futures

Soybeans	January, March, May, July, August
Bonds	March, June, September, December
Gold	February, April, June, August, October, December
British Pound	March, June, September, December

CRITERIA FOR DEVELOPMENT OF A FUTURES CONTRACT

Why is futures trading limited to certain markets? Although futures trading has been attempted in many commodities, there are reasons why it is successful in cocoa, silver, grains, and Swiss francs while there are no major organized futures markets for such goods as tea, tobacco, and steel.

A number of conditions are required for the successful launching of a futures contract. First and foremost, the supply and demand factors should not be dominated by just a few concentrated interests. A broad, orderly, and continuous free cash market must exist. Sulfur, for example, would not be suitable for futures trading because the world's supply is controlled by a few large producers. A second requirement is the trade's cooperation in establishing and then using a futures exchange for the purpose of hedging. Until the OPEC oil embargo in 1973 triggered substantial industrial (and speculative) interest in the potential use of petroleum futures to offset increased risk, the development of an oil futures contract was doomed to failure because of the reluctance of leading producers to participate in futures trading.

A major stimulus to trade hedging is a relatively stable relationship between the cash and futures markets. This relationship is most consistent when both the cash and the futures are in the same basic form. As a traditional commodity moves from the raw to the finished state, the price relationship between the two tends to deteriorate—as, for example, between cotton grower and shirt manufacturer—which renders hedging more complicated and less effective.

Hedging is also facilitated when the commodity is generally produced in surplus, with at least a moderate carryover remaining at the conclusion of each production year. If a commodity were in such short supply that producers could be assured of selling their entire production each year, then their risk of ownership and, by definition, the need for hedging, would be reduced.

Another important prerequisite for futures trading is that the commodity be clearly classifiable as to grade and quality and that this classification be uniform throughout the industry. This means that any two bushels of No. 2 yellow corn must be, at all times, interchangeable. One reason futures trading is not conducted in tea, for example, is the extreme difficulty in defining and classifying its diverse grades and qualities.

Finally, a commodity should be reasonably storable. Generally, the more perishable the good, the less stable its ownership, which greatly increases the risks of dealing in the item. Most fresh fruits and vegetables are considered too perishable for exchange futures trading. When the citrus industry sought a hedging market for domestic orange production, it developed an exchange contract (now traded on the Cotton Exchange) in frozen concentrate orange juice (FCOJ), rather than one based on a particular type of fresh orange.

CHAPTER 3

FUTURES EXCHANGES IN ACTION

Having examined the futures contract, we now turn our attention to the venue in which it is traded. Futures exchanges have varying by-laws and specialties, but their universal function remains that of bringing buyer and seller together within a regulated setting and, in conjunction with their associated clearinghouses, guaranteeing that the traded contracts are consummated.

THE CHICAGO BOARD OF TRADE

> To maintain a commercial exchange; to promote uniformity in the customs and usages of merchants; to inculcate principles of justice and equity in trade; to facilitate the speedy adjustment of business disputes; to acquire and disseminate valuable commercial and economic information; and generally to secure to its members the benefits of cooperation in the furtherance of their legitimate pursuits.

With this statement of purpose, the preamble to the Rules and Regulations of the Board of Trade of the City of Chicago was adopted in 1848 by its 82 founding merchants. In terms of this statement, little has changed since its adoption nearly 150 years ago. The preamble has helped to guide the operations and development of one of the most important exchanges in the world, where trading in futures contracts and futures options contracts is conducted daily in wheat, corn, oats, soybeans and bean products, financial (interest rate) instruments, stock indices, and metals. Today, the Chicago Board of Trade constitutes the world's largest futures and futures options market, which includes a successful evening session (Sunday through Thursday) in T-bond futures that began in April 1987.

Organization of the Chicago Board of Trade

As the world's oldest futures and options exchange, the Chicago Board of Trade accounts for some 49 percent of all such trade in the United States. It accounts for more than 90 percent of all trading in agricultural futures and options and more than 75 percent of all trading in interest rate futures and options. In addition, the Chicago Board of Trade's volume accounts for more than 50 percent of all the options on futures traded in the United States.

As mentioned in Chapter 1, the Chicago Board of Trade is a designated contract market regulated by the Commodity Futures Trading Commission, which was created by Congress in 1974. The exchange is a not-for-profit association consisting of 1,402 full members, 725 associate members, and approximately 1,400 membership interest holders who have limited trading privileges.

The exchange does not engage in buying or selling futures or options. Its primary function is to conduct a public marketing institution, which provides facilities for producers, money managers, merchants, manufacturers, and speculators or their designated agents to gather in a free, auction-type market to trade futures and options. The prices discovered by transactions in the exchange's trading pits reflect the balance of supply and demand around the world.

Membership is a personal privilege and carries with it ethical and pecuniary responsibilities. Applicants must be at least 21 years of age and of acceptable moral and financial character. Prospective members must be approved by the exchange. The applicant must find a current member who is willing to sell his or her membership at a mutually agreeable price, before or after approval of the membership application.

The Chicago Board of Trade is self-governing, with a chairman and vice chairman elected each January. A 24-person board of directors, including three nonmember directors, sets policy and guides the management of the exchange. Directors serve for three years, with approximately one-third of them elected each January. These officials receive a fee for their services. Operational and administrative control of the exchange is vested in a management team consisting of the president, an executive vice president, a vice president/treasurer, a vice president/secretary, 14 other vice presidents, and a general counsel, each responsible for a particular area of the operation. Forty member committees are responsible for the many phases of exchange activity, overseeing the work of approximately 675 paid staff in 32 different departments.

The exchange's primary sources of income are transaction fees, revenue from the sale of quotations, and real estate rentals (the exchange leases office space). Other income-producing sources are membership dues and charges for services.

Facilities of the Chicago Board of Trade for use by members include the following:

- The **Economic Analysis and Planning Department,** which designs new futures contracts to meet the needs of market participants and monitors existing contracts for necessary revisions as markets change.
- The **Education and Marketing Service Department,** which plans and implements marketing and educational programs ranging from the promotion of new and existing contracts to communicating principles and strategies used in the marketplace.
- The **Office of Investigations and Audits,** which monitors market activity and member adherence to the exchange's Rules and Regulations and financial requirements.
- The **Communications Department,** which uses news releases, feature articles, telephone contacts, audiovisual materials, news conferences, and a variety of special projects and publications to disseminate information about the exchange worldwide.
- The **Market Information Department,** which acts as the official information clearinghouse and the source for

current price quotes, daily price moves, delivery sched-
ules, volume records, cash sales, and other statistical information compiled by the exchange.

- The **Floor Operations Department,** which constantly
records the changing prices in each pit on the floor and
transmits them to a central quotations computer for near-
instantaneous flashing on quotation boards on the trading
floors around the world.

- The **Washington, European, and Asian offices,** which
serve as liaisons for the exchange in the nation's capital
and throughout the world.

At the heart of the Chicago Board of Trade are the exchange's
two trading floors, which are vast rooms that stand three stories
high. The newest floor, completed in 1982 as part of a 23-story
annex to the 45-story 1930 landmark Board of Trade building,
has 32,000 square feet. The old trading floor has 19,000 square
feet. A third floor serves the Mid-America Commodity Exchange,
an affiliate of the Chicago Board of Trade since 1986.

Futures trading involves contracts for future delivery that
are entered into verbally and confirmed later between two members of the exchange, either for their own accounts or as agents
for others. As discussed earlier, *a futures contract is an agreement to buy or sell a commodity of a standardized amount and
standardized minimum grade, during a specific month, under
terms and conditions established by the exchange, at a price established in the trading pit.* In the cash market, all terms of a
contract are negotiable and are determined by the individual
buyers and sellers for immediate or future delivery of the commodity.

TRADING IN THE "PITS"

Futures trading is conducted in areas on the exchange floor
called **pits.** Each pit consists of a large, raised octagonal platform with ascending steps on the outside and descending steps
on the inside. There is a pit for each commodity traded. Traders
generally position themselves on steps in each pit according to

the month in which they are trading. Brokers trading the **flash,** or nearest delivery month, stand in a section beginning on the top step, with a clear view of telephones and price reporters, while those trading in later deliveries stand in other designated areas. Buyers and sellers stand side-by-side, as each member may buy or sell at any given moment.

Futures trading on the exchanges is done directly among members. All **bids** (solicitations to buy) and **offers** (offers to sell) are stated aloud by public outcry so that any trader in the pit can take the opposite side of any trade. The pits are usually extremely active and noisy during trading hours, when as many as several hundred brokers strive feverishly to buy and sell.

To effectively communicate with other pit brokers, floor traders simultaneously make use of a system of simple and efficient hand and finger signals (see Figure 3.1), in addition to shouting their bids and offers as required by exchange regulations. A trader with his palm facing inward wishes to buy. Conversely, a trader with his palm facing outward wants to sell. Each finger held vertically indicates quantity. Fingers extended horizontally express the price at which the trader wants to buy or sell.

Traders are aware of the current price, constantly updated on the price boards on the trading floor. The minimum price movement for each contract is referred to as a **tick.** Traders' signals indicate the number of contracts involved, and, in the case of the financial futures, prices are quoted according to the specifications of the individual contract. For example, U.S. Treasury bond futures are quoted in percentages of the $100,000 of the contract, with each percentage point broken into 32 32s (that is, 32 $\frac{1}{32}$s, or 32 equal parts). Hand signals in the bond pit reflect the purchase and sale of long-term Treasuries in terms of thirty-seconds.

There is no central auctioneer. Each trader plays that role individually, which may give the impression to the outside observer that floor trading is chaotic. However, this system, evolved and perfected over the history of the exchange, provides the fairest, most efficient markets to users.

Each trader is required to record all trades, either on his personal trading card or on brokerage order forms. Information included on the forms includes the commodity involved, the

FIGURE 3.1
Traders' Hand and Finger Signals

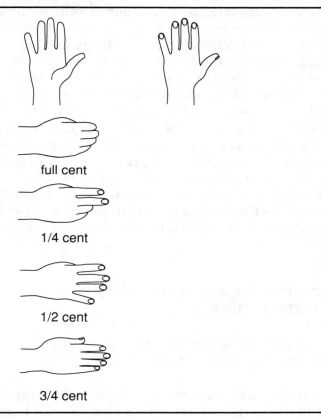

full cent

1/4 cent

1/2 cent

3/4 cent

quantity involved, the delivery month, the price, the number of the opposite trader's clearing firm and his trading acronym, and the letter indicating the half-hour period in which the trade occurred.

Above each pit is a raised platform from which two or more **exchange quotation reporters** constantly observe the changing price picture. As trades are made at prices differing from the preceding trade, a reporter records and time-stamps the new price and transmits it electronically to the central quotation computers. Central quotation then transmits the price information to electronic price boards facing the trading floor and around the world to thousands of offices via phone and satellite link-ups.

These quotations are transmitted as quickly as possible, but are always fractionally behind the actual market in the pit.

To accommodate the thousands of calls coming from trade houses and brokerage firms daily, batteries of telephone stations strategically surround each pit on the exchange floor. Typically, the large institutional and speculative orders flow to the booths closest to the actual trading ring. The close proximity of these phone stations to the pit enables the phone clerks to save precious time by using hand signals to communicate large buy and sell orders to the floor brokers. Smaller orders—typically from commission house speculators—may be phoned to desks farther from the actual trading pit. Located out of range of visual signals, the phone clerk must write the order on a piece of paper and hand it to a messenger who then carries it to the broker in the pit. Once the trade is executed, the messenger reports back to the phone clerk, who then calls the client with the details of the fill.

ENTERING, EXECUTING, AND REPORTING FUTURES ORDERS

The Chicago Board of Trade: Anatomy of a Transaction

Many people are quite surprised to learn how rapidly a market order to buy or sell futures can be executed and reported back to the customer. The procedure for receiving, transmitting, executing, and reporting futures orders has been so refined that, under normal market conditions, the entire operation can and should be completed within a matter of minutes. Let's examine a typical transaction on the floor of the Chicago Board of Trade. Except for some minor details, the procedure outlined could involve either a hedging or a speculative transaction on any of the major futures exchanges.

Mr. Smith, a futures speculator located in New York City, maintains a speculative trading account with a large commission house, which is a clearing member of the Chicago Board of Trade. Mr. Smith has been closely following the bond market.

On the basis of his fundamental analysis of the economy of the United States, consisting of weak economic data reported by various government agencies, a slowdown in his own business sales, and a growing sense that consumer confidence continues to wane, Mr. Smith has grown increasingly convinced that interest rates must fall further if the economy is to avoid a serious recession. In other words, he is **bullish** on the bonds (bond prices rise, interest rates decline).

To gauge his entry into bond futures, Mr. Smith relies on his futures charts, which provide him with a "bird's-eye view" of the price action during the past six months. Although bond prices have climbed sharply since September–October 1990, Mr. Smith projects additional strength and would like to buy March bonds at around 95-16 (quoted in 32s) in preparation for an advance to the 100.00 area in the weeks to follow. On such a **position** Mr. Smith intends to place a stop-loss order at 94-16, representing a risk of 32/32s, or $1,000 per contract.

Although the price of March bonds has been running about 10/32s above his preferred entry price, Mr. Smith has noticed that prices have eased in the past three sessions, and that slightly lower levels could be reached in the upcoming hours. Upon telephoning his account executive and inquiring, "How are March bonds?" Mr. Smith is informed that March bonds are trading at 95-24 and that the market is relatively quiet. Mr. Smith instructs his account executive to phone him if March bonds trade at or below 95-18 before the trading day ends. About 45 minutes later, Mr. Smith receives a phone call from his account executive, who informs him that the bond market is under a bit of pressure due to the news that the latest monthly data indicates the 1991 federal budget will be slightly larger than either Wall Street or the government had expected. The account executive tells Mr. Smith that immediately after the information was released, March bonds **sold-off** from 95-24 to 95-17. Mr. Smith checks his charts and concludes that the small price decline in response to this relatively minor economic report likely represents a buying opportunity. Mr. Smith instructs his account executive to "buy five March bonds at the market."

The account executive handling Mr. Smith's account immediately writes up an order to "buy five March bonds at the market," on a special order ticket, noting Mr. Smith's account number and name. He then immediately time-stamps the order and picks up the phone as he presses the speed dial number for the bond pit at the Chicago Board of Trade.

Amid constant background trading noise, the phone clerk adjacent to the bond pit answers in a loud voice, "Hello, bonds." The account executive quickly repeats Mr. Smith's order to "buy five March bonds at the market for account 428-15879," at which time the account executive stamps the order ticket a second time to record the exact time the order was placed. The phone clerk then time-stamps the order on his end and says to the account executive, "Order number 681, hold the phone," as he turns to whistle or shout to attract the attention of the pit broker, to whom he then hand-signals the trade instructions.

The pit broker, upon receiving the order to buy March bonds, turns into the bond "crowd." The last trade was 95-17. With a market order in hand, the broker shouts out, "Seventeen for five," simultaneously signalling the bid with his hand. A nearby broker with orders to sell March bonds gestures to the broker and shouts, "Sold!" In that brief instant, the pit broker, acting as Mr. Smith's agent, has purchased five contracts of March bonds for the account and risk of Mr. Smith.

The quotation reporter, in the pulpit adjacent to and above the bond pit, notes the transaction. Meanwhile, both the buying and selling brokers note their respective trades on trading cards, one side of which designates **bought** and the other, **sold.** Any trade that has been **carded** shows the commodity, the number of contracts involved, the delivery month, the price, the name of the clearing firm with whom the trade was made, and the initials of the other pit broker. These trading cards constitute the original record of each transaction and become an essential part of clearing records in the offices of the buying and selling firms. Even before the trade is verbally checked between the two brokers who executed the order, Mr. Smith's pit broker flashes news of the completed transaction back to the phone clerk, who time-stamps the order. The clerk then tells the account executive that he's "filled," meaning that he purchased five March bonds at 95-17.

At some point before the end of the trading session, the pit broker's trading card is matched against Mr. Smith's office copy of the order as a double check in the clearing process. Once the trade is checked, the commission house inputs the trade on its in-house computer system, which enters the particulars of the transaction in Mr. Smith's futures account.

The account executive time-stamps the order ticket, for the third and final time, to note the moment when the fill was received and then tells Mr. Smith, who has remained on the phone, the price at which the March bonds were purchased. Mr. Smith then instructs the account executive to enter his stop-loss order to sell five March bonds at 94-17 stop, and also to call his office in 30 minutes for a progress report on the new long position.

Mr. Smith's entire transaction has taken 70 seconds.

The Coffee, Sugar, and Cocoa Exchange: Anatomy of a Commercial Transaction

Mr. Brown is president of XYZ Corporation, a large international sugar dealer headquartered in New York City. The XYZ Corporation is known in the trade as an **operator,** a company whose business involves the purchase of raw cane sugar (primarily from Western Hemisphere producers) and the subsequent resale of these sugars to overseas consuming interests.

Let us say that during the first half of October, XYZ purchases one cargo (12,000 metric tons) of raw cane sugar from Brazil. XYZ would like to resell this sugar, on a profitable basis, as quickly as possible. (The sugar is kept in storage in Brazil and shipped from there directly to the home port of the buyer.) Through its overseas agents, XYZ offers these Brazilian raws to consuming interests in European centers.

Using the world sugar price of approximately 10 cents per pound, the 12,000 metric ton cargo represents a commitment of $2,645,112. For XYZ Corporation, this entails both a considerable cash outlay, and the risk of substantial loss should the prevailing price decline before the sugar is sold. Since XYZ often has several sugar cargos in various stages of purchase and sale, its total investment and risk is considerable. In fact, XYZ, as a prudent business concern, will typically finance (borrow money using its sugar inventory as collateral) a major portion of its inventory, and also hedge (or "lay off") its market risk because of price fluctuations. Actually, even though XYZ is a well-capitalized, experienced international sugar dealer with an excellent record of sales and earnings, its bankers insist that the bulk of its sugar inventory be hedged or sold ahead as a condition for large-scale inventory financing.

As it turns out, XYZ is unable to immediately resell this sugar to its regular customers. Nevertheless, because of the workings of the Coffee, Sugar, and Cocoa Exchange (CSCE), XYZ is not denied the opportunity to hedge at a profitable price basis. By hedging its inventory position on the futures market, XYZ will be setting its sales basis on the position, and will ultimately have the option of resolving its short futures hedge position in any of the following ways:

- It may deliver this cargo, or some other cargo of sugar, against its short futures position.
- It may sell this cargo to one of its regular customers, simultaneously covering (buying in) its short futures position.
- It may, when its short futures position becomes due, switch (roll forward) its hedge by covering the existing short futures position and simultaneously selling another, more distant, futures position.
- It may sell the cargo to another buyer, and the sugar will be priced at the average price, which the buyer of the raw sugar purchases an equivalent quantity of futures contracts for the account of the original seller (XYZ, in this case).
- It may arrange for an A.A. (against actuals) trade wherein the seller and buyer swap futures positions in return for the sale of the actuals.

At the moment, however, XYZ's problem is to get the position hedged. To accomplish this, Mr. Brown, using a direct telephone line from his desk to his broker's booth on the floor of the CSCE, queries the broker's clerk concerning the market.

The clerk advises Mr. Brown that the market is fairly firm, with some commission house buying underlying the current price activity. This is just the type of market situation into which Mr. Brown would like to sell his inventory (he certainly does not want to sell into a weak or declining market). Mr. Brown asks the clerk for a price quote and range on March sugar (No. 11 world sugar). The quote comes back at 998 (9.98 cents per pound) bid, 999 offered, with the day's high and low for the session thus far at 1001 and 979, respectively.

Mr. Brown gives the phone clerk a verbal order to sell 240 contracts (equal to 12,000 metric tons) of March sugar for 998 (or better, of course). When the phone clerk on the exchange floor receives the verbal sell order, he writes it up on a sell ticket, indicating the number of contracts, the month, and the price limit. He then time-stamps the order and immediately turns to hand-signal the order to his floor broker for execution in the pit.

With the order in hand, the broker quickly assesses the market, noting that March is still quoted at 998 bid. Three brokers, with a total of 22 contracts, are bidding 998.

(At this juncture, we shall simulate the broker's ring trading, presenting both his actual **trading voice** and his **sotto voice,** which represents his thoughts.)

> **(Sotto voice)**   This market has been probing the 1000 resistance area for 40 minutes now, and feels tired—better hit those bids.
>
> **(Trading voice)**   Sold! Sold! Sold!
>
> **(Sotto voice)**   A total of 22 lots sold—no more wanted at this price—and bids at 998 are small. The market is very thin right here, and here come other offers at 998. Better get what I can right away at 998.
>
> **(Trading voice)**   Sold those six at 98! Sold those two!
>
> **(Sotto voice)**   Only eight lots at 998—no real demand here—I'd better relay the weak tone to the client.

At this point, the broker motions to the clerk that he has sold a total of 30 lots at 998, and that the market is taking on a softer tone. The phone clerk relays the information to Mr. Brown, who has been following the action on his desktop computer terminal. Based on his need to hedge, and on his perception that the 1000 level is impenetrable at the current time, Mr.

Brown is a bit anxious to sell the entire 240 lot position sooner rather than later. With that in mind, he cancels the order to sell the remaining 210 lots at 998, and tells his broker to offer them at 994 (or better).

> **(Sotto voice)**   Two brokers bidding 95 on a total of 30, I'd better hit those immediately.
>
> **(Trading voice)**   Sold! Sold!
>
> **(Sotto voice)**   Across the ring, 94 bid for 15, go for it.
>
> **(Trading voice)**   Sold you 15 at 94.

With 75 lots sold, and another 165 to go, the broker once again relays the pit conditions to the clerk, who, in turn, tells Mr. Brown that the ring has gone 93-bid for about 20 lots. Furthermore, his suspicion is that sell-stop orders are bunched together in the vicinity of a key chart support point at 968, which, if hit, will pressure the market quickly down to the 940 support level.

Mr. Brown decides that he had better sell the bulk of the remaining contracts at the market, lest he risk selling at a much lower price than he wanted to originally. He tells his broker to sell the remainder of position "at the market, broker not held."

Mr. Brown's broker, who is on the phone with Mr. Brown and the floor simultaneously, immediately conveys the new instructions to the phone clerk that the pit broker should use his judgment to unload the remaining 165 lots as close to the current price as possible. The clerk then signals to the pit broker to "go to the market on the remaining 165 lots of March sugar."

> **(Sotto voice)**   Let's see what, if anything, is still available at 993.
>
> **(Trading voice)**   Sell 20 March at 93!
>
> **(Sotto voice)**   Only 12 lots now bid at 93, no real demand here. Better get rolling in a hurry before competitive selling takes the market away from us.
>
> **(Trading voice)**   Sold you 12 at 993! Sell 50 more at 993! At 91, okay, done—sold you 50 at 91. Sell 100 at 91! No? Forty at even? Sold! Sold you 40 lots at 90. Sell 50 more, right? No—30 at 88? Done! Sold you 30 at 988.

(Sotto voice) The last 70 lots I sold brought in much heavier offers. The sell side is picking up momentum. Additional sellers are offering the market lower. Bids have fallen to 885. Let's clean up the rest of this position now!

(Trading voice) Sell 33 March! Ten at 84, okay, sold! Sell 23! At 79, done, sold you a total of 23 March at 79!

Summarizing this transaction, the XYZ Corporation has just hedged 240 lots (12,000 metric tons) of raw cane sugar as follows (in cents per pound):

30 lots @ 9.98
30 lots @ 9.95
15 lots @ 9.94
12 lots @ 9.93
50 lots @ 9.91
40 lots @ 9.90
30 lots @ 9.88
10 lots @ 9.84
23 lots @ 9.79

Floor trading, however, represents just one aspect of the total transaction. From the moment that the floor broker reports the trades to Mr. Brown and to the clearing firm that clears XYZ's trades (all trades must be cleared by a member of the exchange, who is a member of the Coffee, Sugar, and Cocoa Exchange Clearing Association, Inc.), the floor broker is responsible for the fulfillment of those contracts. After the market closes, the floor broker or his clerk writes up brokerage slips giving the names of the clearing firm buyers of these contracts, the quantity sold, the month, and the respective prices to XYZ's clearing firm (the seller).

After the close, the clerks submit their respective purchase/sales slips directly to a member of the clearing association, who will, later in that day, match up the contracts and clear them. In case certain contracts do not match properly, the traders involved will correct the errors on the following day. At this point, the responsibility of the floor brokers to their respective principals ceases. The responsibility, at this juncture, now exists solely between the respective clearing firms. Each clearing firm will then receive from the clearing association a copy of its purchase/ sales slips, a recapitulation of open positions and other relevant matters, as well as a draft or check for margins required or variation margin payable or receivable. In this fashion, the clearing association substitutes itself as the buyer to the selling clearing firm, and as the seller to the buying firm.

SECTION 2

REGULATION OF FUTURES MARKETS

CHAPTER 4

GOVERNMENT INTERVENTION IN COMMODITY TRADE AND FUTURES MARKETS

Donald W. Westfall
Vice President, Abel, Daft & Earley

Anthropologists and economists may debate whether markets—the exchange of goods for other goods, for services, or for money—predate the type of human association we identify today as "government." More certain, however, is that the large-scale commodity trade and organized futures markets we see today exist at the sufferance *of* governments. In this century, government involvement in futures markets and commodity trade ranges from the total control exercised by many developing country marketing boards to the comparative freedom of such regions as the European Community, Japan, and the United States.

Governments are involved in markets in two distinct ways. The first is market intervention, operating programs that affect supply or demand for traded commodities. This includes agricultural price support programs, consumption subsidies (i.e., artificially low prices), surplus removal, strategic stockpiles, and so forth. The other role of government involvement is as a regulator of the trading mechanism itself. This is accomplished through oversight of markets to assure that the system operates fairly.

Enthusiasm for both sorts of involvement waxes and wanes depending on the most recent or memorable experience. This is where politics enters the picture. Fortunately, fashion in economic theory and regulatory practice is beyond the scope of this discussion. Nevertheless, it may be worth noting that a dichotomy exists. World trade seems set on a path toward greater liberalization and less control of domestic production and overall economic activity. On the other hand, in the United States at least, market volatility in the past few years seems to have sparked a resurgence of interest in more tightly regulated financial markets of all types.

One should not underestimate the influence technological change has on the need or desire for government involvement in futures markets. Recent concern about insider trading in the stock market may make consumers wary about computer-assisted trading because of the distance the new system imposes between individuals and the traditional free and open outcry method. Whether traders are virtuous or governments wise in their attempts to enforce virtue is not our concern. What we must be attentive to is how intervention and regulation may influence the play of market forces.

GOVERNMENT SUPPORT FOR AGRICULTURE

Government involvement in agriculture has a long and well-documented history. In the United States, agricultural programs may focus on maintaining or stabilizing supplies by supporting prices or providing direct support for farmers' incomes. Other efforts may focus on controlling supplies by limiting acreage. Assistance is also provided through a group of programs that concentrate on the international arena, either by stimulating exports, limiting imports, or attempting to eliminate or reduce trade barriers. In the following section, we will provide an overview of each of these approaches and the programs employed to achieve the government's goals.

The reader should keep in mind that this is a broad sampling of U. S. government agricultural programs. Even a simple list of the many activities the U.S. Department of Agriculture (USDA) undertakes to influence commodity markets could run several pages. Our objective is to describe those that have the greatest influence. With time, the relative importance of some may shift, as the policy objectives of Congress and different administrations adjust to changes in market conditions. Thus, the concept of parity prices, once the foundation of agricultural policy, is outmoded today, whereas those such as triple base or set-asides are ascendent. We will confine the scope of this discussion to programs that directly affect commodities traded in futures markets.

Price Supports

Since 1938, the Commodity Credit Corporation (CCC), a branch of the USDA, has been making loans to farmers who use their crops as collateral. The loan, plus interest and storage costs, is usually repayable within a specified period, usually 9 to 12 months. Depending on market conditions at the time the loan matures, the farmer may either redeem the loan or forfeit the collateral to the CCC. Since the CCC has no recourse but to accept the commodity as payment, these are frequently referred to as **nonrecourse loans.**

Loan programs are currently in effect for wheat, corn and feed grains, soybeans, cotton, and sugar. Each program establishes a floor under the price of the respective commodity because once the price approaches the loan rate, the government is a willing buyer of all commodities under loan. (Sugar is something of a special case, since the USDA has been encouraged by Congress not to acquire sugar. Therefore, an import quota is used to restrict supply and keep prices high enough to discourage forfeitures.)

Loan programs have two principal objectives. The first is **price stabilization.** When prices are high, the CCC is able to release stocks. Conversely, when prices are low, acquisitions through forfeitures will support the market. A secondary objective achieved by extending credit to farmers at the beginning of the season is the **reduction of harvest pressure on prices and more-orderly marketing arrangements.**

While largely successful at achieving these ends, the loan rate mechanism has proven to be an imperfect tool for influencing market prices. If loan rates are set consistently above equilibrium prices, as in the early 1980s, they can stimulate excess production and large forfeitures to the CCC. The same forces may also cut exports if the domestic price remains above the market-clearing international price. The result is the accumulation of large government-held reserves. The loan rate reductions included in the 1985 farm bill reflect an attempt to deal with this problem. Further adjustments in the 1990 farm legislation address imbalances among the loan rates for commodities that may provide incentives to grow certain crops and not others.

Income Support Programs

The principal form of income support for U.S. farmers is the **deficiency payment,** which covers the difference between an established income objective (the target price) and the loan rate or market price, whichever is higher. **Target prices** were introduced in the early 1970s as a replacement for the parity price concept, which became increasingly irrelevant as a price support mechanism. Target prices were to be set in relation to the cost of production and yield for each commodity. However, establishing a workable formula has been a difficult task. By the late 1970s and early 1980s, it proved politically difficult to adjust target prices downward to reflect the strong upward trend in yields, resulting in powerful incentives to overproduce. Disposal of the large stocks this generated raised government costs and ultimately provided the impetus for reduced target prices for most commodities in the 1985 and 1990 farm bills.

A modification to the loan program adopted in the 1985 farm bill is the so-called marketing loan. This nonrecourse loan is actually an income support program because the loan is made at one rate but repayment is permitted at a lower level. For cotton and rice, the only two commodities with marketing loan programs in effect, the lower repayment rate is the world price. In effect, the difference between the loan rate and the repayment level acts as an export subsidy and dampens the tendency of the U.S. loan program to limit exports in times of oversupply. By the same token, the cost to the government of such a program can be excessive if the volume of loans redeemed at the lower level is large and the spread between the loan rate and the world price is high.

Just as incomes can be supported by government programs, they can also be limited by others. Typically, payment limitations establish a maximum deficiency payment a person may receive while participating in government farm programs. Payment limitations have been a politically popular way to appear to limit government budget exposure from farm programs and to avoid the transfer of large sums to only a few individual farmers. However, the incentives created by a wide gap between target prices and loan rates or market prices resulted in a certain amount of "gaming" of the regulations, as producers looked for loopholes such as subdividing farms or creating ownership networks to maximize payments. The large number of farmers affected by payment limitations was partly responsible for the popularity of the marketing loan concept under which the limit on the subsidy below the regular loan rate was removed.

Supply Controls

One of the most effective tools the government has to support prices or lower outlays in the short run (either objective or both may be important at any given time) lies in the power to restrict supply. A number of options, which can be used individually or in various combinations, are at the disposal of the USDA. At any one time, a farmer's decisions on what and where to produce may be affected by a wide range of supply-controlling policies. The most important devices fall under the general heading of **Acreage Reduction Programs (ARPs).** These may also be referred to as **set-asides** or **diversion programs.** An ARP usually requires that the producer idle a share of acreage in order to receive other program benefits such as price support loans or deficiency payments. Alternatively, producers may be induced to participate in a set-aside with the offer of diversion payments. The amount of acreage to be idled is calculated by multiplying the set-aside percentage by the producing unit's base acreage (an amount determined by the farm's production history).

Although a diversion program can cut production sharply for a brief period, it has the side effect of pushing producers out of the price support program. If enough farmers fail to participate, either because of payment limitations or expectations of market prices high enough to offset the disadvantages of nonparticipation, ARP effectiveness is compromised. These programs are also politically sensitive, as they are frequent targets for the criticism that farmers are being paid not to farm. It has also proven rather difficult to estimate the impact of an ARP when a large amount of acreage is in production. This is because most of the acreage reduction is likely to come on the least productive land and producers will tend to farm the remaining acreage more intensely. Finally, traditional ARPs, with their focus on base acreage, limit a farmer's flexibility to respond to changes in relative prices of competing crops.

Another type of supply control involves allocating production or access to markets with marketing quotas and acreage allotments. Both devices were used extensively in the 1950s and 1960s but have fallen from favor because they tend to raise prices and may result in surpluses of other commodities planted in non-quota acreage. The 1990 farm bill continues the use of marketing quotas for peanuts and tobacco and has a stand-by provision for marketing allotments for sugar in the event that imports are reduced to a minimum level of 1.25 million short tons.

Long-term idling of land for conservation purposes is also a form of supply control. These efforts are trained on highly erodible land or endangered wetlands. Marginally productive land is usually enrolled in land retirement programs. The duration of the commitment may vary but is usually at least 10 years, again greatly reducing a farmer's ability to respond to changing market circumstances. These programs may also be used to support the price of agricultural land by reducing supply in certain key areas.

International Trade Programs

To the extent that U.S. agriculture is exposed to the forces of the world market, either as exporter or competitor for a share of the domestic market, programs and policies designed to affect the way markets function will influence prices for commodities traded in futures markets. The types of programs most likely to play a role in community pricing are those that stimulate exports through various forms of assistance (some of which may extend to outright subsidization), protection of domestic markets through use of quotas or tariffs, and participation in multilateral and bilateral trade arrangements designed to reduce impediments to trade or to provide preferential treatment for select countries.

The USDA has considerable latitude under the terms of the 1985 and 1990 omnibus farm legislation to use commodities or cash as incentives to expand, preserve, or recover lost export markets. The Targeted Export Assistance (TEA) Program and the Export Enhancement Program (EEP) provide cash and CCC commodities, respectively, to increase U.S. competitiveness in overseas markets. Aggressive use of CCC commodities to subsidize exports under the EEP has had a significant effect on commodity markets, particularly for wheat and feed grains. The EEP is seen by the USDA and the U.S. Trade Representative (USTR) as an integral part of the U.S. negotiating strategy to reduce trade-distorting practices of the European Community. In addition to direct export subsidies, there is a range of indirect credit subsidies available to U.S. exporters or importers of U.S.-produced commodities. These include the GSM-102/103 short- and intermediate-term guarantee programs.

For the most part, the United States is an exporter of the major agricultural commodities traded on futures markets. As a result, tariffs and quotas play a minor role in establishing prices. There are, however, two important exceptions. Quotas on sugar and beef are important factors in the markets for those commodities. For sugar in particular, a quota can exert a significant influence on both the thinly traded domestic market (NY No. 14) and the world market (NY No. 11). A large import quota may depress the domestic market and buoy the world price, or a small allocation can push U.S. prices higher and add supplies to the world market, thereby depressing values.

A complex group of mechanisms for resolving trade disputes is also available to protect domestic industries from unfair foreign competition in U.S. markets. Under the joint authority of the executive branch and the independent International Trade Commission (ITC), investigations are carried out to determine whether any imports are damaging to or likely to damage domestic industries. In the past few years, ITC countervailing duty and dumping investigations have dealt with pork, durum wheat, sugar, and several other traded commodities.

Since 1947, the rules of international trade have been established in a multilateral forum called the General Agreement on Tariffs and Trade (GATT). The principal objectives of the GATT have been to codify the rules of international trade and to reduce barriers to trade. Negotiations have reduced tariffs on a wide range of agricultural and manufactured products. The most recent set of negotiations began in 1985 in Punte del Este, Uruguay, and is called the Uruguay Round. A principal goal of the United States and many other major agricultural trading countries is to reduce the degree of government interference in commodity markets, particularly on the part of the European Community. The EC's Common Agricultural Policy protects its internal markets from competition while simultaneously generating surplus commodities that are exported to the world market, sometimes with heavy subsidies. The United States also enters into bilateral agreements such as the U.S.-Canada Free Trade Agreement. In addition, the United States offers preferential access to U.S. markets for some countries under the Generalized System of Preferences and the Caribbean Basin Initiative.

Policy Trends

The 1985 farm bill employed several provisions that, because of their attractiveness, resulted in a sharp reduction in plantings of major crops and record participation by farmers in crop programs. By 1987, government payments were equivalent to 31 percent of net cash income. By 1990, however, they were down to about 16 percent.

The 1985 farm bill encouraged record farmer participation in commodity programs. For example, participation rates for wheat and corn reached 88 and 91 percent, respectively, in the 1987–88 crop year. In line with the reduced importance of government payments in net cash farm income, they have declined somewhat since then. Nevertheless, rates are still high relative to the longer-term historic participation of 60–70 percent for wheat and 40–50 percent for corn.

The 1985 farm bill also cut land use for crop production significantly. In 1981, the last year there were no set-aside requirements, farmers planted 370 million acres. In the following years, excluding 1983, when there was a massive one-year land idling (the Payment-in-Kind, or PIK, Program), plantings of major crops declined gradually to 314 million acres by 1987 and idle land increased to 76 million acres. Since then, there has been a small increase in total plantings and a corresponding decline in idle acreage. The increase over 1981 in total planted and idle area reflects the fact that portions of the acres idled are "phantom" land—little more than a measurement problem related to the overlap in government programs and the imperfect computation of base acres for program crops. It is important to remember that these phantom acres will not be available for production if land set-asides are reduced.

The 1990 farm bill is similar to the 1985 act in many ways. There are still provisions to restrict plantings through use of ARPs; target prices used to calculate payments have been frozen at the 1990 level; and loan rates will be based on a percentage of average prices received by farmers during the past five years, excluding the high and low years (as a result, loan rates should remain below market prices in most years). In other respects, the 1990 bill represents a watershed in U.S. farm policy by limiting the entitlement nature of commodity payments and by allowing directly and indirectly for greater flexibility among crops. These changes came about because of the severe budget pressures to limit outlays on commodity programs.

Congress dealt with the budget crisis in agriculture by adopting what is called a triple base or payment acres approach to limiting outlays on commodity programs. Under this system, producers receive payments on only part of their permitted plantings of program crops (crop base less acreage idling requirements). The provision is called triple base because a farmer's base acres end up in three categories—idled acres, payment acres, and permitted acres on which no payments are made. Farmers are free to plant other crops on the difference between permitted and payment acres. There are no payments on these acres, but program crops may be eligible for crop loans and planting decisions will be based on market prices.

The payment acre approach also makes it easier to reduce acreage idling requirements without inflating budget costs, since the difference between permitted and paid acreage does not receive payments. Restricting payments may force some farmers out of the program, and those farmers will be free to plant all their land on market price considerations. This further enhances the market orientation of the bill. Given the limited ability to expand U.S. farm acreage and relatively low carryover stocks at the beginning of the period covered by the 1990 bill, many analysts feel the new program will introduce additional price volatility in the event of crop problems in the United States or other major producing regions.

OTHER GOVERNMENT PRICE INTERVENTIONS

The Strategic Petroleum Reserve

One measure of the importance of direct government intervention is the share of the market it affects or controls. But, unlike the actions of private traders, government market policies are often set in a relatively public way. In the case of the Strategic Petroleum Reserve (SPR), these two characteristics converge. The government's objective in holding reserves of crude oil is to accumulate supplies sufficient to meet the nation's needs in the event of a national emergency. The maximum size of the reserve is set by law, and acquisitions occur at a fairly predictable rate set by the capacity of facilities to accept oil and the speed with which Congress releases the funds to purchase the reserves.

The strategic reserve is a response to the energy crisis of the mid-1970s, which spawned a number of government attempts to deal with U.S. dependence on imports. Programs as various as subsidies for alternative energy sources (e.g., ethanol, oil shale, methanol), conservation through downsizing automobiles, solar energy tax incentives, and the accumulation of crude oil reserves, were designed to increase U.S. energy independence and cushion vital industries in the event of another oil shock.

The Energy Policy and Conservation Act, the legislation that established the reserve, made it U.S. policy to build a reserve of up to one billion barrels of petroleum (one barrel is equal to 42 gallons, or 159 liters). The oil is stored in massive underground caverns created from salt domes concentrated along the Gulf Coast. Authorized in late 1975, the reserve received its first infusion of oil in July 1977. A period of rapid growth followed, as the reserve increased to nearly 500 million barrels by 1985. In the following five years, as the threat of tight supplies seemed to recede, fewer than 100 million barrels were added to the stockpile. In the fall of 1990, after Iraq invaded Kuwait, Congress mandated that the maximum size of the SPR be increased to the originally envisioned level of one billion barrels. It is important, however, to distinguish between the legislative authorization and actual funding. The Department of Energy estimated that in 1991, the cost of expanding storage facilities would be $1.3–$2.3 billion in addition to the cost of acquiring the crude oil. On that basis, the department expected to begin purchases in 1996–97 and to complete filling the reserve by the end of the century.

Just how important is the SPR to the market? When the fill level reached 577 million barrels in 1989, it accounted for less than 12 weeks of imports. Under the most recent legislation, the largest single offering that can be made from the SPR is five million barrels. The quantities available may be sufficient to meet the needs of critical industries during a brief national crisis, but the impact on a fast-moving market of sales from the reserve is open to question. The test sale of 3.9 million barrels carried out in the wake of the Iraqi invasion of Kuwait involved a comparatively modest amount of oil—less than a quarter of a day's requirements, or about half of one day's imports—but the sale preceded a significant decline in market prices. It is arguable as to whether the price movement was a reaction to the administration's signal that reserves would be released if the international situation became grave enough or to other political or market conditions. What is certain, however, is that policy makers in years to come will look at the price movement and see cause and effect.

Strategic Metals Stockpile

In the years immediately after World War II, concern about possible shortages of critical materials for defense prompted Congress to authorize the accumulation of a wide variety of products for the National Defense Stockpile.

The stockpile consists of about 100 different items, ranging from opium paste and diamonds to sisal cordage and lead. The reserve also contains a number of metals traded on futures markets, including sizable holdings of silver, platinum, and palladium, and comparatively modest stocks of tin and copper. In September 1990, the value of the stockpile inventory was about $9.4 billion, about 10 percent of which was represented by silver and the platinum group metals. Strategic reserves of silver totaled 93.0 million troy ounces in 1990. Nearly 1.3 million ounces of palladium were also on hand.

The inventory of platinum group metals is about 1.6 million ounces less than the official goal, but no attempt to raise the reserve levels has been made in recent years. In contrast, the entire silver reserve is technically superfluous. However, by law, the stockpiled silver cannot be sold on the open market, and its use in coinage is restricted to specially authorized commemorative issues. However, the existence of potential revenue from the sale of reserve silver (though inconsequential when juxtaposed with the size of the federal deficit) inspires the belief that a more relaxed international political climate may provide the justification for more rapid liquidation of these stocks at some point in the future.

Financial and Debt Instruments

Currencies and interest rate instruments constitute a special category of markets over which governments have an unusually high degree of influence. This should not come as a surprise, as a government might be viewed as producer, consumer, and regulator of its own currencies and debt obligations. Ironically, the rise of trade in financial instruments is a direct consequence of government attempts to regulate currency trading through a system of fixed exchange rates.

In the United States, the Federal Reserve operates as the central bank. To the extent that the Fed's activities are isolated from the agendas of the executive or legislative branches, the influence of government politics on markets is minimized. But the reality is that political considerations usually play a significant, sometimes primary, role in sensitive decisions affecting interest rates, money supply, and the like. Without question, then, macroeconomic policies of government, particularly those such as tax and spending programs that affect incomes, are the most important forces influencing the markets for financials and currencies.

REGULATION OF FUTURES MARKETS

To the casual observer, most futures transactions appear to occur in almost classically free markets. However, the boisterous pandemonium of the trading ring is far from unfettered. Not only are actions of traders constrained by the contracts they enter into, but rules and regulations imposed by the exchange itself and the government also limit the size and number of positions they may take and the amount of price volatility permitted in a given period. There are also regulations governing disclosure of trades and rules that guarantee that markets are accessible to all members on the floor. The role of government agencies has evolved over the years to one of making sure that exchange rules ensure competitiveness, efficiency, and integrity of markets by protecting all traders from market manipulation and fraud. Today, markets offer a wide and ever-expanding array of sophisticated tools for hedging or speculation. This proliferation of products had increased the importance of government regulation. In the minds of some important blocks of market participants, federal oversight has emerged as a crucial element in ensuring that all segments of the industry get a "fair deal" on the floor. Thus, while traders may sometimes bridle at the regulations and reporting requirements involved in futures trading, there is little likelihood that the influence of government agencies will decline precipitously in years to come.

Until the 1920s, futures markets were essentially self-governing bodies. Oversight was provided by exchange directors who sometimes adopted a rather narrow view of the public interest. Absence of neutral party regulations resulted in a high degree of suspicion among farmers that futures markets were manipulated by exchange members and traders. This issue came to a head with the speculative frenzy in grain markets following World War I. After an abortive attempt to regulate futures markets directly, Congress passed the Grain Futures Act of 1922, under which exchanges were licensed. The law also imposed specific responsibilities on exchanges for the first time, to guard against manipulation of markets. Exchanges that failed to provide adequate controls risked the loss of a license to operate in interstate commerce.

In 1936, a newly created Commodity Exchange Commission assumed responsibility for regulating futures markets under the terms of the Commodity Exchange Act. After World War II, the commission was reconstituted as the Commodity Exchange Authority, with expanded responsibility to provide market information to the trading public. Then, in 1974, during a particularly volatile period in the grain markets, Congress again addressed the question of market regulation by creating the Commodity Futures Trading Commission. The new agency was given expanded enforcement powers and a wider scope of markets to oversee. Previously unregulated markets for currencies, metals, and financial instruments came under the CFTC's umbrella. A unique provision of the authorizing legislation requires that the commission's activities be reviewed every four years. These "sunset" reviews regularly place the CFTC and futures trading in the legislative spotlight and have more than once resulted in an expanded mandate for the commission.

The CFTC is principally a regulatory agency. It investigates alleged violations of CFTC regulations and the Commodity Exchange Act. Although prosecution of criminal violations is the responsibility of the Justice Department, the commission may initiate quasi-judicial administrative actions. These cases usually arise from complaints or investigations and involve remedial sanctions or reparations due individual investors. In dealing with exchanges, the CFTC has broad authority over any extension of futures markets into new areas. The commission reviews proposed futures contracts to determine if they serve a valid economic purpose and conform to cash market practices. It monitors exchanges' rules and disciplinary proceedings. It also monitors trading on all contract markets to detect actual or potential manipulation or price distortion. In this last capacity, the CFTC is a source of market information on positions and commitments of traders. Long-term research on market activities also provides the public with data on market performance and functionality.

Finally, under the auspices of CFTC regulation, exchanges and clearinghouses maintain daily trading records and publish daily figures on trading volume.

As the number of investment vehicles proliferated in the late 1970s and early 1980s, some products—such as financial futures options and stock index futures contracts and options— fell into a regulatory gray area over which neither the CFTC nor the Securities and Exchange Commission seemed to have effective authority. The 1982 reauthorization of the CFTC appeared to resolve the issue by giving this commission exclusive jurisdiction over stock index futures and their options. The SEC assumed sole responsibility for options or index trading (including foreign currencies) that occurs on a U.S. securities exchange.

Concerns about program trading and the influence that trading in stock index futures and options may have had in increasing stock market volatility expanded in the wake of the October 1987 stock market collapse. Consequently, the question of who should regulate these instruments surfaced again during the 1990 CFTC reauthorization hearings. As of this writing, both the House and Senate Agriculture Committees have agreed on language that vests oversight of margins for stock index futures with the Federal Reserve. The Federal Reserve, in turn, would delegate this responsibility to the CFTC. Still at issue is the question of whether the CFTC will have jurisdiction over swap and lending transactions conducted by banks. These trades may employ instruments composed of products traded or tradable on futures markets but which are not themselves traded on a market regulated by the SEC or CFTC.

In the future, federal regulation of commodity markets is almost certain to increase. These regulations may be intrusive and disrupt orderly markets, or they may serve the interests of traders by facilitating fair and open trading. Among the most pressing questions are the following:

- Should the CFTC be reauthorized permanently, as are other regulatory agencies?
- How do exchanges and government regulate conflict of interest and insider trading provisions in a way that does not paralyze markets but ensures equitable treatment of all market participants?

- How should the industry address the perception that new products have created what one observer describes as a "speculative playground" that discourages serious investors and hedgers from participating in traditional futures markets in agricultural commodities?
- How will 24-hour electronic trading affect markets? Will it spell the end of the traditional open outcry system?

The issues that confront industry and government will be complex and possibly contentious, and new and unforeseen problems are certain to arise as conditions evolve. Their resolution will require cooperation and a good faith effort on the part of legislators, regulators, exchanges, and individual investors.

CHAPTER 5

INTERNATIONAL COMMODITY AGREEMENTS

Since World War II, governments of sovereign states the world over have accepted wider responsibility for economic stability and growth, both domestically and, as a necessary corollary, in the sphere of international trade and development. Arguably, the most important aspect of governmental responsibility has been the increased attention paid to primary products (raw materials), which play an ever-increasing role in the export earnings of the so-called developing nations.

For the wealthier industrialized nations, an interest in commodity problems does not necessarily reflect a benevolent concern for the welfare of poorer lands. Many developed nations are themselves major exporters of primary goods. Apart from any direct economic involvement, they are often motivated by political considerations. Above such considerations stands the economic interdependence of nations. The developing countries are major markets for those that are more industrialized, and any severe contraction in the former's purchasing power affects the latter's trade and well-being. Today, it is generally accepted that problems with production and procurement of raw materials (from lumber to crude oil to sugar) have broad ramifications affecting the health of the international economy in general and the aspirations of poorer countries in particular. In other words, commodity problems are believed to be part and parcel of the broader problem of economic development.

Furthermore, the economic literature that followed World War II crystallized several other related concepts. First, it was recognized that measures designed to heal or relieve stress in a particular commodity market are often means of supporting or raising export earnings of producers of raw materials. This led to explicit recognition that "commodity arrangements" often constitute an important form of aid to developing nations.[1] Such aid is obvious when importing countries agree to measures that will make them pay more for the primary products they buy. A transfer of purchasing power also occurs when prices are maintained at higher levels than they otherwise would be.

But if commodity arrangements are to be viewed as, at least in part, aid instruments, then it is only reasonable to consider the efficiency of such arrangements compared with other forms of aid. Much of the criticism of commodity agreements in recent years has focused on their alleged inferiority compared with direct aid measures.

The critics of commodity arrangements contend that it is better to provide loans or grants to build highways, exchange guarantees to spur private investment, or technical assistance on a project basis. The supporters of such commodity action plans argue that these specific aid forms are warranted, but commodity arrangements are valued complements as well.

Aside from these differences, all parties now agree that commodity arrangements constitute only one possible set of prescriptions for dealing with the trade and economic needs of developing countries. At times, other aid techniques may offer similar benefits without posing obstacles to market adjustment, and without involving the magnitude of operating costs required of some commodity controls.

Finally, specialists in this area recognize that not all commodity arrangements entail quota restrictions or other mandatory controls. Rather, there exists a full spectrum of possible measures, ranging from mild methods to nondirective techniques to strict controls.

Before we survey this spectrum of alternative measures, it may be useful to recall some of the classic problems that gave rise to commodity arrangements, and also to highlight recent milestones in the evolution of commodity policies.

---

[1]The term *commodity arrangements* is used here to encompass the entire spectrum of policy initiatives described later in this chapter.

IMPETUS TO COMMODITY ARRANGEMENTS

Symptoms of malaise in world trade involving primary commodities have been evident in varying degrees throughout this century. But, as in the case of the United States, the most powerful impetus to national and international government agricultural involvement was the Great Depression of the 1930s. During this period, a host of international commodity agreements came into being (e.g., in wheat, sugar, tin, and other markets), paralleling the domestic agricultural supports instituted in the United States and Western Europe.

Depression-born anxieties lingered until well after World War II. A major source of concern was the extreme reaction of commodity markets to the cyclical fluctuations in the developed countries. The comparative vulnerability of primary commodity markets was starkly revealed in the 1930s. By and large, prices for primary commodities sank far more than prices of more highly processed goods.

The economist saw the explanation for this greater weakness in elastic supply and demand characteristics of most primary commodities. As we observed earlier, demand and supply are said to be inelastic when a given percentage price change does not evoke a corresponding change in supply or a proportionate and opposite change in consumption. Because demand and supply are inelastic, a relatively modest surplus is difficult to deplete. Barring a natural crop disaster, prices must drop to extremely low levels before usage rises enough or output falls enough to close the gap. For agricultural commodities, the problem is sometimes compounded by a tendency on the part of some producers to increase output when prices decline, in a self-defeating effort to retain income.

The spread of depression influences from developed to developing countries proceeded not only via direct changes in demand for primary products, but also through a tendency for protectionist forces to grow stronger, leading to restrictions on competing imports from developing countries.

Through mechanisms of this sort, cyclical contractions or expansions in demand in developed countries are transmitted in magnified form to the primary trade and balance of payments of developing countries. Thus, according to a United Nations estimate, in the first economic downturn after World War II, the 1957–58 recession in the United States and other western countries—coupled with slight increases in the cost of goods purchased in industrialized lands—led to a loss in import capacity. This loss was equal to six years of lending to the developing countries by the International Bank for Reconstruction and Development (at 1956–57 rates).[2]

Instability in the earnings of primary exporters originates in cyclical and year-to-year variations in supply, as well as in fluctuations in demand and changes in import policy of developed countries. If, for example, one year sees a bumper crop 25 percent above that of the preceding season, prices may drop 50 percent or more, with the paradoxical result that producers earn less for growing and selling more. From a longer-term standpoint, the problem of supply instability takes a different form. Periods of high prices lead to general expansion in capacity—by the time output reaches a peak, prices weaken, setting the stage for the next cycle phase.

The problem of achieving greater output and price stability remained the core concern of international commodity thinking from the early 1930s to well after World War II. This concern was reflected in the Havana Charter, drawn up at the 1947–48 meeting of 50 countries participating in the United Nations Economic and Social Council. The Havana Charter projected that one aim of international commodity agreements was to moderate cyclical fluctuations in price without interfering with long-term trends. It went one step further, however, and foresaw the need for facilitating an increase in consumption or for transferring resources from overexpanded to new industries. The charter set the principle, honored in virtually all subsequent commodity actions, of **cooperation on equal terms between producers and consumers.**

Through the 1950s, commodity discussions still focused their attention largely on the question of stabilizing producer returns. However, by degrees, attention shifted perceptibly, though never completely, to the problem of raising the level and

---

[2]*United Nations World Economic Survey* (1958), pp. 6–7.

growth rate of export earnings. Two factors contributed to this elevation of goals. First, on the positive side, some reduction occurred in the need for stabilization as such, largely because of reduced cyclical variations in industrialized lands. For this reason, fluctuations in the exchange earnings of developing countries have been less acute since the 1950s.

The second reason for thinking more about the level and trend of earnings, and less about stability alone, originated in one of the more disturbing trends of the 1950s, the marked tendency for the "terms of trade" of primary producers to deteriorate. In other words, prices of primary goods that developing countries exported declined relative to the cost of the more sophisticated goods they purchased. Hence, the **real value,** or purchasing power, of primary commodity exports shrank. Accordingly, commodity-producing countries found themselves in the unenviable position of having to offer larger quantities of primary commodities to obtain a given "bundle" of manufactured goods. Factors contributing to the adverse trend included the following: production efficiencies permitting greatly expanded output of many primary products; technological innovations leading to synthetic development of substitutes for some primary products, or permitting processors to obtain more usable extract from each unit of raw material; and, lastly, the broad tendency of demand for primary products to grow slowly (or more nearly in line with population) while demand for other finished goods rises at a faster rate.

During the 1950s and 1960s, it came to be widely appreciated that unless something was done to accelerate the earnings growth of the less industrialized countries, or to otherwise provide them with purchasing power, any hopes for accelerated development would quite likely be shattered.

The beginning of the "development decade" of the 1960s saw leading nations commit themselves to programs for supporting and raising income of poorer countries, rather than simply stabilization. Prominent in its support for commodity agreements, France envisioned measures that would boost commodity prices above 1962 levels, thus raising the income of primary producers. Without accepting such a blanket commitment, the United States moved toward sympathetic consideration of commodity agreements as one possible trade-and-aid package for developing countries.

A significant landmark in the evolution of U.S. policy was the August 1961 meeting of the Alliance for Progress at Punta del Este, Uruguay. Here, the United States and other American republics agreed not only on the desirability of commodity price stabilization, but also on a need to overcome "secular deterioration" in the terms of trade of hemisphere producers and the need to promote growth in foreign exchange income received from exports. One outgrowth of Punta del Este was greater consideration of "compensatory finance" plans designed to help make up declines in export earnings of developing countries. Also, after Punta del Este, the United States gave its decisive support to successful negotiation of an international coffee agreement, which became a particularly significant pact in commodity history. While selectively accepting commodity agreements or other international commodity controls, the United States has remained flexible in its approach, evolving a policy of case-by-case study of commodity problems in full awareness of the range of difficulties and the wide spectrum of prescriptive alternatives.

TYPES OF COMMODITY AGREEMENTS

Commodity agreements are usually classified according to the type of control instrument on which they depend most heavily. The three main types are the **quota agreement,** which governs the international coffee agreement and entails restrictions on shipments, exports, sales, and sometimes imports of a particular commodity; the **production agreement,** whereby producers introduce output controls, such as in the case of member oil production within OPEC; and the **buffer stock agreement,** under which a central authority, such as the international cocoa buffer stock manager or the finance ministers for the Group of Seven (G-7) industrialized nations, buys or sells a commodity or currency at the boundaries of a predetermined price range. Regardless of the actual control instrument, all international commodity agreements have as their principal objective achievement of stabilization by confining prices to a prescribed, and relatively narrow, trading range.

International Coffee Agreement: Quota Controls

In the 1960s, the case for an international commodity agreement was strongest for coffee. Here was a commodity of particular significance to developing nations. Moreover, this commodity faced a clear and present danger of declining to price levels that would seriously impair earnings and adversely affect world trade.

Thus, the new International Coffee Agreement (ICA) came into being in 1962 with tremendous and unprecedented political backing. It was supported by the trade (i.e., the National Coffee Association of the United States) as well as by the overwhelming majority of producing and consuming countries. This agreement differed from earlier stopgap efforts in that it sought longer-term statistical equilibrium, as well as an immediate defense against price weakness.

The main control mechanism was an agreement on export quotas. Every two years, the 74-member International Coffee Organization (ICO) predetermines additions to, or subtractions from, beginning coffee-year quotas (October 1 to September 30) to "smooth" price volatility in the event prices rise above or fall below a composite indicator price for an extended period of time. The most recent agreement, which was adopted in 1983 and ended in 1989, attempted to maintain prices in a range between $1.20 and $1.40 per pound.

As a tool for enforcing quotas, the agreement provided that all shipments of coffee from member countries be accompanied by **certificates of origin.** Importing countries agreed not to admit coffees lacking the appropriate certificate, and also to limit the imports from nonmembers whenever the ICO deems necessary.

Exempt from the quota limits are exports to a stipulated list of new markets, such as China, for promotional purposes. The intention of this clause was to encourage growth of consumption in new geographic areas. However, the agreements to date have had a difficult time blocking shipments of significant amounts of coffee at discount prices to non-ICO markets such as the former

Soviet Union, which has had the effect of diluting the overall agreement (more on this problem later in the chapter).

Periodically during the 30 years since the ratification of the first ICA, frost-damaged and drought-damaged crops— particularly in Brazil, the world's largest coffee-producing nation—effectively rationed available coffee supplies, thereby obviating the need for export controls. In these situations—for example, in 1975 and more recently during the 20 months between February 1986 and October 1987—prices increased dramatically to reflect actual or anticipated frost-related supply shortages in Brazil. On those rare occasions, supply and demand considerations and concerns about severe shortages naturally dominated the external pricing mechanisms, or **outside intervention.** Under such circumstances, quotas were suspended altogether to encourage maximum exports (supply) to drive prices back into the price band specified in the agreement.

However, during most of the past 30 years, coffee production has exceeded consumption on an annualized basis, which has elevated the importance of the quota arrangements, especially to the foreign-exchange-starved coffee-producing nations.

Over the years, for the most part, the concept of a coffee agreement has been successful and well-received in the international community largely because it has specified the time period, quantity, and support and resistance measures that are crucial to price stabilization. Over the long term, the discipline of the agreements has enhanced producer incomes, despite a chronic tendency to overproduce year after year. Because coffee is relatively inelastic (meaning that consumption will stay constant despite a sharp move in price) at any given time, without an agreement the actual or perceived burdensome worldwide supply situation could depress coffee prices significantly, which would severely damage the export earnings of many developing nations.

Coffee's relative price stability has benefited consuming nations, as well, over the years, although their participation in the specific coffee agreements perhaps is less critical than the larger aim of trade cooperation in a number of commodity and natural resource relationships with other countries. In the complicated web of international trade, the U.S. government views the coffee agreement as but one of a number of relationships that demonstrate "interest in constructive efforts at international economic cooperation with developing country producers of primary commodities."[3]

Periodically, however, problems have emerged, threatening the survivability of the agreements. Strict export restrictions can be the source of great frustration to smaller coffee producers in particular, who desperately need the income from all the coffee they have available for export, not just from the coffee exports permitted under the agreement. These income pressures have compelled ICO members to lobby for larger quota shares within the agreement, and denial of such requests has been known to push small producers into secretive sales of coffee at discounted prices to non-ICO members. Such sales, if suspected and confirmed by the coffee trade, anger ICO members in general and consuming nations in particular, and could serve to undermine the entire agreement.

In fact, in September 1989, the U.S. government refused to support a new ICA unless and until the producing nations agreed to institute more intense policing methods to discourage deeply discounted sales to non-ICO members and thereby eliminate the two-tier pricing system. Furthermore, in the 1989 negotiations, the United States expressed a desire for greater consumer access to higher-quality washed arabica coffees, asking that 48 percent of the total quota be allocated for those coffees, rather than the 43 percent specified in the 1983 agreement. Such a change, however, would have necessitated an increase in the export quotas of Colombia, the world's largest producer of mild, washed coffees, most likely at the expense of Brazilian export levels. Needless to say, Brazil vehemently opposed any change in the quota system in general, and in its export share in particular. (One side issue concerned illegal drugs. In the 1989 negotiations, it appears that the United States was attempting to secure higher coffee earn-

[3]U.S. Congress, House of Representatives, *Message from the President of the United States Transmitting the International Coffee Agreement, 1983* (Washington, D.C.: Government Printing Office, 1983). Signed by the United States on March 23, 1983. Treaty Doc. No. 98-2, 98th Congress, 1st Session.

ings for Colombia for the purpose of, or in exchange for, greater efforts to fight the flow of cocaine. However, Brazil completely rejected the concept.) Until the ICO adequately deals with the issues of greater access to higher-quality coffee and the two-tier pricing system, the United States—the world's largest coffee-consuming nation—may not become a signatory to any proposed ICA, which, undoubtedly, will continue to be a major roadblock to its implementation.

OPEC: Production Controls

Over the years, OPEC has become a noteworthy example of an international production agreement that has come "unhinged" periodically as a result of member self-interest. In the early 1970s, when the majority of the world's industrialized nations depended upon oil imports from the Middle East for their energy supplies, OPEC unity created a powerful stranglehold on the allocation and pricing of petroleum. However, during the past 10 to 12 years, certain actions—including efforts to develop alternative fuels, creation of meaningful conservation measures, and, most important, tactics that are, in effect, cheating on OPEC production quotas—have undermined the efficacy of the cartel itself. In the case of OPEC, the constant elevation of self-interests of members Iraq, Iran, Kuwait, the Arab Emirates, and Saudi Arabia above the greater interests of the cartel at one time or another has weakened the resolve of the agreement. As a result, this has precipitated the flooding of the shipping lanes with abundant and cheaply priced crude oil, all in direct defiance of predetermined and agreed-upon daily production agreements. With the exception of periods during the Iran–Iraq War (1980–88) and the initial market reaction to the invasion of Kuwait by neighboring oil producer Iraq in August 1990 (which threatened the oil-producing facilities or the Persian Gulf shipping lanes), the price of crude oil has declined steadily since 1980, despite OPEC's best efforts to the contrary.

Usually, members of OPEC gather twice yearly in a European city such as Geneva or London to review, extend, or modify the most recent production agreement. The members discuss (debate) current output levels (cheating included) within the scope of existing world demand for oil, and then proceed to determine total output as well as output levels of each of its individual members for the upcoming six-month period. The most recent agreement was rubber-stamped in July 1990, less than one month before the Iraqi invasion of Kuwait, and specified export quotas for the 13 member states totaling output of 23.2 million barrels per day (see Table 5.1).

The majority of the time, however, OPEC politics obscure OPEC economics. At any given moment, one producer or another is dissatisfied with either its output limitations or the low "benchmark" price of crude oil specified in the agreement. Nearly every meeting involves conflicts between the larger producers, such as Saudi Arabia, and the smaller ones, such as the United Arab Emirates, as well as a heated price debate between the moderate and hard-line Arab nations.

After hours, sometimes days, of disagreement and bickering, OPEC members manage to patch up their differences, if not in sub-

TABLE 5.1

OPEC Crude Output before and during the Persian Gulf War (000s of barrels per day)

	July 1990	December 1990	Change
Algeria	770	800	4%
Ecuador	280	295	5%
Gabon	280	300	7%
Indonesia	1,280	1,440	13%
Iran	3,000	3,200	7%
Iraq	3,100	450	-85%
Kuwait	1,750	250	-86%
Libya	1,300	1,470	13%
Nigeria	1,700	1,900	12%
Qatar	370	375	1%
Saudi Arabia	5,450	8,400	54%
United Arab Emirates	1,900	2,300	21%
Venezuela	1,970	2,330	18%
Total	23,150	23,510	2%

Source: *London Financial Times.*

stance then certainly for the sake of appearance, and emerge from the meeting with a new, and presumably workable, oil output and minimum price agreement. Such was the case for the July 1990 agreement, which ratified an output ceiling of 22.5 million barrels per day, despite threats from Iraq's president, Saddam Hussein, demanding that Kuwait halt its excess production policies. At that time, several petroleum newsletters noted that in July 1990, actual OPEC production was approximately one million barrels per day above the agreed-upon quota (see Table 5.1).

Most OPEC production arrangements, however, fail to satisfy the desires of all the members, and invariably lead to some form of cheating or subterfuge within weeks or months of the signing of the new pact (as was the case in 1990). Indeed, it is a rare agreement that truly binds the cartel to a specified output level for an extended period of time. Once one of the many OPEC production-monitoring organizations detects the slightest rupture in the agreement, futures prices respond swiftly, and the news is in the next day's financial press.

The Group of Seven: Buffer Stock Management

The final example of an international commodity agreement should be considered as a hybrid case of buffer stock management. The treasury secretaries of the G-7 industrialized nations—including Germany, Japan, Great Britain, France, Canada, Italy, and the United States—convened in September 1985 at the Plaza Hotel in New York to introduce a dynamic program for international cooperation in the area of exchange rate stability. In response to the problem of exchange rate volatility, and for the first time since the dismantling of the Bretton Woods agreement by the Nixon administration in 1971, separate governments attempted to cooperate for the purpose of managing free-floating exchange rates through coordination of domestic policy goals and, when necessary, direct intervention into the world's foreign exchange markets.

When the historic meeting at the Plaza Hotel disbanded, the signatories, led by U.S. Treasury Secretary James Baker, had consummated an unprecedented agreement to resist, as a group, attempts by the market to drive the U.S. dollar higher in relation to the values of the yen, the Deutsche mark, the pound, and other currencies of the G-7. (Subsequently, it was learned that they had agreed that their central banks would intervene together to sell a predetermined amount of dollars if its exchange rate climbed above an agreed-upon level—for example, 250 yen per dollar.)

The Plaza Accord represented an international effort to halt the relentless, meteoric five-year climb in the value of the U.S. dollar. Between 1980 and 1985, the dollar climbed from 110 yen to over 260 yen and from 1.65 Deutsche marks to 3.55 Deutsche marks, a rise that, in its latter stages, caused severe economic dislocations, mostly in the United States but throughout the world as well. By definition, the historically high value of the dollar made the cost of U.S. goods exorbitant outside of American borders. American exporters had increasing difficulty selling their high-priced goods abroad and, as a result, were unable to compete with the foreign manufacturers of similar products. By 1985, the situation became so bleak that many U.S. exporters had moved part or all of their operations overseas or had gone out of business altogether. Particularly hard hit was the American farmer, who produces the majority of his crop for export to foreign countries. With the dollar's value soaring, foreign buyers bought grains much more cheaply from other exporting countries, such as Argentina, Brazil, and France, which left the American farmer with large agricultural surpluses and on the verge of widespread bankruptcy.

The high value of the dollar also had negative consequences for the industrialized countries of Europe and Asia. With the price of their goods and services relatively inexpensive on an exchange rate basis, demand soared, and the export sectors of the German and Japanese economies, for example, boomed in the early 1980s. However, the prolonged period of robust export growth produced overheated economies and expectations of rising inflation. Such a situation made foreign governments' task managing domestic fiscal and monetary policy extremely difficult and was reason enough, from their perspective, to call for a stable (as opposed to rising) U.S. dollar.

Certainly there were compelling reasons for the world's finance ministers to meet at the Plaza Hotel in 1985 and for the creation of the Plaza Accord. The G-7 agreed that their separate and sovereign central banks should make available a portion of their dollar reserves for the purpose of entering the foreign exchange markets periodically (frequently, if necessary), in a coordinated effort to sell the dollar if its value continued to climb.

The combined psychological impact of the unprecedented Plaza Accord and G-7 intervention in the foreign exchange market drove the dollar considerably lower (to what many foreign exchange specialists think was a secret G-7 downside target exchange rate for the dollar) in the months following the meeting. By February 1986, the dollar had fallen by an average of 30 percent against the other currencies of the G-7. The Plaza Accord had achieved its intended goal of putting an upper boundary on the value of the U.S. dollar. Its secondary goal, foreign exchange stability, was another matter altogether, and turned out to be much more elusive.

In view of the evidence, one could conclude that the Plaza Accord achieved its primary goal. By September 1987, two years after the accord was signed, the dollar was still rapidly depreciating, and significant G-7 intervention was required to stop the fall.

During and immediately after New Year's weekend 1988, the central banks of the G-7 vigorously purchased dollars on foreign exchange markets. Starting on Sunday night in the Far East and continuing in Europe and the United States Monday morning, G-7 bought an unprecedented amount of dollars for its own accounts—reportedly in excess of $15 billion—and succeeded not only in breaking the dollar's fall but also in driving it 5–7 percent higher during the four subsequent trading sessions. Given the volume and tenacity of the G-7's commitment during that five-day period, the foreign exchange market was put on notice that governments of the industrialized nations considered 1.55 Deutsche marks, 120 yen, and 1.92 pounds sterling as "absolute" and impenetrable lower limits to the dollar's value.

Essentially, the G-7 had come full-circle, from capping the dollar's climb in 1985 at 260 yen, for example, to breaking its fall at 120 yen two years later. Although the more than 50 percent drop in value of the dollar in 24 months can hardly be considered a stable exchange rate environment, the G-7 nevertheless employed (and still employs) its resources in a cooperative effort to protect member currencies from extreme dislocation.

Domestic fiscal and monetary policy coordination among G-7 governments is sometimes difficult, if not impossible, to reconcile. For example, in February 1991, robust economic growth and fears of rising inflation in Germany prompted the Bundesbank to raise interest rates at the same time the Federal Reserve was reducing interest rates to fight a severe recession. Over the years, however, its frequent high-profile meetings and communiqués have preserved its integrity and enhanced its influence in the international investment community. To this day, the G-7 looms as a formidable participant in foreign exchange markets.

Although the G-7 accord sought to regulate world exchange rates (and to some degree interest rates), the principal mechanisms employed to achieve its goals—use of central bank foreign exchange reserves and, at times, "secret" price targets—were sensitive to the same supply and demand considerations that were used in the International Coffee Agreement and by members of OPEC in its ongoing efforts to regulate oil output. The buffer stock manager, or in this case the finance ministers, authorized the use of central bank reserves to either increase or reduce supplies of a particular currency (mostly dollars) on the open market and to send a psychological message to the foreign exchange markets that, at some point, disequilibrium would be recognized and corrected.

The G-7 accord has been subject to the same pitfalls as the coffee and petroleum agreements discussed earlier, namely, self-interest. While the combined efforts of the world's central banks certainly can make an imprint on the foreign exchange markets, each participant is an autonomous nation-state that, at any time, might choose not to take a course of action that it deems detrimental to its larger domestic concerns. During the six years since the Plaza Accord was consummated, there have been several instances when one of the signatories has failed to intervene in the markets along with the others or has taken some unilateral action that effectively subordinated the goals of the G-7 to some domestic policy initiative.

CONCLUSION

Theoretically, a strong case for commodity control agreements exists when an immediate threat is posed to the exchange earnings of lesser-developed countries, when alternative aid measures are not available, and when widespread support exists among both producing and consuming countries of a particular product. Furthermore, external market regulations designed to stabilize prices should be complemented with long-term measures that seek to restore fundamental equilibrium by redressing supply or demand imbalances. This would be the ideal objective in a near-perfect, altruistic world. As we all know, however, in an imperfect and self-serving world, our experience with international commodity agreements has taught us that each control mechanism has its particular susceptibility to weakness. Buffer stock arrangements, whether agricultural (i.e., cocoa) or monetary (i.e., G-7), are expensive, entail high financing, and might exhaust the buffer stock itself in times of unusual stress. Additionally, the choice and defense of an appropriate price range is difficult and often has the effect of weakening the resolve of the underlying members.

Production and export quota agreements (i.e., OPEC, coffee) have met with more success than buffer stock arrangements. They are, however, extremely difficult to enforce and tend to be frail vehicles that break down under the pressures of economic, political, and weather-related disturbances or, most commonly, because self-interests dominate international agreements.

Nevertheless, such problems do not preclude the usefulness of international commodity agreements at particular times when unusual price volatility or fundamental disequilibrium require periodic outside intervention.

SECTION 3

FUTURES AS A VIABLE PRICING MECHANISM

CHAPTER 6

SEASONAL FACTORS IN THE FUTURES MARKETS

Many traders like to think that if prices of a particular commodity behave in a similar way two consecutive years, or even three out of five years, such behavior reflects a strong seasonal propensity. The fact is, however, that under such circumstances, the possibility of prices behaving similarly the following year is no higher than a coin flip, at best. In other words, unless there is an economic explanation for the behavior, then there is no reliable seasonal pattern at work. In a traditional sense—and by definition—a seasonal price pattern is one that emanates from recurrent, seasonal fundamentals, to which we now briefly turn our attention.

SEASONAL CASH AND COMMODITY TENDENCIES

The production and marketing of agricultural commodities is, on the whole, a seasonal business. Unlike manufacturers who may be able to regulate their production to conform to variations in seasonal or cyclical demand, the farmer can exercise little discretion concerning when to plant his crops. Planting time is determined by the type of crop, the geographic location of the farm, and the weather. Nor can the farmer significantly advance or defer harvest to take advantage of market conditions. As an example, the bulk of the U.S. corn crop, averaging eight billion bushels annually, must be harvested between October 1 and November 15, even though the corn will be consumed during the entire year.

Harvesting of U.S. agricultural commodities occurs, in most years, as follows:

Wheat	May through August
Oats, barley, and cotton	July through September
Soybeans	September through November
Corn	September through December

Therefore, from the time that the Texas winter wheat crop begins moving to market in volume late in May, harvest of agricultural commodities expands as the combines work northward. Around September, when the harvesting of wheat, oats, cotton, and barley has been pretty much completed, the soybean crop is about ready to move in commercial quantities, to be followed in a month by the corn crop. Weather sometimes delays harvest past these dates, and early portions of crops are sometimes ready for market sooner. Corn in Texas is ready considerably earlier than corn in the Corn Belt, and soybeans on sandy soil in central Illinois are harvested ahead of soybeans in other areas.

A portion of the harvest is marketed directly to mills, processors, exporters, and terminal elevators, but the bulk of the grain that is not actually consumed on farms is transported directly to the thousands of country elevators that dot our farmlands. Generally, these elevators do not have the facilities to store this vast quantity of grain. Their primary function is to serve as the initial staging area in the distribution of agricultural commodities, and they can operate profitably only by expeditious handling and marketing of the grain. During the height of harvest, long lines of trucks can be seen waiting to unload in front of country elevators. This grain must be either sold and delivered or shipped on consignment in order to make room for newly arriving supplies. Even the large terminal elevators located adjacent to the principal grain marketing centers of Chicago, Duluth, Kansas City, Minneapolis, and Buffalo frequently become congested as thousands of grain-laden railroad cars continue to arrive.

It follows, therefore, that cash prices of agricultural commodities tend to be under pressure during the period of harvest and its accompanying heavy marketing. Gradually thereafter, the pressure of harvest abates as farmers begin harvesting a later crop and preparing to plant next season's crop. Concurrently, commodity cash prices tend to experience a seasonal recovery as the current production begins to move out through the regular channels of distribution into the hands of exporters, processors, millers, terminal storage centers, and consumers.

From time to time, the government loan program has been a major depository for surplus agricultural production. Low commodity prices not only encourage heavier utilization but also attract an expanded volume of grains into the government loan program and, eventually, into the government's hands. This, plus the policy by which the government grain holdings may not be resold in the domestic market except at prices generally above the level of support prices, tends to create a condition of artificial scarcity in commercial channels, giving additional impetus to the postharvest price recovery.

Even nongrain agricultural commodities exhibit such seasonal price tendencies. Cash values tend toward weakness during periods of heavy marketing, with higher prices likely later in the season. Table 6.1 presents the normal seasonal cash price patterns for a number of commodities. It should be emphasized that this data represents an average of cash commodity price movements over many years, and that deviations from this long-term seasonal pattern may occur during any given year.

TABLE 6.1
Normal Seasonal Pattern of Cash Commodity Prices

Commodity	High	Low
Cocoa	January–March	June and December
Corn	August	November–December
Cotton	July	October–December
Potatoes	June–July	October
Soybeans	May	October–November
Wheat	May	July–August

CROP YEARS: OLD AND NEW CROPS

Agricultural commodities are harvested annually and, in each commodity, one month is designated as the beginning of the crop year. For example, July 1 is the beginning of the crop year for wheat, oats, and rye in the United States, even though their harvests may have been in progress before July 1. The reason for this statistical designation is that during the month of July there is a sufficient flow of newly harvested grain to terminals to fully affect prices based on new crop conditions. Statistics of carryover from the preceding crop represent only old crop grain.

The distinction between old and new crop futures follows logically. An old crop future is one whose delivery period expires prior to the full-scale harvesting of the new crop, whereas a new crop future trades during the period when substantial new crop supplies are available for delivery. Trading is conducted simultaneously in both old and new crop futures. For example, in November, trading in wheat on the Chicago Board of Trade is conducted in the December, March, May, July, and September futures. December, March, and May wheat are old crop futures, because any wheat delivered against them will represent old crop grain harvested the previous summer. On the other hand, the July and September futures represent new crop months, inasmuch as the harvest should be sufficiently advanced by that time to permit the delivery of newly harvested wheat.

Although domestic consumption of agricultural commodities will not usually vary appreciably from year to year, even a small variation (particularly toward the end of the marketing year) can be a most important influence on the size of the old crop carryover. This will exert a direct effect on the price of the expiring old crop future in relation to the price of new crop futures. On the other hand, the size of successive crops (representing supply) can show marked variations. Old crop futures normally will sell at premiums to new crop when there is a relative tightness, or the expectation of relative tightness, in old crop supply. During the severe drought of 1988, concerns about crop loss and scarcity of wheat drove up prices of the contracts deliverable between July 1988 and May 1989. However, the price of wheat for delivery in July 1989—the first delivery month in the following crop year (1989–90)—traded between 8 percent and 25 percent below the various contract months in the delivery period directly after the drought. For example, on July 12, 1988 (in the middle of the drought), old crop Chicago wheat for delivery in December closed at $3.98/bu, while new crop July 1989 wheat closed at $3.52/bu on the same day. This 46¢/bu premium for December over July wheat was due largely to the market's expectations that old crop supplies would prove to be scarce relative to supply and demand considerations six months in the future.

The distinction between old and new crop futures is not quite as simple in the case of soybeans and corn. Although October 1 is technically considered the beginning of their crop year, the corn and soybean harvests frequently commence early enough to render new crop supplies available for delivery against the September future and hence to influence the price of that future. Although more applicable to the soybean crop (since soybeans normally are harvested several weeks earlier than corn), the September future of these two commodities can represent either old or new crop futures. This distinction is important to the pricing of the September future. In the case of soybeans, when the carryover is small, old crop futures (July and August) will likely trade at premiums over new crop futures (November and January). This type of situation encourages farmers to harvest as early as possible in order to benefit from the premium prices on old crop futures, so that the September future could be considered new crop. On the other hand, when carryover is expected to be ample, resulting in old crop futures being priced below new crop futures, there is little incentive for new crop soybeans to be rushed to Chicago for delivery against the September future. The result is that the bulk of deliveries would be made against the November and January futures. In this case, the September future would be considered old crop.

COPPER: A NONAGRICULTURAL SEASONAL

Although we tend to associate seasonal price trends with agricultural commodities that are subjected to the influences of planting, harvesting, and marketing, copper prices have also exhibited a strong seasonal price pattern over the years. Since the 1970s, copper prices have tended to exhibit seasonal strength in the early part of the year and weaken during the summer. First- and second-quarter average price levels for the period are generally higher than the lows reached during the summer and early fall.

These relative price particularities seem to occur year after year, regardless of general economic conditions, because of the underlying supply and demand relationships in the copper business. The first and second quarters of the year tend to be seasonally strong periods of consumption (see Figure 6.1), which causes inventory draw-down (see Figure 6.2), which, in turn, results in upward price pressures (Figure 6.3) between the

FIGURE 6.1
Worldwide Refined Consumption Seasonals

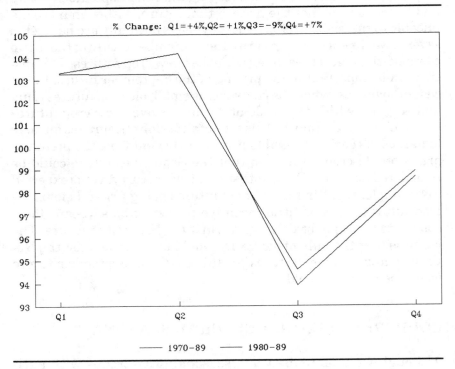

% Change: Q1=+4%,Q2=+1%,Q3=−9%,Q4=+7%

——— 1970−89   ——— 1980−89

Source: Chart courtesy of Paine Webber.

FIGURE 6.2
Worldwide Reported Inventory Seasonals (exchange, producer, user in K tonnes)

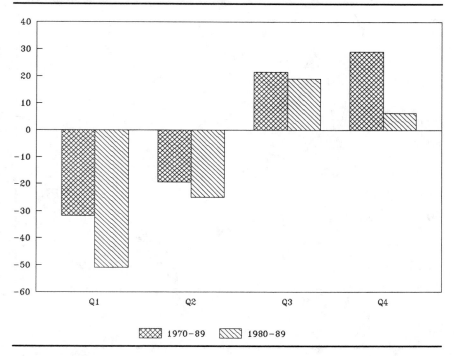

☒☒☒ 1970–89   ⧄⧄⧄ 1980–89

Source: Chart courtesy of Paine Webber.

months of January and April. Conversely, during the third and fourth quarters of the year, consumption slows, inventories rebuild, and cash prices tend to moderate.

While seasonal relationships tend to reflect everything from weather patterns to construction expenditures across the United States, the relatively long-term documented changes in price at particular times during the year provide invaluable background information to the futures trader or hedger in planning his entry and exit from the copper market. Of course, there is always the chance that an aberration in the seasonal pattern could occur because of some sudden interruption in availability, such as the outbreak of war, which is another way of saying that no particular pattern works 100 percent of the time. Nevertheless,

FIGURE 6.3
COMEX Copper Price Seasonals

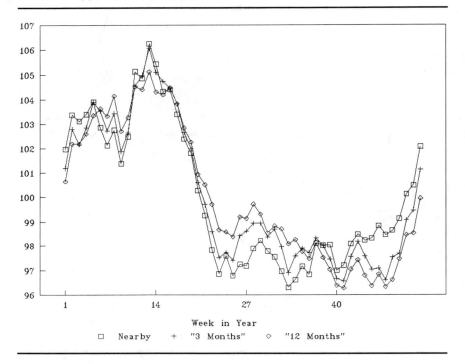

Source: Chart courtesy of Paine Webber.

knowledge of the seasonals has significant value and should be considered part of the trader's arsenal of information prior to entering the market.

CHAPTER 7

THE RELATIONSHIP BETWEEN THE CASH AND FUTURES MARKETS

The cash and futures markets are two separate but closely related commodity markets. The cash market refers to the regular commercial channels for buying, selling, storing, and distributing actual (cash) agricultural, industrial, and financial commodities such as corn, silver, and Swiss francs. The futures market refers to the organized exchange trading of standardized contracts for the future delivery of commodities and financial instruments.

An important distinction between the cash and futures markets is that *less than 5 percent of the total volume of futures transactions is settled by delivery of the actual commodity, whereas virtually all cash transactions result in physical delivery.* Another difference is that, in cash transactions, the precise grade and quality of the agricultural or industrial commodity are specified, whereas in a futures transaction, the seller has the option of delivering any one of several tenderable grades. Commodity exchanges establish a **basis grade** for each commodity, which is deliverable at contract price. Other grades of the commodity may be delivered, but at specified premiums or discounts to the contract price.

Trading is conducted differently in the cash and futures markets. Cash transactions may take place anywhere in the world, at any time, and between any individuals. Furthermore, cash transactions are privately negotiated between the buyer and the seller, so that the trade terms are likely to vary with each transaction. Futures transactions, on the other hand, may be executed only by exchange members in the designated exchange ring or pit, during established trading hours. All trades must be publicly announced by open outcry, and a record of the transaction is immediately noted and disseminated to interested parties. Finally, most of the important terms of the futures contract are standardized, so that the only details that vary for each trade are the names of the buyer and seller, the delivery month, and the contract price.

The most important relationship between the cash and the futures markets—and certainly the one commanding the greatest attention on the part of both hedgers and speculators—concerns price. The difference in price between the actual (cash) agricultural, industrial, or financial commodity and a designated future (in the same commodity) is called the **basis** (sometimes referred to as the **swap rate** in the foreign exchange market). At any given time, there exist various bases for each commodity, regardless of whether it is agricultural, industrial, or financial, which reflect the following variable factors: the cash price for the deliverable grade commodity, the length of time to delivery day, expectations about interest rates (time value of money), the price of the future, and, for agricultural and industrial commodities, the destination.

With respect to traditional commodities, corn and silver, for example, the basis is quoted as the number of points or cents at which the actual commodity is trading above or below the price of the corresponding future. When the price of the cash commodity is trading higher than the future, it is said that the basis is **on**. When the price of the cash commodity is trading lower than the future, the basis is **off**. The basis of each commodity can fluctuate, and during the life of any given future it may change from on to off, or vice versa, in response to changing fundamental or technical factors.

The basis and its fluctuations are major factors that directly influence the many operating decisions of commodity trade firms. It is through changes in the basis that trade firms either profit or lose on their hedging operations. Trade firms attach such importance to it that the price of the actual commodity is frequently quoted in terms of the basis rather than in dollars and cents. For example, the price of a particular grade of cash corn may be quoted "two cents off December." As long as this quotation is maintained, the price of that particular cash corn will fluctuate directly with the price of the December future, always two cents lower.

As for financial instruments, such as bond and Japanese yen futures, the relationship between the cash, or **spot,** price, and the price of the future is equally as important to their operations as the basis is to the farmer. To someone in the import-export business, or an international money manager, the relationship between the spot price of yen, Deutsche mark, or pound sterling and the price of the future will vary over time and reflect changing conditions and perceptions about the value of those currencies in the international marketplace.

No matter what the commodity, and although the price of the cash commodity may be higher or lower than the price of the distant future, the spread between cash (spot) and futures prices must narrow as each future approaches expiration. Ultimately, the cash and expiring futures prices must coincide on contract terms because of the possibility of traders accepting or making delivery of the cash commodity against the expiring future. If the cash commodity was priced below the expiring future, a trader would have a guaranteed profit by buying the cash commodity, selling the expiring future (short), and delivering the lower-priced cash commodity against his short futures commitment. This spreading would continue until the discount of cash to futures was eliminated. Conversely, if the price of the cash commodity were higher than the expiring future, a trader could buy the expiring future and sell the cash to-arrive. He could accept delivery of the actual commodity against his long futures position and deliver it against his short to-arrive commitment. This spreading would continue until cash lost its premium to the expiring future. Cash versus futures spreading is an intricate operation and is usually the exclusive province of experienced, well-financed professionals.

TYPES OF FUTURES MARKETS

There exist three basic types of futures markets (classified by price structure): a **carrying charge** (premium or contango) **market** refers to a market where each future sells at a premium

TABLE 7.1
Futures Quotations of Three Markets (April 19, 1991)

Premium Market		Discount Market		Flat Market	
Soybeans		Copper		Sugar	
May 1991	590.25	May 1991	110.85	May 1991	7.90
July	603.75	July	109.00	July	7.84
Sept	612.25	September	107.50	October	7.83
January 1992	632.75	November	106.50	March 1992	7.88

over the previous future; an **inverse** (discount) **market** refers to a market where each future sells at a discount from the previous future; and a **flat market** refers to a market where all futures trade at approximately the same price (see Table 7.1).

Carrying Charge (Premium) Market

The carrying charge market is the most common type of market structure, existing when the current supplies of a commodity are in excess of requirements (see soybean prices in Table 7.1). In such a buyer's market, the excessive stocks tend to depress the cash price and, therefore, the price of the nearest future, and buyers have no incentive to aggressively bid for supplies. Under these conditions, where each future is priced higher than the preceding one, the price spread between the successive futures should theoretically reflect the costs of owning and storing the cash agricultural or industrial commodity, namely, interest on capital, storage charges, commissions, insurance, and transportation and handling charges. In practice, carrying charges vary, depending on the commodity and its location, the competitive position of its buyers and sellers, and whether the cash commodity owner has his own storage facilities. Premiums in a carrying charge market cannot exceed full carrying charges (except in certain situations, as noted in the next paragraph), and they rarely even equal the full charges. If they did exceed the costs of carrying the commodity, trade houses would buy the near future and sell the distant. They would accept delivery of the cash commodity against their long position, store the cash commodity, and deliver it against their short commitment in the distant future. Their profit would be the price spread between the two futures minus the costs of owning, storing, and delivering the cash commodity. This type of spreading would continue until the premium of the distant future over the nearby future narrowed to less than full carrying charges.

Back in the "old days," in the case of perishable commodities such as potatoes and iced broilers, the premium on a future could exceed full carrying charges, but this was a rare situation. Where there exists a threat of the cash commodity spoiling or being reduced in grade, traders may be reluctant to risk taking delivery of the cash commodity for storage and eventual redelivery against a short futures position. Under such circumstances, traders might not initiate this buy spot versus sell future spread until the premiums exceeded the normal carrying charges by a sufficient margin to justify the additional risks.

Of course, financial instruments are not subject to spoilage or storage charges per se; however, prices are influenced by the opportunity cost of money and expectations about interest rates. Table 7.2 shows the spot and futures prices of the dollar index contract on April 19, 1991.

Just as in our soybean example above, each successive price in Table 7.2 is higher than the preceding price. Although the premium market structure does not reflect the supply and demand of dollars in the same way as with soybeans, the difference between the spot price and the deferred delivery dates (every 90 days) reflects the expected rate of return in the future. The differential between the spot price and the higher-priced June con-

TABLE 7.2
Spot and Futures Quotations of U.S. Dollar Index

Spot	92.69
June	93.55
September	94.43
December	95.33

tract reflects a **cost of carry**, or an **opportunity cost**, of 0.9 percent for a period of 60 days. Sixty days represents one-sixth of a year. Based on 12 months, the market should pay about 5.6 percent interest. It should come as no surprise that at the time 60-day U.S. Treasury paper yielded 5.65 percent (on an annualized basis).

Just as subtle shifts in the differentials between contract prices in soybeans (narrowing of the premiums between months), would reflect changes—real or perceived—in the supply and demand balance, subtle shifts in the structure of the dollar index spot and futures prices could alert the professional trader that the marketplace would be anticipating lower or higher interest rates in the future. In other words, the shape or the slope of the yield curve changes. Armed with this "price discovery" information, presumably, the professional trader can make more informed and rational investment decisions.

Inverse Market

An inverse market is likely to develop when current commodity stocks are below anticipated requirements; when there exists a tightness of deliverable supplies relative to the open interest in the expiring future; or when the forthcoming new crop is expected to be very large. In such a seller's market, cash buyers are forced to bid up prices in order to secure their current requirements, while shorts in the nearby futures, especially in the expiring future, must aggressively cover their positions to avoid the anticipated difficulty of obtaining deliverable supplies in the cash market. This tightness of actuals, and the ensuing demand for nearby futures, inverts the normal price relationships, causing each later future to sell at a discount from the preceding one.

Unlike a premium market, where the maximum premiums on the distant futures tend to be limited by the carrying charges, in an inverse market there exists no such limit to the potential premium of the near futures over the distants. The extent of inverse premiums is largely determined by the degree of scarcity of the cash commodity. If deliverable stocks of a commodity are small relative to existing demand, as expressed by the open interest in the expiring future, shorts will be forced to cover by buying the expiring future, whatever the price. From time to time, we witness a **short squeeze**, where the price of the expiring future vigorously advances to substantial premiums over distant futures. The short squeeze is one of the risks involved in being short an expiring future, especially in a flat or inverse market.

The foreign exchange market, however, is one place where an inverted market has virtually nothing to do with the potential for a short squeeze. You can see from Table 7.3 that the British pound is an inverted market structure. Far from a shortage of pound sterling, the inversion largely reflects two conditions: the relationship between British and U.S. interest rates and the shape of the British yield curve. Taking the second condition first, at the time of this writing relatively high inflation and a falling currency unit created an inversion in British interest rates. Short-term government paper yielded a higher return than did longer-term paper. Second, and concurrently, interest rates in the United States were less than half the British rates, within a normal, rather than an inverted, U.S. yield curve environment.

The inverted price structure of pound sterling prices reflects both of the above-mentioned conditions. An investor exchanging current dollars for pounds would forego an annualized 6 percent return in the United States to buy a currency that could be invested at an annualized rate of 9 percent in London, which certainly would be a logical and rational step to take. However, if it were that easy to enhance our rate of return, everyone would be doing it.

As you might imagine, it is not so easy. For someone who exchanges current dollars for pounds, the risk lies in the fluctuation in the value of the currency itself. In fact, the inverted price structure is telling us that, for various reasons that have nothing to do with supply and demand considerations and ev-

TABLE 7.3
Futures Quotations of British Pound (April 19, 1991)

Spot	$1.7205/pounds sterling
June	1.7028
September	1.6826
December	1.6672

erything to do with expectations about interest rates and inflation, the pound sterling is worth less in the future than it is in the present. What if, during the course of the following 12 months, sterling declines from 1.7205 to 1.6000, or about 7 percent? At the end of one year, and at the time our investor converts his pounds back to dollars, an individual (or corporation) who invested pounds to capture a 9 percent return actually witnessed the erosion of more than 75 percent of his expected return, because of currency exposure. Furthermore, after taking into account an inflation rate of 5 percent in the United States, his real return on investment would actually be negative.

With that in mind, the following year he will think twice about converting dollars into pounds sterling merely to chase high nominal yields, and most likely will keep his money in dollars, which will earn him a positive rate of return.

Of course, in our example, if during the course of the year the pound appreciated by 5 percent against the dollar, the investor would have realized a 9 percent yield on investment plus an additional 5 percent return, purely because of exchange rate movements. In this situation, with a total return of 14 percent before inflation, clearly he received the best of both worlds.

But, in the marketplace, the vast majority of currency trading represents hedged transactions. Unlike our investor who might speculate in British pound futures and who is subject to possibly wild fluctuations in the value of the currency, most investors (corporations or individuals) use the futures markets to transfer the risk involved in complex, multifaceted transactions.

To continue our example, if our investor had to pay for services in pounds in three months, and he wanted to protect himself against the uncertainties of currency exposure (and, therefore, to forego the potential for greatly enhanced returns), one strategy would be for him to convert dollars into pounds and to invest the money in a 90-day certificate of deposit (CD) at the prevailing interest rate of 9 percent. Simultaneously, our investor could sell British pound futures—at a discount to the spot price—for delivery in three months to provide protection against his spot sterling (which is tied up in a 90-day CD). At the end of 90 days, if no major adjustments have occurred between U.S. and U.K. interest rates, or in the shape of the U.K. yield curve, then our investor would have earned approximately 2 percent on his 90-day CD and lost about the same amount of money on his short futures position. Why? Because during the 90-day period, the three-month forward British pound exchange rate climbed from 1.6900 to 1.7200, which eliminated the prior discount as it moved into the spot position.

In our example, the investor's currency hedge accomplished its mission to provide protection against adverse price movements. Had the value of sterling declined during the 90 days, the investor would have realized a profit on his short futures but an equivalent loss on the value of the spot sterling tied up in the CD.

Regardless of which permutation and combination of price moves occurred with respect to our hedging example (which will be discussed in greater detail in a later chapter), the investor must be aware of the inverted price structure of the British pound futures market—as well as the general reasons for the inversion—to successfully accomplish his investment objectives.

Flat Market

A relatively rare situation, a flat market exists when supplies of the cash commodity are adequate to meet the existing demand and the commodity is produced throughout the entire year. In such a market, carrying charges are usually of minor importance because production can often be geared to match the near-term demand, so that minimum supplies need be stored. During 1991 generally, and in the spring of 1991 in particular, the sugar market represented a flat market price structure (see Table 7.1).

CONCLUSION

Before closing this discussion of commodity price relationships, it should be emphasized that commodity prices are constantly fluctuating in response to free-market forces of supply and demand or, in the case of the financial markets, in response to changing perceptions about economic growth, interest rates, and inflation. The commodity pricing mechanism tends to efficiently regulate production and allocate consumption by means of the changing price relationships between the cash and the futures markets, as well as between the various futures. These changing price relationships guide traditional, nonfinancial commodities through trade channels from producers to ultimate consumers by inducing smaller production and greater consumption when prices are low and greater production and lesser consumption when prices are high. In practice, a carrying charge market encourages commodity firms to buy and store the cash commodity and to hedge in a distant future. In such a situation, the futures market pays at least part of the carrying costs (trade firms will normally carry actuals only if they are paid to do so). On the other hand, an inverse market, with premiums for the cash commodity and the nearby futures, encourages commodity firms to sell their excess commodity stocks and to secure their required supplies through buying hedges in the discount futures.

CHAPTER 8

HOW FUTURES PRICES ARE ESTABLISHED

Prices of commodity and financial futures, like the weather, are always subject to change. At any given moment, the price of a futures contract represents the collective estimates of all buyers and sellers of the future supply and demand for the commodity, and price fluctuations reflect the continuous revision of these supply and demand estimates. This premise, however, calls for some qualification. It cannot account for an error in prevailing collective thinking; those who are wrong, at times, may represent the dominant market force (this occurs often in stock index trading, for example). It also neglects to account for the influence of hedges, which, at times, may be placed in the market with no thought as to whether prices are likely to advance or decline. Forceful trading, too, can distort prices. Also, at times, speculators may be responsible for temporarily running a market out of proportion to its basic economic value.

THE INFLUENCE OF SUPPLY AND DEMAND

Regardless of the occasional (and often very frustrating) aberrations that occur throughout the scope of the markets on any given day, the underlying determinant of the value of a commodity or financial instrument centers around the relationship between supply and demand. In the case of traditional agricultural commodities such as corn, soybeans, and wheat, pricing for future delivery begins even before the commodity is planted.

This can be of great assistance to producers, who are able to use price as a guide to planting. It also enables livestock producers to plan feeding requirements, and foreign buyers to determine where and when to buy needed supplies.

In a free market, the supply of a commodity consists of the carryover from the previous crop, production from the current crop, and imports. On the other side of the balance sheet is the demand, consisting of domestic usage, exports, seed requirements, and the reserve required for the year-end carryover. (This basic equation ignores, for the time being, the role of the USDA or the agencies of other governments in buying, storing, and marketing vast quantities of commodities.)

Before planting, during the growing season, and after harvest, the USDA continually assesses crop conditions and supply levels and makes those findings public on a regular basis throughout the year. "Planting Conditions" and "Crop Production Reports" are two of the more important government surveys that are closely followed by participants in the futures markets. As each report is issued, futures prices adjust to the newly estimated supply and demand relationship and to its comparison with previous estimates.

Once the crop has been planted, weather and disease are two principal factors that influence the final size of the crop. Many substantial corn and soybean rallies have been sparked by unexpected droughts and heat spells during the crucial growing period prior to harvest.

Once the harvest actually commences, traders keep a close watch on its progress in the important producing areas, and they monitor yields to determine if the crop size is substantially above or below previous estimates.

After harvest, when the final production has been established, traders' attention shifts more to the question of demand. Export sales, weekly reports of exports, crush (in the case of soybeans), stocks on hand, and movements into and out of terminal storage are carefully scrutinized and analyzed in arriving at the current and future "value" of the commodity in question.

A similar supply and demand framework is employed for the price determination of the nonagricultural commodities as well. Copper prices provide a case in point—on the supply side, government and private agencies report on the estimated yearly mine production of copper and on the amount of copper processed (refined) and delivered into the market. In addition, the prior year's estimated carryover stocks and the COMEX and London Metal Exchange warehouse stocks must be added to the equation to complete a composite view of the supply side of copper.

On the demand side, market participants keep their eyes on brass and rod mill consumption statistics, as well as the rate of housing starts, automobile sales, and industrial production.

The statistical data provide the backdrop for the determination of the value of copper. However, other extraneous factors, such as mine worker strikes, political upheaval, and negotiation of labor contracts can, and often do, cause significant price moves and perceived shifts in the supply and demand balance.

THE INFLUENCE OF PERCEPTIONS

Financial futures prices, such as currencies, bonds, and stock indices, and the price movement, if any, of those instruments, are not determined by supply and demand data in the traditional sense (with respect to corn, for example), but by determinants such as changing perceptions of interest rates, business conditions, and economic and political stability. Those perceptions determine whether British pounds at $1.7200 are inexpensive or expensive, whether bond prices at 95-00 (8.25 percent yield) accurately reflect the market's expectations about inflation, and whether 372.50 in the June S&P is considered overvalued or undervalued.

In the traditional sense, freely fluctuating commodity prices tend to coordinate production and consumption, because low prices of an oversupply commodity tend to induce a greater rate of consumption, frequently at the expense of higher-priced substitutes. High prices, on the other hand, tend to price a scarce commodity out of the market by reducing consumption and encouraging the use of lower-priced substitutes. Corn and other feed grains and cottonseed and soybean oils are two sets of commodities that, for many purposes, are interchangeable depending on relative prices. High prices, moreover, tend to allocate supplies of a scarce commodity over a longer period of time, pending the arrival of a new crop or of additional supplies of the same crop, which may have been attracted to the market because of higher prices.

THE INFLUENCE OF PRICE CHANGES

Besides being influenced by supply and demand for the actual commodity, prices are influenced in a more direct sense by the buying and selling of futures contracts. A major factor in this respect is the prevailing psychology of the trade and the public. Notwithstanding economic supply and demand factors, changing prices can directly induce additional buying or selling. Price fluctuations caused solely by previous price changes are considered **technical** in nature. They are usually of temporary duration, and can be precipitated by large-scale speculative liquidation or short covering, heavy spot month deliveries, or the triggering of large stop orders. This type of technical price fluctuation will not change the basic longer-term price trend. Nevertheless, it can cause considerable discomfort to those traders who, although having a position in accordance with the major market trend, may be too thinly margined or too nervous to withstand the adverse technical price move.

Regardless of their cause, price fluctuations and the active effort to profitably anticipate them constitute the principal interest of both trade firms and the public and so will receive major emphasis throughout much of this book.

SECTION 4

FUTURES PRICE ANALYSIS

CHAPTER 9

THE QUEST FOR PROFITS IN FUTURES TRADING

It's easy to make money on Wall Street. All you have to do is buy when the price is low. Then, as soon as the market goes up, sell and take your profit.

— Mark Twain

Section 4 of this text focuses upon one central theme: how to make money in the futures markets. It can be done. In fact, there are individuals who have won the commodity game consistently, converting modest margin accounts into substantial fortunes. Such success, however, does not come easily, except in the imagination. For a great many nonprofessional traders, the pursuit of profits in futures trading is, at best, frustrating and elusive. Many are called by the lure of high leverage in the commodity markets. Few are chosen to reap the glittering rewards.

THE PROBLEM OF PREDICTION

The average trader's chance of success will be much greater if he or she has a thorough and realistic understanding of sound trading technique and of the pitfalls likely to be encountered along the not-so-primrose trading path.

One fundamental difficulty concerns the problem of prediction. To make money in the futures markets, it is not sufficient to forecast prices with mediocre accuracy. To be successful, your conclusions must be different from, and better than, the forecasts of your competitors. In fact, most serious futures traders use publicly available tools (charts, the latest technical analysis software, and brokerage house reports), but they keep their ideas and conclusions to themselves, especially if they are successful. The successful futures trader must continually outguess the market. That is just the nature of the business.

This point merits reiteration and reflection. A futures market is usually a fairly accurate price barometer of all the facts and opinions that are known, surmised, or guessed about a particular commodity or financial instrument. Today's futures price reflects the consensus of all the people who are trading that market; it mirrors their evaluation of a commodity's present and future price outlook. If we think that the price of a particular future is going to rise or fall, it is either because we believe that our judgment—usually with respect to technical analysis—is better than the market's, or because we think we know something about the fundamentals that most people in the market do not know or are not yet focusing on.

There is still another reason why a trader may believe that a market will either rise or fall— the (disastrous) "method" of price analysis that can be called the *into-wishing* approach, not to be confused with a trader's *intuition*. It is based primarily on the trader's existing market position, rather than on solid research or compelling reason. In such a case, a trader may believe that prices will rise or fall simply because he is already long or short. This market approach is widespread, particularly among small, inexperienced speculators who may not understand that recognizing mistakes—and taking losses—is a necessary part of the discipline of the futures game. Although it will be discussed in detail in subsequent chapters, let us say at this point that *a trader should be long in the market because he is bullish and not bullish because he happens to be long.* Of course the same logic applies concerning a short position and a bearish market viewpoint.

Tomorrow's price changes are likely to depend on tomorrow's news—or anticipated news—the next reported bits of economic data, the next change in the weather, the soon-to-be-released crop estimate, or the unforeseen strike or revolution. From the perspective of most traders, it is a matter of pure chance whether tomorrow's news will be bullish or bearish. Since futures respond to such news, price changes in futures have an important random element.

Ordinarily, news that is published in the daily press is of little actual trading value, other than providing the astute trader with the prevailing sentiment that might be underlying the markets during a given period of time. Any really relevant market news most likely was reported by the various wire service hours before the media disseminated it and, consequently, has already been discounted by professional traders. The more swiftly and perfectly the market reacts to the news, the less will be its remaining bullish or bearish significance.

We will see later that even when a market seems to be following a clear trend, there may be a lack of momentum in the indicated direction; more than that, there may not even be a directive force underlying the apparent "trend." Chance, the careless artist, may simply have drawn an intriguing but meaningless line on the chart of time.

Fortunately, difficulties of this kind do not preclude successful trading, but they do complicate the game and make it a difficult one to beat without good methods, discipline, and access to channels of important market information and technical expertise.

INSIDERS AND OUTSIDERS

What sort of players are best suited to win the frequently irrational Monte Carlo of the futures markets? One would think, quite naturally, that the odds would favor the "insiders," the professionals. In each market, trading in the cash commodity and in futures is the constant preoccupation of people trained to buy or sell on behalf of large, specialized trade houses or large, diversified futures funds. Each of these entities (trading desks) invests a great deal of time and money in an effort to remain cognizant of every factor that might influence its particular markets. The object, wherever possible, is to stay one jump ahead of the market in order to maintain the competitive edge that will enable the firm to profit from its dealings.

For example, on the cash side, a large cocoa importer or chocolate manufacturer may have a private representative in the cocoa growing areas whose duty it is to keep close tabs on crop conditions and developments. In addition, the same firm likely has European connections that provide firsthand information about demand conditions in important consuming areas, while the firm's trading desk is in constant communication with buyers and sellers throughout the world.

By contrast, the large commodity funds that base their decision making on fundamental information might have staff economists and meteorologists who provide in-house forecasts and recommendations concerning agricultural prices. This is the type of important information that eludes the typical individual speculator but at times provides an invaluable edge to the professional trader.

Even such "insider" firms do not consistently make money. From time to time trading desks suffer losses, occasionally quite serious ones. Some of these losses flow from correctable errors. Perhaps better statistical analysis could have made better use of the available information. Or, maybe the loss was due to some market aberration, a one-time "shock" that no forecaster could have predicted. For example, in May 1991, during Far East trading on one otherwise dull evening, Nissan Motor Company announced that it had found an inexpensive substitute material (palladium) to use in the manufacture of catalytic converters. In response to the Nissan announcement, platinum prices nosedived by $34 per ounce over the course of the next 12 hours.

It would seem, however, even with optimum methods, and even with an insider edge on market news, anyone who trades regularly must often lose. The difficulties are enough to prevent most people in the futures business from regularly relying on outright speculation as the main source of their profits.

In contrast to a professional, the speculator is usually an outsider. He or she may not have the necessary time to dedicate to following the markets. The speculator must, as a rule, work with second- or third-hand information, received after it has already been scrutinized and acted upon by large dealers and other professionals. This speculator has no special representatives in critical growing areas, no economists on staff, inferior channels of information, and, most likely, inferior computer capabilities.

Can this market participant approach the speculative success, albeit not very consistent, of the professional, whose everyday business involves dealing and trading in futures? If so, by what means? One possible solution for the amateur trader is to place reliance on the counsel of futures brokers or advisers.

SOURCES OF TRADING GUIDANCE

Before searching for and selecting a broker or trading adviser, your first—and possibly most important—task will be to determine your place in and proximity to the decision-making process. If you are the type of person who feels compelled to make the final decision to buy or sell, and you have enough tools and information at your disposal to do so, then all you require is an executing broker, perhaps even a discount broker, to fill your orders.

On the other hand, if you have the money but neither the time nor the inclination to step into another stressful occupation, you might be wise to find yourself a trading adviser or futures money manager to make the decisions for you.

A list of futures brokers, commodity trading advisers (CTAs), introducing brokers (IBs), advisory market letters, and commodity funds open for public participation can be obtained from a number of sources. Three of the more prominent sources are the National Futures Association[1]; Managed Account Reports[2]; and Futures Magazine Annual Reference Guide.[3]

Each of these adviser categories serves sometimes similar, but most often very different, functions for the individual speculator. Most commission house brokers merely execute buy and sell orders for their clients, whereas other brokers might be registered with the Commodity Futures Trading Commission as CTAs. Then again, some CTAs are not registered brokers but are paid a commission or a percentage of trading profits based exclusively on the accuracy of their forecasts. Some CTAs write market letters in exchange for subscription fees and have absolutely no contact with their clients' trading or order execution.

The large futures funds invest (manage) your money based on a particular investment philosophy, such as a technical analysis within a computerized mechanical framework, or a fundamental, hands-on interpretive approach to the markets. Both

---

[1]Phone: (800) 621-3570
[2]Phone: (301) 730-5365
[3]Phone: (319) 277-6341

disciplines have their benefits and drawbacks, both take you out of the decision-making process totally.

Once you have determined your investment temperament and philosophy, if you want your money managed for you take the time to investigate a number of trading advisers and money managers. Solicit recommendations from friends who might be knowledgeable about trading. Obtain lists of eligible advisers or fund managers; call them and ask for an audited track record (disclosure document), description of their trading philosophy, and even the résumés of the principal decision makers. Use all of this information to determine where and with whom to place your money.

Once you have arrived at a decision, at first place only a portion of your available speculative funds with that adviser or money manager. If you are satisfied with the choice after a few months, then increase the investment.

THE FOLKLORE OF WALL STREET

For the individual investor who desires to experience the decision-making process, the "folklore of Wall Street" is the Street's heritage of commodity trading ideas, written and unwritten. It is a blend of commonsense economics, trading maxims, and helpful hints, garnered over long years of market experience. It is a folklore rather than a science because it is subjectively formulated in a way that appeals to the intuition but is not easily tested.

These Wall Street trading ideas are part insight and part myth. For the commodity economist, there is a great deal of work to be done separating the useful insight from the mythical chaff. To an increasing extent, this means formulating trading concepts and ideas in ways that can be tested—a real challenge to brokers and advisers.

Earlier, we suggested how one might select a broker or adviser to help guide trading decisions. But what if you intended to do it yourself? In that case, your quest must be for rational and workable methods that might help you trade with some justifiable confidence and hope of success. You will also need a broker who will execute your orders and maintain your account efficiently and reliably.

It is useful to start with a critical but not unfriendly view of the maxims commonly accepted on Wall Street. Of these, the following are perhaps the most popular.

- **Go with the market; do not buck the trend.** It is usually unwise to try to pick the top or bottom of a major bull or bear market. It is often better to buy on signs of an uptrend market and to sell on indications of a downtrend.
- **Stop your losses; let your profits run.** Bad trades are inevitable. The important thing is to terminate them before they grow costly and jeopardize your account. Be prepared to admit you are wrong. When you are right, be patient. Do not permit a good profit to turn into a loss.
- **Watch out for a turn when market opinion seems extremely one-sided.** Inevitably, bullishness is overdone at the top of a market, and bearishness at the bottom. This truism encourages the **contrary opinion philosophy**, which holds that a very high index of opinion in one direction, particularly when accompanied by a record-high open interest, is often a prelude to a market reversal.
- **Confine your trading to situations of unusual appeal.** In other words, do not overtrade. There is wisdom in patience. Wait for situations in which profit potential seems unusually high. Trade infrequently, unless your particular plan reasonably requires you to take positions often.

If there is a flaw in these maxims, it is that they are so obvious in implication but not so obvious in application. Certainly, we would all like to let our profits run and severely limit our losses. However, in practice, as soon as we begin trading, a funny thing happens —if we limit our losses too closely, we may incur a great many losses. If we let our profits run too freely, we may lose many of them by overstaying our welcome on the right side of the market. The challenge is in designing specific trading tactics that, in practice, will keep the magnitude of losses low in relation to the magnitude of profits.

Other Wall Street maxims appeal to the intuition but, once again, do not suffice to objectively guide trading decisions. For example, the adage "Trade with the trend" seems straightforward and simple enough. However, without specific rules, it is not so easy to identify trends that are not, in actuality, "false starts" or temporary reversals in an existing trend. We would all like to pick trends that will continue. The question, again, is how. (A question we shall tackle in detail in ensuing chapters.)

These criticisms of Wall Street's maxims should not be overdone. There is something to be said for this conventional wisdom, even if it is often somewhat vague. It offers an informed viewpoint, an attitude that is probably conducive to a healthy trading psychology.

One should be prepared to accept losses and not permit them to grow beyond a predetermined limit. As a general rule, it is probably unwise to buy in the absence of a sign that a downtrend has run out of steam, or to sell in the face of an apparently unchecked bull market. If, as an exception to this rule, you have a specific scale-down buying program, then it is wise to decide in advance whether you are prepared to carry the resulting position indefinitely and pay the cost. If you consider selling scale-up, remember that there is no limit to the extent to which the market can go against you. It is probably wisest to decide firmly at what point you will admit to being wrong, and exit the market resolutely, if not happily.

WHO WINS AND WHO LOSES IN FUTURES SPECULATION?

We have combined some of the Wall Street trading maxims with our own trading experiences to draw a profile of "winners" and "losers" in futures trading, as shown in the table on the next page.

So far, the trading precepts we have discussed have only broadly indicative value. They tell you to "let your profits run," but offer no precise advice as to when to take them. They advise limiting losses, but without saying how much. In short, they remain maxims rather than specific trading guides.

Let us see how we go about devising rules of market behavior that are clear-cut, objective, and more realistic.

Winners tend to:	Losers tend to:
Buy or sell as part of an overall plan combined with viable risk-control strategy.	Buy on weakness and sell on strength. No plan, no risk-control strategy.
After a major upswing, wait for evidence of a top formation before selling. After a major decline, wait for evidence of a bottom before buying.	Sell when prices seem too high. Buy when the price seems "cheap" enough.
Let profits run, but when they begin to fade markedly, liquidate.	Take profits quickly, but if they begin to fade, hold tight.
Protects positions with "stops" or liquidation.	Once a loss develops, wait for market to come back to permit liquidation on more favorable terms.
Enter a spread position only when spread itself has merit.	Spread a loss position to avoid taking a loss.
Know as much as possible about market traded and method used.	Rely on tips and intuition to a particular market situation.
Prevent a good profit from turning into a loss.	"Watch" as profits erode.

DECISION RULES FOR FUTURES TRADING

Formally speaking, one solution to the problem of how to trade profitably entails formulating "decision rules." These rules should be rational and unambiguous, and should be testable. We'll see that some of the rules in popular use are more subjective and more difficult to test than others.

Following established precedent, we can classify decision rules into two main types: fundamental and technical.

The Fundamental Approach

The fundamental approach is based on an analysis of the economic factors and the environment in which they operate. It seeks to determine the underlying causes of price changes, as rooted primarily in the relationship between supply and demand. It addresses itself to one main problem, that of gauging value. It asks the primary question, *What should the price be under the indicated economic conditions?*

The Technical Approach

The technical approach is concerned with the behavior of the market itself. It seeks to predict tomorrow's price in today's and yesterday's observed price pattern, as well as through analysis of mathematical formulas that are designed to detect changes in underlying buying and selling pressure. It focuses its attention on the problems both of gauging the actual price trend and of evaluating its momentum. The basic question it raises is, *Where is the market heading?*

We shall devote our attention in the next chapters to the technical approach, which is broader and more straightforward than fundamental analysis. It links readily with the general trading principles and precepts we have discussed in this chapter. We shall see that the decision rules of the technical analyst are, to a large extent, efforts to implement in an objective, highly organized manner the popular trading maxims discussed earlier.

CHAPTER 10

INTRODUCTION TO TECHNICAL ANALYSIS

TECHNICAL ANALYSIS: ART OR SCIENCE?

Simply stated, **technical analysis** is the study of price behavior. The technician relies upon the past action of the market to help determine future price direction. Just as an experienced medical doctor can recognize sometimes subtle mental or physical symptoms in a patient prior to recommending treatment, the market technician specializes in identifying cause and effect relationships through the study of price change. Chart pattern recognition accompanied by the study of underlying technical and sentiment indicators provides the astute market observer with valuable information necessary for intelligent and profitable decision making.

Although, in the strictest sense of its definition, technical analysis embraces the study of numerical and mathematically derived measurements based on price, volume, and open interest, data interpretation, in fact, is more important than the data itself. The supreme challenge of technical analysis is that it can be, and more often than not is, a subjective discipline—part science and part art form. The correct interpretation of raw data in conjunction with expertise in chart pattern recognition can yield exciting and rewarding insights into future price direction, not to mention improved trading habits.

The student of technical analysis need not have a degree in mathematics to master the technical approach (although a rudimentary understanding of statistics would be helpful). However, to become an accomplished technician, there is no substitute for experience and recall, discipline and creativity.

In this section we shall examine important elements of technical analysis, from simple tools of the trade to more esoteric material involved in evaluating market psychology.

COMPONENTS OF TECHNICAL ANALYSIS: THE CHART

It has been suggested by many knowledgeable people that consistently profitable futures trading cannot occur without the aid of price charts. The chart represents a visual price history, a forecasting tool, and a microcosm of market psychology all in one. To the active trader or the serious investor, charts convey sometimes vital messages about future price action. But it is up to the technician to discover the contents of the messages that are hidden literally right beneath his or her nose and, with that information in hand, take the appropriate market action. It is considered relatively simple to become a chartist (which should be differentiated from someone who aspires to become an accomplished technician) and to absorb the basic principles of charting. With little more than a brief indoctrination, and supplied with a pencil, a straightedge, and a subscription to one of several chart services, any budding trader can join the ranks of the futures chartists. Let's examine these challenging visual aids, beginning with the popular daily bar chart.

The Daily Bar Chart

As indicated by its name, the bar chart is a graphic that shows each day's (or week's or month's) price action contained in a single bar. With the vertical axis representing price and the horizontal axis representing time, the daily price range can be easily viewed by scanning the distance from the top to the bottom of the bar, with the daily settlement price indicated by the protruding horizontal nub (see inset in Figure 10.1). The larger chart in Figure 10.1 shows the daily high, low, and settlement of October 1991 sugar prices and correlates with the last 30 days of data listed in Table 10.1.

FIGURE 10.1

October 1991 Sugar with Moving Averages

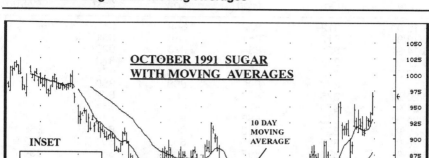

Source: Chart courtesy of FutureSource, a division of Oster Communications, Inc.

All the data needed for the maintenance of a daily bar chart is published in *The Wall Street Journal* as well as in many major city newspapers that provide coverage of the futures markets. Over time, plotting daily, weekly, and monthly price activity on respective bar charts presents a comprehensive profile of market action that spans different time frames.

The Point-and-Figure Chart

Whereas the bar chart plots price against time, the point-and-figure chart records the chronological succession of price changes without regard to date, recording only price direction as well as significant reversals in price direction. Figure 10.2 is a 60-minute point-and-figure chart of September 1991 crude oil. The vertical axis represents the price scale and the horizontal axis is used to input a series of columns in which successive price changes are recorded. One day's trading activity may be

TABLE 10.1 Tabular Data: October 1991 Sugar (June 12–July 26)

Date	Open	High	Low	Last	Average
6/12/91	812	822	809	813	
6/13/91	817	851	810	851	
6/14/91	854	864	828	829	
6/17/91	836	877	835	873	
6/18/91	880	889	860	876	
6/19/91	877	890	868	880	
6/20/91	875	877	865	872	
6/21/91	870	878	837	851	
6/24/91	845	853	841	848	
6/25/91	857	860	848	858	855.1
6/26/91	862	897	862	891	862.9
6/27/91	896	897	860	869	864.7
6/28/91	875	880	840	852	867.0
7/01/91	850	859	841	846	864.2
7/02/91	845	853	836	844	861.1
7/03/91	846	871	846	861	859.3
7/08/91	880	955	880	951	867.1
7/09/91	957	958	940	949	876.9
7/10/91	922	925	901	914	883.5
7/11/91	916	920	907	919	889.6
7/12/91	915	924	907	924	892.9
7/15/91	916	929	905	905	896.5
7/16/91	898	901	865	881	899.4
7/17/91	890	895	878	891	903.9
7/18/91	920	954	919	946	914.1
7/19/91	928	933	916	918	919.8
7/22/91	911	945	911	930	917.7
7/23/91	922	932	915	920	914.8
7/24/91	926	936	907	907	914.1
7/25/91	910	916	906	909	913.1
7/26/91	917	935	917	933	914.0

contained in a single column or in several columns, depending on the volatility and succession of price changes during the session.

Price changes are recorded in appropriate squares, using "X" to mark any advancing prices and "O" to mark declines. As long as prices are headed in one direction, either Xs or Os would be entered in the same vertical column. However, should prices reverse direction (from up to down or vice versa), a new column would be started immediately to the right of the previous one. The extent or magnitude of the reversal in price direction determines when a new vertical column should be started. The special versatility of the point-and-figure chart is that it permits the chartist to select the appropriate interval for price fluctua-

FIGURE 10.2
60-Minute September 1991 Crude Oil

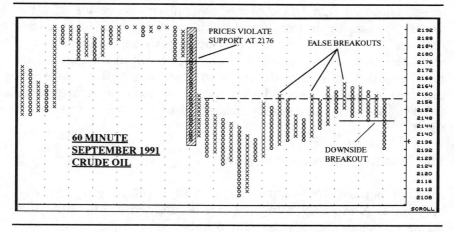

Source: Chart courtesy of FutureSource, a division of Oster Communications, Inc.

tions. The smaller the interval selected, the more incidences of reversals in price direction and, therefore, the more detailed and fine-tuned the point and figure chart.

Conversely, the larger the scale selected, the less frequent the reversals in price direction but the broader and more substantial the price movements. Usually, traders with a short-term orientation (minutes and hours) prefer smaller, more sensitive intervals, while longer-term traders prefer broader intervals for the purpose of generating major reversal signals. Figure 10.2 shows a value of two points per box and a reversal of six points (three boxes). The chartist advances to the next column to the right after prices reverse by six points (cents).

Although for the purpose of illustration we have chosen a short-term horizon, in construction and use of point-and-figure charts the choice of reversal parameters is virtually limitless, since two distinct variables—box size and reversal increment—are involved. It is the technician's objective to select a reversal combination that will maintain sensitivity to price moves but seeks to minimize losses due to whipsaw (by eliminating premature breakout signals triggered by random minor fluctuations). The example in Figure 10.2 has both valid signals and whipsaws. Notice how prices accelerated to the downside upon a violation of major support at 2176. September crude oil prices dropped precipitously from 2176 to 2136 before any buying interest emerged. On the other hand, notice the series of false upside breakouts that occurred in the vicinity of 2160 to 2164. Although the short-term trader would have capitalized on the big move downward from 2176 to 2136, he might also have lost small amounts of money during a succession of "false starts" on the upside, which might be corrected by experimenting with different box and reversal parameters of the point-and-figure chart.

The Moving Average Bar Chart

Another popular tool for the technician is the moving average bar chart. A **moving average** can be defined as the sum of a series of prices divided by the number of components in the series. For example, in a simple 10-day moving average, the technician adds the closing prices for the past 10 days and then divides the sum by 10. On each successive day, he would add the new value to the 10-day total and then subtract the last, or oldest, closing price. Upon dividing the new aggregate by 10, an updated value for the 10-day moving average is calculated. There are many uses and benefits to calculating a moving average, the most important of which is that it enables the technician to "smooth out" the sometimes volatile short-term price gyrations, which helps identify the path of the underlying trend on the bar chart. Once the underlying trend is recognized, the angle of ascent (or descent) of the moving average might offer clues about the strength (or weakness) and probable support (or resistance) levels inherent in the price structure.

In addition, the moving average can be used as a momentum gauge. As long as the removal values are known, the technician can project what future price levels must be added to maintain a rising, falling, or flat average. For example, in Table 10.1, it is clear that future daily prices below 9.00 will begin to damage the upward slope of the moving average, whereas daily prices above 9.40 will steepen the slope and, in so doing, strengthen the trend. In such cases, the moving averages would shift from positive to neutral (and then possibly to a negative mode) or continue to forge upward.

The parameters of the moving average can be varied to identify different trend lengths. A 10-day moving average might be examined alongside a 40-day moving average of the same price series to show the different characteristics of the short-term versus intermediate-term trends. In addition, the movements of the average itself, and in combination with other moving averages, can provide the astute technician with valuable information about future price direction.

In the next chapter we will elaborate on the analytic uses of moving averages. However, for the purpose of the current discussion, moving averages should be recognized as an important ingredient in chart analysis and should be calculated and regularly plotted on a bar chart (see Figure 10.1). In this way, the technician can observe the moving average and the price action simultaneously, to help him form conclusions derived from his chart analysis.

CHART ANALYSIS: BASIC RULES

Basically, there are two functions that charts fill: a record of past price behavior and a tool that can be used to forecast future price direction. Although there is little reason to question the contribution of charts in their role as a historical record of market action, there is an ongoing and probably never-ending debate about the predictive value of this widely used technical device. Usually, however, it is not the value of the chart that is in question as much as the ability of the interpreting individual.

In the following pages, we will examine some basic but indispensable rules and concepts necessary for successful chart interpretation, introduce advanced technical analysis, and form a working methodology that will help discipline the aspiring student of chart analysis.

Rule #1: *Keep an open mind in the study of technical analysis.* This is more a state of mind than it is a trading rule, but the point remains that if you enter the discipline of technical analysis with preconceived notions about its efficacy, you will be disappointed, and that will probably prevent you from exploring areas within the field that could otherwise be exciting and potentially rewarding.

Rule #2: *In analyzing price charts, first identify the major trend of the market (the basic direction in which prices are moving).* One of the most frequently used phrases within technical circles is "The trend is your friend." It also happens to be a bit of indispensable advice that is most often ignored.

Trend analysis is one of the most important aspects of charting, and success or failure in technical analysis is largely dependent upon timely and accurate recognition of price trends. Markets move in three possible directions—up, down, or sideways. Although this might seem elementary or obvious, it remains that, at times, it is very difficult to determine the trend or direction of a given market.

An **uptrend** is characterized by prices fluctuating in a succession of higher highs and higher lows, while a **downtrend** is characterized by a succession of lower highs and lower lows. A market that moves indecisively in a broad horizontal direction is referred to as a **sideways trend**, which is where markets spend much of their time.

An important characteristic of major price trends is that, once established, they tend to persist for long periods of time, usually for much longer than traders anticipate. Many speculators establish market positions near the beginning of a major price move. Regrettably, nearly all take their profits or even reverse positions long before the original move has run its course. If only they would remember that the trend is their friend, such mistakes would occur less frequently.

Rule #3: *After the trend direction has been determined, draw a trendline.* The **trendline** can be a very useful tool in making an objective determination of price trends. A trendline is a penciled line on a chart, tangent to the trading lows in an uptrend or to the trading highs in a downtrend. As soon as the chart pattern develops two successive highs or lows, an initial trendline can be drawn. In general, the greater the number of price points and the wider the distance (elapsed time) between the points, the stronger the confirmation of the underlying trend direction. In Figure 10.3, which depicts the weekly Deutsche

FIGURE 10.3
Weekly Deutsche Mark (nearest futures)

Source: Chart courtesy of FutureSource, a division of Oster Communications, Inc.

mark (nearest futures contract), prices were supported by a strong intermediate term up trendline for 18 months prior to a dramatic trend violation in February 1991.

Rule #4: *After the trendline has been drawn, identify and draw a parallel channel line.* Some price trends are sufficiently orderly to enable the chartist to draw a line parallel, or very nearly parallel, to the trendline and tangent to the rally tops in an uptrend or to reaction bottoms in a downtrend. The two lines constitute a trend channel, with trading activity largely confined within the two lines. Short-term traders may be inclined to trade against the trend channel by liquidating long positions at the upper line with the idea of rebuying on a reaction, or covering short positions at the lower line and then reselling on a rally. Trend channels tend to indicate short-term price objectives, based on the assumption that prices will continue to find support at the lower boundary line (points A, C, E and G in Figure 10.4). Price dynamics within the trend channels exhibit some interesting characteristics that can alert the astute market observer to impending price acceleration or deceleration.

FIGURE 10.4
Daily September 1991 Coffee

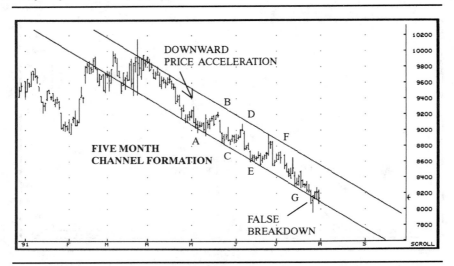

Source: Chart courtesy of FutureSource, a division of Oster Communications, Inc.

The breaking of a trendline, regardless of whether it is the upper or lower boundary line, indicates to the technician that change in price direction or momentum could be taking place and that his outlook and strategy should be altered accordingly.

Rule #5: *Recognize and respect congestion areas of support and resistance.* A **congestion area** can be defined as a range within which price is considered to be in equilibrium. In other words, from a fundamental point of view, supply generally equals demand for a particular commodity. In terms of the dynamics of the congestion area, the lower end of the range is considered a support zone where purchases are made, whereas at the higher end of the range (the resistance zone) sales are made within the overall congestion area. This back-and-forth price pattern continues until technical supply and demand factors and perceptions related to a commodity or future change sufficiently to trigger a surge of buying (new buying and short covering) or selling (new selling and long liquidating), which propels prices out of the congestion area. This could be the result of, or indicate anticipation of, a price-influencing development, such as crop damage, a revised consumption or production estimate, or military or legislative action affecting the availability of a particular product. This news, if not already anticipated and therefore discounted in the prevailing price level, may significantly alter the existing technical supply and demand equilibrium.

After the breakout occurs, the prior congestion area represents either a level of inexpensive prices (because an influx of buyers propelled prices up through the resistance zone) or a level of expensive prices (because an influx of sellers drove prices down through the support zone).

Over an extended period of time, the market role of support and resistance levels reverses as the trend of the market changes. A support area in an uptrend reverses to become a resistance area in the succeeding downtrend, and, conversely, a resistance area in a downtrend will become a support area in a succeeding uptrend.

In Figure 10.5 we can see that December 1991 cotton prices traded in a wide, 300-point range between mid-May and late June 1991. During the six-week time frame, buyers emerged near or below the 7300 level, while sellers contained prices at or above 7600.

FIGURE 10.5
December 1991 Cotton

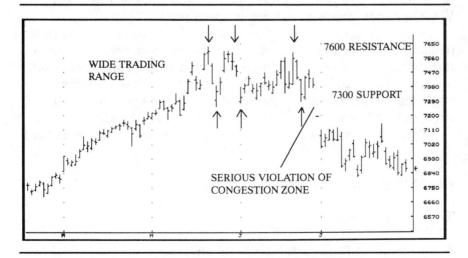

Source: Chart courtesy of FutureSource, a division of Oster Communications, Inc.

On June 28, 1991, however, the congestion period ended abruptly as prices violated the 7290 support level, triggering long liquidation as well as new selling pressure. As a result, prices plummeted nearly 500 points from the breakdown point to the 6800 level.

Once cotton prices broke down from the congestion area, they fell sharply by one and one-half times the 300-point range of the initial congestion area, which represented a significant technical "event" for cotton prices. Although there are no absolute rules about potential price objectives in the aftermath of a breakout from a congestion area, prices usually tend to move in the direction of the breakout by a distance equal to the height of the congestion area itself, and sometimes considerably more. (We will further develop the idea of breakout and follow-through in the section devoted to continuation patterns.)

Rule #6: *Determine if the price configuration is, or has the makings of, a recognizable technical pattern.* Imagine yourself atop a peak in the northern Rockies, on a cool, crystal clear summer night. When you tilt your head back and gaze into a sky full of heavenly bodies, you are likely to see outlines of the Big and Little Dippers, bulls, bears, gods, and goddesses. This is not unlike the experience of the commodity chartist, who looks at his charts and sees price configurations that resemble pennants, flags, human heads and shoulders, and a variety of other designs. Whether they point anywhere is the question.

Rather than study each individual chart pattern as an independent analytic tool, we prefer to place chart pattern analysis in its proper place, which is within the broader concept of market trend analysis. This can be achieved through the development of a thorough understanding of the primary components of chart patterns, such as trends and trendlines and support and resistance areas.

(Two further basic rules will be presented later in the chapter.)

CHART FORMATIONS

Tops and Bottoms

A key element of successful technical analysis is the chartist's ability to locate a significant technical "event." Once found, an analysis of the event will help the chartist to get his bearings and, more often than not, enable him to project future price direction. Tops, bottoms, and middles (continuation patterns) are formations that we should consider "main technical events" because they alert us to the potential for a major reversal in, or acceleration of, an established price trend. (Middles will be discussed later in the chapter.)

By way of definition, a top can be thought of as the upper boundary of a congestion area, in which resistance to a price advance appears insuperable; conversely, a bottom is the lower boundary of a congestion area, in which support during price declines turns out to be unyielding. Tops and bottoms have opposite but identical technical characteristics. The most common formations and their names are shown in Figure 10.6. Keep in mind that these formations are main technical events, which often terminate and reverse price action of the underlying price trend.

Crown Top/Saucer Bottom
Prices slowly round into an impenetrable resistance or support zone that has the power to reverse the underlying trend. (See chart A in Figure 10.6.)

FIGURE 10.6
Major Top and Bottom Price Formations

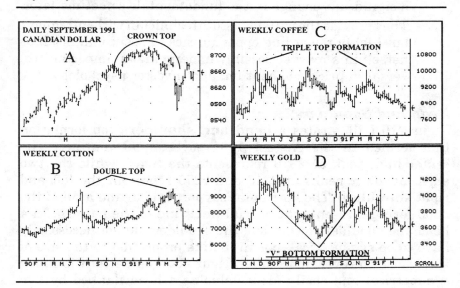

Source: Charts courtesy of FutureSource, a division of Oster Communications, Inc.

Double Top/Double Bottom
A new high (low) price followed by profit taking often leads to a failed test of the previous peak (low), which will result in an exhaustion of the underlying trend. (See chart B in Figure 10.6.)

Triple Top/Triple Bottom
This is an extension of the double top/double bottom resulting in two consecutive failures to penetrate highs (lows). A highly reliable reversal pattern. (See chart C in Figure 10.6.)

The V Top/V Bottom
An infrequent major reversal occurs after the establishment of highs (lows). This pattern is the least dependable because prices usually test their highs (lows) prior to a significant reversal in trend. However, occasionally prices will be driven too far in one direction, which causes a violent reaction in the opposite direction. (See chart D in Figure 10.6.)

Here are some observations about major reversal patterns:

- The longer they take to develop, the more significance they have.
- They represent a transition phase that usually anticipates a significant change in the fundamentals sometime later.
- They provide the patient, astute technician with infrequent but highly rewarding opportunities to position himself or herself in a market possibly undergoing an important reversal in price, momentum, and investor psychology.

Head and Shoulders
Figure 10.7 illustrates a **head and shoulders** top formation that formed in the August 1991 soybean oil contract. The center high peak at 2370 represents the **head**, while the two adjacent lower peaks at 2315 and 2275 represent the left and right **shoulders**. The horizontal support line in and around the 2200 level represents the crucial **neckline** of the pattern. In a head and shoulders formation, the shoulders do not necessarily have to be symmetrical, nor in lifelike proportion to the size of the head. However, more often than not, the pattern is fairly symmetrical and easily identifiable as a head flanked by two

FIGURE 10.7
August 1991 Soybean Oil

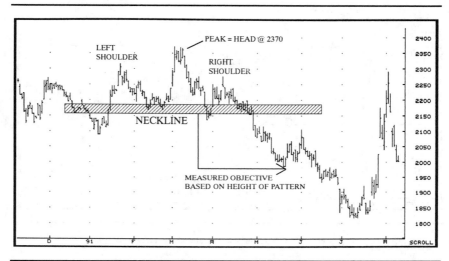

Source: Chart courtesy of FutureSource, a division of Oster Communications, Inc.

shoulders. Of all the formations generally associated with major trend reversals, head and shoulders stand above the rest in terms of reliability.

In the example in Figure 10.7, the pattern took over three months to develop prior to the violation of the neckline support area at 2200 in April 1991. Once the neckline violation occurred, prices stair-stepped to the downside relentlessly for nearly a month and finally found support in the area of 2000. Notice that prices declined about 200 points, which approximates the distance between the neckline and the top of the head.

Figure 10.8 shows an example of a head and shoulders bottom formation in September 1991 crude oil. Left and right shoulder congestion areas developed between 1850 and 1930 over a three-month period, while the lows on February 19, 1991 (the end of the Persian Gulf War), were established at the 1690 level. Once the price structure penetrated 1950 and clearly breached the horizontal neckline, on an up-gap opening at 1982 on the morning of April 10, an advance commenced that propelled prices toward 2200. As with the August soybean oil, prices

FIGURE 10.8
September 1991 Crude Oil

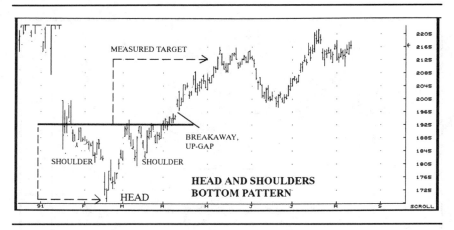

Source: Chart courtesy of FutureSource, a division of Oster Communications, Inc.

moved toward a measured objective equal to the distance between the tip of the head and the neckline, which, in the case of
the September crude oil, covered about 210 points.

In both examples (soybean oil and crude oil), the head and
shoulders patterns represented major market turns and led to
large percentage moves in the direction of the breakout.

The Parabolic Rise and Fall

Parabolic rise and fall action can be considered cousin to the V bottom and top formation. Parabolic action is exemplified in the following market situation. Between March and the end of June
1988, several commodities launched enormous and lightning-fast
price increases. The weekly Commodity Research Bureau (CRB)
index, shown in Figure 10.9, is representative of the price advances of sugar, soybeans, and silver—to name a few—which rose
by 15 percent in an eight-week period between May 14 and June
27 of that year. Speculation was rampant as traders bought with
impunity mostly agricultural commodities that were subjected to
severe drought conditions in the central United States.

Such a steep price rise usually reflects a market panic as traders try to cover short positions or reverse into longs at any price.
Prior to May 1988, enormous excess grain and soybean supplies

FIGURE 10.9
Weekly Commodity Research Bureau Index

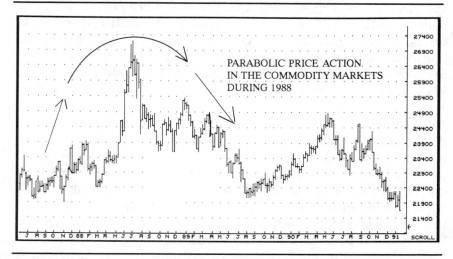

Source: Chart courtesy of FutureSource, a division of Oster Communications, Inc.

tempered the potential for inclement weather conditions. However, as the summer of 1988 approached, and as forecasts of precipitation became more scarce, the price of grains and soybeans climbed in anticipation of a severe drought. Throughout the month of June, each rainless weather forecast produced increasing amounts of fear in the hearts and minds of farmers, traders, and speculators, who pushed prices relentlessly higher for five consecutive weeks.

However, when the rains did come in early July, and after a few hours of reflection, massive liquidation of long positions occurred, pressuring prices all the way back down to their "preparabolic" lift-off levels, which occurred at 240.00 on the weekly CRB chart. Besides the obvious damage inflicted on undercapitalized traders, parabolic chart patterns and price behavior are usually considered significant top formations and could take months, if not years, of subsequent price stability to repair.

Continuation Patterns: The Key to Successful Trading

By definition, major top and bottom patterns occur infrequently and generally require several weeks, if not months, to develop.

The trend that develops after the maturation of a major top or bottom unfolds in a series of down-moves or up-moves interspersed with periods of rest along the way. These rest periods, or pauses within the trend, are referred to as **continuation patterns**. During these rest periods, the price structure chisels out highly recognizable, relatively short-lived but extremely powerful geometric formations that perpetuate the underlying trend. We will review briefly the most common continuation patterns.

Rectangles
A rectangle is a congestion area consisting of a combination of multiple tops (resistance level) and multiple bottoms (support level), with prices fluctuating within the confines of the rectangle formation. The chartist is concerned with determining in which direction prices are likely to break and how far the move is likely to carry. The minimum anticipated price objective from the breakout point of a rectangle equals the height of the rectangle. Specific market factors, peculiar to each situation, tend to add or detract from the total move. The longer the rectangle takes to develop, and the greater the total number of new positions initiated within the congestion area, the more significant the ultimate breakout should be. Figure 10.10 shows a rectangle formation on a 120-minute chart and on a daily chart of the September 1991 Deutsche mark. The rectangle developed during a 10-day period within a strong intermediate term uptrend in the Deutsche mark. The height of the pattern was approximately 110 points (5630 to 5740). Once the price structure broke out to the upside, it climbed to a height of 5842, or 102 points, which almost exactly equaled the height of the rectangle.

Triangles
Triangles are frequently encountered chart formations that tend to occur while a trend is under way. They often mark the midpoint of a move and are more likely to represent a continuation pattern than a reversal pattern. Triangles can be symmetrical, ascending, or descending. A **symmetrical** triangle is a congestion area bounded on top by a down trendline and on bottom by an up trendline. Trading activity consists of a number of descending tops and ascending bottoms, with values converging

FIGURE 10.10

120-Minute September 1991 Deutsche Mark and Daily September 1991 Deutsche Mark

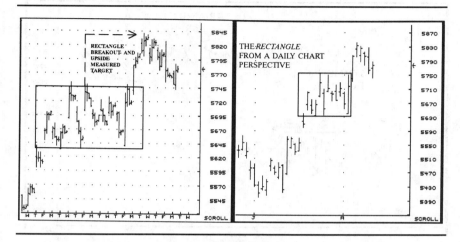

Source: Charts courtesy of FutureSource, a division of Oster Communications, Inc.

toward the apex of the triangle. Prices could break out of the triangle in either direction, although, as noted, the formation is more likely to represent a continuation of the underlying trend, rather than a reversal pattern. A price breakout from a triangle pattern (any type of triangle pattern) will be more reliable if the breakout occurs before prices get into the apex. A breakout from the apex is frequently a false alarm and must be watched very carefully.

An **ascending** triangle is a congestion area bounded by multiple horizontal tops (resistance) and an uptrend of rising lows. This pattern of a flat top against a rising bottom is usually very bullish and tends to break out to the upside.

The third triangle formation, the **descending** triangle, is the reverse of the ascending triangle and consists of a level bottom (support level) and a down trendline, which has a tendency to break to the downside.

Figure 10.11 shows a five-month uptrend in September 1991 crude oil, which exhibited various types of triangle continuation patterns within a bull market environment.

FIGURE 10.11
September 1991 Crude Oil

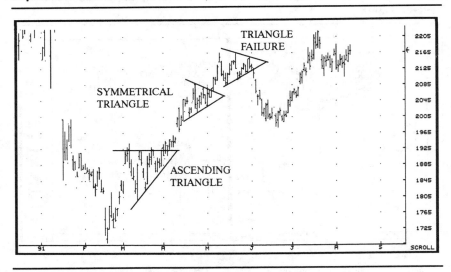

Source: Chart courtesy of FutureSource, a division of Oster Communications, Inc.

Flags and Pennants

Flags and pennants are two other relatively common geometric chart patterns that, like triangles, usually occur during the course of a major move and are usually continuation patterns marking the midpoint of the prevailing move. Particularly following a steep, uncorrected price move, a flag or a pennant resembles a "pennant on a pole." In the majority of cases, these two patterns are continuation formations rather than reversal formations. A downward-sloping flag or pennant seems to break out more frequently on the upside, while an upward-sloping flag is more likely to turn downward. Figure 10.12 shows an intraday 15-minute chart of the September 1991 S&P that exhibits short-term flag and pennant formations that should be recognized and capitalized upon by active traders.

Let us stress, once again, that all of these patterns—rectangles, triangles, pennants, and flags—are simply names applied to differently shaped congestion areas. These variations may well have occurred by chance. It seems clear that if conges-

FIGURE 10.12
15-Minute September 1991 S&P

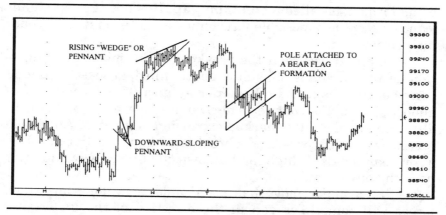

Source: Chart courtesy of FutureSource, a division of Oster Communications, Inc.

tion areas are randomly designed, many could be conveniently framed in one or another of the above configurations. Therefore, we do not place great value on "shape identification" alone. Greater significance attaches to a composite evaluation of the support and resistance levels of the congestion area, the level and location of activity in this area, the relation of this area to trendlines and channels, and chart price objectives.

Market Gaps

The final family of chart formations to be discussed is a group notable for its "absence." Although occurring in several forms, the **gap** is basically a price range within which no trading occurred.

In an **upside gap**, trading will open one morning above the previous day's high, and a **downside gap** occurs when prices open below the low of the previous session. Some gaps are "closed" during the same trading session, or within a few days, whereas other gaps may not be closed for weeks or months. Gap openings are usually caused by heavy public buying or selling at the opening of the market, precipitated by some unexpected news or by the execution of heavy stop orders. A gap caused by stop orders, without the support of substantial follow-through buying or selling, will often trade back to close the gap after the stop orders have been satisfied. This gap, closed shortly after being formed, is called a **common gap**. It is not of great significance, except as a possible forerunner of more volatile impending price action.

A gap that occurs at the breakout of an important congestion formation and is not subsequently filled, at least for a long period of time, is called a **breakaway gap**. This formation frequently marks the commencement of a major move and is usually accompanied by a marked expansion of volume. An upside breakout that leaves behind a breakaway gap is inclined to close at or near the day's high, and a downside breakaway gap at or near the day's low.

After a major move has been under way for some time, prices will sometimes gap in the direction of the underlying trend. This may be caused by some unexpected news or by an accumulation of stop or market orders at the opening of a market. This is known as a **runaway gap**, frequently occurring at or around the midpoint of a major move. The technician may "guesstimate" a price objective for the move on the assumption that the runaway gap represents approximately the halfway point of the entire move.

Even major price moves do not continue indefinitely. An important type of reversal formation, especially following a steep move, is the **exhaustion gap** or **key island reversal gap**. During the latter stage of a bull move, an exhaustion gap would begin to develop just like a runaway gap, where prices open higher than the previous session's high, but the day's high is not sustained and, toward the close, prices begin to decline, closing at or near the lows for the day.

The key reversal from a bear market occurs in inverse fashion. Key reversals are usually accompanied by a sharp increase in trading volume. Unless new trend-continuing incentives come into the market on the following day, the key reversal gap is likely to attract additional liquidation, as well as new countertrend positions, and will very likely signify the termination of the existing price trend. As noted previously, a major top reversal from a bull market usually takes less time to develop than a major bottom formation following an extended

FIGURE 10.13
December 1991 Corn

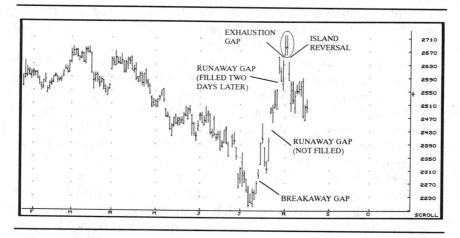

Source: Chart courtesy of FutureSource, a division of Oster Communications, Inc.

bear market. Figure 10.13, a daily chart of December 1991 corn, clearly exhibits the various types of gap formations discussed here.

CONVENTIONAL MEASUREMENTS: PROJECTIONS AND RETRACEMENTS

Rule #7: *Once a congestion area is identified, determine the parameters of retracement and follow-through.* The analysis of continuation patterns requires the recognition that a particular price trend has entered a consolidation period. This brings two important questions to mind:

- How much of the original gains are vulnerable to profit taking?
- What is the likely follow-through potential when the consolidation period ends?

After examining thousands of charts, a rough guideline emerges that suggests that continuation patterns usually retrace from one-third to two-thirds of the previous advance (decline) before resuming the underlying trend. Generally, the more shallow the retracement, the more mature and powerful the underlying trend direction. The thrust out of a congestion area frequently approximates the distance of a prior up-leg (down-leg), including preceding gap areas.

Figure 10.14 illustrates the retracement-consolidation-follow-through sequence that occurred during both the uptrend and downtrend periods of the September 1991 silver contract. Notice the different types of continuation and gap patterns, the size of the retracement, and the magnitude of the subsequent thrusts within the existing trend channel. While not all charts will follow the price action shown in Figure 10.14, the example is representative of technical action in today's actively traded markets.

Rule 7 is important to the technical trader largely because it enables him or her to establish measured expectations about the anticipated price behavior of the underlying trend. In addition, it helps the trader to employ money management guidelines concerned with the positioning of stop-loss orders, market exposure, and target levels for the purpose of profit taking.

Rule #8: *Remain cognizant of, and consistently monitor, volume and open interest in conjunction with ongoing trend analysis.*

FIGURE 10.14
September 1991 COMEX Silver

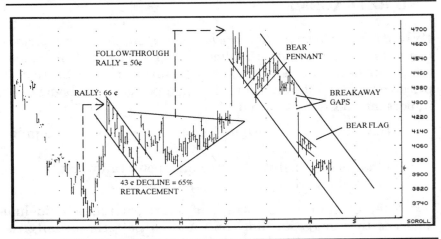

Source: Chart courtesy of FutureSource, a division of Oster Communications, Inc.

Technicians and chartists are volatility seekers. They are ever on the lookout for two inviting omens:

- A pronounced price change
- An indication that the price change in question is significant

One obvious sign that new forces may be stirring is a quickening tempo of activity. In stocks as well as futures, traders who watch market action closely become intrigued when volume buyers and sellers suddenly appear. Where the action is, price movement is apt to be worthwhile. In such circumstances, a dollar ventured may be either expanded by a significant multiple, or quickly lost.

For the watchful trader, an ideal situation might be one in which a commodity has been dormant for many weeks or months. All at once, volume begins to expand, and prices move out of their long-established trading range. Aggressive new buyers and overwhelmed sellers scurry to position or exit the market, which increases the pace of trading and the volume of contracts that change hands.

Figure 10.15 shows a classic example of total volume expansion (all active contracts, including the most active December contract) and price acceleration that occurred in December 1988 corn during the drought-strickened summer of 1988. For nearly five months, December corn prices remained in a tight sideways-to-rising channel that was accompanied by average daily volume of approximately 40,000 contracts. However, starting with the up-gap opening on Monday, May 16, the price structure burst out of the trading channel on relatively high volume of 63,000 contracts, which inaugurated the vertical thrust from 2.25 to 3.70. Notice that daily volume levels expanded during the entire month of June and peaked at 126,000 contracts, or over four-and-a-half times the levels recorded in previous months.

The volume/price behavior of December corn is representative of all the futures markets and instructs us that dramatic price changes are accompanied by significant changes in volume. In other words, high volume packs "go power" and is particularly worth considering as a sign of impending price change. As was the case with corn, this may be true not only at the beginning of

FIGURE 10.15

December 1988 Corn (total volume expansion and price acceleration)

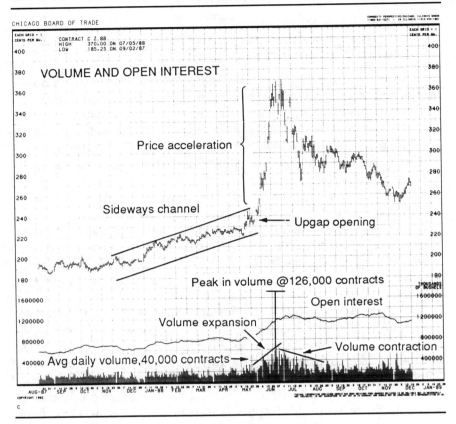

Source: Chart courtesy of Commodity Research Bureau, a Knight-Ridder Business Information Service.

a move, but also near its end. Thus, it is a popular hypothesis that *after a sustained price advance, a period of exceptionally heavy volume marked by an inability to advance, followed soon by a price reversal on high volume, will often portend a significant trend reversal.* In the same way, after a sustained steep decline, a high-volume reversal may be climactic.

A coindicator, often interpreted together with variations in volume, is change in open interest (number of contracts outstanding). Just before a delivery month commences trading, the open interest in that futures position is zero. Once trading begins, the **open interest** rises as buyers and sellers come into the market. For each outstanding contract, there exists one buyer and one seller. Thus, if a new buyer and a new seller enter the market, the open interest increases by one contract. When a new buyer replaces an old one (by purchasing a contract from a previous long), there is a change in ownership, but no change in the number of contracts outstanding. When an existing long sells one contract and an existing short buys one contract, the pair have liquidated one lot, and the open interest drops by that figure.

A buildup in open interest is most often associated with a rise in the volume of hedge-selling, and, on the other side of the ledger, with an increase in the speculative long interest. Ordinarily, hedging is the dynamic element. As a crop movement expands, dealers and processors hedge purchases of actuals, and prices move to the levels needed to attract adequate speculative buying demand. However, the situation may be reversed, with an expansion in open interest coming from speculative buying.

Speculators are most often biased to trading from the long side. A consequence of this preference is that once open interest builds significantly, the number of speculative longs in a market is generally high, often to a degree that technically weakens the market (increases the market's vulnerability to sharp reactions). So long as speculators continue to buy, the potential for a market reversal may be obscured. But once new speculative buying falters, weakness can suddenly develop, with prices declining to a degree beyond any apparent fundamental justification.

Regardless of whether the large open interest position was generated by speculative or hedge interests, it may be a precursor to a trend violation. When open interest stands at a relatively high level, a penetration of an established trend (usually on high volume) should be regarded as a warning of an impending price reversal.

Figure 10.16 shows the price and open interest behavior during a 10-month uptrend in the March 1991 Treasury bill contract. Open interest peaked during the first week of February at the 60,000 contract level, right before a significant breakdown in the price structure through the intermediate term up trendline. Given the extent of the price rise over such an extended period of time, the violation of the up trendline triggered

FIGURE 10.16
March 1991 3-Month T-Bills

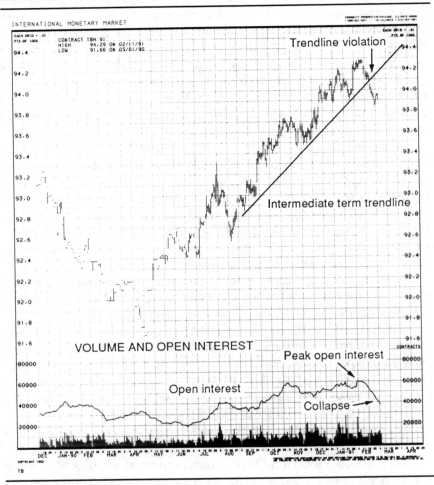

Source: Chart courtesy of Commodity Research Bureau, New York.

liquidation of long positions and a virtual collapse in open interest from 60,000 to 34,000 contracts within a five-week period. In this particular case, the price breakdown scared many weak holders of long positions, which served to "squeeze" the speculative excess out of the market prior to a resumption of the bull market.

In evaluating the significance of changes in open interest, one logical approach is to analyze how any given change is produced. It is usual for analysts to consider the four following possibilities:

IF price and open interest change as follows:	THEN the main market influence is judged to be:
price rises and open interest rises	new buying
price rises and open interest declines	short covering
price declines and open interest rises	new selling
price declines and open interest declines	long liquidation

Recall that every time a futures trade occurs, there is an equal number of contracts bought and sold. However, when price and open interest rise together, then it seems plausible to regard new buying as the predominant force. Similarly, when open interest is rising and price is declining, we may consider the dominant influence to be new selling.

Technicians generally consider trading volume (in addition to open interest change) in gauging the significance of a given technical formation. Generally, the combined impact of open interest and volume produce two principal assertions:

1. In an advancing market, rising open interest and high volume tend to confirm the validity of the uptrend (the market is considered technically strong).

2. In a declining market, rising open interest and high volume tend to confirm the validity of the downtrend (the market is considered technically weak).

As a corollary of the above, the following are considered:

1. A declining open interest in a rising market represents strength primarily because of short covering (the market is considered technically weak).

2. A declining open interest in a falling market represents price weakness primarily because of long liquidation (the market is considered technically strengthening as the open interest is reduced).

Furthermore, we may state the following:

1. When price and open interest move together, the market is considered technically strong and, therefore, either actually or potentially bullish.

2. When price and open interest diverge, the market is considered technically weak and, therefore, either actually or potentially bearish.

Critics of this conventional perspective of volume and open interest point out that it has not been easy to validate it statistically. The relationships involved are probably more subtle and complex than the foregoing hypothesis implies. For example, it is not uncommon for a top or bottom to be made on high volume accompanied by rising open interest. At such times, the combination of an extended price move accompanied by expanded open interest and volume may indicate that the market has become overconfident and is becoming increasingly vulnerable. Whether or not this is so must be judged, in part, from other evidence, including the behavior of the "crowd." That is, one must give consideration to the contrary opinion view, which holds that a very one-sided public conviction is often a prelude to a significant market reversal.

Taking these criticisms into account, we might suggest that the technician focus on significant and sudden changes in volume and open interest, and that a combined rise (fall) of price and open interest on high volume has bullish (bearish) implications in the early stages of an up-move (down-move), but this bullish (bearish) significance diminishes as the speculative public assimilates the factors that fueled the advance (decline).

SUMMARY: RULES OF TECHNICAL ANALYSIS

With our discussion of volume and open interest, we have concluded the introductory material on technical analysis. The elementary tools, concepts, and rules of technical analysis, such as charts, trends, and pattern recognition, are indispensable elements of futures analysis and must be understood and mastered by any serious trader. Here we list our eight introductory trading rules, which should be studied before moving on to more esoteric studies or advanced technical analysis, to which we will next turn our attention.

Rule #1: *Keep an open mind in the study of technical analysis.*

Rule #2: *In analyzing price charts, first identify the major trend of the market.*

Rule #3: *After the trend direction has been determined, draw a trendline.*

Rule #4: *After the trendline has been drawn, identify and draw a parallel channel line.*

Rule #5: *Recognize and respect congestion areas of support and resistance.*

Rule #6: *Determine if the price configuration is, or has the makings of, a recognizable technical pattern.*

Rule #7: *Once a congestion area is identified, determine the parameters of retracement and follow-through.*

Rule #8: *Remain cognizant of, and consistently monitor, volume and open interest in conjunction with ongoing trend analysis.*

CHAPTER 11

ADVANCED TECHNICAL ANALYSIS AND PATTERN RECOGNITION

The previous chapter acquainted us with the basic tools of technical analysis. We now consider variations and extensions of the basic theme of trend analysis that can provide the technician with additional invaluable information about the profile of the market under examination.

CYCLES, WAVES, AND OTHER ASSORTED ESOTERICA

Cycle Analysis

It will only be a matter of time before the discerning chartist discovers, deliberately or inadvertently, the discipline of cycles—that is, the belief that prices behave similarly over defined, measurable periods of time. Just as winter follows fall or Halley's Comet streaks through our skies once every 76 years, futures prices have been observed in basing or peaking price patterns at regular intervals, from eight hours to 54 years. The *Random House Dictionary of the English Language* defines a **cycle** as a "recurring period of time, especially one in which certain events or phenomena repeat themselves in the same order and at the same time intervals." Frequently, price action over time fits that description.

A textbook example of cyclicity occurred in the copper market in 1988 when multiple cycles of varying lengths bottomed within a six-month period. Although the charts in this chapter depict price action that occurred some years ago, they are, nevertheless, extremely instructive. The chart of December 1988 copper (Figure 11.1) illustrates short-term cyclicity. For the 11 months between February and December 1988, copper prices established short-term trading lows every 22 market days. By examining the chart we can identify a regular period of price activity that repeated itself roughly every 22 days, or every four to five weeks. Armed with this information, the copper trader can identify a "window of expectation," which, when combined with other forms of analysis, can greatly enhance the timing and decision-making processes concerning entry and exit from the copper market.

Figure 11.1 also shows the short-term cycle activity of copper prices against a backdrop of trendline and channel analysis. Until upside price acceleration took place beginning in late September 1988, prices had been confined to a seven-month up-slanted trading channel. Notice that each time prices touched the lows of the channel line, it coincided with an average 22-day cycle low. Minor lows were established in each 19-to-23-day period. It appears, however, as though deeper, more meaningful lows (but not damaging to the health of the underlying trend) occurred at every third short-term cycle bottom, or, in other words, every 60 to 67 days.

Based, once again, on examining the chart, we add a recurring, intermediate-term cycle to our arsenal of growing information about copper price behavior, which, thus far, contains information that instructs us to expect meaningful lows approximately every 22 days and again every 64 days.

From the perspective of market timing, in the spring of 1988, profitable trading on the long side of the copper market would have had the highest likelihood of success during the period of the simultaneous bottoming of both the 22-day and 64-day cycles. As long as the up trendline remained intact on a closing basis, buying against the trendline support at multiple cycle lows provided excellent market entry points.

It is important to recognize, however, that once the cycle period is identified with any degree of confidence and reliability, the technician must await a bona fide confirmation signal prior

FIGURE 11.1

Short-Term Cyclicity (Daily December 1988 Copper)

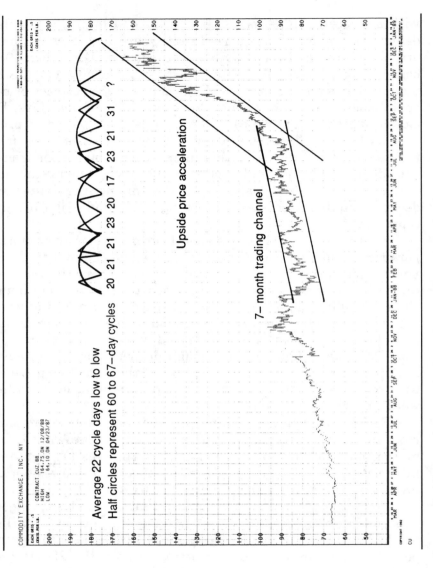

Source: Chart courtesy of Commodity Research Bureau, a Knight-Ridder Business Information Service.

to entering the market. In the case of copper prices illustrated in Figure 11.1, notice that most, if not all, of the cycle lows between February and September made intraday upside reversals or gapped higher the session following a cycle low, confirming that an important upside reversal and short-term trend change had occurred. Upon recognizing the cycle-low confirmation signal, entry on the long side of December copper was justified from a technical perspective.

In the absence of a confirmation signal, however, entering the market based solely on a projected low that may or may not have occurred would have been insufficient evidence upon which to base a decision to employ—and risk—one's hard-earned equity. Remember, *cycles are valuable secondary technical tools only if conventional technical price activity confirms their existence.*

The cycle phenomenon in commodity price behavior can be observed occurring over longer periods of time as well. To continue our example using copper prices, Figure 11.2 shows that copper prices have a reasonably reliable 30-month, or two-and-a-half-year, cycle (+/−four months). Thirty-month cycles are considered significant longer-term time intervals, and impact with commensurate cyclic force. As such, the bottoming of an intermediate-term cycle can be, and usually is, accompanied by extreme price pressure that more often than not has downside blow-off characteristics.

Extreme long-term cycle activity can be observed as well, and is considered a significant technical event that reverses the direction of prices for years to come. Figure 11.2 also shows the approximate five-year recurring cycle lows (shown in shaded areas) in copper prices since the mid-1970s. After each major cycle low, prices experienced a relatively brief basing period prior to an explosive vertical advance.

The information gleaned from cycle behavior can be extremely helpful to traders and investors, provided it is used properly, and can be incorporated into a disciplined approach to chart analysis. With that in mind, we add another trading rule of technical analysis:

Rule #9: *Price/time cycle observation should complement conventional trend analysis.* After examining a particular

FIGURE 11.2
30-Month Cycle (Monthly Copper Prices)

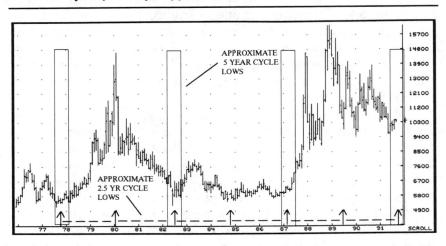

Source: Chart courtesy of FutureSource, a division of Oster Communications, Inc.

chart to determine trend direction and to insert trendlines and channels, the chartist should search for periodicity in short-, intermediate-, and long-term cyclic activity, note various important cycle time periods, and extrapolate or project the next series of lows. Once that is accomplished, it can be determined whether the dominant underlying cyclic direction is up or down, and positive or negative.

Copper prices provide a valuable case study, as examination of copper price charts of various duration revealed a major cycle low every five to six years, and shorter-term cycle lows every 28–31 months and each 11–13 weeks.

Based on long-term cycling expectations for a five- to six-year low due between June 1987 and June 1988, and based on intermediate-term cyclic expectations for 30-month lows due around December 1986 (+/−four months), the cycle work was projecting a possible significant buying opportunity sometime during the 12-month period between early 1987 and early 1988. Furthermore, add to the long-term cycle information the reliability of the 11–13-week cycle, and you have an identifiable window of expectation mapped out for future reference.

Between August 1986 and April 1987, copper prices formed a **saucer bottom** pattern during the projected time period for important cycle lows (see Figure 11.3). Once the upside breakout occurred in May 1987, with the penetration of a five-year down trendline that confirmed the cyclic lows (see Figure 11.2), copper prices exploded from $0.63 per pound and raced toward $1.50 per pound in less than six months. To anyone who followed cyclic price behavior, the power exerted by rising copper prices was no coincidence, especially in view of the bottoming process of the five-and-a-half year and 30-month time cycles.

From the breakout point in copper, the overriding technical considerations should be juxtaposed against a backdrop of upside cyclic pressure until such time as projections of cycle peaks can be made, alerting the trader to the possibility of approaching "natural" resistance.

This explanation of the cycle analysis is a simple representation of a fairly complex subject but, nonetheless, one that provides the reader with the flavor of the discipline. Any aggressive technician should integrate the study of cycles into his or her overall chart analysis.

FIGURE 11.3
Saucer Bottom Pattern (Weekly Copper Prices)

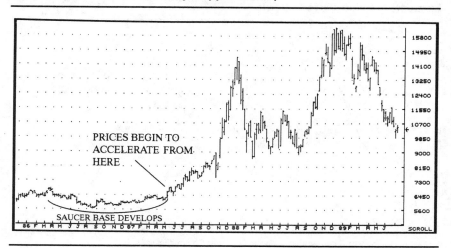

Source: Chart courtesy of FutureSource, a division of Oster Communications, Inc.

Wave Analysis

The **Elliott Wave Theory,** an esoteric body of technical work, was first published in 1938 by Charles J. Collins as the Wave Principle, based on the original work of Ralph Nelson Elliott.

After studying years of stock market price behavior, Elliott discovered that prices (represented by the Dow Jones Industrial Average) move in repetitive sequence. Quite apart from market watchers who believed that prices move randomly, Elliott's study concluded that stock prices rhythmically chiseled out stair-step advances or declines in sequences of fives and threes (see Figure 11.4). Bull market advances, he observed, consist of five distinct movements (three up and two down), whereas corrections within a bull market environment consist of three separate price moves (two down and one up). Conversely, in a bear market environment, declines are characterized by sequences of five distinct moves (three down and two up), followed by upside corrections of three moves (two up and one down). It was Elliott's determination that bull and bear markets—at least with respect to stock prices—are governed by a natural repetitive order that manifests itself in observable, even predictable, patterns.

FIGURE 11.4
Elementary Elliott Wave Patterns

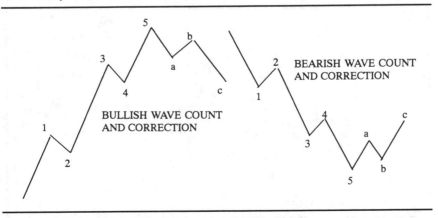

Source: Courtesy of FutureSource, a division of Oster Communications, Inc.

Although there were no financial futures markets for Ralph Elliott to analyze back in the 1930s, his theory of price behavior transcends stock price behavior, and can be applied to commodity and futures prices as well.

Whereas Elliott recognized the repetitive and ongoing nature of stock market waves, we have found that not all futures markets exhibit reliable wave characteristics at all times. But most futures markets—especially the financial markets—do, at certain times, exhibit patterns that conform to traditional Elliott wave structure. It is precisely at those times that a working knowledge of Elliott's basic principles can provide the technician and trader with the edge that could prove significant in approaching a particular market and trading strategy. Elliott pattern recognition applied to futures price behavior will enhance the technician's ability to recognize—and participate in— unfolding bullish or bearish trends, and will help in the timing of entry and exit points.

As you might imagine, applying the wave principle to one's price analysis is a very subjective exercise, as one chartist's third wave can be considered another's fifth. Nevertheless, although Elliott himself could not explore futures price behavior, there are many examples where the wave discipline has been applied to futures price analysis with very rewarding results.

Figure 11.5 shows a monthly chart of the S&P 500 stock index (nearest futures) from mid-1982 to mid-1991. The overall pattern exhibits three distinct up-legs separated by two down-legs (the crash of 1987 and the minicrash of 1989).

From a slightly shorter-term perspective, Figure 11.6 is a weekly chart that shows the unfolding of a primary down-leg in the silver market between 1990 and 1991. After prices peaked at $5.35 per ounce in August 1990, a well-defined downside five-wave pattern unfolded in a classic Elliott wave format. Notice that each minor down-leg within the overall decline subdivided into five waves. Such a disciplined pattern should alert the technician that the market (in this case, silver) is in the grasp of a **primary bear market** structure and, therefore, that short positions should be considered or maintained.

FIGURE 11.5
Wave Counts (Monthly S&P 500 [nearest futures])

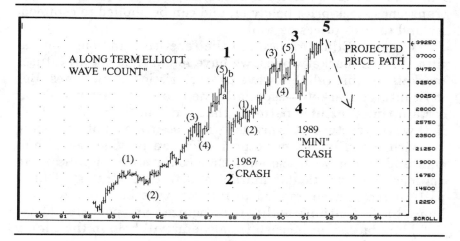

Source: Chart courtesy of FutureSource, a division of Oster Communications, Inc.

FIGURE 11.6
Primary Down-Leg Unfolding (Weekly Silver Prices [nearest futures])

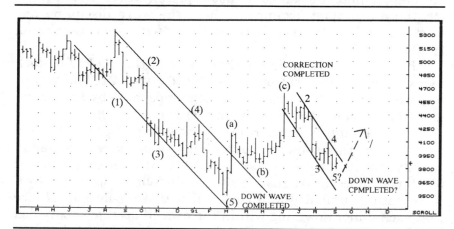

Source: Chart courtesy of FutureSource, a division of Oster Communication, Inc.

The weekly silver chart also depicts two important Elliott rules of pattern recognition:

1. The third wave is usually the longest and most powerful of the primary legs.
2. The unfolding wave form usually creates defined channels of operation that can be used as confirmation of the wave count.

As far as the first rule is concerned, if the chartist can determine that the first wave unfolded in a five-wave structure, ideally he wants to participate in the subsequent five-wave price move in the direction of the original five-wave structure (third wave), which he expects will be considerably longer and more rewarding. Having such knowledge enables the chartist to time his entry during a countertrend correction in anticipation of a dynamic third-wave price move, which Elliott observed to be at least as long as the first wave, and often 1.618 times longer. In the silver collapse during the second half of 1990, the third wave traveled 1.30 times the distance of the first wave.

As for the second rule, channel lines often help the chartist get his bearings within the unfolding wave count. The decline in silver prices chiseled out a textbook wave pattern that precisely traversed a well-defined, down-sloping channel, and continued to provide guidance during the subsequent corrective and primary waves. In addition to aiding the chartist in his subjective interpretation of wave structure, the channels can also be used to identify support and resistance levels, and as guides for the determination of money management (risk) decisions.

Our final example of wave form incorporates ratio analysis and shows the textbook development of a bull market in heating oil in the January 1990 futures contract (see Figure 11.7). The key development on the entire chart occurred during the rally immediately following the lows that were established in June 1989 at 4800. The rally from 4800 to 5370 (first wave) unfolded in a five-wave structure after a final vertical down-leg, which itself exhibited a five-wave structure. One of Elliott's main tenets is that adjacent five-wave moves do not occur unless there is a significant change in trend.

To the discerning chartist, once a five-wave decline followed by a five-wave advance has been observed, a major clue exists

FIGURE 11.7
Ratio Analysis of Wave Form (Daily January 1990 Heating Oil)

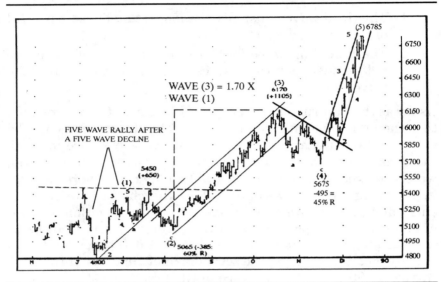

Source: Chart courtesy of FutureSource, a division of Oster Communications, Inc.

that the decline in heating oil prices had come to a close and that a period of rising prices lay ahead. Therefore, to experienced "Elliotticians," the two-week rally should have alerted them to reorient their trading strategy to the long side of the market.

At that juncture, the Elliott trader looked for a setback to buy heating oil in anticipation of a major third-wave advance. Such an opportunity came during a three-week period of sideways-to-downside price action between 5400 and 5100 (second wave), after which prices rocketed to the 6170 highs in eight weeks. The third-wave advance began to accelerate to the upside upon penetration of the first-wave highs in the vicinity of 5450. Once the breakout occurred, prices climbed at a steep 45-degree angle within the confines of a well-defined trading channel. In fact, all the primary up-legs (1, 3, and 5), occurred within progressively steeper channels in a picturesque Elliott wave bull market structure.

In addition to helping us identify a major turn in trend, the wave principle also prescribes for its followers relationships that can be used to project targets through the use of Fibonacci ratios and percentage retracements.

Leonardo Fibonacci was a thirteenth-century mathematician who discovered a number sequence upon which Elliott based his wave theory. In Fibonacci's number sequence—1, 2, 3, 5, 8, 13, 21, 34, 55, 89, 144, 233, 377,. . .—the sum of any two consecutive numbers equals the next higher number in the sequence, and, after the first four numbers, the ratio of any two numbers approaches .618, or 62 percent. The first three Fibonacci ratios—1:1, 1:2, 2:3—represent Elliott's retracement levels of 100 percent, 50 percent, and 67 percent, respectively.

Elliott studied this number series and found that the stock market's wave patterns and the relationship between its legs were governed by the properties of the Fibonacci number series. Elliott also discovered that the length of the waves had various proportional and percentage relationships that could be calculated in advance of an actual rally or decline. For example, one of Elliott's rules states that the top of the third wave can be calculated by multiplying the length of the first wave by 1.618 and adding that value to the bottom of the second wave.

Armed with a working knowledge of the wave principle and its Fibonacci ratios, the chartist would have had an exciting and rewarding experience trading the long side of the heating oil market in the seven-month period between June 1989 and December 1989.

To return to our example in Figure 11.6, the initial five-wave advance was followed by a three-wave correction that successfully held the previous lows and ushered in an explosive subsequent advance. If we add a Fibonacci 1.618 to the length of the first wave, which was 570 points, measured from the bottom of the second wave, our minimum upside target for the third wave would equal 6115. Prices actually climbed vertically and surpassed the initial Fibonacci target at 6115, but not by much. Furthermore, the fourth-wave correction occurred in a classic Elliott wave "a-b-c" retracing 45 percent of the third-wave advance, which was right in the middle of two classic Fibonacci retracement plateaus of 38 percent and 50 percent (38 percent is considered to be a Fibonacci retracement because when any number in the series other than 1, 2, or 3 is divided by the number that is two higher in the series—that is, 8 divided by 21, 144 divided by 377,and so on—the result is approximately .38). Finally, the up-move, or fifth wave, was completed at approximately 6800, within the confines of a tight, well-defined channel, and resulted in a Fibonacci 2100-point advance from the 4800 contract lows.

Esoteric analysis? Perhaps, but there are countless examples of Elliott wave structures and Fibonacci relationships on the futures charts of the past and present. Given a little patience, a firm understanding of conventional trend analysis (which is the prerequisite base of our technical knowledge), and time to learn Elliott's rules, the chartist can explore for himself or herself how prices behave in a specific market.[1]

Rule #10: *The chartist should be able to recognize Elliott wave patterns and have a rudimentary understanding of Fibonacci ratios and retracements.* Having knowledge of wave theory should be considered having an edge over someone who chooses to ignore a body of technical work that can provide clues about the impending price direction of a particular commodity.

Associated Esoterica: Mathematical "Sensors"

Cycle and wave analysis are two disciplines within the larger discipline of technical analysis, which we defined previously as the study of price behavior. Although the bulk of our interest concerns pattern recognition, the use of mathematical formulas to study the relationship among prices can enhance our ability to determine the direction of a trend and its underlying strength or weakness.

For the most part, we are talking about the construction and use of a **price oscillator** (a technical indicator that measures market momentum, where momentum is defined as the rate of change of prices). Several of the more popular oscillators include the following:

- Welles Wilder's Relative Strength Index (RSI)
- Stochastic Oscillator
- Williams's % R
- Moving Average Convergence/Divergence (MACD)

---

[1]For a more extensive discussion of the Elliott Wave Theory, refer to *The Elliott Wave Principle* by Robert Prechter and A. J. Frost (see Bibliography).

For illustrative purposes, and in the interest of simplicity, we will confine our brief examination of oscillators to the one most widely followed, RSI.[2]

The mathematical formula for RSI is expressed as follows:

$$RSI = 100 - \frac{100}{1.00 + RS}$$

$$RS = \frac{Average\ number\ of\ days\ closes\ up}{Average\ number\ of\ days\ closes\ down}$$

Once RSI is calculated and entered into the formula, the resulting value will be expressed as a whole number and plotted on an index graph with coordinates from 0 to 100. Wilder discovered that a climb in the index above 70 would be considered a bullish extreme (prices would turn down) and that a decline in the index to below 30 would be considered a bearish extreme (prices would turn up). An example of RSI behavior (using a nine-day period for the value of the number of days in the formula) with respect to daily October 1991 sugar prices is shown in Figure 11.8.

Each time the RSI index approached or dropped beneath the 30 level, the rate of descent slowed considerably, or prices rallied to relieve the oversold condition. Sometimes a rally developed from an oversold condition, which not only relieved the oversold condition but inaugurated a powerful advance that propelled the index into overbought territory above the 70 level. Once overbought, sugar prices invariably reacted, rested, or declined until the overbought condition was relieved.

In addition to viewing the RSI as an overbought/oversold indicator, it can be used to gauge momentum divergences as well. One such divergence occurred at the August lows. In the early part of August 1991, prices established lows at 810, at which time the RSI recorded an oversold reading of 24. After a very brief rally, prices plunged to new lows at 790, but the RSI managed to hold at its prior lows at 24 (see 1 in Figure 11.8). In other words, although prices declined to new lows, the RSI es-

---

[2]The oscillators listed above are discussed in detail in *Technical Analysis of the Markets: A Comprehensive Guide to Trading Methods and Applications (see Bibliography)*.

FIGURE 11.8
9-Day RSI (Daily October 1991 Sugar)

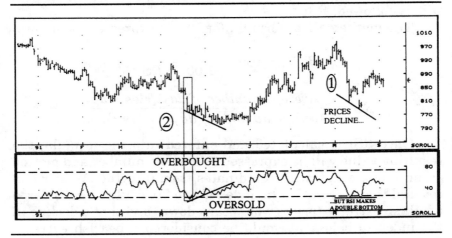

Source: Chart courtesy of FutureSource, a division of Oster Communications, Inc.

tablished a double bottom, and in doing so failed to confirm the price weakness. That price/RSI behavior is referred to as a bullish nonconfirmation and alerts the chartist that downside momentum is slowing or stopping. It also alerts one to seriously question the strength of the underlying downtrend and the wisdom of remaining in short positions.

A third popular use of the RSI oscillator is to employ it to trigger buy and sell signals. When the index climbs from below to above the 30 level, traders can enter the long side of the market. Conversely, once the index falls below the 70 level after having been in overbought territory, traders can enter the short side of the market. Although the RSI can be used by itself to generate buy and sell signals, markets have a tendency to show a delayed reaction to RSI signals, which therefore makes it a dangerous indicator upon which to base one's entire decision. For example, in the case of October sugar in Figure 11.8, in mid-April, with prices at approximately 785, the RSI reversed from 23 to give a buy signal. Although the RSI continued to climb for the next four weeks, prices remained under pressure and did not bottom until mid-May in the 750 area (see 2 in Figure 11.8). Anyone who established long positions at the turn of the RSI had to endure a nearly 50-point loss prior to the upside reversal in prices.

The above example is a vivid reminder to the technician to avoid dependence on one indicator for market entry and exit points, and to use the index as one of many tools to fine-tune one's analysis in general and trading strategy in particular.

Rule #11: *The serious chartist should know how to interpret momentum oscillators.* Most subscriber chart services calculate and plot the RSI as well as one or two other oscillators and momentum formulas each week. However, most moderately sophisticated technical analysis software packages have programed the formulas for numeric oscillators and indicators, and using them is a very efficient way to calculate and track them on a real-time basis.

SUMMARY: MORE RULES OF TECHNICAL ANALYSIS

Before we turn our attention to the world of computers and their impact and use in technical analysis, we review a list of our more advanced trading rules:

Rule #9: *Price/time cycle observation should complement conventional trend analysis.*

Rule #10: *The chartist should be able to recognize Elliott wave patterns and have a rudimentary understanding of Fibonacci ratios and retracements.*

Rule #11: *The serious chartist should know how to interpret momentum oscillators.*

CHAPTER 12

INTRODUCTION TO JAPANESE CANDLESTICK CHARTING

By Steve Nison

Chartered Market Technician, Vice President, and Director of Research at Nikkhah Group at Refco, Inc., New York. Adapted from Japanese Candlestick Charting Techniques *by Steve Nison © Steve Nison, 1991.*

Japanese candlesticks are a tool for charting and technical analysis older than bar charts and point-and-figure charts. The candle charts were almost unheard of in the United States until recent years, yet they have been used for generations in Japan.

As you will discover, the candles furnish unique insights into the markets. Gauging by all the services now offering candles to their subscribers, Japanese candlestick charts are now joining bar charts and point-and-figure charts as a standard charting tool. Why have the candles created such interest? Some reasons include the following:

- Candlestick techniques can be used for speculation and hedging; they can be used by all time frame traders and in any market where technical analysis is used.
- Candlestick charts are flexible. Users include first-time chartists as well as seasoned professionals. This is because candlestick charts can be employed either as a standalone tool or combined with other technical methods.
- Whereas the bar chart shows the direction of the move, the candle chart shows both the direction and the force underpinning it.

- The primary reason for the widespread attention aroused by candlestick charts is that using them instead of, or in addition to, bar charts is a win-win situation.

As we will soon discuss, the same data (the open, high, low, and close) is used to draw the candlestick charts as is used for the bar charts. This is very significant. It means that any of the technical analyses used with bar charts (such as moving averages, trend-lines, Elliott wave, and retracements) can also be employed with candlesticks. But—and this is the key point—*candlestick charts can send signals not available with bar charts.* In addition, there are some patterns that may allow one to get the jump on those who use traditional Western charting techniques.

CONSTRUCTING THE CANDLESTICKS

Figure 12.1 shows the familiar bar chart. Figure 12.2 is a candlestick chart using the same price information as in the bar chart. What is immediately noticeable is that on the candlestick chart, prices seem to jump off the page. It presents a stereoscopic view of the market as it pushes the flat, two-dimensional bar chart into three dimensions.

Since candlestick charts are new for most people, I will place them in a familiar perspective by using the most common Western chart, the bar chart, as a reference in learning how to draw the candlestick lines. Drawing the daily bar chart line requires the open, high, low, and close. The vertical line on a bar chart depicts the high and low of the session. The horizontal line to the left of the vertical line is the opening price. The horizontal line to the right of the vertical line is the close.

Figure 12.3 shows how the same data would be used to construct a bar chart and a candlestick chart. Notice how differently the lines are drawn. The thick part of the candlestick line is called the **real body.** It represents the range between the session's open and close. When the real body is black (i.e., filled in) it means the close of the session was lower than the open. If the real body is white (i.e., empty), it means the close was higher than the open.

FIGURE 12.1
Bar Chart

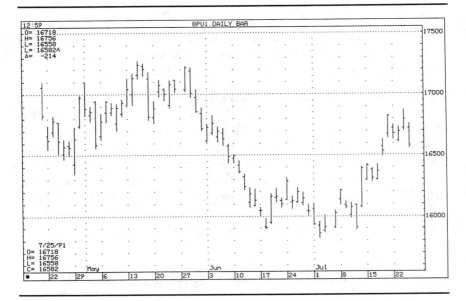

Source: © 1991 CQG, Inc.

FIGURE 12.2
Candlestick Chart

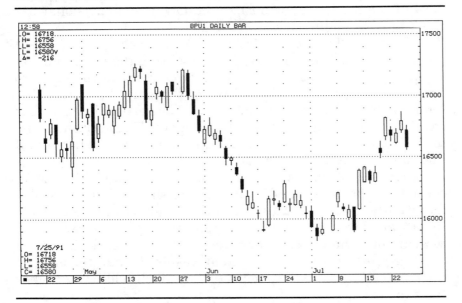

Source: © CQG, Inc.

FIGURE 12.3
Bar Chart Compared with Candlestick Chart

Time Period	Open	High	Low	Close
1	20	30	15	25
2	25	25	10	15
3	30	35	15	20
4	45	50	35	40
5	25	40	25	35

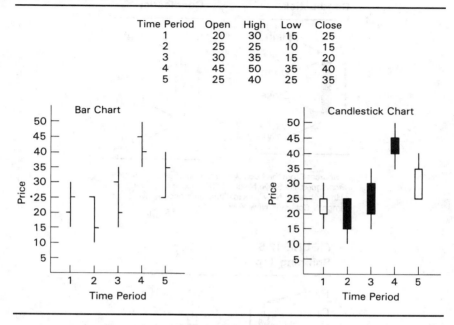

Source: From the book *Japanese Candlestick Charting Techniques*. By Steve Nison © 1991. Used by permission of the publisher, New York Institute of Finance/A division of Simon & Schuster, New York.

The thin lines above and below the real body are the **shadows,** which represent the session's price extremes. The shadow above the real body is called the **upper shadow** and the one below the real body is the **lower shadow.** Accordingly, the peak of the upper shadow is the high of the session and the bottom of the lower shadow is the low of the session. We can clearly see why these are named candlestick charts—the individual bodies often look like candles with their wicks. If a candlestick line has no upper shadow it is said to have a **shaven head.** A candlestick line with no lower shadow has a **shaven bottom.**

The long black candlestick in Figure 12.4 reflects a bearish session in which the market opened near its high and closed near its low. Figure 12.5 shows the opposite of a long black body and thus represents a bullish period, during which prices had a wide range. The market opened near the low and closed near the high of the session.

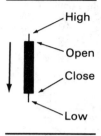

FIGURE 12.4
Bearish
Candlestick

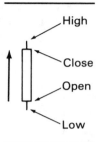

FIGURE 12.5
Bullish
Candlestick

Source: From the book *Japanese Candlestick Charting Techniques.* By Steve Nison © 1991. Used by permission of the publisher, New York Institute of Finance/A division of Simon & Schuster, New York.

FIGURE 12.6
Spinning Tops

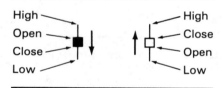

Source: From the book *Japanese Candlestick Charting Techniques.* By Steve Nison © 1991. Used by permission of the publisher, New York Institute of Finance/A division of Simon & Schuster, New York.

The candlesticks in Figure 12.6 have small real bodies; as such, they represent uncertainty or rest. They are called **spinning tops** and are neutral in lateral trading bands but, as shown later, do become important when they are part of star formations. The spinning top can have either a white or a black real body.

Figure 12.7 shows spinning tops for September 1991 silver. The spinning top on June 7 had a high-volume session. Although there was heavy buying, the small real body of the spinning top shows that the selling pressure was aggressive enough to keep

FIGURE 12.7
Spinning Tops (September 1991 Silver)

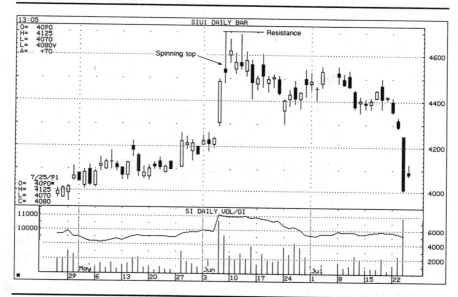

Source: © 1991 CQG, Inc.

the bulls in check. The spinning tops over the next few days reflected a market that was unable to show follow-through to the upside. In addition, on three out of four sessions the market neared $4.70 and failed, which set up a resistance area. These factors gave clear warning that the bull force was dissipating.

In Figure 12.8 there are no real bodies on the candlestick lines, instead, they have a horizontal line. These are examples of **doji lines.** A doji is when the open and close for that session are the same (or very close, e.g., two or three 32s in bonds, a quarter cent in grains, and so on). The lengths of the shadows can vary.

The doji is a distinct trend change signal. However, the likelihood of a reversal increases if subsequent candlesticks confirm the doji's reversal potential. Doji sessions are important only in markets where there are not many doji.

Doji are valued for their ability to call market tops. This is especially true after a long white candlestick in an uptrend. The

FIGURE 12.8
Doji Lines

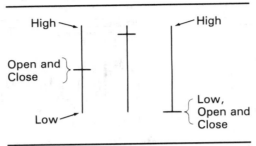

Source: From the book *Japanese Candlestick Charting Techniques.* By Steve Nison © 1991. Used by permission of the publisher, New York Institute of Finance/A division of Simon & Schuster, New York.

reason for the doji's negative implications in uptrends is that a doji represents indecision—indecision, uncertainty, and vacillation by the buyers will not maintain an uptrend. It takes the conviction of buyers to sustain a rally. If the market has had an extended rally and then a doji surfaces, it is read as indecision and could mean that the scaffolding of buyers' support will give way.

As good as doji are at calling tops, based on my experience they lose reversal potential in downtrends. The reason for this may be that, as mentioned above, a doji is synonymous with irresolution. With ambivalent market participants, the market could fall of its own weight. Thus, an uptrend should reverse, but a falling market may continue its descent.Because of this, doji need more confirmation to signal a bottom than they do a top.

A doji after a long white candlestick (See Figure 12.9), especially after a prolonged uptrend, tells us that the forces between the bulls and the bears are in a state of balance. It is often a forewarning that a top is near. Here we see a sharp rally unfolded from late April to late May 1990. During the week of June 4, a doji arose following a tall white candle. This doji showed that the market was in a state of equilibrium. In other words, the bulls had lost control of the market (it does not reflect that the bears have yet taken over). From this doji session, the market stalled before it fell and retested the April lows. Note that in October there was another doji following a long white candle.

FIGURE 12.9
Doji after a Long White Candlestick (Weekly Bonds)

Source: © 1990 CQG, Inc.

The following week's candle closed at a new high for the move, and the market then resumed its upward course. This brings out the point that *if the market closes above the high of a combination of white candle and doji it negates the bearish implications of the pattern.* This is because it shows us the market has moved from a state of balance into one where the bulls have regained control.

So far, we have seen that the relationships among the period's open, high, low, and close alter the look of the individual candlestick line. More importantly, we can now see a major advantage of the candles—like a bar chart they give the trend of the market, but, unlike the bar chart, the candles also show the force behind the move. It is important to note that all the candle examples above can be for intraday to monthly charts. Thus, for a 60-minute candle the open, high, low, and close of the 60-minute period would be used for that candle line; for a daily chart it would be the open, high, low, and close for the day. For the weekly chart the candle would be based on Monday's opening, the high and low of the week, and Friday's close.

REVERSAL PATTERNS

Technicians watch for price clues that alert them to a shift in market psychology and trend. These technical clues are **reversal patterns**. Western reversal indicators include double tops and bottoms, reversal days, head and shoulders, and island tops and bottoms. Most of the candle signals are reversals.

The Hammer and the Hanging Man

Figure 12.10 shows candlesticks with long lower shadows and small real bodies (the real bodies can be black or white), with the real bodies near the top of the daily range. The variety of candlestick lines shown is fascinating in that either line can be bullish or bearish, depending on where it appears in a trend. If either of these lines emerges during a downtrend, it is a signal that the downtrend could end. In such a scenario this line is labeled a **hammer**, as in, "The market is hammering out" a base (see Figure 12.11).

If either of the lines in Figure 12.10 emerges after a rally, it means that the previous move may be ending. Such a line is ominously called a **hanging man** (Figure 12.12) because it looks like a hanging man with dangling legs.

Both the hammer and the hanging man can be recognized by a real body that is at the upper end of the trading range, a long lower shadow that should be twice the height of the real body, and a very short upper shadow or none at all.

Note that the shape of the hanging man line and the hammer are the same, but the implications of the line are completely dependent on where the line is in relation to the trend. For a hanging man line there must be a previous uptrend (even a short-term one), and for a hammer there must be a downtrend preceding it.

FIGURE 12.10
Hammer and Hanging Man Candlesticks

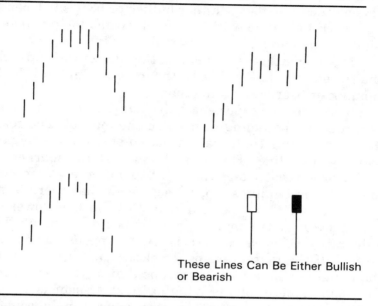

These Lines Can Be Either Bullish
or Bearish

Source: From the book *Japanese Candlestick Charting Techniques*. By Steve Nison © 1991.
Used by permission of the publisher, New York Institute of Finance/A division of Simon &
Schuster, New York.

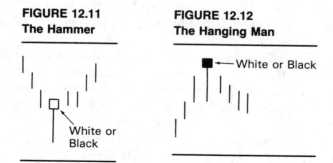

FIGURE 12.11
The Hammer

White or
Black

FIGURE 12.12
The Hanging Man

White or Black

Source: From the book *Japanese Candlestick Charting Techniques*.
By Steve Nison © 1991. Used by permission of the publisher, New York
Institute of Finance/A division of Simon & Schuster, New York.

It may seem unusual that the same candlestick line can be both bullish and bearish, but think about island tops or bottoms. This pattern can also be either bullish or bearish, depending on where it is in a trend, with an island top and top reversal and an island bottom and bottom reversal.

The longer the lower shadow, the shorter the upper shadow; and the smaller the real body, the more meaningful the bullish hammer or bearish hanging man.

Based on my experience, the hanging man must be confirmed before becoming bearish on the market. The reason for the need for this confirmation has to do with the shape of the hanging man line. This line shows that the market sold off during the session and then rallied to close at, or near, the highs. At first impression, it may seem that there is nothing bearish about this type of action. But the long lower shadow does show that the market, once it begins to break, becomes vulnerable. Of more concern is what happens during the next session. If the market opens (or closes) under the real body of the hanging man session, it means that anyone who bought at the open or close of the hanging man session is in a losing position. From this point on, the market may come under pressure.

Figure 12.13 is an excellent example of how the same line can be bearish (as in the hanging man line on July 2) or bullish (the hammer on July 23). Although both the hanging man and the hammer in this example have black bodies, the color of the real body is not important.

Figure 12.14 shows a series of bullish hammers numbered 1 through 4 (hammer 2 is considered a hammer in spite of its minute upper shadow). The interesting feature of this chart is the bullish signal given early in 1990. New lows were made at hammers 3 and 4 as prices moved under the July lows at hammer 2, yet there was no continuation to the downside. The bears had their chance to run with the ball. They fumbled. The two bullish hammers (3 and 4) show the bulls regained control. Hammer 3 was not an ideal hammer because the lower shadow was not twice the height of the real body. Yet, this line did reflect the failure of the bears to maintain new lows. The following week's more classic hammer reinforced that a bottom reversal was likely.

FIGURE 12.13
Hanging Man and Hammer (December 1990 Soybean Oil)

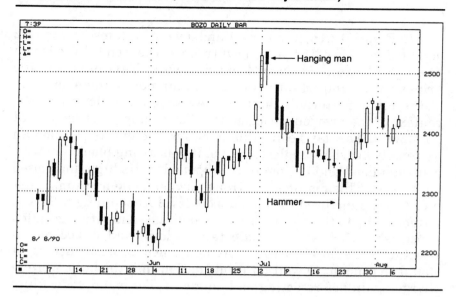

Source: © 1990 CQG, Inc.

FIGURE 12.14
Bullish Hammers (Weekly Copper)

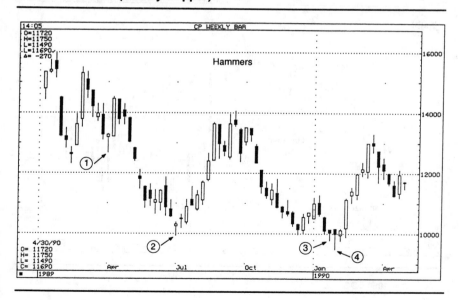

Source: © 1990 CQG, Inc.

In Figure 12.15, hammers 1 and 3 were bottoms. Hammer 2 signaled the end of the prior downtrend as the trend shifted from down to neutral. Hammer 4 did not work. This hammer line brings out an important point about hammers—and about any of the other patterns I discuss: they should be viewed in the context of the previous price action. For example, let us look at hammer 4. The day before this hammer, the market formed an extremely bearish candlestick line. It was a long black day with a shaven head and bottom (i.e., it opened on its high and closed on its low). This manifested strong downside momentum. Hammer 4 also punctured the old support level from January 24 and formed a gap to the downside (as we'll discuss later, this is called a bearish "window" in candle terminology, and it becomes a resistance area). With the aforementioned bearish factors, it would be prudent to wait for confirmation that the bulls were in charge again before acting on hammer 4. For example, a white

FIGURE 12.15
Hammers (May 1990 Lumber)

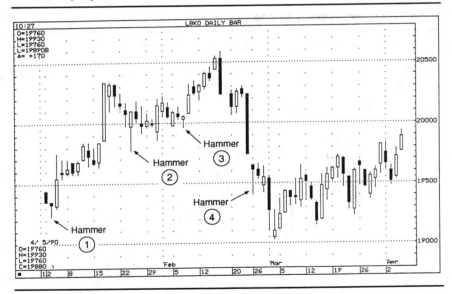

Source: © 1990 CQG, Inc.

candlestick that closed higher than the close of hammer 4 might have been viewed as confirmation.

A classic hanging man is charted in Figure 12.16. There are new highs for the move, via an opening gap, on the hanging man day. Then, the next day, the market gaps under the hanging man's real body. This means that all those new longs who bought on the hanging man's open or close are left "hanging" with a losing position.

An extraordinary advance took place in the orange juice market from late 1989 into early 1990 (see Figure 12.17). Observe where this rally stopped—at the hanging man made in the third week of 1990. This chart illustrates an important point: *a reversal pattern does not necessarily mean that prices will reverse. All a reversal indicator implies is that the previous trend should end,* which is what happened here. After the appearance of the hanging man reversal pattern, the prior uptrend ended; the new trend was sideways.

FIGURE 12.16
Classic Hanging Man (September 1991 Oats)

Source: © 1991 CQG, Inc.

FIGURE 12.17
Hanging Man (Weekly Orange Juice)

Source: © 1990 CQG, Inc.

Another hanging man appeared in July. This time, prices quickly reversed from up to down. As discussed, you should not always expect this scenario with a top trend reversal.

The Engulfing Pattern

The hammer and the hanging man are individual candlestick lines that can send important signals about the market's health. Most candlestick signals, however, are based on combinations of individual candlestick lines. The **engulfing pattern** is one of these multiple candlestick line patterns. It is a sign of major reversal composed of two opposite-color real bodies.

Figure 12.18 shows a bullish engulfing pattern. The market is in a downtrend, then a white bullish real body engulfs the previous period's black real body. Figure 12.19 illustrates a bearish engulfing pattern. Here the market is trending higher. The white real body engulfed by a black body is the signal of a top reversal.

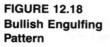

FIGURE 12.18
Bullish Engulfing
Pattern

FIGURE 12.19
Bearish
Engulfing Pattern

Source: From the book *Japanese Candlestick Charting Techniques*. By Steve Nison © 1991. Used by permission of the publisher, New York Institute of Finance/A division of Simon & Schuster, New York.

For an engulfing pattern to be valid, the market has to be in a clearly definable uptrend or downtrend—even if it is a short-term trend.

The closest Western analogy to the Japanese candlestick engulfing pattern is the reversal day. A reversal day occurs when, during an uptrend (downtrend), a new high (low) for the move is made and then prices close under (above) the previous day's close. Because the engulfing pattern requires only that the second real body engulf the previous real body, but it need not engulf the shadows, this pattern will give a signal not available with the Western reversal pattern. This may allow a jump on those who use traditional reversal days as a reversal signal.

The more technical clues there are about a support or resistance area, the more significant that technical zone becomes. Figure 12.20 shows how a bullish engulfing pattern took on extra significance because it was also a successful retest of the previous week's lows.

Let's examine how a candlestick chart might be an advantage over a bar chart. Figure 12.21 shows two bearish engulfing patterns. Since the upper shadows of the black candles of these patterns didn't make new highs, there were no signs of top reversals by using the traditional Western reversal pattern as a gauge. Yet the candlesticks did provide bearish reversal signals with the bearish engulfing patterns.

FIGURE 12.20
Bullish Engulfing Pattern (May 1990 Copper)

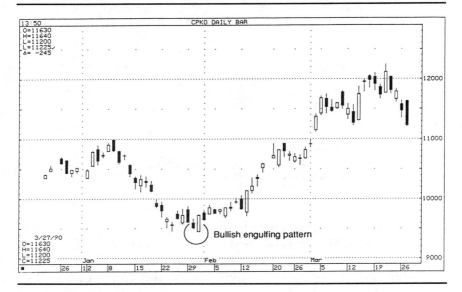

Source: © 1990 CQG, Inc.

The Dark Cloud Cover

The next reversal pattern we will examine is the **dark cloud cover** (see Figure 12.22). It is a two-candlestick pattern that is a top reversal after an uptrend or, at times, at the top of a congestion band. The first day of this two-candlestick pattern is a strong white real body. The second day's price opens above the previous session's high (i.e., above the top of the upper shadow). However, by the end of the second day's session the market closes near the low of the day and well within the previous day's white body. The greater the degree of penetration into the white real body, the more likely a top. Some Japanese technicians require more than a 50 percent penetration of the black real body into the white real body. If the black candlestick does not close below the halfway point of the white candlestick, it may be best to wait for more bearish confirmation on the session after the dark cloud cover.

FIGURE 12.21
Bearish Engulfing Patterns (Monthly CRB)

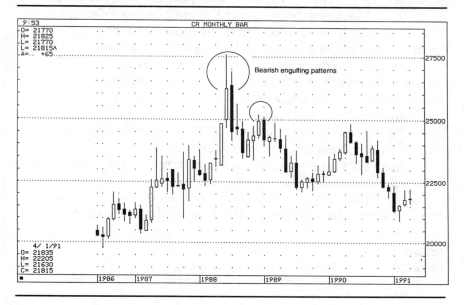

Source: © 1991 CQG, Inc.

FIGURE 12.22
Dark Cloud Cover

Source: From the book *Japanese Candlestick Charting Techniques.* By Steve Nison © 1991. Used by permission of the publisher, New York Institute of Finance/A division of Simon & Schuster, New York.

The greater the degree of penetration of the black real body's close into the previous white real body, the greater the chance for a top. If the black real body covers the previous day's entire white body it would be a bearish engulfing pattern. The dark cloud cover's black real body gets only partially into the white body.

Think of the dark cloud cover as a partial solar eclipse that blocks out part of the sun (i.e., it covers only part of the previous white body). The bearish engulfing pattern can be viewed as a total solar eclipse that blocks out the entire sun (i.e., it covers the entire white body). Consequently, a bearish engulfing pattern is a more meaningful top reversal.

Figure 12.23 shows three dark cloud covers. Other bearish signals confirmed each of these covers. Let's look at these individually.

Dark cloud cover 1 is a variation on the ideal dark cloud cover pattern. In this cover, the second day's black real body

FIGURE 12.23
Three Dark Cloud Covers (July 1990 Crude Oil)

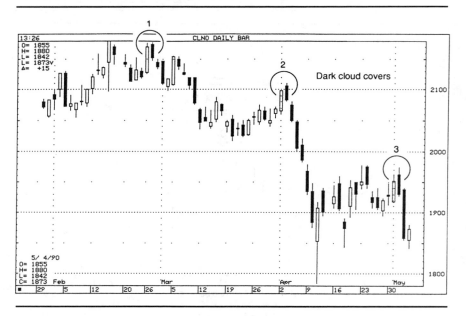

Source: © 1990 CQG, Inc.

opened at the previous day's high instead of above it. It was still a warning sign, and there was an added negative factor. This dark cloud cover also signified a failed attempt by the bulls to take out resistance at the mid-February highs.

Dark cloud cover 2 is not the only reason for caution at this $21.00 level. Consider this technical axiom: a previous support level, once broken, can convert to new resistance. That is what unfolded at $21.00. Notice how the old $21.00 support, once breached on March 9, converted to resistance. The failed rally attempt during the dark cloud cover pattern on the first two days of April proved this.

Dark cloud cover 3 was also a failure at a resistance zone made at the late April highs.

The Piercing Pattern

The bullish pattern in Figure 12.24 is composed of two candlesticks in a falling market. It is the opposite of a dark cloud cover. The first candlestick is a black real body day and the second is a long white real body day. This white day opens sharply lower, under the low of the previous black day. Prices then push higher, creating a relatively long white real body that closes above the midpoint of the previous day's black real body.

A compelling reason to use candle charts is that they pictorially (and quickly) display who is winning in the battle between the bulls and the bears. Let's look at how this relates to the psychology behind what is called the **piercing pattern**. First we observe that the market is in a downtrend; the bearish black real body reinforces this view. The next day the market opens lower via a gap. The bears are watching the market with contentment. Then the market surges toward the close, managing not only to close unchanged from the previous day's close but well into the previous black session's open–close range. The bulls have proved that they can mount a strong counteroffense. The market now takes on a different composure. Those who are looking to buy would say that new lows could not hold; perhaps it is time to step in from the long side. And those who are short will be second-guessing their position.

FIGURE 12.24
Piercing Pattern

Source: From the book
Japanese Candlestick Chart-
ing Techniques. By Steve
Nison © 1991. Used by per-
mission of the publisher,
New York Institute of Fi-
nance/A division of Simon &
Schuster, New York.

Figure 12.25 shows that a piercing pattern in early March was a successful retest of the previous week's lows that were put in place via a bullish engulfing pattern. Here we see the consequence of getting two bullish signals near the same price area.

Stars

One group of fascinating reversal patterns includes **stars**, which are small real bodies that gap away from the previous large real body (Figure 12.26). It is still considered a star as long as the star's real body does not overlap the previous real body. The color of the star is not important. Stars can occur at tops and bottoms.

The star is a warning that the previous trend may be ending. This is because the star's small real body reflects a diminution of buying force (in an uptrend) or selling force (in a down-

FIGURE 12.25
Piercing Pattern (July 1991 Cocoa)

Source: © 1991 CQG, Inc.

FIGURE 12.26
Stars

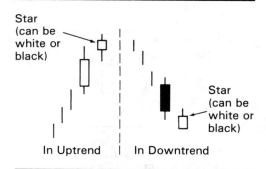

Source: From the book *Japanese Candlestick Charting Techniques.* By Steve Nison © 1991. Used by permission of the publisher, New York Institute of Finance/A division of Simon & Schuster, New York.

177

trend). The star should be respected especially after an extended trend or a rapid price move. Stars are usually more important if the line that precedes the small real body is a large real body.

The star is part of two reversal patterns—the **evening star** and the **morning star**. In either of these star patterns the real body of the star can be white or black.

The Morning Star

The morning star (Figure 12.27) is a bottom reversal pattern. Like the real morning star (the planet Mercury) that foretells the sunrise, it presages higher prices. It is composed of a tall black real body followed by a small real body that gaps lower (these two lines constitute a basic star pattern). The third day is a white real body that moves well within the first period's black real body. This pattern signals that the bulls have seized control. Let's break down this three-candlestick pattern into its components to understand the rationale behind the seizure.

The market is in a downtrend when we see a black real body. At this time the bears are in command. Then a small real body appears, which means that sellers are losing the capability

FIGURE 12.27
Morning Star

Source: From the book *Japanese Candlestick Charting Techniques.* By Steve Nison © 1991. Used by permission of the publisher, New York Institute of Finance/A division of Simon & Schuster, New York.

FIGURE 12.28
Classic Morning Star (Japanese Yen)

Source: © 1991 CQG, Inc.

to drive the market lower. The next day, the strong white real body proves that the bulls took over. An ideal morning star would have a gap before and after the middle line's real body (ie., the star). However, the absence of the second gap does not seem to vitiate the power of this formation.

Figure 12.28 shows a classic bullish morning star pattern developed from March to May 1990. Note how the first and third candles of the morning star resemble a piercing pattern because the white candle pushes well into the black real body.

The Evening Star
The evening star is the bearish counterpart of the morning star pattern. It is aptly named because it appears, like the true evening star (the planet Venus), just before darkness sets in. Since the evening star is a top reversal, it should be acted upon

if it arises after an uptrend. Three lines compose the evening star (see Figure 12.29). The first two lines are a long white real body followed by a star. The star is the first hint of a top. The third line is a black real body that moves sharply into the first period's white real body. The third line corroborates a top and completes the three-line pattern of the evening star. (At first glance, Figure 12.29 may look like an island top reversal as used by Western technicians.)

The evening star pattern can be compared to a traffic light. The traffic light goes from green (the bullish white real body) to yellow (the star's warning signal) to red (the black real body confirms the prior trend has stopped).

By analyzing the evening star more closely, one can see that it furnishes a reversal signal not available with an island top (see Figure 12.30). For an island top, the low of session 2 has to be above the high of sessions 1 and 3. Yet, the evening star requires only the low of the real body 2 to be above the high of real body 1 to be a reversal signal.

An evening star pattern in early May (Figure 12.31) called the high of the market just before the major break. This chart is a classic example of an evening star in which the second session's real body is not touching the first and third session's real bodies.

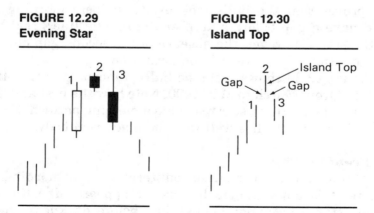

FIGURE 12.29
Evening Star

FIGURE 12.30
Island Top

Source: From the book *Japanese Candlestick Charting Techniques.* By Steve Nison © 1991. Used by permission of the publisher, New York Institute of Finance/A division of Simon & Schuster, New York.

FIGURE 12.31
Evening Star (August 1991 Crude Oil)

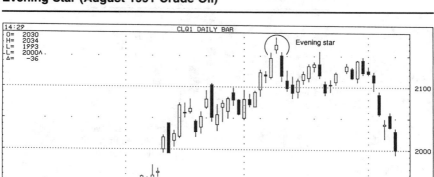

Source: © 1991 CQG, Inc.

Windows

The Japanese commonly refer to a gap as a **window.** Whereas the Western expression is "filling in the gap," the Japanese would say "closing the window."

A window is a gap between the previous and the current session's price extremes. Figure 12.32 shows that for an open window to be made in an uptrend there must be a gap between the previous upper shadow and the current session's lower shadow. A window in a downtrend is displayed in Figure 12.33. It shows no price activity between the previous day's lower shadow and the current day's upper shadow.

It is advised to always go in the direction of a window. Windows can also become support and resistance areas; thus, a window in a rally implies a further price rise and should be a floor on pullbacks. If the pullback closes the window and selling pres-

FIGURE 12.32
Uptrend Window

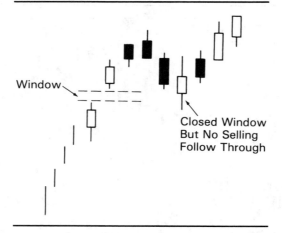

Source: From the book *Japanese Candlestick Charting Techniques.* By Steve Nison © 1991. Used by permission of the publisher, New York Institute of Finance/A division of Simon & Schuster, New York.

FIGURE 12.33
Downtrend Window

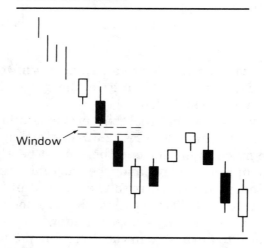

Source: From the book *Japanese Candlestick Charting Techniques.* By Steve Nison © 1991. Used by permission of the publisher, New York Institute of Finance/A division of Simon & Schuster, New York.

sure continues after the closing of this window, the previous uptrend is voided.

A window in a declining price environment implies still lower levels. Any price rebounds should run into resistance at this window. If the window is closed, and the rally that closed the window persists, the downtrend is over.

Traditional Japanese technical analysis (i.e., use of candlesticks) asserts that corrections go back to the window. In other words, a test of an open window is likely. Thus, on a window in an uptrend one can use pullbacks to that window as a buying zone. One should vacate longs, and even consider shorting, if after the window closes the selling pressure continues. The opposite strategy would be warranted with a window in a downtrend.

Remembering that up-gapping windows can become supportive, we see in this example that the sell-off that commenced with the evening star (see Figure 12.34) found a solid band of support at the window that opened in mid-April.

FIGURE 12.34
Window as Support (August 1991 Crude Oil)

Source: © 1991 CQG, Inc.

FIGURE 12.35

Window as Support and Resistance (September 1991 Copper)

Source: © 1991 CQG, Inc.

Figure 12.35 provides a wealth of information. On June 3 a hammer appeared. The next session opened a window that became a support throughout June. The rally that started with June's hammer ran into trouble in early July near the $1.0350 area. This level was a window in a downtrend (and thus resistance) that formed between May 2 and 3. The early July rally that stopped at the window was also a Fibonacci 62 percent retracement of the sell-off from A to B.

CONFLUENCE: WESTERN SIGNALS AND CANDLESTICKS

Candlestick methods by themselves are a valuable trading tool. Yet they become even more powerful when they confirm Western technical signals. We saw an example of this in Figure

12.35 when we discussed the window confirming a Fibonacci retracement.

The more technical signals you have coinciding at the same price area (this could mean candle patterns or Western signals or both) the more technically significant that area becomes. I call this a confluence of technical indicators. Figure 12.36 and 12.37 illustrate this concept.

Figure 12.36 shows a trendline joined with candles. Dark cloud covers 1 and 2 produced a resistance line. Dark cloud cover 3 intersected at this resistance line and thus confirmed the line's importance as a supply area.

Figure 12.37 shows how a group of candle signals coincided in the 68–69 cent area. First was the bearish engulfing pattern, then a dark cloud cover a few weeks later, and then the coup de grace via an evening star (the last two candles of this evening star were also a bearish engulfing pattern). This 68–69 cent zone was a major top.

FIGURE 12.36
Candles with Trendlines (Monthly Platinum)

Source: © 1991 CQG, Inc.

FIGURE 12.37
Cluster of Candlesticks (Weekly Deutsche Mark)

Source: © 1991 CQG, Inc.

   The power of candles is in their flexibility; they can be used alone or melded with any Western technical tool. They can be joined with retracement levels and trendlines, and they can be merged with such indicators as RSI, stochastics, volume indicators, Elliott waves, moving averages, and so on. By using candle charts one can remain with whatever technical tool or system one is most comfortable with—the candles will add an extra dimension of analysis unavailable anywhere else. This is the basis for my prediction that candles will largely replace bar charts. For experienced technicians the union of Eastern and Western techniques creates a wonderfully exciting synergy.

CONCLUSION

Some wonder if candlesticks will lose a portion of their technical significance if they become too popular. I might view two candlestick analysts as two doctors who go to the same medical school. Both may have the same knowledge about how the body works, yet they may read a patient's symptoms differently and treat a patient with different methods. This is because each doctor has unique experiences, philosophies, and perceptions that he or she brings to diagnosis and treatment. So it is with each investor. How you read the market's health through the diagnostic tool of candlestick analysis, and how you react to the symptoms of the market's health through candlestick techniques, may not be the same as how another candlestick practitioner does so. How you trade with candlesticks will depend on your trading philosophy, your risk aversion, and your temperament. These are very individual aspects.

In addition, each market has its own unique personality. As the Japanese express it, "The pattern of the market is like a person's face—no two are exactly alike." By studying your market's personality you will uncover the candlestick formations that appear most and work best for that market.

I hope that this brief introduction to the candles has opened new avenues of analysis. I am sure that you, like I, after spending some time with candlesticks, will not trade without the insights they offer.

CHAPTER 13

FUNDAMENTAL ANALYSIS

Donald W. Westfall
Vice President, Abel, Daft & Earley

WHAT IS FUNDAMENTAL ANALYSIS?

The price at which a commodity changes hands is established by the interaction of the supply of the item and demand for it. The fundamental analyst focuses on two facts about this transaction. First, that, other things being equal, a current higher price results in a larger supply at some future time (this is the law of supply). And, second, though no less important, a higher price will, at some point in the future, impede the sale of the item (this is the law of demand). Of course, both of these propositions are assumed to be reciprocal with regard to lower prices.

Fundamental and technical traders disagree about techniques for forecasting the future and perhaps even about when the "future" really is. For the trader who relies principally on fundamental tools, the future may be the next crop year or the next month or even the next week. Rarely is it the next day, hour, or minute, as is so often the case for the technician. The "fundamentalist" assumes that, within limits, enough information is available to predict the direction of prices for some period of time. Consequently, the fundamental view incorporates the idea that the market is not perfect. In a perfect market, all traders would have equal knowledge and the ability to apply that knowledge, and no one would be able to gain from it consistently. In fact, as Holbrook Working has noted, difference of opinion is the source of much trading. According to Working, differences of opinion arise because "the amount of pertinent information potentially available to traders in most modern markets is far beyond what any one trader can both acquire and use to good effect."[1] Thus, traders are selective about the information they use, or circumstances dictate that they have access to only a limited range of information. Either way, differences of opinion and consequent transactions occur.

The fundamentalist also diverges from the technician in emphasizing the importance of underlying economic forces in establishing price—in "knowing" why price changes happen. Although some technicians may view the attempt to explain price movement with supply and demand balances, carryover stocks, and reports of economic activity as hopelessly naive, in fact few successful technical traders operate purely on the signals emanating from the charts.

At its base, **fundamental analysis** is nothing more than trying to figure out whether the forces of supply and demand will result in a price level higher or lower than the one prevailing at the time of analysis. In that sense, looking at the fundamentals is always a relative proposition. The analyst asks: "Will supplies be tighter or demand less intense a year from now? A month from now? Tomorrow?"

Analysts, regardless of their level of sophistication, rely on a model of the market. This may be as complex as multiple equations running on high-speed computers or as basic as an estimate of production and consumption derived from a cursory reading of the newspaper. Good fundamental analysis requires good information, however, and the first prerequisite for obtaining it is the judgment necessary to sort the meaningless from the meaningful in a blizzard of information.

Computer models play an increasing role in fundamental price forecasting. Elaborate equations describing the reaction of the market to changes in supply and demand of both the commodity itself and competing or complementary items can be devised to forecast prices. Some models are extremely successful, but even the best must be adjusted frequently to take into account changing market structures. The cost and complexity of econometric models gener-

---

[1]Anne E Peck, ed., *Selected Writings of Holbrook Working* (Chicago: Board of Trade of the City of Chicago, 1977), p. 37.

ally places them out of the reach of the average trader. Many are developed and run by firms with sizable research staffs and direct access to information on physical trades.

Even so, it is possible for the layman to collect sufficient data to develop an informed view of the market. The success of the individual analyst depends largely on the intensity of study, but a healthy dose of inspiration is often helpful. It is hard to be a successful generalist. For the novice, after reviewing a range of commodities for potential, the wisest course should be to focus on one or two and to get to know the factors that are most likely to drive prices up or down from current levels. At this point, the serious trader regularly follows the data that will move the market. A loose-leaf notebook divided into sections for each of the factors to be followed is enough, if it is kept religiously.

The sad truth of fundamental analysis is that you can be right about the direction of the market and still miss the move. How many fundamental analysts have moaned, "I was right on the fundamentals, but my timing was off." In too early. Stopped out. Chasing a market you "knew" was going to take off. It happens. But worse and far more dangerous than missing the move is becoming so wrapped up in supply and demand numbers that "unarguable" fundamentals fuel a speculative fever. That is precisely the time when the prudent trader turns to basic risk/reward and technical analysis for guidance.

Finally, we need to realize what fundamental analysis is not. It is not a premature peek at a sensitive government report that makes possible a killing on the floor of the exchange. The film *Trading Places* is a fundamentalist fantasy in which audacious junior traders outwit crooked Big Money and triumph in one incredible hour of frenetic activity in the orange juice pit. Reality puts the good fundamental trader in the market after studying weather conditions, reviewing private forecasts, talking to knowledgeable growers, and so forth.

WHY DO IT?

Why look at the fundamentals? The short answer is to avoid being surprised by the market. If we accept the basic laws of economics, in any given year the balance between supply and demand will shape prices. Therefore, having some idea of how these factors are aligned, or are likely to be aligned, should be a valuable trading tool. There are also times when the fundamentals allow one to get a jump on a major move. Correctly anticipating the impact of news on the market is one aspect of fundamental trading.

However, as noted earlier, being buried alive in carryover stocks or nourished only with an alphabet soup of PPIs, CPIs, Ms and GNPs can easily put the fundamentalist out of touch with market perceptions or expectations. In those all-too-frequent cases, the fundamentalist can wake up far behind or well in front of the forecast move.

Fundamental analysis is all about discovering the primary factors involved in establishing supply and demand and determining the influences those forces will have on the price of a commodity. It is obvious that no analyst can know everything about even one market. Moreover, there is virtue in keeping things simple. More than one analyst has discovered that every variable added to the equation introduces the opportunity for error. Timeliness is important, too, but it is possible to overemphasize the advantage gained by being among the first to possess a particular nugget of information. Markets, particularly modern futures markets, are efficient discount mechanisms. As information that has a price impact percolates through a market, it is quickly incorporated into the price. Irwin Shishko, co-author with Stanley Kroll of *The Commodity Futures Market Guide,* has noted that "the central problem of attempting to base trading decisions on an analysis of changing fundamentals . . . [is that] it is difficult or impossible to gauge prices better than the collective wisdom of all traders, a wisdom that is already pretty accurately reflected in the market."

Difficult—but not futile. Good fundamental analysis depends on selective use of available information and careful interpretation of the data. The only way to develop the foundation is to read, listen and diligently study the forces shaping market prices. Although some general rules apply to all markets, success comes with an understanding of the unique features of individual markets. And, as we shall see in a detailed look at the sugar market later in this chapter, one often-overlooked element of the analysis is keeping an eye on the expectations of other traders. Taking a position on the basis of a detailed review of supply and demand numbers—even when the analysis is correct—can be costly rather than profitable if no one else believes it at the time. There is small satisfaction in being ultimately right, if it costs you money.

HOW THE FUNDAMENTAL ANALYST LOOKS AT MARKETS

Obviously, markets are affected by different forces. The good analyst is attuned to the most important general influences—such as interest rate fluctuations, leading economic indicators, and the general state of the economy. This is information available in the popular press and financial publications such as *The Wall Street Journal, Barron's, Business Week,* and others. More specific information may come from brokerage house reports. In addition to primary data, government publications are also an excellent source of analysis. The USDA, the Federal Reserve, and the Departments of Commerce and Labor publish reports that are the basis of even the most sophisticated models, and this information is available at a relatively low cost and in a timely fashion. Government agencies also provide analysis of long-term trends, and although these reports tend not to focus on price effects, they can be useful in formulating a view of the market.

Another outstanding compendium of information on commodities traded on futures markets is the *Commodity Yearbook,* published by the Commodity Research Bureau. It contains hundreds of tables of relevant information on the full range of commodities and clearly written articles on individual markets that outline the basic elements of supply and demand, and the role each plays in establishing price levels. Finally, the Chicago Board of Trade publishes a *Commodity Training Manual* that briefly describes the fundamental factors for many important futures markets.

The trader who wishes to concentrate on an individual commodity may consider subscribing to a specialized service that reports on supply and demand developments or physical transactions in a given market. Unfortunately, such services are usually expensive, and can cost anywhere from a few hundred dollars to several thousand annually. Most employ a staff of analysts to assemble information on changing production and consumption expectations. They may also describe market sentiment and physical trading activity—knowledge difficult or impossible to obtain from the popular press. Information on the leading private reporting services is available from the research department of any major brokerage house.

We have touched on supply and demand, but what factors should we include in analyzing them? First, let's look at *demand*. In general, demand is reflected in data on consumption, or "disappearance." The main factors influencing demand are population growth, income levels, and economic cycles. On the *supply* side, we are nearly always interested in production of the commodity. Stocks or inventories are a crucial element of supply and are often quite difficult to estimate. In fact, inventory data for a broad range of commodities, particularly agricultural products, are less reliable than those for production or use because they are frequently calculated from production and consumption information. Thus, any error in supply or use figures gets included in stocks. Over time, the data can be distorted. However, inventory figures tend to be most accurate when stocks are lowest (i.e., during periods of high prices). Stocks at those times usually provide a good indication of the level of minimum "working" inventories. Imports and exports—trade flows—are an aspect of both supply and demand and should be watched carefully if the commodity is internationally traded.

The careful fundamental analyst recognizes that not all factors are equal, that all markets are affected by general economic conditions, and that different causal keys open the doors to understanding different markets. Figure 13.1 identifies the most important factors at work in major markets. We call these the **high-impact variables**—those with the most immediate or serious effect on prices.

AN EXAMPLE: THE SUGAR MARKET, 1979–1981

To illustrate how one goes about working with market fundamentals, let's look at the sugar market for a 14-month period beginning in late 1979 and ending in early 1981. A quick look at

FIGURE 13.1
High-Impact Variables

High Impact Variables
Factors That Influence Futures Markets

Market Group	Fundamental Variables
Agriculturals	■ Acreage and yield ■ Government programs ■ Food and Industrial Crop Use ■ Relative Prices ■ Production Cycles
Fiber, Food, and Forest Products	■ Housing Starts ■ Interest Rates ■ Government Programs ■ Population and Income Growth ■ International Agreements ■ Price Cycles
Metals	■ Economic/Political Climate ■ Industrial Demand ■ Interest Rates ■ Inflation
Energy	■ World Political Situation ■ Production Levels ■ OPEC Stability ■ Supply – New Discoveries ■ International Economy
Financial Instruments	■ Inflation ■ Interest Rates ■ Money Supply ■ Monetary and Fiscal Policy ■ Economic Outlook ■ Political Climate

the price chart for this period gives some indication of what's in store—a 230 percent run-up followed by a precipitous 49 percent drop, all in the space of a year and a half. Underlying the move was a solid fundamental disruption in supply and a significant demand response, but there were other forces at work that confused and complicated the situation and made the analyst's life a nightmare of second-guessing. At the time, being right on the fundamentals and wrong on the market seemed like a fact of life. Nevertheless, fundamental analysis was useful in identifying the basic trend and the market's staying power at critical junctures.

Our example will cover the life of the March 1981 delivery for the sugar Number 11 contract traded on the New York Coffee and Sugar Exchange (now the Coffee, Sugar, and Cocoa Exchange, or CSCE) (see Figure 13.2). For a significant portion of the roller coaster ride of 1980 and 1981, the March contract was the most closely watched and most active delivery. The contract came on the board in October 1979 at an initial settlement price of 13.87 cents per pound for a lot composed of 50 long tons (112,000 pounds). When it expired at the end of February 1981, the settlement price was 23.25 cents per pound. If a trader placed a buy order on the first day and then retired to a desert island (without a newspaper or even a Quotron) for the next 14 months, he or she would have had a 67.6 percent gain before commissions and probably without margin calls. But no one has that much discipline—even computers take profits and get stopped out.

FIGURE 13.2
March 1981 Sugar "11"

Source: Commodity Research Bureau.

The Supply and Demand Balance

Before we begin our review of the situation in 1979, let's take a brief look at some of the important statistics and structural factors that a sugar market analyst focuses on; that is, the day-to-day fundamentals. First, the supply and demand balance.

The basic tool for any analyst of sugar market fundamentals is a supply and demand balance. The one shown in Table 13.1 was issued in August 1979 and covers the period from the price surge in the mid-1970s through the collapse late in the decade. At the top are the elements of supply: initial stocks, production, and imports. Next come the demand factors: exports and consumption. These are aggregated from estimates for virtually every country producing sugar.

The key measure in the balance is the ratio of ending stocks to consumption. A number of studies have demonstrated conclusively that there is an inverse relationship between the stocks-to-consumption ratio and season average prices. That means when the ratio is high (large stocks relative to global consumption), prices tend to be low, and, conversely, when stocks are low

TABLE 13.1
World Sugar Balance, 1974–1980

	1979/80	1978/79	September / August 1977/78	1976/77	1975/76	1974/75	1973/74
	Estimate						
			(1000 metric tons, raw value)				
Initial Stocks	30 412	30 065	24 900	20 585	17 478	15 984	16 051
Production	88 054	91 196	90 935	86 883	81 756	78 450	79 489
Imports	28 738	27 079	28 220	27 534	23 844	24 141	23 902
Total	147 204	148 340	144 055	135 002	123 078	118 575	119 442
Exports	28 779	27 545	28 247	28 323	23 365	24 707	24 627
Consumption	91 580	90 383	85 743	81 779	79 128	76 390	78 831
Final stocks	26 845	30 412	30 065	24 900	20 585	17 478	15 984
±1000 tons Production .	− 3 142	+ 261	+ 4 052	+ 5 127	+ 3 306	− 1 039	+ 3 801
± per cent	− 3.45	+ 0.29	+ 4.66	+ 6.27	+ 4.21	− 1.31	+ 5.02
±1000 tons Consumption	+ 1 197	+ 4 640	+ 3 964	+ 2 651	+ 2 738	− 2 441	+ 2 968
± per cent	+ 1.32	+ 5.41	+ 4.85	+ 3.35	+ 3.58	− 3.10	+ 3.91
Stocks in per cent of consumption	29.31	33.65	35.06	30.45	26.01	22.88	20.28

Source: F. O. Licht, *International Sugar Report*, December 18, 1979, p. 1.

relative to consumption, prices will be relatively higher. If that seems simplistic, it is. As we shall see, the role of expectations must be factored in.

Next, a word about the data. In this abbreviated example we will rely on two sources: F. O. Licht, a highly regarded private forecasting service based in Germany, and the USDA. Licht is the Bible of the sugar world, and most financial wire services carry Licht supply and demand forecasts in a timely manner. Brokerage houses subscribe to Licht's service and publish estimates based on the company's data. The USDA publishes world production and consumption estimates on a crop-year basis. Licht figures cover a September–August marketing year. During the period we are reviewing, the USDA was occasionally criticized for having incomplete figures, but on the whole the government data were reliable and available at low cost.

Market Structure

With this brief look at the supply and demand balance behind us, let's move on to the sugar market. The description that follows is a highly condensed version of market structure descriptions, adapted from USDA information available at the time.

The central fact of the sugar market for most traders is that historically sugar prices have moved in a pronounced cyclic pattern. Three factors cause prices to behave this way: the nature of sugar crop production, the way producers make their decisions about investing in new processing facilities, and market distortions on the demand side.

Nearly two-thirds of the world's sugar comes from sugarcane, a perennial crop—a grass, really—that yields economical quantities of sugar for two to six or seven years. It usually takes at least 15 months after planting before the first crop can be harvested. Sugar yields generally decline after the second harvest of the same stand. Cane sugar planting and output increase slowly in response to gradually rising prices, and when prices fall there is not much incentive to reduce production until new planting is required. Sugar beets, however, are an annual crop, so production can be varied in response to changing market conditions in a relatively short time.

Investment in sugar production tends to be limited to periods when prices for sugar are high, particularly in developing countries. High sugar revenue produces the resources to expand area, replant, and build new mills. To some extent, the same is true for sugar beet growers and processors.

Consumption is also affected by price changes. The responsiveness of consumption to price (the price elasticity of demand) is generally low in developed countries. In other words, consumption is not affected much by changes in price. In developing countries where demand is quite elastic, government policies frequently insulate consumers from market forces. Thus, it takes a significant price increase to ration available supplies because the burden of the adjustment falls on those countries where consumption responds least to price changes.

So, the cycle works like this: high prices spark a burst of production followed by a prolonged period of low prices. Low prices stimulate consumption growth, which, when combined with stable production (because output is slow to adjust), erodes stocks and sets the stage for a shortage.

Market Developments

In 1979, the sugar market looked like it was ready to begin a slow period of price recovery before another surge. Prices had been low since the run-up in 1974–75. That bull market stimulated huge investments in production in cane-producing countries and in the European Community (with an assist from the Common Agricultural Policy). High production depressed prices, but consumption rose slowly in response to population and income growth, particularly in the developing countries. A survey of analysts in early 1979 would probably have put a cycle-induced price rise in 1982—far enough in the future to use up some of the large stocks accumulated in the late 1970s.

However, midway through 1979 sentiment began to change. As analysts and traders began to focus on production prospects for the coming year, they saw a sudden significant drop in output. Nevertheless, forecasts of stock levels by the USDA in September put inventories at nearly 35 percent of global consumption, large enough to moderate potential price increases. By September, weather started by play a role as hurricanes in the Caribbean damaged the crop in the Dominican Republic. Then, in October, the Soviet Union emerged as a buyer, driving prices higher. The path was not smooth, however. Prices took a one-day half-cent drubbing when the House of Representatives rejected a sugar program, and the erosion of forward premiums slowed as the market became aware that when prices rose over 15 cents, quota restrictions limiting exports by members of the International Sugar Agreement would lapse, making more sugar available to the market in 1980.

By mid-December, spot prices broke above 15 cents per pound and the March 1981 futures price stood over 16.50 cents, 20 percent above its first sale price barely three months earlier. Clearly, something was going on, and the market, acting as an efficient discounting mechanism, was internalizing some important news. But what was it?

The USDA's year-end report forecast a 4 percent drop in production due to "decisions in some countries to reduce output, and unfavorable weather conditions in some other countries." But the USDA still expected only a slight rise in consumption and a modest drop in the ratio of stocks to consumption. But this cautious view seemed at odds with the data. In Figure 13.3, which appeared in the USDA's December 1979 Sugar and Sweetener Report, the relationship of prices to production in 1974 must have given encouragement to some who were already long sugar.

Licht was more bullish, however. A December sugar balance showed stocks in 1978–79 lower than previously estimated, and in the forecast for 1979–80 the stocks as a percentage of consumption were under 30 percent for the first time since 1975–76.

On January 4, 1980, the United States suspended grain exports to the Soviet Union in retaliation for the Soviet invasion of Afghanistan. The grain markets were closed in Chicago, and as bears sold sugar in New York, prices dropped. Within a few days, however, rumors of substantial physical sugar purchases by China and the Soviet Union began to push prices up. The reason for these purchases became evident as results from the Cuban harvest emerged; over 25 percent of what had been expected to

FIGURE 13.3
World Sugar: Price and Change in Production

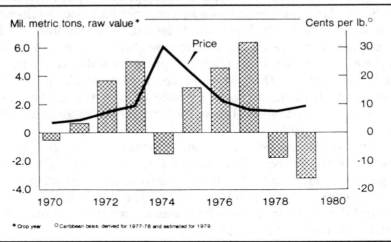

Source: USDA, Economic Research Service, *Sugar and Sweetener Report,* Vol. 4, No. 12, December 1979.

be a bumper crop for the Cubans was affected by rust, a sugarcane disease. Eradication was possible only by planting new cane varieties. In the meantime, it would be difficult for Cuba to meet free market and preferential supply contracts.

Then the fundamental situation got tighter. Peru, an exporting country, emerged as a buyer. Thailand encountered difficulties. High oil prices forced Brazil to divert cane to alcohol production and to suspend exports from the two main bulk loading ports in the southern part of the country. Then Turkey and Iran bought large tonnages for spot delivery. Through February, the nearby delivery positions led the way. Little, if any, carrying charge was in the market as the market rose on nearby demand for actual sugar. This pattern would not persist throughout the year.

In March, the market broke as March 1981 futures fell from a high of just over 30 cents to a low of about 22 cents. But what a ride! In 21 trading days, the March contract registered day-to-day limit moves 17 times—6 times up and 11 times down. Technically, the market was ripe for a correction. But what could the fundamentals tell about this situation? On the supply and demand side, not much—the market still seemed constructive. Physical buyers continued to emerge, especially as the market plummeted. But, if we broaden our view of the "fundamentals," it is possible to see that other forces had begun to exert unexpected influences in the sugar market. In particular, we see the convergence of a debacle in silver with high interest rates. Interest rates in the United States were approaching 20 percent and it was becoming difficult for short hedgers to make margin calls as prices rose. Then, a crisis in silver forced some traders and institutions to liquidate long sugar positions to generate cash to cover deteriorating silver positions. Much of this was not known until some months later. For the fundamental trader, the market was fraught with risk. For the technician, it was slightly more transparent. But the technician with a solid background in the fundamentals could be reasonably confident that, while trading from the short side, the bullish fundamental picture would reassert itself.

An opportunity for the fundamental trader to bring reason to bear on a volatile market came in February, when Coca-Cola announced that high-fructose corn syrup would be approved for use in Coca Cola itself. The market dropped the one-day limit on fears that this would reduce sugar demand. For those with an understanding of the sugar and sweetener complex, this was absurd. Plants that produced high-fructose corn syrup were already operating at capacity and no new production facilities were scheduled to come on-stream for at least two years. The important implications of this announcement lay well in the future.

The market surged again in May and rose to 36 cents, basis March futures, before dropping in July. This time the decline seemed more soundly based on fundamental factors. In particular, physical sugar began to trade at increasing discounts to the terminal market as it became clear that prompt sugar was available. Then, expectations about the following year, the 1980–81 season, came into play. As a report from F. O. Licht noted, "Estimates of production and consumption imply a further call on stocks in 1980–81 . . . [and] stocks could shrink to the take-off point for another price surge." This sentiment seemed to be confirmed when the Soviets again surfaced as buyers ahead of the October expiration in New York. March futures climbed from 35 cents to 41 cents in September. But despite the bullish potential noted by Licht, March 1982 futures were lagging by 10 cents per pound. Clearly, something was up.

Interest rates, an easy-to-overlook fundamental factor, were haunting the market. Prices collapsed in November, and, in the case of the March contract, they never recovered. The free-fall began at 45.65 cents and ended 76 trading days later at expiration—22.40 cents lower. Remember the sugar cycle and the role of demand elasticities? By the autumn of 1980, there was no question that in countries where consumers were exposed to world prices, the rise was affecting consumption. In addition, political instability and the shift of demand to alternative sweeteners played a part in reducing world market buying. But these developments were not enough to satisfactorily explain the weakness in worldwide demand and remain consistent with generally accepted demand elasticities. The culprit was interest rates. The soaring cost of money during most of 1980 raised the price of holding inventories and therefore the price of sugar (see Figure 13.4). For a free market importer, the difference between an interest rate of 10 percent and one of 20 percent is significant. In a greatly simplified sense, at 45 cents per pound this difference added about 4.5 cents per pound to the price paid if a large purchase were financed over a year's time. In effect, at a 20 percent rate of interest, spot sugar at 45 cents could cost as much as 54 cents with long-term financing. For this reason, users reduced invisible stocks to absolute minimums and producers became increasingly eager sellers of their inventories.

Finally, it turned out that production responded to high prices about as expected. Instead of a stocks-to-consumption figure approaching 25 percent, the 1980–81 season wound up at 28.4 percent, a comfortable margin and on the way up again.

CONCLUSION

What can we conclude from this odyssey through the life of one contract in one very volatile market? First and most obviously, causes and effects are always easier to divine in retrospect. Sec-

FIGURE 13.4
Sugar Prices and Interest Rates

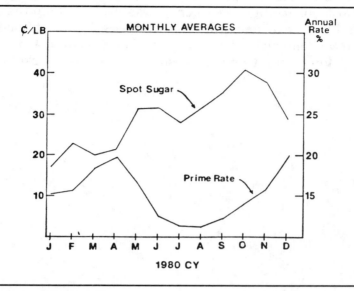

Source: Abel, Daft & Earley.

ond, the important fundamental variables to follow can change through time, even over a span as brief as a year. Who would have thought in the fall of 1979 that interest rates would play such a role in market conditions only a year later? Third, it is possible to follow the fundamentals and forecast a major move, but the magnitude of the price change may not be apparent when the analysis is first undertaken. The USDA and Licht supply and demand data were as accurate as could be expected at the time, and they failed to justify a price forecast above the levels that prevailed when they were issued. Fourth, the fundamentals can change over the long run, too. Today, an analysis of the world sugar market that did not allow for high-fructose corn sugar would be dangerously unreliable. In the United States alone, corn sweeteners now account for more than half of all sweetener consumption. And new high-intensity sweeteners with significant market potential are being introduced regularly. Some analysts have argued that the sugar cycle has been altered by new sweeteners and by government policies in ways that will prevent, or at least dampen, the periodic surges that have characterized sugar markets for nearly a century. Fifth, and most important, fundamental analysis can help the astute trader identity a major, durable change in market conditions and, in tandem with diligent application of technical principals, an individuals can trade successfully in futures markets.

CHAPTER 14

PUTTING IT ALL TOGETHER

THE GAME PLAN

Successful futures trading involves far more than deciding to allocate speculative funds to the hottest "trade of the month" touted by some large brokerage firm. To trade successfully, an investor must have a game plan, a methodology that should be followed strictly every time a trading decision is made. In the following pages, we will pull together elements of the preceding chapters to arrive at such a methodology that incorporates elements of technical analysis, fundamental analysis, and money management.

Establish the Major Trend of the Market

Regardless of whether you are interested in trading soybeans, silver, or stock indices, every market of interest should be examined to determine the direction of the long-term trend (six months to five years), the intermediate-term trend (three months to six months), and the short-term trend (less than three months). By examining and determining trend direction on the monthly, weekly, and daily charts, you will discover where prices have been and, perhaps, be able to make a judgment as to where they might head in the future.

For example, the monthly chart pictured in Figure 14.1 shows that cocoa prices have been bound by a powerful 15-year resistance line. Every rally to the trendline since 1977 resulted in a price reversal and resumption of the bear trend. The length and apparent power of the down trendline is one of

FIGURE 14.1
A View of the Long-term Bear Market (Monthly Cocoa [nearest futures])

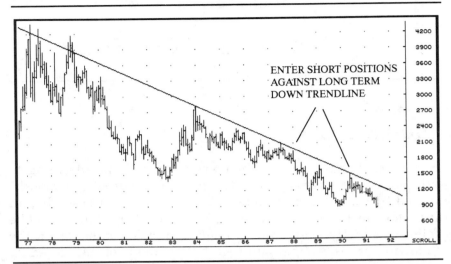

ENTER SHORT POSITIONS
AGAINST LONG TERM
DOWN TRENDLINE

Source: Chart courtesy of FutureSource, a division of Oster Communications, Inc.

the most salient features of the longer-term technical picture, and warns us against taking unnecessary risks on the long side of the market and to seek opportunities to establish short positions when the price structure approaches long-term resistance levels.

Figure 14.2 shows the weekly chart of cocoa. Once again, note the long-term resistance line that has capped each rally attempt within the four-year time frame of the chart. Although the rally efforts in late 1988 and early 1990 were sizable at $400 and $600 per ton, respectively, they represented countertrend price movements and, in the end, were turned back by the downward-sloping resistance line. Furthermore, each down-leg after a countertrend rally pushed prices to new bear market lows, providing additional evidence that the cocoa market was in the grasp of a particularly powerful downtrend. The examination of the long- and intermediate-term charts leaves little doubt that the overriding price trend in the market has been bearish.

FIGURE 14.2
Weekly Cocoa (nearest futures) with Three Technical Oscillators

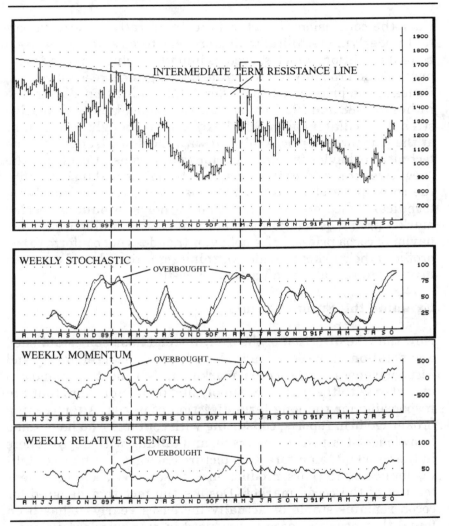

Source: Charts courtesy of FutureSource, a division of Oster Communications, Inc.

Examine the Technical Data for Trend Confirmations and Divergences

Near the conclusion of each countertrend rally, several important underlying technical indicators registered an extreme overbought condition, which served as important clues that the price
move would probably fail to hurdle the long-term resistance line.
Beneath the price chart in Figure 14.2, notice that during the
rallies in 1988 and 1990, the stochastic, momentum, and relative
strength oscillators all reached extreme overbought levels right
at the point where prices collided with the down trendline. This
technical behavior is important for two reasons: it confirms the
"negative strength" of the resistance trendline and it shows that
the cocoa price structure is very responsive to the underlying
technical indicators. This information helps to build a specific
market profile using those factors that seem to influence the behavior of cocoa prices. Price behavior that does not conform to the
profile of the market provides warning signs that should cause an
investor to reevaluate a particular position.

Examine the Fundamentals

Now that the direction of the overall trend has been established
and notations have been made about the technical reliability and
responsiveness of the cocoa market, it is time to become acquainted with the pertinent supply and demand factors that are
responsible for the long-term direction of prices. After reading
brokerage firm reports, consulting with contacts who have some
knowledge about the cocoa trade, and talking with floor brokers
in the cocoa pit, an interesting picture emerges. With prices falling for nearly 15 years, production excesses have been the salient
feature of the cocoa market. Despite the fact that demand for
cocoa remains stable or actually increases yearly, it has been
found that because cocoa is produced in many underdeveloped,
foreign-exchange-starved African and South American nations,
government subsidization perpetuates output even though prices
are constantly falling. (In a more "rational" free market environment, presumably, falling prices would weed out marginal,
weak producers, lowering output and, eventually, pushing prices

higher.) To put it in a nutshell, most of the world's cocoa output comes from low-cost subsidized producers, which could pressure prices indefinitely.

With that as a backdrop to the market, it is understandable why the value of cocoa has been declining for many years. We also understand that, in the past, weather-related crop failures, or suspicions thereof, account for nearly all of the rallies that have emerged within the ongoing bear market. Therefore, it would seem that, barring the removal of government subsidizations from the farmers, poor growing conditions, crop disease, or crop failure in one or more of the world's leading cocoa production areas, the downtrend in prices should remain intact and unyielding.

Unless crop conditions deteriorate, the likelihood of another year of excess production is high, which will translate into lower prices in the future. As far as supply and demand balance, major rallies are opportunities to establish intermediate-term short positions. Once in the market, it is important to pay particularly close attention to and have a broker monitor all available new information that emerges about the cocoa market and about crop conditions. With that in mind, the next challenge is timing the entry into the short side of the market.

Market Timing and Strategy

Although it has been determined that both the longer-term technical trend and the fundamental trend in the cocoa market are bearish, entering a position in the direction of the trend—but into the final stages of a powerful countertrend advance—requires a large dose of fortitude. Selling into a rally or buying into a decline can be an exciting, but initially uncomfortable, experience, albeit one that is necessary to become a successful trader.

Our examination of trend direction and the underlying technical behavior of the market has produced some powerful tools that should help determine where to enter the short side of the cocoa market. Our discovery work tells us that short positions have been most rewarding when established into a countertrend rally, and as close to the long-term down trendline as possible.

FIGURE 14.3
Monthly Cocoa with Resistance Band

Source: Chart courtesy of FutureSource, a division of Oster Communications, Inc.

Based on the monthly charts shown in Figure 14.3, during May 1990 the intersection of the 15-year downtrend with the vertical (price) axis should occur at approximately $1,550/ton (see chart annotations). Furthermore, every attempt to move above the trendline since the highs in 1984 at 2805 has failed and formed a lower, parallel resistance line to the longer-term trendline. The two parallel lines form a **resistance band** that is approximately $100 in width and should be used to initiate short positions as well as to gauge protective stop placement.

Establishing a Position

Our strategy was to enter the short side of the September 1990 cocoa contract at nearest futures equivalent to the $1,530/ton area, placing the price structure at the lower side of the resistance band. Furthermore, we planned to place a reversal stop protection $120 above the entry price—or outside the top of the band. In effect, prices would have to climb through the 7-year parallel resistance band and break through the 15-year down trendline to stop us out of the short position. Such a powerful advance, and the penetration of long-term down trendlines, would argue forcefully that the technical profile of the market had changed and that the cocoa market was most likely undergoing a significant (bullish) improvement in its underlying fundamentals. At that juncture, the huge bear market might be coming to an abrupt close, which would be justification to reverse to the long side of the market.

As it turned out, we established our short position in the September 1990 cocoa contract at $1,500/ton, and after just a few days of discomfort that pushed prices to the $1,541/ton level, cocoa prices reversed to the downside with a vengeance. Within four weeks of entry, December cocoa prices had collapsed nearly $350/ton, which retraced about two-thirds of the countertrend advance, and prices kept falling. Clearly, the bear market was alive and well.

Although the resistance band provided the key for market entry and money management discipline, a more conservative approach would have been to enter the short position after the market provided a technical signal that the countertrend advance had ended. In the case of September 1990 cocoa, a bearish confirmation might have provided the basis for sell signals that occurred on May 15, 1990, when September cocoa prices climbed to new countertrend highs prior to reversing $60/ton during the same session. That key reversal day (see Figure 14.4), or the subsequent violation of the near-term up trendline at $1,360/ton, represented very negative signals and could have been used either to establish initial short positions (along with the seven-year parallel resistance band), or to add to existing short positions.

Typically, the more conservative and risk averse you are, the greater the number and quality of confirmations you will require before entering the market. A more aggressive trader who enters a trade based on less corroborating evidence may experience the pain of false starts. However, a trader who minimizes exposure on the false starts by using tight stops will eventually be rewarded for his or her discipline and persistence.

Maintaining the Position

Concurrent with initiation of the position and entering protective stops, it is useful to determine a target window. Target measurements can be derived by calculating "swing objectives" and by employing Fibonacci ratios to determine the projected

FIGURE 14.4
September 1990 Cocoa

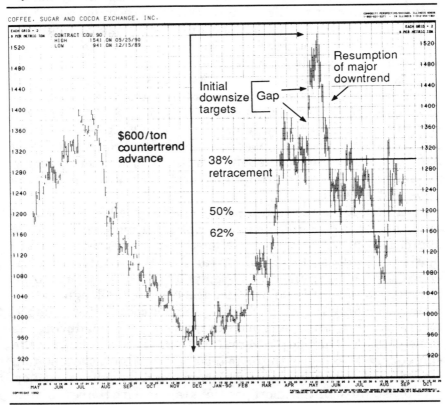

Source: Courtesy of Commodity Research Bureau.

distance of a price move. It is a good idea to note the minimum and maximum expected target prices and to consider exiting part of your position at each successive target. Furthermore, the balance of the position should be protected with trailing stops to avoid relinquishing significant profits.

In the case of the short cocoa position, the initial downside targets were identified by the gap areas left behind during the final up-leg of the countertrend advance (Figure 14.4). In addition, the most common Fibonacci retracement percentages were calculated from the previous $601/ton advance and then marked on the chart as potential downside price objectives.

The gap areas and the Fibonacci targets proved very useful. In Figure 14.4, notice that the price structure managed to find support in the Fibonacci retracement window between 1311 (38.2 percent) and 1169 (61.8 percent). Although prices eventually plunged beneath the 62 percent retracement levels to 18-year lows, for the purposes of the short position, it provided a place to cover part of the short position as well as a place to adjust stop protection on remaining positions.

DISCIPLINE, DISCIPLINE, DISCIPLINE

Even before the anticipated price action confirms a turn in the direction of the underlying trend, you should have already determined how much money you are willing to risk on the trade, the appropriate stop-loss level, and the intended target window. Of course, this requires that you know and respect your risk tolerance and just how much money is available for such a speculative endeavor.

Once the trade is established, avoid being influenced by unsubstantiated floor gossip, press comments, or volatile intraday price action. Every day, you will be exposed to "extraneous market noise" that causes doubts about the wisdom of your position. But, if you have the courage of your convictions, and maintain discipline, you should not close out the position prematurely or adjust stop-loss levels to increase your exposure, which are two serious mistakes often repeated by both experienced and inexperienced traders.

THE LOGICAL APPROACH

What we have tried to put together in the preceding pages is a disciplined way to think about, and successfully enter and exit, the futures market. Although you may not agree with some of these elements, the most important thing to understand is the need to have an organized system to help narrow your choices to a few potentially rewarding situations among the dozens out there. In addition, we have tried to emphasize that maintaining discipline in market analysis, carefully determining entry and exit points, and giving due consideration to money management decisions are all essential ingredients of success. Without a systematic approach, there is no discipline and you will probably lose money. However, taking a disciplined, systematic approach to the markets means that you have

- Identified a trading opportunity in the direction of the underlying trend;
- Reviewed and are aware of the pertinent fundamentals;
- Awaited particular price action and technical confirmation that help you time market entry;
- Determined risk tolerance and entered stop-loss orders; and
- Projected price objectives, partial exit strategy, and potential stop adjustment levels.

If all of the steps mentioned above have been taken prior to committing funds to the market, then you are following a systematic, disciplined approach and can consider your involvement in the futures market to be consistent with sound money management and strategic considerations. That is, the game plan is set, major contingencies have been thought out, and money management disciplines have been implemented.

SECTION 5

THE COMPUTER IN TECHNICAL ANALYSIS

CHAPTER 15

INTRODUCTION TO COMPUTER ANALYSIS

Thomas E. Aspray
President and Research Director, Aspray, Parsons and McClintock Asset Management Corp.

WHAT COMPUTERS CAN DO

The boom in computer technology over the past few years has been astounding. In the early 1980s, only a small percentage of individual investors owned computers. Now, because of the lower cost and the advancement in the areas of graphic capability, increased speed, and data storage, the computer has become an essential tool of the financial markets.

Any successful trader will tell you that commodity trading is an arduous occupation requiring discipline, concentration, and extensive analysis. It is almost impossible to completely analyze the broad spectrum of commodity markets without a computer. The amount of time that is required to look at monthly, weekly, and daily charts, as well as the technical indicators, may not allow ample time to trade. This has changed dramatically with the use of computers and the development of software to manipulate financial data. A computer allows the serious trader to analyze current and past market data in a very short period of time.

One popular misconception among individual traders is that sophisticated computer equipment and the right software will necessarily make them better traders. This is a questionable assumption. In order to utilize a computer successfully, one must first have a basic knowledge of the underlying principles of commodity trading. Without this understanding, computerized commodity analysis can confuse the individual trader and even be detrimental to his or her trading.

In addition, many novice traders feel that if they have a computer, they don't have to think. This attitude reflects a serious misunderstanding of the advantages and disadvantages of a computer. If given reasonable and logical instructions, the computer can repeatedly carry out complex mathematical calculations without errors; the results of these calculations are then available to the trader. If, however, the principles behind the calculations are not understood, the results are useless. On the other hand, if the instructions to the computer are not logical or reasonable, the results are of little value. Hence the saying, "garbage in, garbage out."

With the drop in computer prices and the availability of analytical software, computers have become an essential tool for the professional trader or analyst. For those who cannot afford to upgrade periodically, however, these new developments in computer technology can also cause frustrations, as equipment or software can become obsolete within a year or so of their purchase. (On a personal note, the first home computer I purchased in 1979 cost about $3,000; a comparable system would now cost under $500. Though this particular computer is no longer being used, it was well worth the original investment.)

In my office, I perform extensive computerized analysis of both daily and weekly data. Within two hours after the markets close, I collect the day's data, which is then added to my existing files. The analytical routine begins as the computers review 30 weeks of daily data, running at least 12 calculations on each commodity. Results of each of these calculations are then printed. After completing the analysis on one commodity, the computer automatically moves on to analyze the next market. In about three hours, over 25 commodities are analyzed and the results are then available so reports can be written that evening for my clients. Four or five years ago this would have been impossible, except for firms that had large mainframe computers.

BASIC REQUIREMENTS FOR
COMPUTERIZED ANALYSIS

Hardware and software combinations available for carrying out commodity analysis are virtually limitless, but there are some basic requirements common to all levels of expertise. The main thrust of financial programming in recent years has been toward the IBM-compatible and Macintosh computers.

Among professional traders, IBM compatibles are used by more analysts; though, for the beginner, the Macintosh does have distinct advantages. For the computer novice, the Macintosh seems to have a shorter learning curve, and one can quickly become comfortable using the Mac. Currently, there are many more software programs available for the IBM than for the Macintosh, though this is changing rapidly.

The basic hardware requirements in addition to the IBM or Macintosh computer are a printer and a modem. The capability to print a copy of the data or charts is very helpful because it is often necessary to send copies to clients. A modem allows the computer to communicate over phone lines, which is necessary for collecting data from one of the many computer networks. To accomplish this, the user needs to establish an account with the data vendor, who will then issue an identification number and password. To collect data via a modem, the user connects with the main computer through a phone line, and the data is then transferred from the mainframe to the personal computer.

For data storage, most computer systems now have built-in hard drives. The cost of a hard drive has dropped significantly in the last few years. A hard drive has become standard equipment on most computer systems, and it offers distinct advantages over a single disk-drive system. Depending on its size, a hard drive can store the equivalent of 30 to 100 floppy diskettes, and the user avoids the continual swapping of individual disks.

The availability of computerized data on a wide range of markets has also expanded significantly in the past few years. During the 1970s the principal source for computerized financial data was the Dunn & Hargitt Company. It formed the basis for many of the commodity and stock financial data services that now exist. These services send the user data on a diskette, or one can collect the data using a modem.

Some traders may choose to enter data manually, which is inexpensive but time-consuming. Doing so, thereby avoiding data charges, can be more cost-effective for the smaller capitalized trader. Manual data entry, despite its limitations, does have some positive factors, as any type of data from any source can be entered. This allows flexibility for original research, as one is only limited by imagination. The most convenient source for obtaining data is the local library, as one can record past data from the financial journals for later entry into the computer. The primary drawback is the time required to manually enter a year's worth of data. Collecting the data using a modem could take less than 10 minutes, while manual entry would take several hours. If one compares the time required and the increased possibility for errors, the purchase of data via a modem is advisable.

There are now many competitive services providing data and therefore costs are becoming more reasonable. For example, daily data charges for one commodity might range from $7 per month to $70 for 20 years. There are several different types of file formats available. Data compatibility and cost are both important criteria in selecting a data service.

After choosing the appropriate equipment and data, the next step is to select the software that will be used to analyze the markets. There are two major types of software: spreadsheet programs such as Lotus 1-2-3™ and Excel™, and specific technical analysis programs such as CompuTrac™ and MetaStock™. These programs already contain a series of indicators and analytical capabilities.

Spreadsheet Analysis Software

A spreadsheet program is essentially a series of rows and columns, similar to an accountant's columnar pad. While its use for technical analysis of commodity markets is not so readily apparent, the advantages of such a program for business forecasting can easily be seen. One such program is Excel™, developed by Microsoft™ for both Macintosh and IBM computers. It has a wide range of uses and applications, from balancing one's checkbook to financial planning and forecasting. The formulas must be input by the user before calculations can be performed. When the formulas in the spreadsheet are changed, any values that were based on these formulas are automatically recalculated.

For the commodity analyst, the main advantages of the spreadsheet program are that the cost is moderate and no knowledge of programming is required. To enter formulas, only a rudimentary knowledge of mathematics is necessary. For testing with a spreadsheet, one must first either enter the data manually or collect the data to be tested. Once data is available, the formulas to be studied can be entered using a simple mathematical format. The analyst can easily develop personal indicators and test them using market data to see whether or not they will work.

For example, a very simple calculation would be to run a 10-day moving average of prices. For this example we will look at April 1989 gold prices from the period of February 1–28, 1989 (see Figure 15.1). Since we will be using closing prices for the moving average, our first column will be the date, the second column will be the closing price, and the third column will be the moving average. Because we have selected a 10-period moving average, our first moving average value is not available until the tenth trading day, or February 14. The formula for a simple moving average (SMA) is quite straightforward. The closing prices are added for the past 10 days and the total is divided by 10. To get the moving average value for the next day, one inserts the new closing price, totals the last 10 closing prices, and divides by 10. From a spreadsheet standpoint, this can be expressed as the value of the sum of B2 through B11, with that sum divided by 10. The spreadsheet software allows you to copy this formula to each successive day; therefore, as new data is added, the moving average is automatically recalculated over the 10 most recent data points.

Of course, moving averages are a very simple type of calculation. Most spreadsheet programs will allow more complex and extensive formulas. Mathematical functions are generally built into the program, which can easily be copied into a formula. (Most of these formulas are found in chapter 18 and can be converted into spreadsheet format.)

FIGURE 15.1
Spreadsheet Calculation for 10-Day Moving Average (April 1989 Gold)

	A	B	C
	A	**B**	**C**
1	DATE	APRIL GOLD	10 DAY MA
2		CLOSING PRICE	
3	2/1/89	397.2	
4	2/2/89	395.9	
5	2/3/89	396.3	
6	2/6/89	396.9	
7	2/7/89	395.5	
8	2/8/89	399.1	
9	2/9/89	398	
1 0	2/10/89	391.7	
1 1	2/13/89	389.7	
1 2	2/14/89	389	394.93
1 3	2/15/89	388.2	394.03
1 4	2/16/89	387.1	393.15
1 5	2/17/89	384.3	391.95
1 6	2/21/89	389.4	391.2
1 7	2/22/89	390.2	390.67
1 8	2/23/89	394	390.16
1 9	2/24/89	392.6	389.62
2 0	2/27/89	389.8	389.43
2 1	2/28/89	390.4	389.5

Technical Analysis Software

Over the past few years, many technical analysis software pack-ages have been released. These packages offer many advantages over the spreadsheet form of computer analysis, the first being that many of the indicators that the analyst might wish to use are already programmed into the software. The analyst can save time, as the formulas do not have to be developed or manually entered into the computer.

The second advantage, which is essential for the serious analyst, is the ability to automate the analytical routine. This allows the analyst to set up a predefined series of steps and calculations that will be run with the data. Once these are de-fined, the computer can be set up to run this series of calcula-tions over any number of different markets. The results from these calculations can then be output on a printer.

Another distinct advantage is the ability to do historical testing. Many of the software packages allow the analyst to design a trading system that will generate buy or sell signals. Once these systems are designed, the computer can go through data testing the system. It will then figure the net profit or loss over the entire time period and determine whether a certain method or analytical approach is profitable. (This will be discussed later in the chapter, Designing and Testing the Trading System.)

While software programs have many differences, they do have some similarities. The most simple technical analysis program allows the user to either manually enter data through the keyboard or to retrieve data via modem. Once the data is entered or collected, the program will allow the user to plot the data in a chart form and get a copy via the printer.

The main difference between software programs is the number of technical studies or indicators that are preprogrammed into the software. The possibilities range from simple moving averages to sophisticated volume analysis, cycle testing, and Fourier and regression analysis. With new programs released on a regular basis, anything written about specific technical analysis software could be obsolete within one year. Technical support is also an important criterion for selecting a software program, as operating problems can develop with many software programs. Some vendors have full-time staff members ready to help solve software problems, whereas others have little or no support available.

For monitoring daily, weekly, or monthly data, the price range for technical analysis software is almost as wide as the capabilities. The most sophisticated program can run as high as $3,000 with additional regular maintenance or upgrade fees; other packages are available for only $200. The median price for a technical analysis software package is in the $300–500 range.

INTRADAY ANALYSIS

There has been substantial growth in technical analysis software that analyzes on-line intraday data. Sophisticated equipment is now available to monitor prices as the markets are trading. This can be a basic quote system or an intraday system that allows the analyst to chart the trading throughout the market day. These programs also have a wide range of capabilities, with the simplest being a program that can generate 5-, 10-, or 30-minute or longer charts of the intraday price action. Some of the more advanced software programs will allow the user to perform a number of technical calculations on the data. Most of the indicators discussed in this book are incorporated into these intraday software programs.

The type of intraday analysis software once only available for checking the commodity markets is now available for tracking stocks and major stock indices, as well as stock options and mutual funds.

Intraday systems also require a data source, which is the major cost factor. The most common form of retrieving data is through a small satellite dish. This allows the computer to collect real-time data from a major communication satellite. Over the past two years, other methods of obtaining intraday or real-time data have become available. In some areas, intraday data collection is available through FM broadcast, cable television signal, or dedicated land lines.

With 24-hour trading available in many markets, systems such as Telerate's TeleTrac™ system allow the ability to track cash and commodity prices around the world. When trading ceases in the United States, prices are then picked up in the Far East and London until trading resumes in the U.S. markets. The trader is able to carefully monitor prices in all the world markets.

Many of the intraday systems allow the analyst to easily program custom screen displays to fit individual needs. Figure 15.2 shows an example from Telerate's TeleTrac™ system that features four different bar charts, plus seven lines of news and quotes at the bottom. This type of format allows one to monitor many different markets simultaneously. For example, panel 1 is an hourly chart of cash gold prices; panel 2, hourly yen/$; panel 3, hourly prices for the German bond futures traded in London; and panel 4, the hourly data on Tokyo's Nikkei Dow Stock Index.

Twenty-four-hour trading in the currencies is exhibited in Figure 15.3, which shows British pound prices, hour by hour, for a little over a week of trading. While currency markets have

FIGURE 15.2
Customized TeleTrac Screen

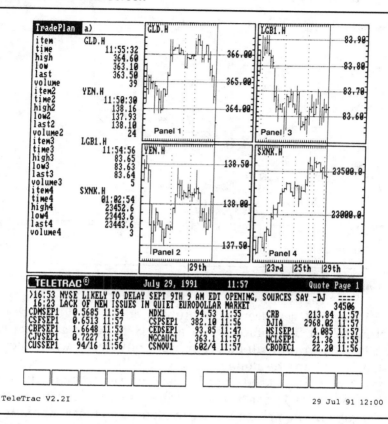

Courtesy of Telerate.

been traded around the clock for many years, it is now possible for traders to track these prices graphically. The currency markets are the world's largest and most liquid markets, and experienced currency traders must have the 24-hour data available. The currency markets will be used as examples for many of the discussions in this section, as it is my primary area of interest. Note that basic charting techniques, including trendlines and chart formations, can also be effective on the hourly data.

In both the cash and futures markets it is important to understand the units in which the data is expressed. For exam-

FIGURE 15.3
TeleTrac Screen ($/STG)

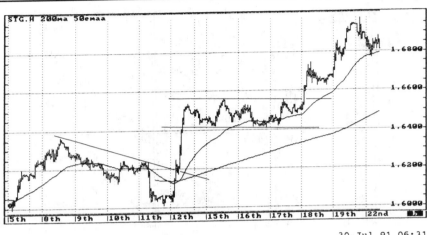

TeleTrac V2.2I   30 Jul 91 06:31

Courtesy of Telerate.

ple, Figure 15.3 represents the number of U.S. dollars per pound
sterling (STG). Therefore, when the U.S. dollar is stronger than
the STG, the graph will be declining. Conversely, when the STG
is stronger than the dollar, the chart will be rising. All traditional technical methods can be used on the 24-hour data, and
the price action is continuous, unlike in the futures markets
where gaps in the price data are evident. The most sophisticated
intraday software allows one to run many technical studies using the 24-hour as well as the intraday data. This has become an
essential tool for currency traders, as the major banks and mul-
tinational companies must be able to hedge their currency risk
on a worldwide basis.

　　As mentioned previously, one drawback of an intraday system is cost. After the initial hardware cost of approximately
$1,000–2,000, one must also pay for the intraday data, including
exchange fees. The total for data, dish lease, and exchange fees
ranges from $400 to $2,000 per month. Because of the possibility
of exchange fees being waived in the near future, these costs may

decline. The reduction in cost of up to 50 percent would make intraday systems available to many more traders. In the interim, if the trader does not mind a 15-minute delay in getting prices, the cost drops sharply, as the exchange fees are not required.

The advantages or disadvantages of tracking prices on an intraday basis are subject to much discussion. Some seasoned traders who began trading well before the technology boom will say that monitoring prices on a trade-by-trade basis obscures the major trend and generates heavy commission costs. Other traders will say that without the ability to track the prices on a short-term basis, one's effectiveness in the market is greatly reduced. However, in coming years the trend will be toward advanced computer technology designed to monitor prices of stocks and commodities on a trade-by-trade basis.

CHAPTER 16

THE COMPUTER AND FUTURES PRICE ANALYSIS

Thomas E. Aspray
President and Research Director, Aspray, Parsons and McClintock
Asset Management Corp.

Computerized commodity analysis can be grouped into two primary types, objective and subjective analysis. In my analysis I use a combination of both, although for many inexperienced traders, objective analysis alone may be more successful.

Objective analysis is a mechanical approach that has become more common in recent years. In this type of analysis, buy or sell signals are generated by the computer using formulas that are either disclosed or not disclosed. Most objective systems also have a built-in risk management feature, which has the computer determine a protective stop-loss point on existing positions.

In **subjective analysis,** the data is analyzed by the trader and then a decision is made. In other words, the trader looks at the indicators, the charts, and so on and then makes his or her own decision. Traditional divergence analysis, in which one compares the price activity with one or more technical indicators, is a type of subjective analysis.

OBJECTIVE ANALYSIS

In objective commodity analysis, trading signals are generated when specific, predetermined criteria are met. This removes the emotion or subjectivity from the decision-making process. The simplest type of objective system is one that utilizes moving averages. Much of the early computer analysis was concentrated on moving averages and moving average systems. The most basic moving average system is one in which longs are established when prices close above the moving average. Longs are then liquidated and short positions established when prices close below the moving average. For example, Figure 16.1 is a chart of April 1989 gold with a 21-day SMA over the prices. On the bottom half of the chart is a histogram that compares the spread, or the difference, between the closing price and the 21-day SMA. If the histogram is above the zero line, it indicates that the close is above the SMA. Conversely, when the histogram is below the zero line, the closing price is below the 21-day SMA. One of the problems with moving average systems and all trend-following methods is that they do not work well in nontrending markets. In choppy or sideways periods of price action, **whipsaws** are often generated. A whipsaw is a signal that is reversed within a short time and usually results in a loss.

As prices dropped below the moving average in early September (point 1), a sell signal was generated. This signal was reversed in October at point 2.

FIGURE 16.1
21-Day SMA (April 1989 Gold)

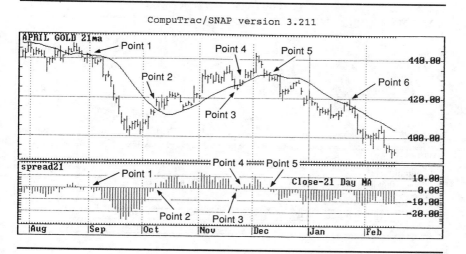

The choppy price action in late November generated a brief whipsaw as prices closed below the SMA at point 3, but the signal was reversed two days later at point 4, as prices closed back above the 21-day SMA.

A more profitable sell signal was generated in early December at point 5, prior to a steep decline. This decline was interrupted by a brief rally in late January 1989 (point 6), as prices moved above the moving average intraday, before closing below the moving average. Most traders utilizing this type of system would have stayed short through this rally, as signals are taken only when the price actually closes above or below the moving average. Intraday violations of the moving average are generally ignored. Gold prices during this period were in a well-established downtrend. Therefore, the number of whipsaws and the resulting losses were not too substantial.

A more recent example of gold prices (Figure 16.2) illustrates a period of nontrending activity, as from February through June 1991 gold prices stayed between $360 and $370 per ounce. Of particular interest is the period from late February to late May, when over 13 signals were given (see arrows), the majority resulting in small losses.

FIGURE 16.2
MA with Nontrending Activity (October 1991 Gold)

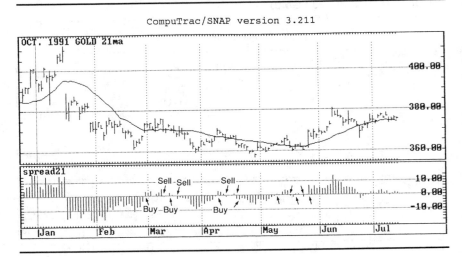

CompuTrac/SNAP version 3.211

In the 1970s, extensive work was performed to determine whether a dual moving average system would be more profitable than a single moving average system. The dual moving average system uses a short-term and a longer-term moving average to generate signals. The longer-term moving average identifies the long-term trend, while the short-term moving average is used for timing. When the shorter moving average moves above the longer-term moving average, longs are established. Conversely, a move of the shorter average below the longer-term average gives a signal to sell long positions and to go short. This type of system, as with most objective trading systems, is always in the market. In other words, it is always either long or short. The dual moving average systems are very effective in trending markets, as they tend to let profits run while losses are generally cut fairly soon.

The primary disadvantage of a dual moving average system occurs in sideways or trendless markets where this type of approach will often generate many trades and few profits. The most comprehensive work on a dual moving average crossover system was performed in 1982 by Frank L. Hocheimer and Richard J. Vaughn in Computerized Trading Techniques, Merrill Lynch Commodities. A summary of these results is shown in Figure 16.3.

The April 1989 gold chart (Figure 16.4) shows the averages that this research found to be the most effective (i.e., 8- and 48-day MAs). On the bottom half of the chart, the histogram represents the difference or spread between the 8 and 48 SMAs. At the beginning of this chart the system was short, as the 8-day MA was below the 48-day MA. A positive signal was given in November (point 1) as the 8-day MA moved above the 48-day MA. This signal was reversed in December with a sell signal (point 2). It should be noted that this work is currently outdated and is included here for illustrative purposes. Even though the table reflects impressive results with some commodities, it should not be used on current markets without further testing. This table provides a good reference source, however, for those who wish to do further research in this area.

There has been much debate and research on how to select the best moving average. Those who use cycles extensively in their trading will say that the length of the moving average should be tied to what has been determined to be the dominant

FIGURE 16.3
Results of Dual MA Crossover System

Commodity	Consistent Weights	Cumulative Profits or Losses (Net)	Largest String of Losses	Number Trades	Number Profitable Trades	Number Losing Trades
British Pound	3,49	117,482	−7,790	160	68	92
Cocoa	14,47	160,226	−8,620	303	128	175
Corn	13,47	83,565	−3,890	258	114	144
Canadian Dollar	4,21	57,430	−13,560	286	124	167
Cotton	22,50	324,719	−7,910	371	176	195
Copper	14,33	254,744	−6,112	473	250	22
Deutsche Mark	4,40	78,631	−3,909	169	78	91
GNMA	17,43	94,476	−12,742	278	126	152
Gold	8,48	482,769	−7,932	334	184	152
Heating Oil	14,40	−4,721	−413	88	6	82
Japanese Yen	4,28	120,899	−4,367	131	74	57
Hogs	18,50	52,888	−8,710	409	182	227
Lumber	6,50	5,022	−10,054	368	127	241
Live Cattle	6,21	113,178	−10,410	936	385	551
Plywood	23,44	8,378	−17,350	436	132	304
Soybeans	20,45	393,390	−18,610	530	247	283
Swiss Franc	6,50	172,454	−7,467	148	66	82
Soybean Meal	22,47	187,264	−8,805	484	217	267
Soybean Oil	13,49	127,399	−6,573	527	206	321
Silver	7,29	386,557	−21,726	1213	478	735
Sugar #11	6,50	475,442	−13,399	500	181	319
Treasury Bills	6,18	74,933	−21,423	535	200	335
Treasury Bonds	25,50	184,487	−10,066	147	81	66
Wheat	11,47	169,640	−5,282	358	140	218

The above table shows the last Merrill Lynch update of the double crossover method. In the column under *consistent weights* are listed the moving average combinations. For example, the British pound shows a 3 and 49 day combination to be the best.

These numbers are meant for information purposes only and are now several years old. The reader is cautioned against using these numbers in current markets without further testing of their validity. Optimized averages must be retested and updated occasionally.

(Source: "Computerized Trading Techniques 1982," Merrill Lynch Commodities, Inc., Frank L. Hochheimer and Richard J. Vaughn.)

cycle length. Other moving averages are then used as a factor of this dominant cycle length. For example, there are generally 20−21 trading days in a month, and for some commodities this is an important cycle. Therefore, moving averages either twice this amount (i.e., 40 days) or half this amount (10 days) are often used in a dual moving average system.

Some analysts believe that Fibonacci numbers work well for moving average systems. Two Fibonacci numbers are often combined into a dual moving average crossover system. Figure 16.5 shows the April 1989 gold contract using 13- and 34-day MAs,

FIGURE 16.4
8-Day and 48-Day SMAs

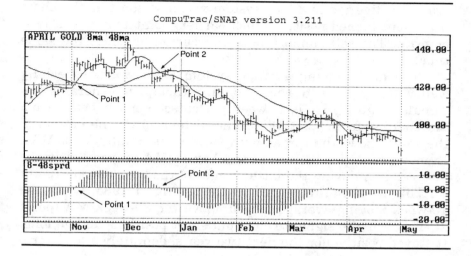

FIGURE 16.5
13-Day and 34-Day MAs (April 1989 Gold)

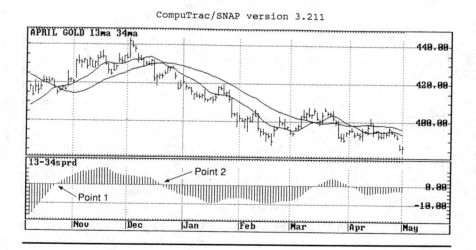

both of which are Fibonacci numbers. One can compare this chart with that of the 4- and 48-day MAs and observe some dramatic divergences. This system was also short as the chart began but turned positive much earlier (point 1) and at a lower price. The sell signal (point 2) occurred at about the same time.

The dual moving average system often works especially well when applied to weekly data, although it generates few signals. Figure 16.6 is a weekly Deutsche mark chart from March 1984 to October 1986. The histogram on the bottom of the chart shows the spread between the 10- and 30-week MAs. It shows that the shorter-term 10-week MA stayed below the 30-week MA during the latter stages of the bear market (point 1). This bear market ended in the spring of 1985, when the 10-week moving average moved above the 30-week MA (point 2). This was the signal to close out short positions and go long. It stayed positive for the next two years, definitely a long-term approach.

FIGURE 16.6
10-Week and 30-Week MAs (Weekly Deutsche Mark)

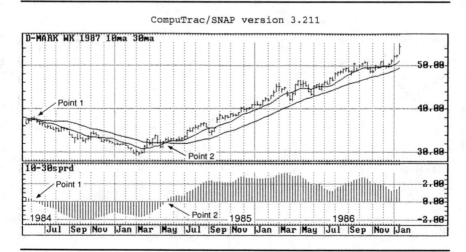

CompuTrac/SNAP version 3.211

SUBJECTIVE ANALYSIS

The most common type of subjective analysis is traditional chart analysis, in which the trader looks for significant chart formations or trendline violations in order to anticipate a change in trend. (On the other hand, most objective systems attempt to identify a trend after it is already under way.) The sharp increase in the number of computers and technical analysis programs has also caused a dramatic increase in the number of computerized technical indicators, or tools. These technical tools can be grouped into two major areas, price-based, or momentum, indicators and what I call demand-type indicators that use volume or open interest in addition to price. The use and application of these indicators varies from analyst to analyst. This is central to the question of subjective analytical decisions.

Divergence analysis is one of the more popular types of subjective analysis. A divergence is formed when an indicator, whether a momentum or demand indicator, acts stronger or weaker than prices. Positive or bullish divergences are associated with market bottoms, whereas negative or bearish divergences are formed at market tops.

Figure 16.7 is a weekly chart of the Deutsche mark from November 1989 through July 1991. On the bottom half of the chart is a typical momentum indicator. In early 1991 (point 3), the Deutsche mark made new highs against the dollar, exceeding the November 1990 highs (point 2). The indicator, however, gave a much different picture as it peaked in early 1990 and then declined. This negative or bearish divergence is illustrated by comparing the slopes of lines A and C. As prices were trending higher (line A), the indicator was trending lower (line C). Another more pronounced negative divergence was formed in 1991 (point 3) as, while prices were much higher (line B), the indicator formed sharply lower highs (line D). At major market tops there will often be a series of negative divergences, as was the case in this example (points 1, 2, and 3). The 20% decline in the value of the Deutsche mark over the next five months was one of the more dramatic declines of the last 10 years.

FIGURE 16.7

Momentum Indicator Showing Negative Divergence (Weekly Deutsche Mark)

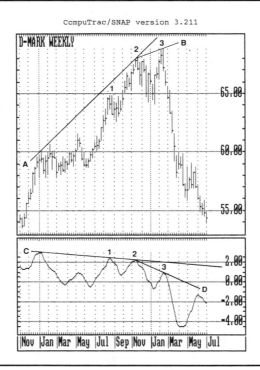

CompuTrac/SNAP version 3.211

Figure 16.8 shows an example of a positive divergence, also using weekly data on the Deutsche mark. The chart covers the period from November 1983 through June 1985 and includes the same momentum indicator as in Figure 16.7. The Deutsche mark, after peaking in November 1980 at the 5800 level, had declined steadily, dropping below 3000 in early 1985 (point 2). Though the Deutsche mark had declined well below the September 1984 lows, the momentum indicator did not make new lows, thereby forming a positive divergence (line B). This divergence was confirmed when the indicator moved above the previous peak (dashed line) at point 3. The 10- and 30-week MAs turned positive in May 1985, also indicating a change in trend. The currencies would move higher and the dollar would move lower

FIGURE 16.8

Momentum Indicator Showing Positive Divergence (Weekly Deutsche Mark)

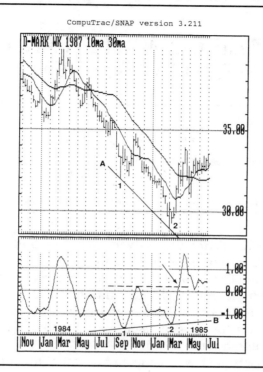

for the next six years. These signals were given over six months prior to the historic G-7 meeting in September 1985, when the world monetary authorities announced their decision to lower the value of the dollar.

In my analysis, I have found that combining traditional chart analysis with divergence analysis is an effective way to identify significant turning points, which will be discussed in the following chapters.

CHAPTER 17

THE COMPUTER AND TRADING SYSTEMS

Thomas E. Aspray
President and Research Director, Aspray, Parsons and McClintock Asset Management Corp.

The increase in technical analysis software has caused a dramatic surge in the number of computerized technical indicators or tools. CompuTrac, one of the first technical software manufacturers (CompuTrac is also the name of their program), now offers over 30 different indicators in its current version.[1] Some of these indicators have been used for many years, while others have been created since 1990.

In this section, I will concentrate on a few of my favorite indicators and the methods I use to interpret them. The charts in this section were created using CompuTrac software.

THE DIRECTIONAL MOVEMENT INDEX

The most successful trading methods are usually designed to identify changes in the major trend and follow that trend. In our discussion of objective analysis, we looked at single and dual moving average trading systems, which are both trend-following methods.

---

[1]For further information on CompuTrac software, write to CompuTrac, Inc., 1017 Pleasant Street, New Orleans, LA 70115.

Most trend-following systems show poor performance in nontrending (sideways) markets. This type of market is especially difficult to trade, as these systems tend to have a bias toward the long or short side and, as such, are repeatedly stopped out of long or short positions in a sideways market. Different strategies should be used in nontrending markets, although commission costs generally have a greater impact on profits. Therefore, to determine what technique is best suited for trading a market, one must first determine whether the market is currently trending or not.

One tool that is commonly used by analysts to determine trending versus nontrending markets is the directional movement index (DMI), developed by J. Welles Wilder, Jr. (see Bibliography). The DMI is made up of several different parts and the formula is quite complex. The reader should refer to the original work for formulas and methods of calculation. I will concentrate on three components of the DMI: the positive directional movement (+DI), the negative directional movement (−DI), and the average directional movement index range (ADXR).

The ADXR measures the amount of directional movement or trending on a scale of 0 to 100. The higher the number, the greater the market is trending. Low readings, under 30 or so, indicate an environment where most trend-following systems would not be expected to perform well. The slope of the ADXR line is also important because a rising ADXR line is consistent with a trending market, whereas a declining ADXR line suggests a nontrending environment. When the ADXR line is above 30 and starts to decline, it is often an early indication that the market is changing from trending to nontrending. Confirmation occurs when the ADXR line moves below 30. This type of behavior is often evident during corrections within a major trend. The readings from the ADXR can be an important part of a trading strategy because it can help determine what size position should be taken, as larger positions should be taken in trending markets than in nontrending markets. In addition, wider protective stops can be used in trending markets than in nontrending markets.

To calculate the ADXR, +DI, and −DI lines, the trader determines the input for the length of time studied. The time frames commonly used are 9 and 14 days (9 is the interval selected for these charts). Obviously, the shorter the time period selected, the more sensitive the indicator becomes and the signals are therefore more frequent but not necessarily more profitable.

The first chart (Figure 17.1) depicts soybean prices during the bull market of 1988 and includes the ADXR line from the directional movement index. (This is a perpetual contract, which is discussed in detail in a later section.) I have drawn a line at the 30 level and will consider levels above 30 to be trending and those below it nontrending.

Soybean prices consolidated during the January–March 1988 period between resistance (line 1), and support (line 2). During this period, the ADXR line was below 30 and not trend-

FIGURE 17.1
1988 Soybeans with ADXR Line

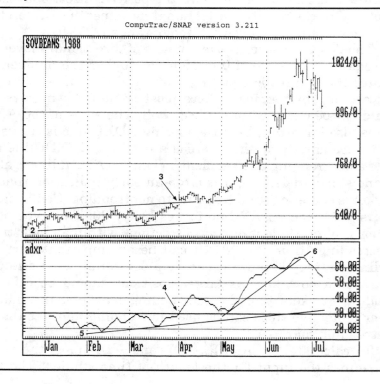

CompuTrac/SNAP version 3.211

ing. Prices gapped higher on April 1 (point 3) and through resistance (line 1). The ADXR line moved through the 30 level on the same day (point 4), which confirmed the price action. Soybean prices retested support (line 1) in the latter part of April, but the ADXR stayed well above the 30 level and its uptrend (line 5). As soybean prices rallied sharply during May and June, the ADXR line continued to rise. The ADXR line turned lower in late June, breaking the short-term uptrend (line 6). This was the first indication that prices were moving from a trending to a nontrending environment.

This use of the ADXR can be applied to all markets, whether cash or futures. The foreign exchange markets are one of the better trending markets, therefore the ADXR readings are especially valuable. The dollar index (see Figure 17.2), which measures the value of the U.S. dollar against a basket of currencies, declined steadily from the May 1989 highs until February 1991, when it began a dramatic rally.

The strength of the rally in 1991 was unexpected by most economists and also surprised many technicians. Those watching the ADXR readings were given early evidence that a strong trend was under way. The ADXR had been moving lower until early February, when the downtrend (line 1) was broken (point 3) as the ADXR moved back above the 30 level. The uptrend in the ADXR (line 2) was intact until late April when it was violated (point 4). The declining ADXR line and violation of its uptrend suggested that the uptrend was maturing.

The signals on the dollar index could have been substantiated by the analysis of the currency futures. There is an inverse relationship between the dollar index and the currency futures; in other words, as the dollar index rises, the individual currencies will be declining. The trader can therefore gain greater confidence in his or her analysis of the dollar's direction by looking at both the dollar index and the individual currencies. Figure 17.3 shows the Deutsche mark futures during the same period as with the dollar index. The Deutsche mark moved to new all-time contract highs in early February before reversing direction. The ADXR line, which had been below 30 and not trending for most of January, turned higher in early February, breaking its downtrend (line 2). By the time the mark violated important

FIGURE 17.2
Dollar Index with ADXR

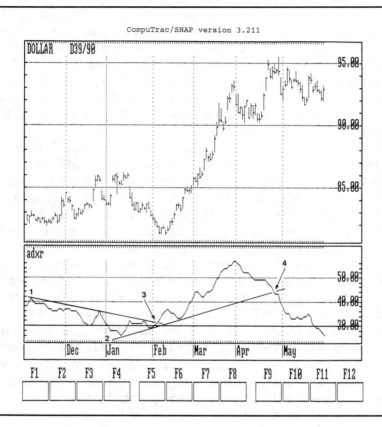

support (line 1), the ADXR line was in a well-defined uptrend
(line 4). The mark was clearly trending until late April, as the
uptrend (line 4) was broken (point 5). The change from trending
to nontrending was confirmed in late May, as the ADXR dropped
below the 30 level.

The values of the ADXR can clearly be used to identify
those markets which are trending, but, equally important, it can
also be used to identify the nontrending markets, which most
traders would like to avoid. For example, the U.S. stock market
rallied sharply in early 1991, making an initial peak in mid-
April. Over the next five months the S&P futures traded nar-

FIGURE 17.3
Deutsche Mark with ADXR

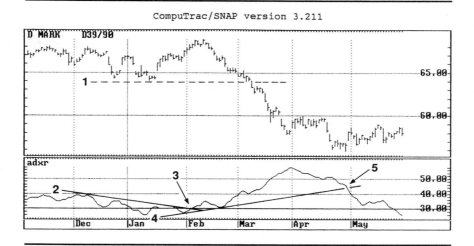

CompuTrac/SNAP version 3.211

rowly in a 30-point range with no discernable trend. This period was very frustrating to both the bulls and the bears alike, as trend-following methods were not successful. Figure 17.4 illustrates how the ADXR line peaked in March and, as the S&P futures were moving higher in early April, dropped below the 30 level (point 1). The ADXR line stayed below 30 for the next five months and indicated that the S&P futures were not trending.

The ADXR line is determined by two initial calculations, the +DI and the −DI. The +DI indicates the positive market action and the −DI measures the negative market action. Buy and sell signals can be generated when these lines cross (+DI over −DI is bullish; +DI below −DI is bearish). The crossing of the +DI and −DI can be converted to an oscillator, which I call the DIOSC. If the DIOSC is above zero it is positive; below zero is negative.

Let's look at what type of signals the +DI, −DI, and DIOSC gave for soybean prices during 1988. Figure 17.5 shows a plot of the +DI line and the −DI line, the DIOSC and the ADXR line. As soybean prices traded between resistance (line 1) and support (line 2) during the January–March period, the +DI and −DI crossed five times (see arrows). These crossings are more easily

FIGURE 17.4
S&P with ADXR

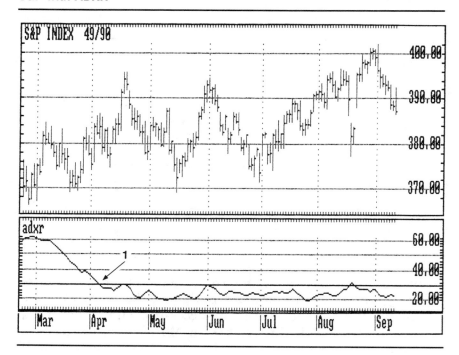

identified on the plot of the DIOSC. These signals resulted in either small profits or losses. In mid-March (point 3) the DIOSC again moved above the zero line (+DI greater than −DI). Other than the single two-day drop below the zero line in April, the DIOSC was above the zero line and positive until early July.

The first three signals occurred while the ADXR line was below 30 and not trending. These signals were, therefore, less important. When the ADXR line moved above 30 on April 1, the DIOSC was already positive (above zero), and this was a much stronger signal. Even during the brief sell signal in April, the ADXR line was above 30 and its uptrend (line 4), so the trend was still intact. The ADXR line can then be used to filter the DIOSC signals, as crossing above or below the zero line by the DIOSC is much more valid and more likely to be profitable when the ADXR line is rising and above 30.

FIGURE 17.5
+DI, −DI, DIOSC, and ADXR (1988 Soybeans)

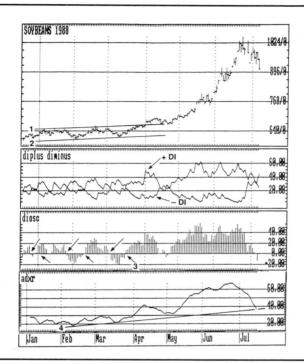

The combination of the DIOSC and the ADXR values helped identify the major uptrend in the dollar index in early 1991. As noted earlier, the ADXR line stayed below the 30 level from early December 1990 through January 1991. Several signals were given by the DIOSC (see Figure 17.6) during this period. In mid-February, the DIOSC once again moved above the zero line (point 3), and, two days later, the ADXR line moved above the 30 level and its downtrend (line 1). It was about three weeks later that the dollar index moved above the December–January highs. The DIOSC stayed positive until mid-April, when the ADXR line was then declining. This suggested the trend was maturing; by late April, the ADXR line dropped below 30, indicating the dollar index was no longer trending.

FIGURE 17.6
Dollar Index with ADXR and DIOSC (D39/90)

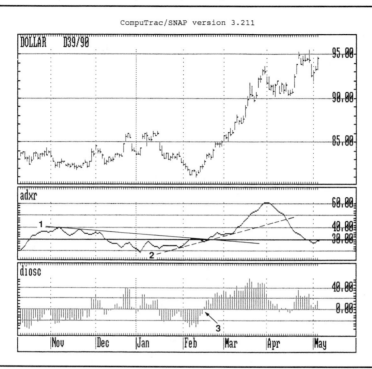

CompuTrac/SNAP version 3.211

Many markets have only one or two trending periods per year. By trading these markets only during the trending periods one can preserve trading capital and reduce the frustration caused by choppy, sideways markets. The last example using the ADXR and DIOSC features gold prices of August 1990–February 1991 (see Figure 17.7). The ADXR line stayed below 30 from late September (point 1) until early February (point 3). The first indication that the market may have entered a trending phase was the violation of the two-month downtrend in the ADXR (line 2). This coincided with a new sell signal from the DIOSC (point 4). By the time the ADXR line moved above 30, the DIOSC was farther below the zero line.

These examples should demonstrate that the ADXR line can be an important tool, either separately or in conjunction with the signals from the DIOSC. The ADXR can be used to

FIGURE 17.7
October 1991 Gold with ADXR and DIOSC

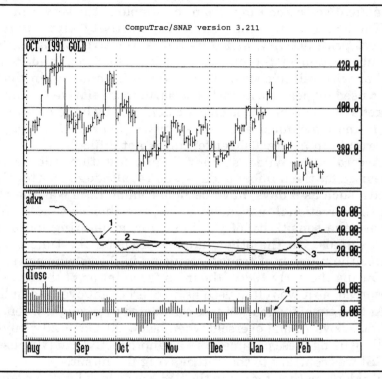

CompuTrac/SNAP version 3.211

filter signals from the DIOSC, or the ADXR line can be used separately to select only those markets that are trending. Since the time that the original work was published by Wilder, this indicator has been modified and fine-tuned by many analysts. The variations on the use and application of the directional movement index are beyond the scope of this text, but this discussion should serve as an introduction to this valuable tool.

THE RELATIVE STRENGTH INDEX

The relative strength index (RSI) is another popular tool developed by J. Welles Wilder, Jr., and discussed in his book, *New Concepts in Technical Trading Systems*. This indicator, one of the most useful, is featured in many of the popular chart services. It is also an indicator that is frequently misused. As is the case with the directional movement index, the methods of its interpretation are diverse and range from the simple to the very complex.

The RSI measures the current day's activity with regard to the past price activity, hence its name, relative strength. (See Formula section at the end of Chapter 18.) Stock traders are familiar with relative strength in a different manner, in that it is also used to measure a stock's performance relative to a major market average. The RSI is easily calculated by hand or is available in most technical analysis software programs. Setting up the formula in a spreadsheet format is not difficult.

According to Wilder's original interpretation, the default value used for the number of days was 14, although shorter time periods, such as 9 days, have become common. As was the case with the directional movement index, the shorter time periods increase the sensitivity of the indicator, generating more frequent signals. On the other hand, increasing the time period reduces the number of trades, resulting in fewer whipsaws.

During the early 1980s, the misinterpretation of the RSI was widespread, as it was often used as an overbought/oversold indicator. At that time, the market was considered overbought when the RSI was above 70 and oversold when below 20. Generally, buying or selling using these parameters was unproductive, and this use of the RSI was contrary to the author's original intent.

Wilder's method for using the RSI was to look for divergences between the RSI and prices when the RSI was above 70 or below 30. A topping signal is generated when the RSI first makes a high above 70, and then prices make a new high but the RSI does not. The topping signal is completed when the RSI drops below the intervening low. I have found that this type of formation generates valid signals even if the RSI is not above 70.

Figure 17.8 shows this type of formation using the April 1989 gold contract. Both gold prices and the RSI made their initial highs (point 1) in early November 1988, and then, as prices made further highs in December (point 3), the RSI made a lower high (also labeled point 3). The RSI therefore formed a negative divergence, and the key support for the RSI was the intervening low (point 2). The violation of the RSI support (point 4) confirmed the negative divergence and the top formation.

FIGURE 17.8
April 1989 Gold with RSI

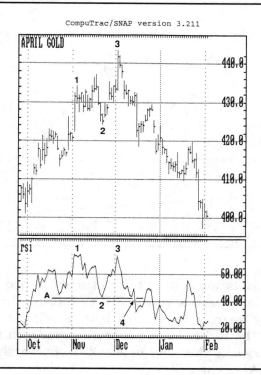

CompuTrac/SNAP version 3.211

A classic bottom signal is given when the RSI is below 30 and a new price low is not confirmed by a new low in the RSI. This signal is completed when the RSI moves above its previous peak. Figure 17.9 shows pork belly prices from late 1988 until May 1989, with the 14-day RSI. The RSI made an initial low below 20 in early April and, on the next decline, prices dropped to new lows (line 2), while the RSI made higher lows (line 2). When the RSI moved above resistance (line 1, see arrow), the bottoming formation was completed. The former resistance in the RSI (line 1) then became important support, which held on the late May decline. Pork belly prices then moved to sharp new highs in late June (line 3). The RSI formed lower highs (line 3) and therefore a negative divergence. This divergence was sup-

FIGURE 17.9
Pork Bellies with RSI

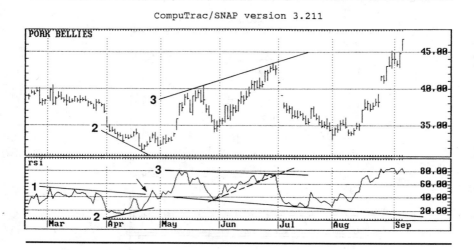

CompuTrac/SNAP version 3.211

ported by the violation of the RSI's uptrend (dashed line), which set the stage for a decline in the RSI to support (line 1).

For many years I have used both moving averages and trendlines on the RSI itself to generate signals. In my analysis I use a 21-period (either day or week) front-weighted moving average (WMA) of the RSI.

$$\text{WMA} = \frac{(X + N) + (X - 1)(N - 1) + \ldots + (N - X + 1)}{X + (X - 1) + (X - 2) + \ldots + 1}$$

where N is the most current data value and X is the number of days in the period.

Figure 17.10 depicts the futures contract on the Nikkei Dow index, the major stock market index in Japan. It includes a 21-day WMA of the RSI. Even more important than whether the RSI is above or below its WMA is the slope of the WMA. When the WMA is rising, prices and the trend in the RSI are up. Conversely, a declining WMA is consistent with declining prices.

Both the RSI and its WMA turned higher in early November, and the RSI stayed above its MA until early December. The

FIGURE 17.10
Nikkei Dow with RSI and WMA

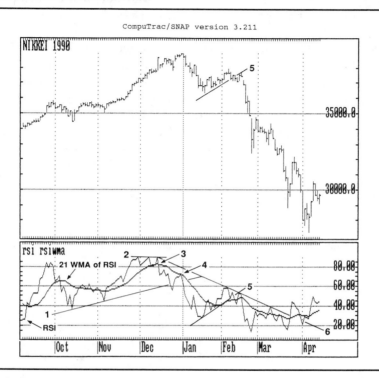

RSI failed to move higher with prices in mid-December (line 2), and then dropped below its MA (point 3). The RSI's uptrend (line 1) was broken briefly several days later. The Nikkei Dow index turned higher once more, making new highs at 39,000 in late December. The RSI, however, was much weaker, as it only rallied back to its declining MA (point 4) and was well below its previous peak. This action confirmed that the top was in place as both prices and the RSI turned sharply lower and the Nikkei Dow lost 2,000 points.

The market stabilized in the middle of January, forming a short-term uptrend in both prices and the RSI (line 5). The RSI moved up to the December lows at the 60 level. Two days later, the price and the RSI uptrends (line 5) were broken. These uptrends were retested a week later before the RSI started to decline sharply and dropped back below its MA. This established a downtrend in the RSI (line 6), which was not broken until late March. During this period the Nikkei Dow declined over 7,000 points.

As with all of the indicators discussed in this section, the signals using weekly data are generally the most accurate. They often last from six months to a year, which is favorable because of the low commission costs. A good example of this is the long-term chart of the Deutsche mark futures, Figure 17.11. Underneath the bar chart is the 9-period RSI with its 21-period WMA. There are many signals to analyze during the five-year history covered, but I will concentrate on just a few selected time periods. The RSI first dropped below the 20 level in mid-1988, when the deutsche mark was at 5300. Almost a year later, in June

FIGURE 17.11
Deutsche Mark with RSI and 21-Period WMA

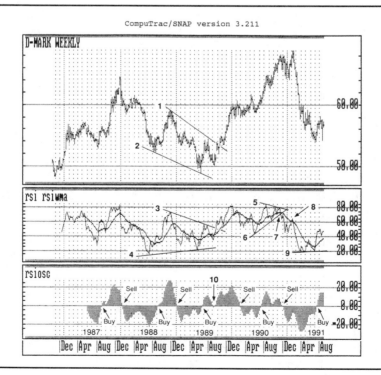

CompuTrac/SNAP version 3.211

1989, the RSI dropped to just above the 20 level, but the Deutsche mark was much lower at 4950. Therefore, the RSI formed a positive divergence (line 4). The strength of the positive divergence is evident by comparing the lower lows in price (line 2) and the higher lows in the RSI (line 4). The divergence was confirmed when the downtrend in the RSI (line 3) was broken. At this time the RSI's weighted moving average was clearly rising. This occurred in September 1989, more than two full months before the events in Europe that resulted in the reunification of the two Germanies, dramatically boosting the mark's value.

The RSI analysis of the Deutsche mark in late 1990 and early 1991 suggested that a major top was being completed. The RSI made an initial peak in August 1990, well above the 80 level as the Deutsche mark was at 6400. By early December 1990, the mark was at 6800, but the RSI was unable to make it above 80, forming a negative divergence (line 5). Shortly thereafter, the uptrend in the RSI (line 6) was broken and the RSI dropped below its MA (point 7). After dropping quickly to the 6400 level, the Deutsche mark turned higher once more, moving to new highs at 6900 in February 1991. The negative divergence at this time was even more pronounced as the RSI rose back to its declining WMA (point 8) just above the 60 level. This formation was very similar to the one that was discussed on the Nikkei Dow and is generally a reliable formation. The RSI was therefore acting much weaker than prices, and the Deutsche mark declined from 6900 to 5400 in the next five months. A positive divergence (line 9) was formed at the July 1991 lows.

If one moving average can be used effectively to determine the trend in the RSI, and therefore in prices, two moving averages can often work better. The RSIOSC at the bottom of Figure 17.11 is the difference between a six-week WMA and a 24-week SMA, represented in a histogram form. When the 6-week WMA of the RSI is above the 24-week SMA, the histogram is above zero and a positive signal is given. Conversely, when the 6-week WMA is below the 24-week SMA, the histogram is below the zero line, and a negative signal is given. In over four years, the RSIOSC generated just eleven signals, which are annotated on the chart. Only one whipsaw was evident during this period, in

September 1989 (point 10). The signals from the RSIOSC often coincided with either positive or negative divergences. The signals from the RSIOSC generated a gross profit of 3154 points, which, at $12.50 per point, is $39,425 per contract. (A complete discussion of the testing results of the RSIOSC on the weekly Deutsche mark will be found in chapter 18.) It should not be assumed that future results using the RSIOSC will equal or exceed past results, and it is provided only as an example, not a recommendation.

The RSI is one tool that all commodity traders should become familiar with. The use of two moving averages of the RSI is an area that warrants some additional research. If it is used in the above manner, the RSI can be one of the more reliable price-based indicators.

ON-BALANCE VOLUME

Volume is an important part of technical analysis that is ignored by many traders. Even basic chart analysis should include volume analysis to add confidence to one's conclusions. For example, the British pound in 1988 (Figure 17.12) appeared to be forming a complex head and shoulders top formation. The initial peak in March (labeled LS1 for left shoulder 1) occurred on the heaviest volume as the pound made further new highs (at LS2 and the head) in mid-April, while the volume declined (line 4). This is what should occur in a head and shoulders top formation. Volume did increase on the decline in early May as the neckline (line 1) was tested at point 2. Volume expanded further when the neckline was broken (point 3), thereby confirming the top formation.

One way to analyze volume is with the on-balance volume (OBV), one of the early technical tools developed by Joseph Granville, a well-known stock market analyst. Originally developed for the stock market and individual stocks, it is now less popular with the advent of new and supposedly more sophisticated technical tools. It is rarely used on the commodity markets, as many other analysts do not find it useful. I would disagree, as I find it to be a very useful and relatively simple technical tool.

FIGURE 17.12
British Pound with Volume

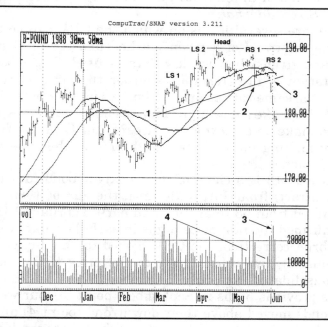

While it is easier to calculate OBV by computer, it can be calculated by hand for individual stocks, market indices, or commodities. Shown below is the method for hand calculation:

1) Pick an arbitrary starting volume number. Most commodities or stocks take the volume for one week for daily plotting or a month's volume if plotting the OBV weekly.

2) To calculate the first OBV value, add in the volume if the price on the first day is higher than that of the previous day and subtract the volume if it is lower. For example:

Commodity Price	Price Change	Volume	OBV
		50,000	
323	+2	10,000	60,000
324	+1	5,000	65,000
322	−2	10,000	55,000

3) After you have 20 or 30 OBV values, they can be plotted on graph paper along with the price of the market you are fol-

lowing. If access to a computer data source is unavailable, the data can be found in financial publications such as *Barron's* or *The Wall Street Journal.*

There are several levels on which the OBV can be used to determine the trend of a given market, and the most reliable signals are given when weekly data is used. The most basic interpretation is to determine whether the OBV is rising or falling at the same rate as prices. If prices make a new high, did the OBV also make a new high? If prices make a new low, did the OBV also make a new low with prices? If the OBV does confirm prices by making either a new high or low, then the current trend is intact.

Figure 17.13 is a chart of the weekly T-bond futures (perpetual contract) from July 1984 until the end of 1986. T-bond prices rallied from 58 to about 72 in early February 1985. The OBV confirmed the new price highs in early February (point 1). After a brief correction, the OBV moved to new highs in May 1985 (point 3), two weeks prior to the price highs (point 2). Prices consolidated from July to October 1985. The OBV moved above its previous highs in September (point 5), four weeks before T-bonds moved above their downtrend (point 4) and eight weeks before prices moved above the early July highs. The OBV in this example was a very good leading indicator, as it was indicating accumulation well before prices moved higher. At each successive new high in prices (points 6 and 7), the OBV made new highs in advance of prices.

Generally, in a valid uptrend, the OBV will be stronger than prices and will lead prices higher. Conversely, in valid downtrends the OBV will be weaker than prices, as the OBV will make new lows ahead of prices. When the OBV fails to make new highs or new lows with prices, it is an early indication that the trend may be changing.

The second level of analysis with the OBV is to use simple trendline analysis on the OBV itself. Though this type of analysis is not common, after many years of using it I have become convinced of its value. Trendline analysis, whether on price charts or the indicators, is clearly a form of subjective analysis. Often, the OBV's trendlines are broken prior to the price

FIGURE 17.13
T-Bonds with OBV

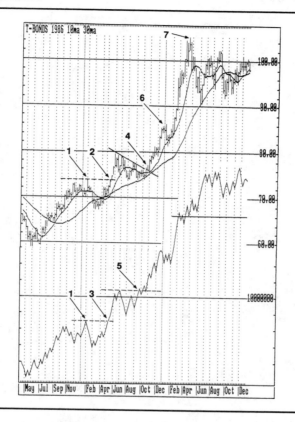

trendlines. The trendlines can be simple uptrends or downtrends or support and resistance levels.

Figure 17.14 of the T-bond futures shows a line of resistance in the OBV (labeled 1), formed during November 1984– February 1985. The breakout through this resistance was bullish (point 2), as prices moved up sharply for the next month. During the summer and fall of 1985, T-bond prices consolidated (line 3). The upside breakout in the OBV (point 4) preceded the price breakout by almost a month, and the OBV moved sharply higher. The OBV moved sideways in late 1985 and early 1986 (line 5), before once again moving sharply higher (point 6). The

FIGURE 17.14
T-Bonds with OBV

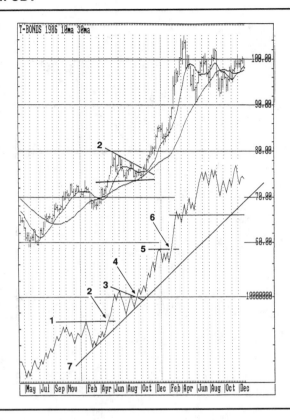

rally from October 1985 until April 1986 was dramatic, as the bonds moved up 30 full points, or $30,000 per contract. This rally lasted almost eight months. An intact long-term uptrend in the OBV (line 7) can be drawn using the May and September 1985 lows.

The third level of analysis is to use a moving average of the OBV to determine whether the trend is up or down. The slope of the moving average is more important than whether the OBV is above or below its moving average. When the OBV is above its rising moving average, it indicates the continuation of the uptrend. If the OBV is below its moving average and the moving average is declining, it is negative.

Through testing I have found a 21-period, front-end WMA works the best. That is either a 21-day for daily data or a 21-week for weekly data. The calculation of a WMA is somewhat tedious by hand, and a simple 21-period moving average works almost as well. The 21-week WMA has been included on Figure 17.14; the OBV stayed above its moving average from September 1985 through September 1986.

In my experience, the weekly OBV can be a valuable tool to help the trader identify major moves in the commodity markets. The weekly chart of soybeans, Figure 17.15, with the OBV and its 21-week WMA, is one good example. The weekly OBV formed a trading range (line 1) during June–November 1987. In September, the OBV moved above its WMA (point 2) and tested its recent highs before declining. The OBV found support at its

FIGURE 17.15
Soybeans with OBV

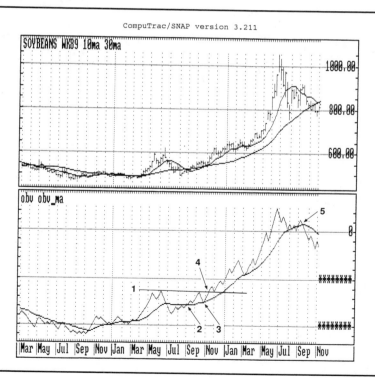

rising WMA (point 3) in November and turned up once more. By late November (point 4) the OBV moved through resistance and to new highs. This occurred two to three weeks before prices made new highs. For the next seven months, the OBV continued to make new highs well before prices. The first sign of a top came in late July when the OBV dropped below its moving average (point 5), and the WMA flattened out.

Using the same methods of analysis, the OBV can also be effective on the daily data, as it can stay positive or negative for several months, helping the trader identify the major trend. Figure 17.16 shows the daily prices of the Deutsche mark futures between November 1990 and May 1991. As the mark turned higher in January 1991, the OBV was in an uptrend (line 2) and above its rising moving average. The OBV formed a short-term

FIGURE 17.16
Deutsche Mark with OBV

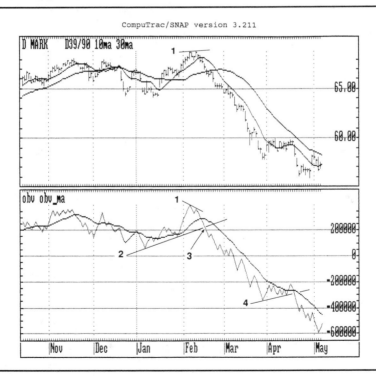

CompuTrac/SNAP version 3.211

negative divergence in February (line 1) and soon after dropped below its moving average. The sell signal was confirmed when the OBV violated its uptrend (line 2, at point 3). Until mid-April the OBV stayed below its declining moving average. The stabilization in the OBV is reflected by line 4. The OBV did move briefly above its moving average, but the violation of OBV support (point 5) signaled the resumption of the decline.

Volume analysis is another important part of technical analysis and the use of a computer makes this type of analysis much easier. Among the many technical tools that use volume in their calculation, the OBV is one of my favorites.

THE HERRICK PAYOFF INDEX

In my opinion, the open interest can also give the analyst or trader valuable information about the price action. The trend of the open interest is examined in a manner similar to volume analysis. Rising open interest and rising prices are bullish, as they indicate that new long positions are being established and pushing prices higher. On the other hand, the open interest declining as prices move higher suggests that the rally is primarily short covering, which is a negative prognosis.

A similar type of analysis is used when prices are declining. If the open interest rises on a price decline, it indicates that new short positions are being established. This new selling should continue to move prices lower. Declining open interest with declining prices is positive, as it indicates that the decline is primarily long liquidation. The absence of new selling indicates that the correction could be an interruption within the dominant uptrend.

One indicator that uses open interest, volume, and prices is the Herrick payoff index (HPI), developed by the late John Herrick. Its formula is quite complex (see Formula section in chapter 18), and is available in several software programs. Basically the HPI is a mathematical method of measuring the money flowing into or out of a commodity by computing the difference in dollar volume each day. The formula includes the value of a one-cent move for the commodity being analyzed. As a general rule, $250 can be used for agricultural commodities and $500 for the financial futures.

I find the HPI to be an excellent short- and long-term tool, although my use and interpretation varies from the original work. In this section, I will concentrate on the intermediate analysis using weekly data.

The relationship of the weekly HPI to the zero line can generate excellent long-term signals. If the HPI is above zero it is positive, which indicates that money is flowing into the commodity. Conversely, when it is below the zero line or negative, money is moving out of the commodity. The formation of positive or negative divergences often precedes the crossing of the zero line and the violation of trendlines or key support and resistance levels further supports the divergence analysis.

Figure 17.17 is a weekly chart of Eurodollar futures from October 1986 until April 1989. The HPI dropped below the zero line in January 1987 (point 1), which indicated that money flow had turned from positive to negative. This signal was in effect until October 1987 (point 2), as the stock market crash caused panic buying of interest rate futures.

This buy signal lasted until late April 1988 when, once again, the money flow turned negative as the HPI violated the zero line (point 3). The market was in a well-established downtrend for the next year. The Eurodollar futures rebounded in September–November 1988, when the HPI moved briefly above the zero line (point 4). This signal was reversed (point 5) as the decline in the Eurodollar futures resumed. The HPI stayed below the zero line until April 1989, when the money flow again turned positive (point 6). During the 32-month time period covered in this chart, the HPI gave only six signals, a very long-term approach.

Figure 17.18 is a weekly crude oil chart from May 1985 until December 1987, with the HPI and its 21-week WMA. The collapse in oil prices from November 1985 until April 1986 was very dramatic, and excellent signals were given by the HPI. As prices moved to new highs in November 1985, the HPI was above the zero line but acting weaker than prices. This weakness was substantiated by the violation of the uptrend (line 1) in

FIGURE 17.17
Eurodollars with HPI

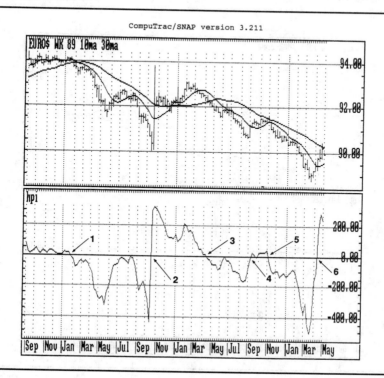

CompuTrac/SNAP version 3.211

the HPI and was confirmed by the drop through the zero line (point 2). This indicated that money was flowing out of the crude oil market, which was bearish.

As prices plunged sharply for three months, the HPI continued to make new lows with prices and stayed well below its moving average. As crude dropped to the $10 level in mid-April, the HPI formed a positive divergence (point 4), as it made a higher low than indicated (point 3), even though prices were almost $1.50 per barrel lower.

During the ensuing six-week rally, the HPI moved briefly above the zero line before prices again dropped back to the $10 level. On this decline the HPI violated the zero line, but on the retest of the lows in the $10 area, the HPI made a much higher

FIGURE 17.18
Crude Oil with HPI

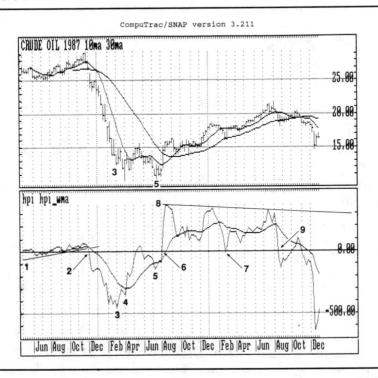

CompuTrac/SNAP version 3.211

low (point 5). This was a very strong positive divergence. The
HPI soon moved quickly back above its moving average and
then above the zero line (point 6).

Early in this rally, the HPI was much stronger than prices,
as it moved well above its previous highs. This strong positive
money flow was a bullish indication. For the next year, despite
one brief interruption (point 7), the money flow stayed positive.

The rally continued until prices reached the $22 area, but as
this rally progressed the HPI made a series of lower highs (line
8), indicating that the volume/open interest was getting weaker
as the rally progressed. Therefore, less capital was supporting
prices. For the next four weeks, prices declined sharply and the
HPI dropped briefly below the zero line before quickly rebound-
ing (point 9). The ensuing technical rebound took the HPI above

the zero line for about four weeks before a stronger sell signal was generated. Crude oil prices then began a major decline.

The intermediate trend, as determined by the analysis of the weekly data, is most important in my work. To select or fine-tune entry points, one must also look at the daily data. In addition, the HPI can be effective on the daily data, as divergence analysis can help the trader identify important turning points as they occur. Once again we will use the April 1989 gold contract as an example (Figure 17.19).

Prices peaked in mid-December and made new rally highs (point 2) in the $445 area. The HPI formed a negative divergence on this rally as it made a lower high (point 2) than it had made in November (point 1). A drop in the HPI below the zero line and its previous lows (point 3) confirmed that funds were

FIGURE 17.19
April Gold with HPI

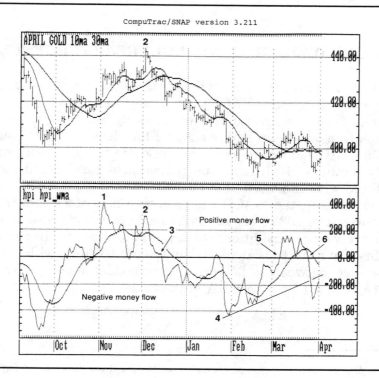

now flowing out of the gold market. The HPI stayed below zero for the next several months as gold dropped almost $50 per ounce.

In late February, as prices were again making new lows, the HPI formed a short-term positive divergence (line 4). The HPI formed higher lows while prices made lower lows, suggesting a reflex rally was likely. The HPI moved above the zero line on this rally (point 5). This signal lasted only two weeks before it was reversed (point 6). During this period, the weekly HPI (not shown) stayed below the zero line, indicating that on an intermediate-term basis, the money flow was still negative.

From these examples one can see that the HPI gives excellent intermediate-term signals when used on the weekly data. It allows the trader to clearly analyze the longer-term trends in the volume and open interest. To better define entry points, both the weekly and the daily HPI should be monitored and used together.

MOVING AVERAGE CONVERGENCE/DIVERGENCE

Another popular technical indicator is the moving average convergence/divergence (MACD), originally developed by Gerald Appel.[2] There are several methods of analyzing this price-based momentum oscillator, and Mr. Appel has done further research on the MACD since his original work. He has his own proprietary methods of utilizing the indicator, which should not be confused with the discussion below.

Originally, the MACD was designed as a stock market indicator, but in 1983 I began to discuss how it could also be used effectively on commodities. The original formula for this indicator first involves the calculation of the MACD line, which is the difference between a 26-period exponential moving average (EMA) and a 12-period EMA of the close.

$$EMA = (N - Y) \cdot alpha + Y$$

---

[2]*The Moving Average Convergence-Divergence Method* (New York: Signalert Corp.), 1979.

where N = the most current data value, Y = yesterday's EMA value, and alpha = 2 / (X + 1), where X equals the number of days in the period.

The signal line is then calculated by taking a nine-period EMA of the MACD line. These variables can be used on daily, weekly, or monthly data. (See Formula section in chapter 18.)

The original interpretation was to use the crossings of these two lines to generate buy or sell signals. For example, a buy signal was generated when the MACD line moved above the signal line, and a sell signal when it dropped below the signal line. When used on weekly data, this indicator often works quite well, as it catches the majority of the intermediate-term swings. Figure 17.20 shows a weekly soybean chart from October 1986 through April 1989 with the MACD (solid line) and the signal (dotted line).

FIGURE 17.20
Soybeans with MACD Lines

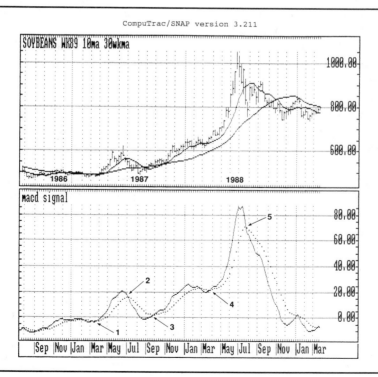

CompuTrac/SNAP version 3.211

The buy and sell signals are noted on the chart, with many lasting four to eight months. I will discuss a few of these in detail to show how the MACD acted during the explosive soybean rally in 1988.

Soybean prices traded in a very narrow range from September 1986 until April 1987, when prices started an upward move. The MACD crossed above the signal line in March 1987 (point 1), with prices in the $4.80 area, thereby generating a buy signal. This signal stayed in effect until July 1987, as prices were in the $5.40 area. After staying negative for about 12 weeks, the MACD line once again moved above the signal line, generating a new buy signal (point 3). Both the MACD lines and the signal lines rose sharply until February 1988. The MACD line dropped below the signal line for four weeks before giving a new buy signal (point 4) in the $6.70 area. This signal lasted until late July 1988, when a new sell signal was given (point 5) in the $8.50 area. The actual price high was over $10.50 per bushel and therefore the sell signal was somewhat late. Later in this section we will look at a modification of the MACD that would have helped to improve the exit or sell signal.

The Japanese yen is another example of how this indicator worked during a long-term uptrend. The yen became the world's currency in many respects during the late 1980s. Figure 17.21 follows the action of the yen from June 1985 until December 1987 with the MACD and the signal line. This chart shows several dramatic moves to the upside, the majority of which were correctly pinpointed by the MACD. Note that in September 1985 the two lines converged (point 1) but did not cross, hence the name convergence/divergence. A brief whipsaw did occur in January 1986 (point 2), as there was a sell signal, quickly reversed by a buy signal, which lasted for the next four months. During the May–August 1986 period, three signals were generated (points 3, 4, and 5). Even though the yen continued to move higher, both the MACD lines and the signal lines did not make new highs, thereby forming a negative divergence (line 6). This made the sell signal in August (point 5) more valid, as crossings of the two lines, when accompanied by positive or negative divergences, are generally more significant.

In choppy markets or prolonged uptrends or downtrends, the results are often less favorable, as the indicator may give

FIGURE 17.21
Yen with MACD

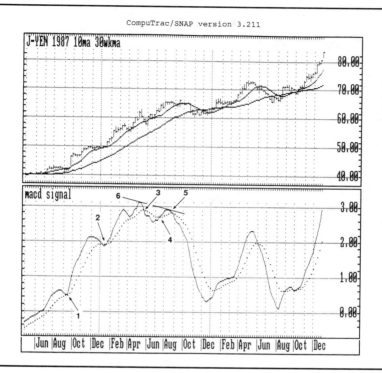

CompuTrac/SNAP version 3.211

false buy or sell signals. This is a common problem with many price-based or momentum-type indicators.

I have completed extensive research in which I analyzed different time periods for the MACD. My findings show that, for some markets, other time periods work better than the original values given above. One can also test or optimize the inputs for the MACD for a specific commodity. In general, I use the difference between a 20- and a 10-period EMA for the MACD line, and a 10-period EMA of this difference for the signal line.

I prefer to look at these two lines in a histogram form by taking the difference, or spread, between the MACD and the signal lines, which I call the MACD-His. Figure 17.22 shows the MACD-His on the same weekly chart of soybeans. The buy and sell signals are more clearly evident and provide additional valuable information. When the MACD-His changes directions,

FIGURE 17.22
Soybeans with MACD-His

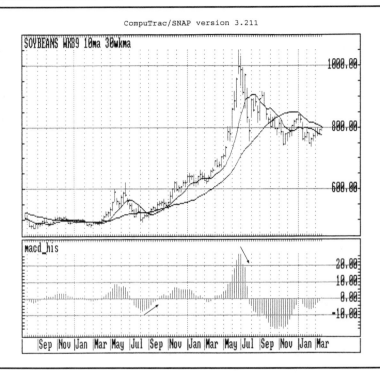

CompuTrac/SNAP version 3.211

especially on the weekly data, it gives the trader an indication that the trend is also changing. In June 1988, after soybean prices had risen over 80 percent in less than three months, the MACD-His, which was well above the zero line and positive, stopped rising and turned down (see arrow). This decline was coincident with the price highs, and an early warning signal to take profits on longs. The MACD-His then declined steadily for four weeks before giving a sell signal.

Many who use the MACD have noted that the actual crossovers often lag the price high or low, especially on the weekly data. In an attempt to generate accurate signals, I have developed the MACD-Momentum, or MACD-Mo. This is calculated by taking a 10-period momentum of the MACD-His. (See Formula section in chapter 18.)

Figure 17.23 shows a weekly chart of the British pound with the MACD-His and MACD-Mo. The MACD-Mo generally moves above or below the zero or reference line, two to four weeks ahead of the MACD-His. As prices are bottoming or topping, the MACD-Mo has already changed direction. For example, in November 1986, the MACD-Mo moved above the zero line (point 1) five weeks before the MACD-His crossed the zero line. In very strong rallies or declines, the MACD-Mo will often top or bottom well ahead of the price highs or lows. It peaked in January 1987, then declined for the next few months, even though the pound continued to move higher. This negative divergence in the MACD-Mo was confirmed by the crossing of the zero line (point 2), which coincided with the price highs. By the time the MACD-His dropped below the zero line five weeks later, the decline was

FIGURE 17.23
British Pound with MACD-His and MACD-Mo

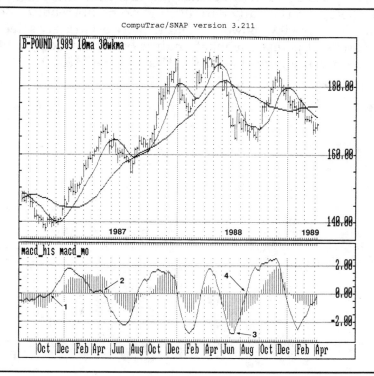

well underway. By looking at the rest of the chart, one can see that changes in the MACD-Mo's direction often precede changes in the price direction.

The British pound declined from $1.90 to $1.65 per pound from May through August 1988. The MACD-Mo bottomed eight weeks before the price lows (point 3). The MACD-Mo crossed above the zero line in late August, while prices stayed flat for the next five weeks before turning higher.

When used together, the weekly MACD-Mo and MACD-His often generate important information about major trend changes. The slope of the MACD-Mo can be used to alert the trader to a change in trend, while the MACD-His can be used for confirmation.

The signals from the MACD-Mo and MACD-His are less reliable when daily data is used. As is the case with many price-based technical tools, whipsaws are often generated in prolonged uptrends or downtrends. Of the two, the MACD-His works better on the daily data during strong uptrends or downtrends. It is my view, however, that to more accurately select the entry and exit points one must analyze both the weekly and the daily data using both the MACD-His and the MACD-Mo.

CHAPTER 18

DESIGNING AND TESTING THE TRADING SYSTEM

Thomas E. Aspray
President and Research Director, Aspray, Parsons and McClintock Asset Management Corp.

DESIGN BASICS

Extensive research and testing is continuously being carried out to develop the "ultimate" trading system. This seems to be the dream of both professional and part-time traders, and this field has been expanded dramatically since 1989. As late as the mid-1980s there were only a handful of systems available and now there are over 100 such systems being sold to the public. Some commodity traders and advisers have found that the development and marketing of their system can be more financially rewarding than trading itself, as many cost $2,000–3,000.

In the design process, the first step is to select the parameters that will be used to generate buy and sell signals. These parameters can be as simple as a dual moving average crossover system. More advanced parameters can also be used, employing volume and open interest, regression analysis, and so on. Once the basic parameters are established, additional filters can be added to enhance the performance.

The second necessary ingredient to any trading system is precise rules for money management. In addition to generating buy and sell signals, a system should determine the protective stops on either long or short positions to limit losses or reduction of profits.

Many experienced and successful commodity traders will tell you that precise rules for money management are at least as important as an effective trading system. Why is money management important? Most traders win on only about 40 percent of their trades. Therefore, profitability requires that losses on losing trades be kept relatively small and winning trades must be held for profits to develop.

There are many methods of determining protective stops. Some utilize a mechanical approach, such as Wilder's parabolic system, which adjusts the protective stops as prices move up or down. Others favor a percentage stop based on the margin requirement. Chartists use a stop that is placed either above or below a recent price high or low. Stops tied to moving averages are also used, and some systems use a fixed dollar stop of $1,000 on any trade.

Money management not only includes the placement of protective stops on long or short positions but should also have rules as to what percentage of the available funds is committed to any one market or group of markets. Extensive research has been done in this area and has shown that a more conservative approach tends to provide the best long-term performance.

A conservative approach would have no more than 50 percent of a trading account allocated to margin requirements. For example, if you were trading with a $30,000 account, no more than 50 percent, or $15,000, should be committed to initial margin requirements at any one time. Rules also suggest that no more than 10 percent of one's account should be allocated to any one market or group of markets. In my experience as a lecturer and trader, I have found that novice traders often violate these rules, often with disastrous results.

One common problem, even after a historically profitable system has been developed or purchased, is that many traders do not have the discipline to follow the system. The conviction to follow their system is especially lacking during periods of adverse performance. Typically, a system, whether objective or subjective, will go through periods of poor performance. It is during these times that many traders stop following their system. This frequently occurs just before the system once again becomes profitable. It is also the case with money managers, as clients generally wish to place funds with a manager who is performing well. A more realistic approach would be to find a manager who has done well consistently and place funds with that person during a period of poor performance.

Another common mistake that many traders make is that they overemphasize trading in one market or in a group of interrelated markets. Over the past several years, the most popular markets to trade have been in the financial futures, specifically T-bond futures and the S&P stock index futures. They are popular because they show the highest volatility with daily swings that range from several hundred to several thousand dollars. This volatility has the allure of great profit potential—unfortunately, most traders look only at this profit potential and not the potential for losses. This is a major mistake in commodity trading. During nontrending periods many traders attempt to establish positions in these markets and take a series of $300–500 losses. At the same time, some of the other markets will be trending more effectively and have much better profit potential. I prefer to recommend a diversified futures account where commodity contracts in several nonrelated groups are monitored.

The **high correlation** factor is a problem in the financial futures. High correlation means that markets will generally tend to move together. The stock market is often sensitive to interest rates and therefore one would expect the T-bond futures and stock index futures to move up or down together, notwithstanding the occasional historical exception. Traders on both exchanges watching these two markets closely can make it financially hazardous to trade just these two markets.

Despite the plethora of horror stories from commodity traders, I am continually amazed at the number of people who do not feel that protective stops should be part of their trading approach. The failure to use protective stops is responsible for the majority of large losses in commodity trading. One of the first things I determine when considering a trade is where the protective stop would be. This tells me the potential risk on the trade. The next step is to look at where the market would move if I were correct. This allows me to determine the potential reward of the trade. Combining these two numbers will provide the risk/reward analysis of the trade. For example, assume you feel that gold prices are going to move up. Gold settled the previous day at $400 per ounce. The recent significant low on the charts was at $390; therefore, a sell stop on the long position could be placed just below this at $389. This is the potential risk on the trade, which works out to be $11 per contract, or $1,100.

Suppose significant upside resistance was evident in the $450 area, which would be the potential reward on this trade. This works out to be $50 per contract, or $5,000. The actual ratio can be calculated by dividing the risk ($1,100) by the reward ($5,000). The ratio would be approximately 1:5, which would be favorable as you are risking only one-fifth of what you have the potential to make. I like to look for trades that have a minimum 1:3 risk/reward ratio. In other words, I am willing to risk one-third of what I have the potential to make. As noted earlier, with only 40 percent of the trades by most traders generally profitable, attention to the risk/reward ratio can be a critical variable in long-term profitable performance. Currently, this type of risk/reward analysis is not a preprogrammed part of technical analysis software packages; however, it is likely that future programs will recognize its importance.

In summary, the design process for a trading system must include two distinct and equally important factors. First, one must determine the parameters and rules that will be used to generate buy or sell signals. Second, money management routines should be an essential part of any trading system. Let's look at an example of a basic system and how it might be modified through the use of filters.

The Four-Week Rule: A Sample Trading System

One well-established trend-following system that I will use as an example is the price channel system. This concept and the most successful application of it to date were developed by Richard Donchian, who is associated with Shearson Lehman Brothers. Donchian's four-week rule is an extremely simple system, which, to many, is a distinct advantage. It states that short positions should be covered and new longs initiated whenever prices move intraday above the highs of the previous four weeks. These long positions are then liquidated and short positions are established when the prices drop below the lows of the previous four weeks.

The primary advantages of this system are the same as those of a dual moving average system; that is, it is always in the market and does not miss a major move either up or down. Second, the trading is quite infrequent; therefore, the cost of commissions is reduced. The disadvantages occur in nontrending or sideways markets, as several consecutive nonprofitable trades or whipsaws can occur.

Figure 18.1 shows how the four-week rule worked on the April 1989 gold contract. The chart suggests that this was a trending market, and one would have expected this method to work fairly well.

The first signal was evident in early September (point 1) as the four-week lows were violated and the system went from long

FIGURE 18.1
April Gold with Four-Week Rule

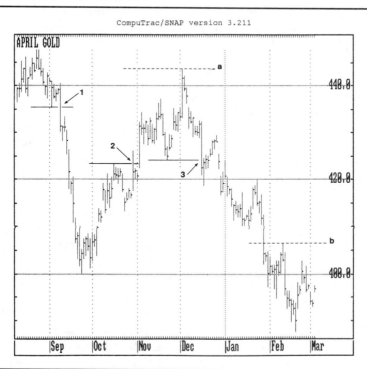

CompuTrac/SNAP version 3.211

to short. This signal was in effect until late October (point 2), when prices moved above the previous four-week highs. This was a signal to cover short positions and go long. These long positions were established in approximately the $423 area. They were held until prices dropped below the four-week low in the middle of December (point 3), at approximately $424, for a $100 loss per contract. As these longs were liquidated in December, new short positions were established with a buy stop above the previous four-week highs or initially at the dashed line (a). Prices then began a rather steady decline keeping one on the short side, as none of the rallies that developed in the latter part of December or in January moved above the highs of the previous four weeks. Currently, this method would still indicate a short position with a buy stop at the dashed line (b) in the $407 area.

One problem with the simple four-week channel approach is that, although the protective stop is clearly defined, it is not calculated with regard to margin requirement, account size, or the risk/reward ratio. For example, if longs were established at point 2 in the $423 area, the initial sell stop would have been below $400, which was the four-week low. Therefore, the risk would be $2,300 per contract. Based on a margin requirement of between $2,500 and $3,000, many would consider this an unacceptably wide stop.

One positive factor with this sort of approach is the infrequency of trading. Although this chart covers almost five months, only two signals were generated. This type of trading takes a long-term approach and might not be popular with your broker since the commissions would be relatively low. This example helps substantiate that this approach works best in a trending market.

In choppy or sideways markets, the results using this system can be disastrous. Figure 18.2 is a recent chart of May 1989 soybean meal. The first signal was given in late September, which was a signal to sell short. This position was closed out for a loss, and longs were established in early November (point 2). This second position (point 3) was also stopped out at a loss. Throughout the entire history displayed on the chart, only the current short position shows the potential for a profit. In fact, the four closed trades on the chart led to a loss of approximately $4,500 per contract. It is obvious from this example that the use

FIGURE 18.2
Soybean Meal with Four-Week Channel

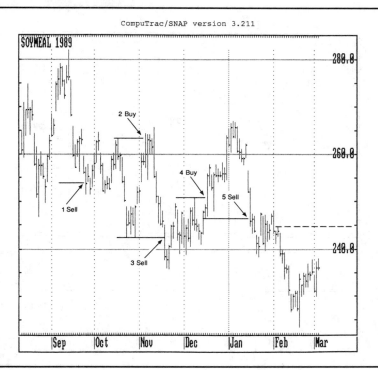

CompuTrac/SNAP version 3.211

of some sort of filter with the four-week channel system would help the trader avoid choppy or sideways markets.

Wilder's directional movement index, discussed previously, is an example of a potential filter. This system has the ability to generate buy or sell signals as well as to determine whether the market is trending. For example, when the ADXR line is below 30, the market is considered to be nontrending; if above 30, the market would be trending. For Figure 18.3, we have added the ADXR line as a potential filter to the gold chart discussed previously in Figure 18.1. Note that the 14-day ADXR line dropped below 30 in early November at the approximate time when the buy signal was given from the four-week channel system. This drop suggested that the market was entering a nontrending period. It stayed below 30 until late January, when it moved back above it, indicating the market was once again trending.

FIGURE 18.3
April Gold with ADXR

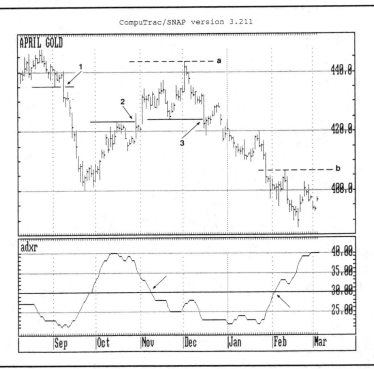

CompuTrac/SNAP version 3.211

Even more interesting is how this filter of the ADXR line would have helped us in the soybean meal. Figure 18.4 shows the same chart of soybean meal and the four-week channel buy and sell signals with the ADXR line below it. You will note that throughout the entire period shown in the chart, the ADXR line was well below the 30 line and flat. Using this as a filter, one could have avoided this market entirely during this period.

As discussed previously, the main problem with moving average systems and the four-week channel system is that they can be disastrous in sideways markets. This was clearly the case in the soybean meal example. The addition of the ADXR line from the directional movement index would be of great help, as one would only take the buy or sell signals on the four-week channel system when the ADXR line was above 30. Other signals would be disregarded.

FIGURE 18.4
Soybean Meal with ADXR

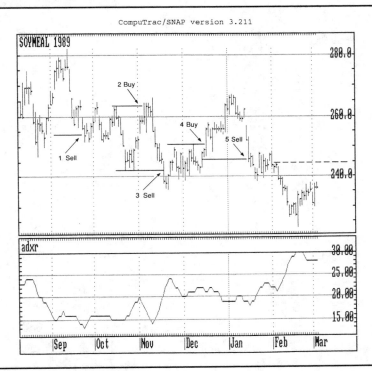

CompuTrac/SNAP version 3.211

Another potential filter for the four-week channel system is the −DI and +DI from the same directional movement index. These can be converted to the DIOSC, as discussed in chapter 17. As indicated previously, when the bar is above the zero line, the +DI line is above the −DI line (buy mode). Conversely, when it is below the zero line, the −DI line is above the + DI line, or in the sell mode. The chart of gold in Figure 18.5 includes the DIOSC. In early September (point 1), the DIOSC moved below the zero line, generating a sell signal. This occurred four days prior to and approximately $7 higher than the four-week channel system sell signal. This DIOSC signal was reversed in the latter part of October (point 2), when the DIOSC moved above the zero line, giving a buy signal. The four-week channel system turned positive on the same day. The sell signal in mid-December (point 3) from the DIOSC also coincided with the sell

FIGURE 18.5
April Gold with DIOSC

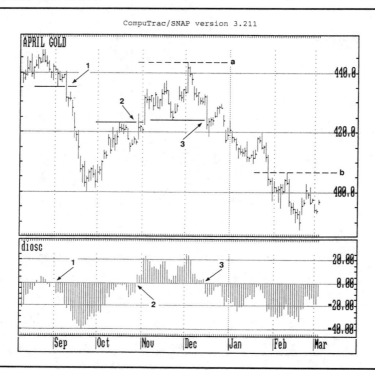

signal from the four-week channel system. Both methods are still negative at the end of the chart.

The plot of the DIOSC for the soybean meal (Figure 18.6) also reflects the choppy action, as quite a few signals were generated. You will note that except for two brief whipsaws (points 2 and 3), the DIOSC was negative from mid-September (point 1) until mid-December (point 4). The sell signal in January from the DIOSC (point 5) came approximately two days earlier, and $1,000 per contract higher, than the sell signal given by the four-week channel system. In fact, for the period shown, the four-week channel system resulted in losses of approximately $4,500. In contrast, the signals generated by the DIOSC resulted in profits of approximately $1,600. It is obvious that the results of the four-week

FIGURE 18.6
Soybean Meal with DIOSC

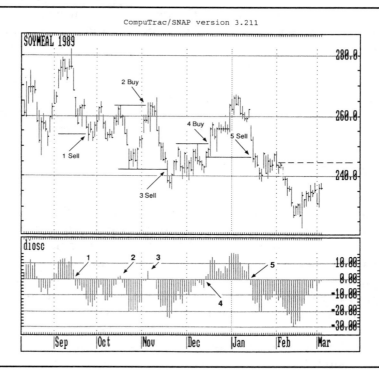

channel system could be improved greatly by the addition of the signals from the DIOSC. Of course, if one used the ADXR lines to determine whether the market was trending, this market would have been avoided entirely. Many of the most successful systems on the market do have a trend-following component, which I believe is essential for a successful trading approach.

The charts of gold and soybean meal are just examples and should not be used to confirm or reject the validity of a trading system. The filters that I discussed are only two of the possibilities that could be used to enhance this system. In fact, later work was done on the four-week channel system to modify it to a two-week channel system, which, for some markets, appeared to show better results.

TESTING

Design is just the first step, as the trading system must then be tested before it can be used. This is impossible without a computer. Some of the commercially available software packages now have built-in testing features, so that once a system or method is developed, one can test it against historical data. Recently, several new programs have been released just to test trading system ideas. There are three key variables in the testing process: data types, length of the period tested, and the report criteria.

Data Types

One problem in selecting the data used for testing is that the specific commodity contracts have a limited trading span and therefore are not well suited to long-term historical testing. There are two primary ways of getting around this problem. The first is what is generally known as a continuation chart, which is a method of linking a number of contracts together to form a long-term historical record. The most common way of doing this is to always plot the price of the nearest expiring contract. When this contract stops trading, the next nearest contract is then followed. The main disadvantage with the continuous contract is that occasionally the nearest contract will be trading at an extreme discount or premium to the next succeeding contract. Once contracts are changed, it can result in a large fluctuation in the continuous chart, either up or down. Large price swings also occur because of the extreme price volatility of the nearest contract or spot month. This, too, can cause distortions in the testing process. Some analysts try to get around this problem by switching contracts a month or two before they expire to avoid the potential volatility in the spot month.

The second method of continuing a long-term historical record, and the method that I favor, is the use of Perpetual Contracts. This method constructs a continuous time series based on a constant forward time period. It is a mathematical extrapolation constructed by taking a weighted average of the two nearest futures contracts. (Perpetual Contracts were first discussed by Robert Pelletier, president of Commodity Systems, in the March

1983 issue of *Futures Magazine*.[1] The name "Perpetual Contract" is a registered trademark of Commodity Systems. The calculation for the Perpetual Contract is quite complex and is discussed more fully in the original article.) The Perpetual Contract alleviates many of the problems that develop with continuous contracts, and I have found it to be an excellent tool for testing trading systems or individual indicators.

Test Period and Cost

Once the type of data is selected, the test period is the next important determination. Many approaches will work well during a short time period, especially if the market is in a pronounced up- or downtrend. However, the same system can be disastrous if a longer test period is selected. Most analysts would agree that a five-year test period is long enough to resolve any short-term distortions.

To assess the performance of any system, one must include the costs of trading (i.e., commissions); an appropriate amount should also be factored in for slippage. Slippage can be defined as the difference between the price you want to enter a market and the price at which your order is actually filled. The effect of slippage can be confined through limit orders but is a significant factor in some types of trading systems.

Report Criteria

One of the earliest technical analysis software programs was put out by CompuTrac/Telerate. CompuTrac was the first to introduce historical testing as part of its Profit Matrix program. Within this program, the subroutine allows the user to specify what criteria have to be met before buy or sell signals are generated. One can also enter percentage protective stops, costs of commissions, slippage, and so on. As an example, we will use the weekly data and the RSIOSC, discussed previously in chapter 17.

---

[1]CSI, Inc., is a commodity and stock data service at 200 W. Palmetto Park Road, Boca Raton, Florida 33432-3788.

The signals were tested using $50 per trade in commission/slippage costs. Figure 18.7 covers the Deutsche mark futures from late 1985 until September 1991, using the Perpetual Contract. Below the bar chart is the RSIOSC, which, as discussed earlier, is the difference between a 6-week WMA and a 24-week SMA of the 9-week RSI. Positive or buy signals are generated when the RSIOSC moves above the zero line; negative or sell signals are generated when the RSIOSC drops below the zero line. The bottom panel represents the signals and shows that only 12 were given during the period.

Using CompuTrac, this system can be tested and the software will provide either a summary or a trade-by-trade report. The summary report is shown in Figure 18.8. A good deal of information is provided, but I will concentrate on just a few items, which I have labeled by line number.

FIGURE 18.7
Deutsche Mark with RSIOSC

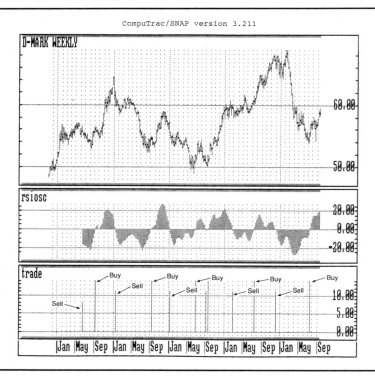

FIGURE 18.8
Summary Report

```
08-Oct-91  04:35:56        D-MARK WEEKLY      > DMOSC.PFT     Page:   1
DATE, OPEN, HIGH, LOW, CLOSE, VOL, OI, RSI:9, WMA:6, SMA:24, SPREAD
-------------------------- Profit / Loss - Summary ---------------------
```

Item	Long	Short	Net
		Per Trade Ranges	
10 Best Trade	6.78	11.32	11.32
..Date	901207	910719	910719
11 Worst Trade	-1.68	-2.35	-2.35
..Date	890908	890922	890922
Max Open P/L	8.75	13.46	13.46
..Date	871231	910705	910705
Min Open P/L	-1.35	-2.23	-2.23
..Date	890901	900511	900511
		Overall Ranges	
Max P/L	19.78	31.10	31.10
..Date	901207	910719	910719
Min P/L	4.09	-0.65	-0.65
..Date	880122	870911	870911
Max Equity	33.37	33.24	33.37
..Date	910920	910705	910920
Min Equity	-1.52	-1.20	-1.52
..Date	871002	870904	871002
		Statistics	
Periods	94	130	255
1 Trades	5	6	11
2 # Profitable	4	3	7
3 # Losing	1	3	4
4 % Profitable	80.00	50.00	63.64
5 % Losing	20.00	50.00	36.36
6 Avg Profitable Trade	4.51	6.68	5.44
7 Avg Losing Trade	-1.68	-1.76	-1.74
Avg #Periods/Profitable Trade	21	31	25
Avg #Periods/Losing Trade	11	12	12
		Results	
Commission	0.20	0.24	0.44
Slippage	0.00	0.00	0.00
8 Gross P/L	16.55	14.99	31.54
Open P/L	2.27	0.00	2.27
9 Net P/L	16.35	14.75	31.10
Net Profitable Trades	18.03	20.03	38.06
Net Losing Trades	-1.68	-5.28	-6.96
Equity	18.62	14.75	33.37

Line 1 indicates that during the period tested, only 11 trades were closed out, of which 7 were profitable (line 2) and 4 were losing (line 3). Lines 4 and 5 show that 63.64 percent were profitable and 36.36 percent were losing trades. The average profitable trade (line 6) was 5.44, or 544 points, which, at $12.50 per point, was $6,800. The average losing trade (line 7) was 1.74, or 174 points, which works out to be $2,175 per losing trade.

The gross P/L (line 8) was 31.54 (3154 points), or $39,425, based on trading one contract. When $50 was deducted for commissions/slippage, the net P/L (line 9) was 31.10, or $38,875. Finally, shown at the top of the table (line 10), the best trade resulted in a profit of 11.32 ($14,150), while the largest losing trade (line 11) was 2.35 ($2,937.50). No stop was used in this testing, as the drawdown during the period was quite small. Obviously, the use of a stop would change the results depending on how tight a stop was used. This is obviously just one example, and one where this system worked quite well. It should not be assumed that this system will work as well in the future or in other markets.

Other systems that have become prevalent in the past few years can be referred to as black box systems. They are so named because the methodology on which they are based is not fully disclosed. Recent objective analysis of the profitability of these systems suggests that a few actually do work quite well. However, many systems claim to generate profits that seem unbelievable. These systems are often quite expensive and range in cost from $500 to several thousand dollars. Of course, when compared with the amount one can lose trading commodities, they do not seem so expensive.

Systems that take a long-term approach seem to be the most attractive. Figure 18.9 shows a sample report from a long-term trading system that has been on the market since 1983; it is a trend-following system and is therefore always in the market. Note that the summary report includes the current positions, the number of positions taken, as well as protective stops and levels at which additional positions or pyramid positions can be added.

Hypothetical or simulated performance results have certain inherent limitations. Unlike an actual performance record, simulated results do not represent actual trading. Also, since the trades have not actually been executed, the results may have under- or overcompensated for the impact, if any, of certain market factors, such as lack of liquidity. Also, simulated trading programs in general are designed with the benefit of hindsight. No representation is being made that any account will, or is likely to, achieve profits or losses similar to those shown in the examples provided. In commodity futures trading there can be no assurance of profit. Losses can and do occur. As with any investment, you should carefully consider your suitability to trade commodity futures and your ability to bear the financial risk of losing your entire investment.

One problem with some of the black box systems is that the trading rules are optimized on a continuous basis. From a statistical standpoint, this casts some doubt on the validity of the results. In the development of a system, optimization can be a

FIGURE 18.9
Long-term Trading System Daily Worksheet (11/22/91)

	Position Long|Short	1 Close	2 Stop	3 1st Pyr.	4 2nd Pyramid	5
LIVE HOGS	3	4288	* 4380	4275	4386	4162
COTTON #2	3	5830	6442	6039	6526	5881
CBT CORN	3	2476	* 2565	2498	2579	2464
COFFEE	2	8259	* 8032	8220	8536	7871
COMEX SILVER	2	417	* 391	410	418	401
SOYBEANS	2	5648	5328	5642	5789	5503
DEUTSCHE MARK	3	6248	5949	6089	6209	5763
CBT WHEAT	3	3684	3295	3580	3670	3423
SWISS FRANC	3	7045	6424	6901	7023	6584
COMEX GOLD	3	3724	* 3499	3640	3713	3565
JAPANESE YEN	3	7705	7434	7680	7721	7542
N.Y. HEATING OIL	3	6079	7236	6473	7013	6218
S&P INDEX	3	37684	43145	38776	39953	37880
SOYBEAN OIL	3	1915	2093	1929	2043	1893

valuable tool. The study on two moving average systems, discussed earlier, was the result of optimization. Through testing, the two moving averages for each commodity were selected for the combination that showed the best profits. Once the parameters for a trading system have been selected, the trader can vary those parameters or optimize them to find the combination that works the best. In the Deutsche mark example, the moving average periods were optimized, and the 6-week WMA and 24-week SMA were found to show the best results.

We can expect to see many advances in the coming years as computers become more powerful and basic computer systems continue to proliferate. Software advancements should come in the area of new and improved trading systems and less expensive technical analysis software programs.

FORMULAS

Relative Strength Index

$$RSI = 100 - (100 \div 1 + RS),$$

where RS is equal to the average of x days up closes divided by the average of x days down closes. Because it is normalized, the values always fall in a range of $0-100$, which alleviates some of the problems in other price-based oscillators.

Moving Average Convergence/Divergence

Exponential Moving Average (EMA)

$$EMA = alpha\,(M) + alpha\,(1 - alpha)\,(M - 1)$$
$$+ alpha(1 - alpha)^2(M - 2) \ldots ,$$

where

$$alpha = 2/(N - 1), \text{ a smoothing constant}$$
$$M = \text{the closing price}$$
$$N = \text{the number of days.}$$

The MACD line is the difference between a 10-period EMA (alpha = 0.182) and a 20-period EMA (alpha = 0.095):

$$MACD \text{ line} = EMA_{0.182} - EMA_{0.095}$$

The signal line is the 10-period EMA of the MACD:

$$Signal \text{ line} = MACD_{0.182}$$

The MACD-Histogram, or MACD-His, is the MACD line minus the signal line:

$$MACD\text{-}His = MACD \text{ line} - signal \text{ line}$$

The MACD-Momentum, or MACD-Mo, is a 10-period momentum of the MACD-His:

$$MACD\text{-}Mo = 100\,(MACD\text{-}His_{current} - MACD\text{-}His_{10 \text{ periods ago}})$$

Herrick Payoff Index

$$\text{HPI} = \frac{\text{Ky} + (\text{K}' - \text{Ky})\,\text{S}}{100{,}000},$$

where

Ky = yesterday's HPI
S = user-entered smoothing factor (0.1 standard)
y = yesterday's value
K′ = CV (M − My) [1 ± 2 I/G]

The ± sign in the right bracket of the formula is + if M (mean price) > My (yesterday's mean price); if M < My, it is −.

M = (high + low)/2
C = value of a one-cent move
V = volume
I = the absolute value of today's open
     interest minus yesterday's open interest
G = today's open interest or yesterday's
     open interest, whichever is greater

The formula requires the dollar value of a one-cent move. If you use the actual value of a one-cent move for some commodities, the changes in the resulting line are so small that the resulting graph is almost impossible to interpret. Therefore, I use $500 for a one-cent move in the financials, including the metals and energies, and $250 for the agriculturals and exotics.

SECTION 6

THE TACTICS OF TRADING

CHAPTER 19

TRADING PRELIMINARIES

BUYING, SELLING, AND DELIVERING

A trader who is bullish on a market might buy one or more futures contracts. Purchase of a futures contract obligates the "long" to do one of two things: (1) accept delivery of the actual commodity or underlying instrument, paying for it in full at the time of delivery at the then-current price, or (2) close out (offset) the long commitment prior to receiving a "delivery notice" by selling a like quantity of the same future.

If a trader is bearish on a market and sells one or more futures contracts, he obligates himself to either deliver one of the tenderable grades of the actual commodity sometime during the delivery period or close out (offset) his short commitment prior to the last trading day in the respective delivery month by purchasing a like quantity of the same future. For example, a trader who is long 5,000 bushels of Chicago March wheat and who does not want to take delivery would close out his long position by selling 5,000 bushels of Chicago March wheat. He could not close out his long position by selling any other month of Chicago wheat, nor by selling March wheat on any other grain exchange.

A futures transaction, therefore, either establishes a new position or liquidates an existing position. Thus, the "open interest" for any given commodity designates the size of the total open commitment—the total number of "long" contracts open, which is also the number of open "short" contracts. For example, in September 1991, the open interest in COMEX silver (New York) was 88,106 contracts—88,106 long contracts and 88,106 short contracts. By definition, the size of the open long position equals the size of the open short position.

Very few speculators are disposed to deliver or accept delivery of a commodity. Because traders are able to offset (by liquidation) their futures commitments, eliminating the necessity of making or accepting delivery, broad speculative participation, without which futures markets could never function, is encouraged. As mentioned earlier, only about 2 percent of the total volume of futures transactions is normally settled by delivery of the actual commodity.

Deliveries against futures contracts are made during the final month of trading. Delivery is at the option of the short, who may deliver any tenderable grade during the delivery period at any of the designated locations. Delivery is effected through the short (seller) passing to the clearinghouse, who passes to the long (buyer), a negotiable warehouse receipt that is accepted as evidence of title to the specified quantity and grade of the commodity. In some commodities, such as cocoa and silver, the warehouse receipt represents a specific lot of a commodity, identified by number. In other commodities, grains being the most prominent, the warehouse receipt merely represents a quantity and quality of the commodity commingled with other grain of like quality.

Since delivery is at the option of the short, longs who are not in a position to accept delivery of the actual commodity or financial futures instrument should either close out or switch their position into a more distant month prior to first notice day.

There are a number of futures contracts that involve cash settlement rather than the traditional delivery of the underlying commodity or financial instrument. The stock indices, for example, settle for cash at the completion of the last trading day of the contract. Cash settlement occurs by transferring funds into or out of the contract holder's account in an amount based on the difference between the settlement price at expiration and the price at the time of entry.

DIFFERENCES BETWEEN THE COMMODITY AND THE SECURITIES MARKETS

There exists a number of interesting and important distinctions between the operations of the futures markets and the securities markets. Futures traders should have a complete understanding of these distinctions.

As futures contracts have a limited term, usually not more than 12 or 18 months, and are never paid for in full until delivery, traders cannot establish futures positions and just "sit with them" as they can with securities. Also, complete price cycles are sometimes compressed into the relatively short life of a futures contract. As a consequence, futures usually offer more extensive and broader short-term price movements than do securities.

Some futures contracts, such as grains and meats, specify maximum daily trading limits, whereas no trading limits exist in the securities markets. (As a result of the stock market crash of October 1987, however, "collars" were established in the stock index futures markets to maintain an orderly trading environment.) In lieu of trading limits, securities exchanges may suspend trading for short periods in any security where there exists such an imbalance of buy and sell orders.

However, no such potential restraint exists in the over-the-counter market, where trading is conducted without recourse to trading limits or intraday suspension of trading.

Each commodity delivery month eventually becomes the **spot,** or **cash,** month. Long positions in the spot month involve the additional risk of receiving delivery, whereas short positions involve risks of a tight situation due to a possible shortage of deliverable supplies. These two important risks are peculiar to the futures markets. The securities trader does not face them, except in the rare instance where "short" stock cannot be borrowed and is called in by brokers.

During recent years, security margins have remained at 50 percent. In contrast, futures margins have rarely exceeded 15 percent. Therefore, with a given amount of capital, a futures trader can take a position involving a much greater market value than can a securities trader. There is no distinction between a new short sale and a liquidating sale in the futures market, nor between a new or a short-covering purchase. For round-lot orders in listed securities, short sales must be made on either an "uptick," or on an unchanged "tick," following an uptick. This means that in a weak market, an order to sell short a round-lot of a listed security may not be executed until the price ticks up. This sometimes results in a delay, or an execution at a lower price than anticipated. In summary, a futures trader can more easily effect a short sale than can a securities trader.

Futures trading requires the knowledge of much more specific detail than does securities trading. For example, futures vary with respect to where they are traded, hours of trading, size of contract, magnitude of price fluctuations, maximum trading limits, margin, commissions, first notice day and last day of trading, and so on. The securities trader is concerned with fewer details.

For any security, the short interest is just a small fraction of the long interest (total amount of stock outstanding). Hence, most investors profit when stocks go up, and few when they go down. In futures markets, the long and short interests are always equal, so that the same amount of money is always made and lost, regardless of in which direction prices move.

Futures margin deposits are technically "earnest money," held by the commission firm as a guarantee that the customer will meet his contractual obligations. There is no debit balance in a futures account, hence no interest is charged. Interest charges are incurred only if the trader accepts delivery of the actual commodity (during the delivery month) and does not pay for it in full. In the securities market, on the other hand, the margin-account investor is charged interest on his debit balance (money owed the broker).

There is no organized "specialist" system in futures trading. Commodity pit brokers trade directly with each other and execute all buying and selling orders entrusted to them, including stop orders. In contrast, securities trading on the listed exchanges involves the use of the specialist system. Specialists are stock exchange members who are designated by the exchanges to maintain an orderly market in specific securities and to execute orders for other brokers.

Many commodities have reduced day trade or spread (straddle) commissions and reduced spread (straddle) margin requirements. There are no reduced day trade commissions in securities trading, although lower margin is required on day trades.

In futures trading, a position is normally closed out at the brokerage firm where the position was initiated, and on the same exchange. In the securities market, an investor may order his stockbroker to deliver his securities position to another broker (even if it is held on margin), and he may liquidate his position at the new broker. Also, a security bought on one exchange may be sold on any other market that lists that particular issue.

SELECTING AN ACCOUNT EXECUTIVE

A futures trader should be very selective in choosing an account executive. Many futures traders have few direct dealings with the futures brokerage firm; it is through their account executive that business is conducted. Not only does the client–account executive relationship involve mutual trust and confidence, it frequently involves transactions representing substantial sums of money. Therefore, traders should not be reluctant to meet and talk with futures account executives of several brokerage firms before opening an account.

An account executive should be experienced, knowledgeable, and should have a keen sense of responsibility for his clients' accounts. He should be available during trading hours, and must be quick and accurate in entering orders. He should be capable of answering, or at least obtaining the answers to, all inquiries, should provide his clients with necessary price quotations, and should be able to advise them concerning significant news events as they occur. It is important that the client and the account executive develop a close working relationship.

Although the client should make his own trading decisions, the account executive should, when asked, provide trading suggestions and should be willing and able to discuss the client's ideas. If the client is a "chartist," the account executive should be chart-oriented and should either keep his own charts or have access to charts.

A commodity account executive should be associated with an experienced, reputable, and well-capitalized commission firm holding memberships on the principal futures exchanges. The Commodity Futures Trading Commission and the individual futures exchanges can provide information concerning large and small futures commission firms.

Another category of broker is the introducing broker (IB). As the name implies, the IB is an independent entity—registered with the National Futures Association—who introduces accounts to a futures clearing merchant (FCM). The IB does not hold client funds but places accounts at a CFTC-registered FCM that is subject to regulatory capital requirements by the CFTC, an agency of the United States government. Because they are independent entities, and usually have lower overhead considerations, IBs generally charge lower commissions than the full-service brokerage firms and, in many cases, provide similar services.

Most futures account executives are busy servicing their clients and have neither the time nor the facilities to conduct their own private research work. However, if those brokers are successful—or plan to be—they should have immediate access to outside technical and fundamental research studies, as well as to modern news-retrieval services that can provide up-to-the-minute details on economic data releases and "spontaneous" events that impact the markets.

Futures traders should scrutinize the clearing firm's trade execution facilities and its ability to handle all orders with speed and efficiency, especially market orders. If you are a sizable trader who buys or sells five contracts or more per order, then your broker should have direct access to the exchange floor when placing orders. Smaller traders may have to place their orders through a centralized service desk, which should be efficient and courteous.

It is probably a good idea to find out if your clearing firm employs its own traders in all the markets in which you plan to trade. If not, then inquire about the staff and reputation of the firm that will be providing **give-up service.** Give-up service refers to independent floor brokers who do not work for the large clearing firms but execute their orders on a contractual basis. For any reason, should you have a problem with the give-up floor brokers, then have your clearing firm recommend someone else who can do the job to your satisfaction.

OPENING AN ACCOUNT

Once an account executive has been selected, an account can be opened. You will be asked to divulge some basic items of personal information and bank references, just as when you open an account at a bank or at a retail store. Since nearly all buy and sell orders are accepted by the account executive verbally, commission firms must assure themselves that their clients are reputable individuals of high personal integrity. Commission firms must also inquire into their clients' financial circumstances to ascertain that they can afford the risks associated with futures trading.

Upon opening an account, a futures trader is required to sign a number of forms, including a customer's agreement and risk disclosure document (see Figure 19.1). These forms detail the mutual obligations of both the client and the brokerage firm, alert the client to the risks inherent in futures trading, and provide the brokerage firm with financial information and safeguards. In addition, the brokerage firm will ask for a margin deposit before opening an account or before accepting orders. Some firms stipulate a minimum acceptable account size, such

FIGURE 19.1
Summary of Required Account Forms

____________________ Account Name   ____________________ Account Number

Prior to opening an account for you at must receive your acknowledgement of receipt or agreement to each of the following documents. **DO NOT SIGN BELOW WITHOUT CAREFULLY READING EACH RELEVANT DOCUMENT.**

A. You must have received, read and understood each of the following documents before opens an account for you:

1. **CUSTOMERS AGREEMENT.** I have received, read, understand and agree to the terms of the **Customer's Agreement** on pages 3-9.	Customer Signature:________ Date:____ Joint Party Signature:________ Date:____
2. **RISK DISCLOSURE STATEMENT.** I have received, read and understand the separate **Risk Disclosure Statement** on page 10.	Customer Signature:________ Date:____ Joint Party Signature:________ Date:____
3. **OPTIONS DISCLOSURE STATEMENT.** I have received, read and understand the separate **Options Disclosure Statement** on pages 11-15.	Customer Signature:________ Date:____ Joint Party Signature:________ Date:____
4. **NON-CASH MARGIN DISCLOSURE STATEMENT.** I have received, read and understand the separate **Non-Cash Margin Disclosure Statement** on page 16.	Customer Signature:________ Date:____ Joint Party Signature:________ Date:____

B. Your acknowledgment of receipt or consent to the following document is only required under the conditions described in the document. **DO NOT SIGN BELOW WITHOUT CAREFULLY READING THE DOCUMENT.**

PERMISSION TO CROSS. I have received, read, understand and agree to the terms of the **Permission to Cross Agreement** on page 17.	Customer Signature:________ Date:____ Joint Party Signature:________ Date:____

C. **Please read and complete the Consent to Arbitration on page 21, if appropriate. You need not sign this agreement to open an account with**

D. Please read and complete, as appropriate, either the **Certificate of Exemption from Reporting and Form W-8,** on page 24-25, or the **Payer's Request for Taxpayer Identification Number and Certification on Form W-9,** on pages 26-27. In addition, your account representative may provide you with other documents and forms which you are required to read and complete prior to opening your account with

E. If you are a foreign customer or broker, please read and complete, as appropriate, the **Foreign Customer Agent Designation,** on page 28, and the **Foreign Customer Special Calls Notice** on page 29.

as $10,000 or more, in order to discourage individuals of inadequate means from speculating in futures.

There are certain forms that commission firms mail to their clients every time a trade is made, a position closed out, and an accounting period (usually a month) completed. Upon receiving any of these forms, the client should verify it for accuracy and should immediately report any discrepancies to the account executive.

A **trade confirmation** is mailed to each client every time he makes a trade (see Figure 19.2). This confirmation contains the client's name, address, account number, the trade date, whether it was a purchase or sale, the commodity and the market, the number of contracts (or bushels of grain) involved, the delivery month, and the price. This confirmation usually does not indicate the total money value of the entire transaction, nor the profit or loss realized on a liquidating trade.

For every liquidating trade the client receives a **purchase and sale** (closeout) form (see Figure 19.2). This form recaps both the purchase and the sale, the round-turn commission, and the net profit or loss. All purchase and sale forms should be retained for future use in preparation of tax returns.

At the end of each month, commission firms mail out **monthly statements** to each of their clients whose accounts showed any activity during the month or contained any open cash or futures positions as of the close of the month (see Figure 19.3). The monthly statement is divided into two sections: one for the open positions as of the last day of the month, the other indicating all "money" entries (cash deposits and withdrawals and profits or losses on closed-out trades) during the entire month. The cash balance as of the first and last days of the month is also included. All monthly statements should be retained for preparation of tax returns.

Shortly after the end of the calendar year, the clearing firm will issue (to clients holding U.S. citizenship) IRS form 1099, which reports net profit or loss on futures transactions only (brokerage firms are not required by law to furnish a 1099 for transactions involving options on futures). Non-U.S. citizens should review IRS form W-8, Certificate of Foreign Status, which alerts the brokerage firm not to withhold taxes on any interest-bearing financial instruments (i.e., Treasury bills).

FIGURE 19.2
Trade Confirmation

SUBJECT TO TERMS AND CONDITIONS
ON REVERSE SIDE

*CODED SYMBOLS ARE EXPLAINED
ON REVERSE SIDE

PERIOD ENDING
JAN 30, 1992

ACCOUNT NUMBER

TAX ID

DATE	BOUGHT / LONG	SOLD / SHORT	CONTRACT DESCRIPTION	*EX	PRICE PREMIUM	AMOUNT DEBIT	CREDIT
1/29/92	ACCOUNT BALANCE -- REGULATED						29000.09
--------	C O N F I R M A T I O N ----------- C O N F I R M A T I O N ----------						
THE FOLLOWING TRADES HAVE BEEN MADE THIS DAY FOR YOUR ACCOUNT AND RISK							
	3 / 3*		MAR 92 NYFE YX INDEX	F	226.95		
			COMMISSION			90.00*	
			CLEARING FEE			.30*	
			EXCHANGE FEE			3.00*	
			NFA FEE			.36*	
			TICKET CHARGE			2.50*	
			TOTAL COMMISSIONS			90.00*	
			TOTAL CLEARING FEES			.30*	
			TOTAL EXCHANGE FEES			3.00*	
			TOTAL NFA FEES			.36*	
			TOTAL TICKET CHARGE			2.50*	
			NET PROFIT OR LOSS FROM TRADES			96.16*	
-------	P U R C H A S E & S A L E ------- P U R C H A S E & S A L E ------						
1/29/92		3	MAR 92 NYFE YX INDEX	F	229.30		
1/30/92	3*	3*	MAR 92 NYFE YX INDEX	F	226.95		
			P&S				3525.00*
			PROFIT OR LOSS FROM TRADES				3525.00*
			NET PROFIT OR LOSS FROM TRADES				3525.00*
CURRENT ACCOUNT BALANCE REGULATED							29317.73*
---------	------ O P E N P O S I T I O N S ----------						
11/07/91	30,000 / 30,000		U.S. T BILL DUE 02/06/1992 912794XY5 MAT- 2/06/92		90.00		27000.00
11/29/91	20,000 / 20,000		U.S. T-BILL DUE 02/27/1992 * 912794YB4 MAT- 2/27/92		90.00		18000.00
			*******************ENDING ACCOUNT BALANCE				29317.73*
			TOTAL EQUITY				29317.73*
			ACCOUNT VALUE AT MARKET				29317.73*
			SECURITIES ON DEPOSIT				45000.00*
			EXCESS EQUITY		74317.73 *		

E. & O.E.   GRAINS IN 000'S   RETAIN FOR TAX RECORDS   PLEASE REPORT ANY DIFFERENCES IMMEDIATELY. THE FAILURE TO IMMEDIATELY EXERCISE YOUR RIGHT TO HAVE ERRORS CORRECTED WILL BE DEEMED YOUR AGREEMENT THAT THIS STATEMENT IS CORRECT AND RATIFIED.

FIGURE 19.3
Monthly Commodity Statement

SUBJECT TO TERMS AND CONDITIONS
ON REVERSE SIDE

*CODED SYMBOLS ARE EXPLAINED
ON REVERSE SIDE

ACCOUNT NUMBER

PERIOD ENDING
NOV 29, 1991

MONTHLY COMMODITY STATEMENT

TAX ID

DATE	BOUGHT LONG	SOLD SHORT	CONTRACT DESCRIPTION	EX	PRICE PREMIUM	DEBIT	CREDIT
10/31/91			ACCOUNT BALANCE -- REGULATED				43050.91
11/01/91	2	2	DEC 91 CBT U.S. BONDS	A	P&S		3439.82
11/01/91	1	1	DEC 91 NYFE YX INDEX	F	P&S	937.44	
11/04/91	1	1	DEC 91 NYFE YX INDEX	F	P&S	937.44	
11/07/91			TBILL MATURE		CASH		29596.57
11/07/91			INTEREST TBILL MATURE		CASH		403.43
11/07/91	30,000		U.S. T BILL DUE 02/06/1992		RECEIVE	29651.18	
11/08/91	30,000-		U.S. T-BILLS DUE 11/07/1991		DELIVER		
11/18/91	2	2	DEC 91 NYFE YX INDEX	F	P&S		1675.12
11/21/91	2	2	DEC 91 NYFE YX INDEX	F	P&S	1724.88	
11/25/91	2	2	DEC 91 NYFE YX INDEX	F	P&S	1124.88	
11/25/91			CXL P&S S2Z 20895VS21055		ADJUSTMENT		1724.88
			15YX				
11/29/91			INTEREST TBILL MATURE		CASH		268.33
11/29/91			TBILL MATURE		CASH		19731.67
11/29/91	20,000-		U.S. T-BILL DUE 11/29/91		DELIVER		
11/29/91	20,000		U.S. T-BILL DUE 2/27/1992		RECEIVE	19784.00	
11/29/91			ACCOUNT BALANCE -- REGULATED				45730.91*
			NET FUTURES PROFIT OR LOSS(-) FOR MONTH			2115.18	
* * * * *	* *	* *	OPEN POSITIONS * * * * * * * *	* *	* OPEN POSITIONS *	* * * *	
11/06/91		4	DEC 91 CBT U.S. BONDS	A	98 24/32	4000.00	
		4*	OPEN TRADE EQUITY		99 24/32	4000.00	
8/30/91		3	DEC 91 IMM CAN-DOLLAR	E	86.880	3450.00	
11/05/91		5	DEC 91 IMM CAN-DOLLAR	E	88.830		4000.00
		8*	OPEN TRADE EQUITY		88.030		550.00
2/06/92	30,000		U.S. T BILL DUE 02/06/1992				27000.00
	30,000 *						
2/27/92	20,000		U.S. T-BILL DUE 2/27/1992				18000.00
	20,000 *						
			TOTAL OPEN TRADE EQUITY			3450.00*	
			TOTAL VALUE OF SECURITIES				45000.00*
			ACCOUNT VALUE AT MARKET				42280.91*

E. & O.E.   GRAINS IN 000'S   RETAIN FOR TAX RECORDS   PLEASE REPORT ANY DIFFERENCES IMMEDIATELY. THE FAILURE TO IMMEDIATELY EXERCISE YOUR RIGHT TO HAVE ERRORS CORRECTED WILL BE DEEMED YOUR AGREEMENT THAT THIS STATEMENT IS CORRECT AND RATIFIED.

WHO TRADES IN FUTURES?

In the broad, actively traded futures markets, orders originate daily throughout the world. The two basic classes of futures traders are **speculators** and **hedgers**. The speculator is motivated solely by a desire to make a trading profit. He buys in anticipation of a price rise and sells in anticipation of a price decline, risking his own capital on his ability to accurately forecast price movements. The hedger, on the other hand, trades primarily either to establish his commodity prices, or to reduce price risks on commodities owned and not yet sold, or sold ahead for later delivery and not yet owned. He is concerned with the changing price spreads between cash and futures, or between different futures months, rather than with the actual price or its fluctuations.

There are two broad classes of speculators: **public speculators,** who usually are not members of futures exchanges, and **professional speculators,** who generally enjoy exchange membership privileges. The public speculator trades through a commission member firm. Public speculators are usually engaged in a business unrelated to futures, although occasionally one of them becomes so absorbed in futures trading or so successful at it that he becomes a full-time trader. Many professional traders are **floor traders,** that is, as members of one or more futures exchanges, they conduct their trading directly from the pits or rings of an exchange.

One type of professional trader that is instrumental in maintaining an orderly trading market is the **scalper.** He is an "in and out" trader who is almost always willing to buy at a small fraction below previous transactions or sell at somewhat above the previous price. Price fluctuations between trades are minimized because of the buying and selling by these scalpers. An adept scalper in an active market may trade into and out of several positions within an hour, being satisfied with a profit on minimum fluctuations. Since he is willing to accept small profits, he must close out or even reverse his position at the first sign of a loss. Except in unusual circumstances, the scalper will "even up" his positions prior to the close of each trading session.

Two other classes of professional traders are **day traders** and **position traders.** They differ primarily in their time approach to trading. A day trader is a speculator who, although not trading for as quick a "turn" as a scalper, will generally not carry open trades overnight. He may "scalp" trades but more frequently will try to trade with the trend when he senses a turn developing in the market. Position traders, on the other hand, most of whom do not trade from the exchange floors but from anywhere in the world that has electricity and telephone service, can be either long- or short-term traders. They will carry open positions over a period of time when they consider the trade favorable.

The fourth class of professional floor trader is the **spreader,** or **arbitrageur.** He is constantly watching price relationships between different futures and will buy one future and sell another any time he feels that the price differential between the two futures is temporarily distorted. Some spreaders scalp trades, while others take a longer-term position anticipating a trend in spread differences between futures, between markets, or even between two related commodities. Spreading is an extremely complex form of futures speculation, requiring a great deal of knowledge and experience.

HOW FUTURES PRICES ARE DISSEMINATED

The rapid, accurate, and widespread dissemination of futures prices is a vital factor in the efficient operation of modern futures markets. Within seconds after each price change on a major futures market, traders throughout the world can see the price change recorded on their electronic quote machines.

Nonprofessional traders without access to the electronic boards at the exchange or electronic quote machines will find a daily financial newspaper to be the primary source of their futures price information. The leading financial dailies provide prices, volume, open interest, and perhaps even daily price charts. In addition, they usually include a daily column that discusses the important features of the previous day's trading.

Futures prices are disseminated in the following ways:

Newspaper Price Quotations

A comprehensive futures price reporting section is included in many of the major daily newspapers. For each future, the opening, high, low, and closing prices are provided daily, plus the net price change from the previous trading session, as well as the life of the contract high and low prices. Figure 19.4 summarizes trading for January 16, 1992, from *The Wall Street Journal.*

Electronic Quote Machines

Desktop quote machines vary in their software packages and aesthetics. However, as a basic feature, all the various vendors enable the user to access and display comparable real-time price and news information similar to the example provided in Figure 19.5. Reading from left to right are the contract symbol and month, the change from the previous settlement, the high of the day, the low of the day, and the settlement from the previous session. Also shown are quotations on options and spread differentials, as well as the most recent news headline.

Typically, the monthly fee for real-time on-line price quotations is $350 to $1,000. The less expensive the fee, the fewer the number of "elective" services. Someone interested in receiving only price quotes will pay considerably less than someone who needs additional services such as news retrieval, technical studies, and option pricing.

SOURCES OF MARKET INFORMATION

Data concerning every aspect of the futures business is continually collected, compiled, and disseminated by various government and private units. With the exception of the advice from private advisory services, this data is available free, or at low cost. Futures traders should take full advantage of the wealth of information available from the following sources.

FIGURE 19.4

Wall Street Journal Futures Prices (January 17, 1992)

FUTURES PRICES

GRAINS AND OILSEEDS

METALS AND PETROLEUM

INTEREST RATE

OTHER FUTURES

308

Source: *The Wall Street Journal*, January 17, 1992.

FIGURE 19.5
Electronic Quote Page

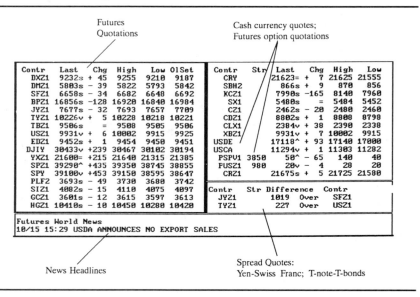

Futures
Quotations

Cash currency quotes;
Futures option quotations

Contr	Last	Chg	High	Low	OlSet
DXZ1	9232s	+ 45	9255	9210	9187
DMZ1	5803s	- 39	5822	5793	5842
SFZ1	6658s	- 34	6682	6648	6692
BPZ1	16856s	-128	16920	16840	16984
JYZ1	7677s	- 32	7693	7657	7709
TYZ1	10226v	+ 5	10228	10218	10221
TBZ1	9506s	=	9508	9505	9506
USZ1	9931v	+ 6	10002	9915	9925
EDZ1	9452s	+ 1	9454	9450	9451
DJIY	30433v	+239	30467	30102	30194
YXZ1	21600=	+215	21640	21315	21385
SPZ1	39290^	+435	39350	38745	38855
SPY	39100v	+453	39150	38595	38647
PLF2	3693s	- 49	3730	3680	3742
SIZ1	4082s	- 15	4110	4075	4097
GCZ1	3601s	- 12	3615	3597	3613
HGZ1	10410s	- 10	10450	10280	10420

Contr	Str	Last	Chg	High	Low
CRY		21623=	+ 7	21625	21555
SBH2		866s	+ 9	870	856
KCZ1		7990s	-165	8140	7960
SX1		5480s	=	5484	5452
CZ1		2462s	- 20	2480	2460
CDZ1		8802s	+ 1	8808	8798
CLX1		2384v	+ 38	2390	2338
XBZ1		9931v	+ 7	10002	9915
USDE		17118^	+ 93	17140	17000
USCA		11294v	+ 1	11303	11282
PSPU1	3850	50^	- 65	140	40
PUSZ1	980	20v	- 4	28	20
CRZ1		21675s	+ 5	21725	21580

Contr	Str	Difference	Contr
JYZ1		1019 Over	SFZ1
TYZ1		227 Over	USZ1

Futures World News
10/15 15:29 USDA ANNOUNCES NO EXPORT SALES

News Headlines

Spread Quotes:
Yen-Swiss Franc; T-note-T-bonds

U.S. Government Statistics

Several agencies of the U.S. government provide statistical information on a variety of subjects that can be important to futures traders. Below is a list of the agencies and their general phone numbers, as well as examples of major publications available to wire services and the public. Interested traders should contact the Office of Management and Budget Affairs in Washington, D.C. (202-395-3093) for a schedule of release dates for principal federal economic indicators.

- Department of Agriculture monthly reports (202) 720-4021
  - agricultural prices
  - crop production
  - grain stocks
  - cattle on feed
  - hogs and pigs
  - plantings
  - world agricultural production

- Department of Commerce monthly reports (202) 523-0777
  - housing starts and building permits
  - wholesale trade
  - advanced retail sales
  - new one-family houses sold and for sale
  - advanced report of U.S. merchandise trade
  - merchandise trade, balance of payments
  - advanced report on durable goods
  - plant and equipment expenditures
  - personal income and outlays
  - composite indexes of leading, coincident, and lagging indicators
  - gross national product
- Department of Labor monthly reports (202) 523-1913
  - employment situation
  - consumer price index
  - producer price index
  - real earnings
  - productivity and costs
  - employment cost index
  - U.S. import and export price indexes
- Federal Reserve Board monthly reports (202) 452-3206
  - industrial production and capacity utilization
  - selected interest rates
  - consumer installment credit
  - money stock, liquid assets, and debt measures (weekly)
- Department of the Treasury monthly reports (202) 208-1434
  - Treasury statement (monthly budget)
  - thrift institution activity

National Weather Service

The National Weather Service prepares and disseminates daily and long-range forecasts for various parts of the country. This information is available through newspapers, wire services, and cable television stations, or directly from the Weather Service on a subscription basis. Also, data are collected on a weekly basis, in cooperation with state statisticians, on the conditions of all important crops in each of the major agricultural states.

Futures Exchanges

Most of the major futures exchanges publish literature concerning their exchange, as well as the individual markets traded. The exchanges also offer, some on a subscription basis, daily or weekly reports concerning futures prices and significant supply and demand developments for each commodity or financial future. Requests for information can be addressed by directly contacting the exchanges (see the table on page 313).

Futures Brokerage Firms

Many of the major brokerage firms issue daily or weekly futures market letters, as well as frequent "special situation" reports. This literature is distributed to the firms' clients and is generally available to prospective clients. Traders can secure this literature by writing or visiting the office of any major futures brokerage firm.

Private Advisory Services

There is a multitude of private advisory services that offer their market letters and chart services for fees ranging from a nominal trial subscription to several thousand dollars per year. In general, futures advisory services can be classified by their analytical approach to price forecasting and by the type of service offered. There are technically oriented (charting) services and fundamentally oriented (supply and demand) services. Some services provide specific buy and sell recommendations, whereas others furnish charts or fundamental information, leaving the trading decisions up to the subscriber. The choice between these types of services depends upon the trader's individual preference and on how much he is willing to pay. Sample literature is usually available from each of the advisory services. An excellent reference guide for such services is published by *Futures Magazine*.

Directory of Exchanges

Chicago Board of Trade (CBOT)	(312) 435-3500	(800) 572-3276
Chicago Mercantile Exchange (CME)	(312) 930-1000	
Coffee, Sugar, and Cocoa Exchange (CSCE)	(212) 938-2800	
Commodity Exchange, Inc. (COMEX)	(212) 938-2000	
Kansas City Board of Trade (KCBT)	(816) 753-7500	(800) 821-5228
MidAmerica Commodity Exchange (MACE)	(312) 341-3000	(800) 572-3276
Minneapolis Grain Exchange (MGE)	(612) 338-6212	
New York Cotton Exchange (NYCE)	(212) 938-2650	
New York Futures Exchange (NYFE)	(212) 656-4949	(800) 221-7722
New York Mercantile Exchange (NYMEX)	(212) 938-2222	
Toronto Futures Exchange (TFE)	(416) 947-4486	(800) 387-1774 Canada
Winnipeg Commodity Exchange (WPG)	(204) 949-0495	

Financial Newspapers

As noted previously, the leading financial dailies, in addition to carrying futures prices, volume, open interest figures, and cash commodity prices, sometimes include a daily column discussing the important features of the previous day's trading. A good financial newspaper provides a convenient, inexpensive means of following market developments. Traders should be cautioned, though, against initiating trades on the basis of information or gossip contained in these public columns. In most cases, news has already been acted upon and discounted by the time it appears in the public press.

Television

News and commentary available from the Cable News Network (CNN) provides national coverage of events that may affect futures prices. Local broadcast and cable stations also offer regional information to their viewers. Many broadcast and cable stations offer daily summaries of trading trends and prices. The broadcast media have the ability to disseminate important or noteworthy information as soon as it is available, whereas delays are inevitable with newspapers.

Books

There are numerous books available discussing agriculture, commodities, financial futures, the futures market, charting, and other related subjects (see Bibliography). Frequently, business and finance sections of large bookstores carry many relevant titles. Industry trade publications usually display publisher book lists and make titles available on a mail-order basis.

FUTURES MARGINS

Margin is a deposit that a futures trader must make as a financial guarantee that he will fulfill his contractual obligations. The short must either cover his short position by buying back a like amount of the same futures or deliver the actual commodity or financial futures instrument during the specified delivery period. The long must either liquidate his long position by selling a like amount of the same future or accept delivery of the actual commodity when tendered to him during the specified delivery period.

There are **initial** and **variation** (maintenance) margin deposits. Initial margin is deposited when the futures position is established. Subsequently, if the market moves against a trader's position by a specified amount (to be discussed later in this chapter), the broker will call for additional margin funds. This additional deposit is called variation, or maintenance, margin.

A futures exchange establishes minimum initial margin requirements for each future traded on its "board." (See Table 19.1.)

TABLE 19.1
Exchange Minimum Margin Requirements (as of October 1990)

	Net Positions Initial/Maintenance		Spread Positions Initial/Maintenance	
	Speculative	Trade Hedge	Speculative	Trade Hedge
Coffee	$ 2000/1500	1000/750	1250/938	625
Cocoa	750/563	375/282	450/338	225
Cotton	1000/1500	1000/1000	500/375	100
Sugar No. 11	750/563	375/282	500/375	250
Silver (N.Y.)	1330/1000	1000/1000	106/80	80
Gold (N.Y.)	1330/1000	1000/1000	106/80	80
Copper	1064/800	800/800	372/280	1080
Yen	1755/1300	1300/1300	0	0
Canadian $	540/400	400/400	0	0
S&P 500	22050/9000	9000/9000	22600[1]	22600
Bonds	2700/2000	2000/2000	0	0
Corn	675/500	500/500	0	0
Wheat	675/500	500/500	0	0
Soybeans	1687/1250	1250/1250	0	0
D-Mark/Yen	—	—	1685/1248	1248
Wheat/Corn	—	—	540/400	400

[1]SP500/Maxi.

This is a fixed sum of money per contract, rather than a specific percentage of the total cost, as with securities trading. In setting margin requirements, futures exchanges consider both the price level and the volatility of the market. Since these two elements can change rapidly, exchanges reserve the right to change their minimum initial and maintenance margin requirements at any time. Margin changes usually become effective the day following the announcement by the exchange. Increases in initial margin requirements and lowered rates apply to all contracts.

Margin requirements may vary from one brokerage firm to another, as brokers sometimes call for a higher margin than the exchange-specified minimum. However, competitive pressures within the industry tend to keep margin requirements fairly uniform. Traders should not select a brokerage firm on the basis of lower margin requirements, as this is one of the least important differences between firms.

Margin for each market varies, depending on whether the transaction represents speculative or trade hedging business, and whether it is a net (outright long or short) or a spread position. A spread position involves concurrent long or short positions in the same or related commodities (i.e., July versus December cocoa, Chicago wheat versus Kansas City wheat, or, within the same grain exchange, one grain versus another). Lower margins are required for spreads than for net positions, inasmuch as a spread position is considered to be less risky than a corresponding outright long or short position. Furthermore, established trade firms engaged in bona fide hedging operations are carried on reduced margins or, in certain markets, on a limited line of credit.

Margin requirements are so mercurial that any listing soon becomes obsolete. Nevertheless, a better understanding can be gained by reviewing a sample listing (see Table 19.1).

In margining a spread, each side of the spread is called a "leg," and margin is required on only one leg of the position. In the case of grain spreads, where the spread margin on each of the two legs is different, margin shall be the higher of the two legs. As an example, spec margin on corn is $675 (see table), with $1,687 the spread margin on soybeans. Therefore, a corn versus soybeans spread would require $1,687 margin (higher of the two legs).

A thorough understanding of margin will be of great assistance to both speculators and hedgers in their market operations. The components of a futures margin account include the following: requirements, realized profits and losses, paper profits and losses, ledger balance, and equity and excess.

Requirements

Requirements refer to the total amount of initial margin required by the commission firm. For example, the minimum speculative requirements as of October 1991 (see Table 19.1) for an account long (or short) two contracts each of cocoa, corn, bonds, and silver is $10,910. Changes in market value of the open position have no effect on requirements. Requirements increase only when additional positions are established or when one leg of a spread is lifted; they decrease when existing positions are closed out or when a net position is spread.

Realized Profits and Losses

There is an important distinction between realized and paper profits and losses. A profit or loss is **realized** only after a position has been closed out. If the net difference between the selling price and the purchase price (including commission) is a positive figure, the account has realized a profit. If the net difference is a negative figure, the account has realized a loss.

Paper Profits and Losses

Paper profits and losses apply only to positions that are still open. A futures position will reflect a paper profit if the future is trading at a higher price than the original purchase price or at a lower price than the original sale price. In figuring paper profits and losses, deduct the entire round-turn commission on the open position (even though the commission is not charged until liquidation). It makes more sense to conservatively value an account rather than overstate it.

There is a latent relationship between realized and paper profits and losses. Within minutes after a position has been established, in even a moderately active market, the market price will probably have changed. This price fluctuation gives rise to a paper profit or loss. During the entire period that a position is kept open, every different price from the original trade price causes the position to reflect a changed paper profit or loss. When the position is ultimately liquidated (assuming delivery of the actual future is not involved), the paper profit or loss that existed at the moment the position was closed out is realized. In summary, the paper (unrealized) profit or loss that applies to an open position becomes a realized profit or loss when the position is liquidated.

Equity and Excess

Equity represents the total worth of the account. It can be calculated by adding cash, treasury securities, and profits on open futures and option positions to the ledger balance, and then deducting all paper losses and round-turn commissions.

After determining the requirements and equity of an account, the trader is able to calculate his **excess** by deducting the total margin requirements from the equity. For example, if an account has equity of $80,000 and margin requirements of $43,000, the excess would be $37,000. Excess represents **buying power** with which to margin additional positions, or cash, which may be withdrawn from the account. Brokerage firms **price** (calculate requirements and equity) each customer's account daily so as to note margin deficiencies as they occur.

A futures trader should know the current financial conditions of his account at all times. He will know whether he can add to his position without being called for initial margin and will be able to anticipate variation margin calls. As mentioned previously, variation (maintenance) margin is a sum that the trader is required to deposit if the market moves adversely to the level where his initial margin deposit is impaired, usually by about 25 percent. As an example, using the account just described, the $37,000 may be used to margin new positions or may be withdrawn from the account. Let's say that our speculator, Mr. E, withdraws the excess of $37,000 and places the money in an interest-bearing account until he plans to use it elsewhere. Should his futures market positions deteriorate to the point that the account sustains paper losses of $10,750, the equity would be reduced to $32,250, or 75 percent of its original level, the point at which the brokerage firm would issue a variation margin call (for $10,750). Within a day or so, Mr. E would have to liquidate at least that amount from his money market account and either wire the funds or mail a check to his account at the brokerage firm. Keep in mind that Mr. E does not have to post additional variation margin until the loss equals or exceeds 25 percent of his initial margin outlay. In other words, his original margin of $43,000 would "carry" unrealized losses between $0.01 and $10,749 before a call is triggered for additional margin.

Sophisticated traders, closely scrutinizing their accounts, can anticipate and sometimes eliminate variation margin calls by reducing positions or by depositing just enough cash (at the close of a given trading session) to maintain equity slightly above requirements.

The margin required on futures positions generally represents about 4 to 12 percent of the market value of each underlying futures contract. However, many adept traders speculate on 4 percent or less. Brokerage firms typically require day-trading clients to maintain in their accounts an amount of money equivalent to at least 25 percent of the overnight margin level of the futures contract(s) involved. For example, if overnight margin required to trade bonds is $2,700, a small speculative day trader would have to show a minimum of $675 (25 percent of $2,700) in his account.

As noted previously, spread positions enjoy reduced margin requirements because they generally involve fewer risks than do outright net long or short positions. This is based on the assumption, generally valid, that a price move in one delivery month will be accompanied by a like move in another delivery month, with the possible exception of spreads involving the spot month or two different crop years of the same commodity. Unfortunately, reduced risks generally involve reduced profit potential. However, there exist reduced margins for spread positions involving two different grains creating, at times, trading situations on reduced margin, limited neither in risk nor in profit potential. For example, a net position in Chicago wheat calls for margin of $675, and $675 is required for a net position in Chicago corn. However, a position involving long wheat and short corn (or vice versa) would require just $540 to margin the entire position. Both the risks and the potential rewards of such high-leverage trading are substantial. One should note, however, that spreads involving old crop versus new crop futures can be extremely risky.

COMMISSIONS

Until 1975, commission rates were set by each exchange for the futures contracts traded on their particular boards. Commission rates have since been deregulated and are now negotiated between client and broker. They fall into two categories, a **regular rate** for a position kept open for more than one day, and a **day rate** (usually a reduced rate) for a position opened and closed during the same trading session.

With the exception of commissions on options, which are also negotiated but can be charged either upon the initiation of a position or upon liquidation, futures commissions are charged on a **round-turn** basis upon liquidation of the position only.

Typical commissions for small speculative clients at one of the large full-service brokerage firms range from $50 to $100 per round turn. Clients with accounts at these firms have access to their research staffs and receive frequent written reports about the fundamental and technical outlook for an entire spectrum of markets, from soybeans to stock index futures.

Discount futures brokerage firms came of age after deregulation in the mid-1970s. They typically charge $25 to $40 per round turn; however, as a rule, they do not have research staffs and do not supply research assistance to their clients. To facilitate their lower commission structures, the discount firms usually operate a centralized order desk that clients access via a toll-free telephone line, rather than hire and assign account executives to service individual clients. The discount broker–client relationship is a basic no-frills account that is advantageous to traders who make their own decisions and do not require the value-added services of the larger brokerage firms.

Commission rates can be negotiable and will vary depending upon volume and frequency of trading. As in other businesses, the greater the volume of trading or frequency of round turns, the lower the negotiable commission rate. For example, a very active individual day trader who enters orders of 10 contracts or more per trade will probably be accorded a more preferential commission rate than the "one-lot" trader (one contract per round turn), who, more often than not, requires nearly as much attention and service as the larger trader. In such cases, the firm will charge the small trader a premium commission rate while charging the large trader substantially less.

A futures position is normally liquidated at the same firm where it was established. However, in instances where the customer transfers the account to another brokerage firm while the position is open, the original firm typically charges an extra round-turn commission to effect the transfer of the position to the books of the new firm.

CHAPTER 20

TRADING TECHNIQUES

In our excursion into the mysterious and sometimes misunderstood economic realm of futures trading, we have sought to provide practical guidelines for those who venture to trade in this often traumatic area. It seems useful and appropriate, as we approach the final lap of our journey, to discuss those decision rules that may help a trader join the winning minority.

Trading rules are essentially of two kinds:

1. **Budget concepts,** designed to carefully control one's risk taking and properly guard one's capital.
2. **Trading concepts,** designed to determine what position to take, in which markets, and when.

BUDGET CONCEPTS

"Budget," in the sense used here, concerns the basic problem of allocating and protecting capital. How much available capital should be earmarked for futures trading in general, and what portion to each specific market? How can one prevent spilling too much down the seemingly bottomless hole of persistent error? How to be sure of maximizing those favorable returns that come our way?

In this area of capital planning and management, there are certain principal elements to keep in mind:

• One's capital should be properly divided among uses that vary in degree of likely risk and rewards. A complete strategy of personal finance necessarily involves a choice, or rather, a weighted participation in real estate, bonds, stocks, commodities, art, and other assets. As a prospective trader, you ought to determine in advance what portion of your capital you are prepared to allocate to the "high-risk money game" of futures trading. This portion should be low enough to preclude your emotional or material ruin even if the preassigned capital is entirely depleted. The ultimate means of limiting losses—if your capital is infringed by a previously stipulated amount—is to merely stop trading. Or, as one old-time sage remarked, "When a market position becomes too large, sell down to a sleeping level."

• It is suggested that the capital you have allocated to futures trading be divided into two portions, one for actual trading, comprising not more than 50 to 60 percent of the total trading capital, and the balance to be held in reserve. The portion devoted to trading should be diversified into at least six different markets, to help ensure a relatively broad mix of investments.

• For each commodity trade you are considering, there are two sets of odds that should be considered ahead of time:

1. **The apparent profit/loss ratio**—that is, the ratio of gain you are targeting relative to the loss-limit you plan to enforce.

2. **The likelihood of success**—your estimate of the odds that the market will attain your profit objective before it reaches your loss limit.

It is sensible to favor those trading possibilities in which both odds seem exceptionally high. As a rule of thumb, consider only those trades in which you envision a profit at least three times greater than your loss limit, and also in which your estimate of the potential for success is markedly greater than 50:50. The higher your "confidence index" based on value analysis and technical measurements of potential, the more you can logically risk.

The moment you initiate a trade, decide as fully as possible what your course of action will be if the market does or does not conform to your expectations. Your plan should include a predetermined point at which you will stop your losses by liquidating an adverse position. You should also predetermine an acceptable target price at which to accept partial profits, or to protect those paper profits against a market reversal. This price objective is, of course, subject to continuous review and revision.

• Your objective in employing speculative capital is to achieve a higher annual rate of return on this capital than on lower-risk investments. Accordingly, you must be concerned not only with profit objectives but also with anticipated "time rates of gain"— that is, the speed with which a return on capital is realized. This points up the need to concentrate on markets in which action seems somewhat imminent. It also argues in favor of closely watching those technical indicators which might suggest when a move is starting.

• For the same reason (and exclusive of tax considerations), you should be willing to accept a more modest profit in a few days or weeks than might be considered satisfactory in six months or a year. In short, the time factor should be considered in determining each trade and deciding on price targets.

• Keep value in mind as an important, although not exclusive, consideration. There is an imperfect tendency, in the very long run, for a market to reflect cost of production or some other refined measure of inherent worth. Remember, however, that in the brief time it takes for your highly leveraged commodity position to achieve a substantial profit or loss, a commodity may trade far above, or below, its true value.

Accordingly, any impulse to buy scale-down "below value" or to sell scale-up, when the price is "too high," must be carefully controlled within the framework of budget principles for conserving capital.

A tactic that can be employed advantageously when a market has begun to seem fundamentally attractive is to divide the assigned capital in each particular market into three portions. Buy the first increment when there is reason to believe that the price is untenably low, if possible, near an indicated floor, or support level. Buy the second unit when acceptable technical indicators have signaled a trend reversal from down to up. And, finally, buy the third unit when profits have begun to be manifest on all previously purchased contracts. (Of course, the same logic—and a corresponding one-two-three selling program—may be appropriate when a market appears overpriced and near some definable upper limit, and when the technical analysis agrees with the fundamental conclusion.)

On occasions, a bullish or bearish spread looms as an attractive alternative to an outright long or short position. In general, a spread is preferred when it seems likely to reduce the risk inherent in an outright net position without comparably reducing the profit potential of that position.

TRADING CONCEPTS

To be successful in futures trading, detachment and objectivity are two crucial attributes. As a futures trader, you must be faithless and irreverent. You do not worship silver and gold nor regard lead as base or sugar as sweet. You have passionate conviction in no market and believe in no "sure thing." You have no predilection for either the long or the short side of a market. And any market view that you may assume today is based on a tentative estimate of likelihood, subject to change tomorrow or on the very next "tick" in the market price.

Our second set of decision rules is concerned with the problem of detecting potentially profitable situations and deciding when to initiate and close out positions. As futures market analysts and price forecasters, we must discover which markets are interesting, where they may be heading, and when.

The ultimate decision to buy or sell is a complex amalgam of fundamental and technical factors:

1. *Fundamental analysis:* oriented, above all, to determining when a market is undervalued or overvalued, based on economic factors related to supply and demand.

2. *Technical analysis:* geared to seeking clues—in the action of the market itself—to its probable future course and to the likely extent of a projected price move. It is a most important tool in recognizing key turning points (reversals) in price trends.

Sound fundamental analysis is a key to profitable position taking, although positions initiated on the basis of fundamental analysis should be undertaken with one eye on the technical picture. For example, if copper appears fundamentally strong, one should carefully watch the technical situation within that market for a chart buy signal. It is most important that the many tools of fundamental and technical analysis be combined into a practical, reliable trading technique.

Acknowledging the importance of fundamental analysis, major technical indicators that run counter to fundamentally oriented conclusions should be seriously heeded. Experience has shown that significant fundamental market changes frequently remain obscure until after the market price has already discounted the change. Stubbornly maintaining a position based on a fundamental analysis, in the face of adverse technical indicators (and an adverse price trend), constitutes a quick method of running up substantial trading losses. In short, do not ignore the technical action of the market, no matter how fundamentally oriented a trader you may be.

Whenever possible, it is helpful to buy or sell in line with an observable seasonal pattern. For example, if soybean meal prices have advanced during the fall and early winter for eight of the past ten years, and if there is reason to believe this pattern may be repeated, then one has a supporting argument for purchases indicated by technical analysis. It is suggested, however, that the "seasonal" itself not be viewed as a completely independent basis for trading.

Whenever forward contracts trade at substantial premiums over nearbys, then such premiums may appear to offer an extra incentive to sell. Whenever forward contracts are at sizable discounts under nearbys, then such discounts may appear to constitute an extra incentive to initiate purchases. However, premiums or discounts are not in themselves sufficient justification for trading. The logic of purchase or sale must be justified on additional grounds, particularly on technical considerations.

Remember that support and resistance levels are often useful guides to buying and selling points. Support may exist at a particular price level either for technical reasons (i.e., because a heavy volume of trading occurred at a particular level at some significant time in the past), or for fundamental reasons (i.e., a prescribed government support or sales level). In the same way, resistance may be anticipated at a particular price level for fundamental or technical reasons.

Let us now relate technical analysis to trading technique in specific terms. In so doing, we shall divide the approach to technical analysis into two significant areas: identification and tactics.

Identification

1. Identify both the major and the minor price trends.
2. Identify the major and minor support and resistance levels.
3. Identify the trend channel, if there is one.
4. Identify both the short- and the long-term price objectives, based on the following:
   - support and resistance levels
   - pattern count or conventional and Fibonacci chart projections
   - 40–50 percent retracement and other chart patterns
   - long-term (continuation) chart analysis

Tactics

Absolute Rules

1. Do not initiate or hold a position that is counter to both the major and the minor trends. There are *no exceptions.* The violation of this elementary maxim probably constitutes the largest cause of speculative trading losses.
2. Limit the risk on every position. Do not permit a good profit (50 percent of margin requirements) to turn into a loss; liquidate the position just ahead of the break-even point. If you have closed out prematurely, you can always reenter the market.
3. On profitable positions, liquidate 40–60 percent of the position at the indicated price objective, and protect the balance of the position with stops (either chart or "money" stops).
4. Have all orders scaled and entered in advance.
5. Do not initiate or liquidate a position because of impatience or boredom.

6. As the equity in an account increases, do not commensurately increase the size of the position. Diversify into other markets and take advantage of other trading techniques (i.e., spreads or options).

Conditional Rules

1. A major problem in trading involves the correct timing of trades. The solution lies in being more accurate in initiating positions so that your percentage of correctly timed trades is greater.

2. Seek to establish positions that are in the direction of both the major and the minor trends. If the major trend is sideways and the major price objective has been substantially attained, trade with the minor trend. (In a major sideways trend, initiate a position on a minor trend signal, with close stop protection.)

3. The major trend invariably persists longer than anticipated. If you miss the first reversal from a major trend, you will often get a second chance to catch the new trend (particularly in an upside breakout from a major bottom area). Do not chase a market.

4. A market will rarely penetrate an important overhead resistance level on the first attempt. Even if it does go through, it may pull back at least to the breakout point. Seek to sell on this rally if the other technical indicators support the sale.

5. In a major downtrend, sell on a minor rally into overhead resistance, or on a 40–50 percent retracement of the last down-leg. In a major uptrend, buy on a minor reaction into support, or on a 40–50 percent retracement of the last up-leg.

6. The minor trend rarely lasts more than seven trading days. Seek to buy bullish flag patterns in a major uptrend and to sell bearish flag patterns in a major downtrend, especially if the flag is five or more days old. Be especially cautious if buying an upflag in an uptrend, especially if near the top of the uptrend channel and/or near the major upside objective—seek to unload some longs on this type of rally.

7. A major move frequently runs three "legs" (Elliott Wave Theory). Start looking for a major top formation on the third major up-leg of a bull trend; look for a major bottom formation on the third major down-leg of a bear trend.

8. Important crop and statistical reports will usually be supportive of the existing major price trend (an important report is likely to continue the major market trend rather than reverse it). Accordingly, when trading with the minor trend, against the major trend, lighten up or go flat before such a report.

9. As a general proposition, avoid averaging a position when previous trades are held at losses, except if the other technical indicators strongly support the added position, and efficient stop-loss protection is maintained for the entire position.

In connection with the above trading identification and tactics approach, it may be useful to introduce Figure 20.1. Although this trading form obviously cannot ensure successful trading results, it can materially assist the trader in objectively viewing and analyzing the technical condition of a market and in timing his trades. When used in conjunction with sound trading principles it should substantially improve overall trading results.

INITIATING A POSITION

In analyzing the technical condition of the market, one should look beyond price, trading volume, and open interest. Consider also a psychotechnical approach, based on the market's response to fundamental events, as follows:

A market can be considered *technically strong* if it rallies on bullish news but does not decline (or declines minimally) following bearish news.

A market can be considered *technically weak* if it declines on bearish news but does not rally (or rallies feebly) following bullish news.

Traders all too frequently buy at the top of a move and sell near the bottom. Common to most traders and analysts is a

FIGURE 20.1
Trading Form

Commodity	Trend		Support		Resistance		Trend Channel		Price Objective		Comment	Take Action
	Major	Minor	Major	Minor	Major	Minor	Top	Bottom	Major	Minor		
Cattle (live)												
Cocoa												
Copper												
Corn												
Deutsche Mark												
Treasury Bonds												
Silver												
Soybeans												
Sugar No. 11												
Wheat												

329

major emotional weakness: sentiment invariably turns bullish on rallies and bearish on declines. A more practical (and generally more profitable) approach, which admittedly requires considerable discipline and courage, involves buying on declines (into support) during a major uptrend and selling on rallies (into overhead resistance) during a major downtrend.

Should one initiate a position on a breakout from an existing trading range (congestion area)? Or wait for a pullback following the breakout? This depends on several factors, including where in the overall price level the market is trading, what type of technical patterns exist, how the open interest recently changed, what the technical action looks like, how large a position one desires to accumulate, and past experience with this market on previous breakout and trading situations.

As a general proposition, one can be more aggressive in selling a reversal from what appears to be a major market top than in buying what appears to be the reversal of a major downtrend. As noted previously, if one misses the exact reversal from a major downtrend, one often gets a second shot at buying. Not necessarily so, however, with breakdowns from major tops, as prices tend to fall more rapidly and surely than they do when reversing from down to up. It has been said that "markets can fall of their own weight, but it takes buying—and lots of it—to put prices up." A bit oversimplified, perhaps, but it does summarize a generally valid phenomenon.

Initiating a market position on a stop order will tend to ensure that you remain uncommitted until a trading range breakout occurs. You will frequently observe a chart formation developing, and may then be inclined to take a position in anticipation of an impending breakout. In too many situations, the expected breakout does not occur. Those eager speculators who prematurely initiate positions in order to save a few extra points frequently end up losers. (This is one of the reasons that so many traders find themselves buying at the tops of trading ranges and selling at bottoms.)

Speculators frequently buy (or sell) futures merely because they seem to be priced too low (or too high) on fundamental grounds. An excellent example of this situation occurred in the world sugar market in 1984–85. Sugar attracted widespread buying support around the 4¢-per-pound level (prices had just completed a huge decline from the 14¢ level), largely because this 4¢ level was "even below the cost of production." Many analysts were referring to the fact that, at that depressed level, the value of the bag and the labor involved in bagging the sugar exceeded the value of the sugar itself. Incredibly, the "value" buyers at the 4¢ level witnessed, in short order, their "investment" tumble down to 2.5¢. Needless to say, many speculators capitulated below the 3¢ level, and those that did not bail out held sizable losses for months before prices turned to the upside.

Noting this example, it is logical to conclude that, when a commodity sells at an "illogical" price level (one that appears to be completely out of line with economic realities), there is probably a valid underlying reason for the apparent discrepancy. Inconveniently, though, the explanation may not become apparent until much later. Although it requires considerable patience and self-control, successful trading calls for attention to sound trading principles based on technical factors, particularly when prices are illogically too high or too low.

There are certain types of markets that should generally be avoided by all but very experienced traders. These include the following:

• Markets where prices can be determined, or even be largely influenced, by an arbitrary decision or action of an individual, organization, or government, may not be possible to be realistically analyzed, since even the fundamentals can be changed at any time. Charts are of limited help, because trend changes can occur so rapidly and unexpectedly that they are virtually impossible to anticipate.

• In very thin, volatile markets such as platinum, orange juice, and coffee, it is frequently difficult to get in—and even more difficult to get out—without sacrificing a substantial "slippage," particularly if positions are large. In addition, these markets are more likely to become distorted (usually to the public speculator's disadvantage) than are the broader, more heavily traded markets.

CLOSING OUT A POSITION

The timely decision to close out a position is at least as important as, if not more so than, the decision to initiate a position.
Successful trading requires that you limit losses and allow profits to run. By so doing, you can make money even though you
may lose on the majority of your trades. This trading maxim is
elementary. It is emphasized in every book and trading primer
ever published, and one wonders why it is hardly ever followed.
If the reader has previously traded in futures, it is suggested
that he review his trading record in light of this particular advisory. Note how the trading results would have been improved
if this tactic had been followed.

After establishing a position, you may be deluged with con-
flicting stories, rumors and tips. Many of these items have already been discounted, some are exaggerated, and some may
even be spurious. Therefore, do not permit yourself to be dis-
suaded from your position. Stand by your commitment as long as
the trend continues to move in your direction, but never hesitate
to abandon the position if the price trend reverses. In setting
your stop placement, try to set the stop close enough to the
market to close out the position if the trend reverses, but not so
close that a purely random fluctuation can set off the stop.

Closing Out a Position at a Profit

Never be reluctant to accept profits, or at least to very closely
protect a position, when it appears warranted. There are two
approaches to managing a position with a paper profit:

1. Place a stop order below the uptrend line and the signif-
    icant support area (in the case of a long position), or
    above the downtrend line and the significant resistance
    area (in the case of a short position). As the market con-
    tinues to move favorably, follow each technical rally or
    reaction and continue to raise your stop (for a long posi-
    tion) or lower it (for a short position). Ultimately, a cor-
    rection will continue to move against you, penetrating
    the trendline and either the support or the resistance
    level. At that point, the stop will close out your position.

2. From your charts, establish a price objective (below the current market if you are short, above the current market if you are long) and liquidate a portion of the position when the market moves to that level.

One practical approach to the problem of closing out a profitable position is to close out half the position based on chart price objectives (as discussed in approach 2) and to close out the remaining half position on stop only in the event that the market reverses course (as noted in approach 1).

When the market appears to be reversing direction, one constructive tactic may be to hedge a position by buying an option (a call option hedges a short position, and a put option hedges a long position) in the same future. However, if the reversal appears to be a major development, it is probably advisable to liquidate the position.

Closing Out a Position at a Loss

A certain percentage of your positions are bound to go against you. Do not procrastinate in taking a loss; the first loss is usually the cheapest. As a famous cotton trader said some 90 years ago, "Run quickly or not at all."[1]

Be objective and honest with yourself. If the market is moving adversely, do not search out reasons to support a losing position. The market will show you when you are wrong; just be humble enough to heed the warning.

As a general rule, avoid meeting a margin call. Instead, close out all or part of the position. You have already erred by allowing the position to have gone so far against you. Putting up additional margin merely compounds the error.

ANTICIPATING THE UNEXPECTED

The market can trade at your limit and you may not receive a "fill."

---

[1]Authors' note: We advise running quickly.

The market can gap, either on the opening or even during the session, filling stop orders at adverse prices and leaving stop limit orders unfilled.

If you have an order open to initiate a position on either a limit or a stop order, and include a contingent protective stop-loss order, an unexpected market gap on an opening could fill your order and stop you out simultaneously.

Limit-bid or limit-offer moves may prevent you from closing out a position, even where you are willing to do so "at the market." Furthermore, the market could open on subsequent days limit-bid or limit-offer.

Resting stop orders may be "cleaned up," after which the market may resume its original course.

TRADING IN THE SPOT MONTH

The spot month may be more volatile and less predictable than distant futures. Prices for spot futures can move out of line with other futures.

Nontrade speculators should normally be out of the spot month before first notice day. Positions can be maintained by switching into a more distant future.

Trading rules can be changed for the spot month, as in the following: (1) certain types of orders, such as stop orders and contingent orders, may not be accepted; (2) regular trading limits are usually revoked during the spot month; and (3) if trading gets too "hot," margin requirements for the spot month may be arbitrarily increased. At times a brokerage house may accept only liquidating orders for the spot month.

Factors to consider if you do have a spot month position: (1) Who are the long and short interests in the market? (2) What is the size of the open position, and how has it been changing during recent sessions? (3) What is the size of the deliverable or certificated stocks and the extent of deliveries thus far in the delivery period? (4) What is the spot month price compared with prices of distant futures? (5) What is the history of previous spot month contracts for the same commodity?

Unless you are prepared to take exceptional risks, do not short the spot month if it begins to widen its premium over distant months. Spot month squeezes may persist until the final minutes of trading, or even as the commodity goes off the board.

CONCLUSION: THE "DON'TS" OF TRADING

Thus far, our counsel has stressed the "dos" of commodity trading. It may be prudent, in parting, to emphasize the "don'ts," even at the risk of some redundancy.

1. Above all, do not allow your losses to run, in the hope that tomorrow you will be right. There should be no tomorrow beyond your preassigned risk limit.
2. Do not hide losses by spreading. If the position has soured, the prudent tactic is to get out. Enter spreads on their own merits only.
3. Do not trade without a plan, which should encompass profit objectives as well as loss limits.
4. Do not neglect either the fundamental or the technical side of the market.
5. Do not overlook those seasonal patterns that have had a high frequency of success in recent years.
6. Do not allow a few successful trades to build overconfidence and undermine meticulous care with respect to profit/loss ratios and likelihood estimates.
7. Do not solicit or accept "tips" from brokers or other traders. Be ready to learn from all qualified sources, however, including a broker with solid research material.
8. Do not permit widely held bullishness or bearishness to dominate your view. Give credence to the contrary opinion doctrine, which says: "Watch out when the overwhelming majority sees things one way."
9. Do not maintain a position when the trend of the market has reversed adversely.

As futures traders, one commitment is central. That commitment is to a rational strategy—one whose key objective is to limit one's losses in some predetermined manner and, with equal foresight and decisiveness, to allow profits to run. This involves the necessity of preventing a good profit from turning into a loss. Success in futures trading is not easy, but it is perhaps more attainable for those who have maximally absorbed, and will practice, the tactics and techniques surveyed herein.

CHAPTER 21

TRADING STRATEGIES AND RISK CONTROL

---

strategy:
*a plan, method or series of maneuvers or stratagems for obtaining
a specific goal or result*
— *Random House Dictionary of the English Language,*
2nd edition, unabridged.

Have you ever fantasized about how nice it would be to have
a copy of the financial newspaper a day in advance—or even two
or three days? Just imagine knowing, ahead of time, the closing
futures prices. That would be some edge, wouldn't it?

Unfortunately, you can't get such information. But other
important information *can* be obtained in advance, which *could*
provide a winning edge.

Suppose you could learn the following well in advance:

- That you are statistically likely to lose money in trading
- What you are likely to do wrong that will contribute to
  your losing results
- What you can do to avoid making these strategic and tactical mistakes
- How you can improve your overall performance to give
  yourself the sought-after winning edge

This chapter is devoted to trading strategy and risk control, and
it will be concerned with addressing the above considerations.

BASIC STRATEGIC TENETS

The most important characteristics for the speculator are **discipline, patience,** and **objectivity.** Discipline is the primary key to successful trading. You must be disciplined to follow the rules and game plan you have selected. A trader must also have patience to stick with positions as long as the market continues to move favorably. Boredom and impatience are major impediments to successful operations. Finally, all traders must know the rules: "Trade with the trend," "Cut losses and let profits run," and "Don't overtrade." Even unsuccessful traders can easily recite these basic tenets, yet most speculators end up losers because they constantly violate them. The few consistent winners, on the other hand, share a disciplined adherence to following these simple strategies.

Keeping Emotions in Check

The trader needs a good sense of emotional balance and market perspective to avoid being "seduced" by his profits or discouraged by his losses. Despite his best efforts at a disciplined and objective approach, the trader will encounter bad periods where nearly every trade goes sour. It is only human to become discouraged, but the trader must redouble his efforts to trade "by the rules" because the way to make losses back, with interest, is by following these rules.

We've all heard the old saying: When the going gets tough, the tough get going. In futures, the true test of a trader's ability is in how he handles the losses and the bad times. Sometimes, after a series of losing trades, the trader should close out completely and get out of the market. Then, when he has cleared his head, has a positive attitude, and has reconfirmed his strategy, he can reenter the market.

One reason paper trading invariably outperforms real trading is that, with paper trading, there is only the desire to win— with real trading, although there is still the desire to win, the fear of losing often becomes dominant. This is the major reason to avoid overtrading or overpositioning.

The trader's worst enemy is himself and his emotions, as he invariably reverses the basic emotions of hope and fear. Here is how it works. A trader buys corn at 2.45, and it quickly advances to 2.53, a profit of $400 per contract. He fears that he will lose his profit, so he liquidates his position. On the other hand, if his 2.45 long position declines to 2.37 for a loss of $400, he starts to hope that his losing position will turn around, and he holds on to the position. This is the perfect example of reversing hope and fear.

What he should do is hold his profitable position, hoping that the market will continue to move favorably and his $400 profit will increase. On the other hand, he should liquidate his losing position, fearing that the market will continue south, and his $400 loss will increase.

Following Trends

The investors who make money on a reasonably consistent basis are the longer-term position traders who have learned how to combine trend following with viable strategy and money management. Instead of trying to pick off tops and bottoms and scalping for small countertrend moves, they concentrate on trying to identify major price trends and trading in the direction of those major moves.

To follow major trends, you should use—in addition to daily price charts—long-term (weekly and monthly) charts. These show more clearly the long-term trends and support and resistance levels, and they provide a good overall perspective of price action.

It is not sufficient to accurately identify a market trend. One must also implement a viable strategy to capitalize on the trend, in order to maximize profits on winning positions and minimize losses on adverse positions. The best approach is a combination of first-class technique and a viable money management (strategic) approach.

Jesse Livermore, perhaps the greatest lone-wolf speculator of this century, said, "Big money is made by sitting, not trading." Knowing how and when to "sit" with a winning position and when to pyramid onto that position, while patiently avoiding excessive trades, is one of the trader's most difficult tasks. Here is another Livermore quote: "You always find lots of early bulls in bull markets, and lots of early bears in bear markets, yet they make no real money out of it. People who can both be right and sit tight—they make the big money." Speculators are invariably trying to sell rallies in bull markets and to buy reactions in bear markets—and losing money on most trades.

A preferred strategy is to trade in the direction of the major trend *and* against the minor trend. In a **major uptrend,** buy on minor trend reactions into support, or on a 40–60 percent reaction from any trading high, or on the third to fifth down-day of the reaction. In a **major downtrend,** sell on minor trend rallies into overhead resistance, or on a 40–60 percent rally from any trading low, or on the third to fifth up-day of the rally. (Note: A 50 percent retracement move represents classical technical analysis; 38 percent and 62 percent represent so-called Fibonacci retracements. These three retracements are worth close scrutiny, as they frequently delineate, and help project, tops and bottoms within trending moves.)

Analyze your markets and develop your tactics and strategies in advance and in privacy. Don't ask anyone's advice and don't offer advice to others. Stick with your objective, disciplined analysis, and make revisions to your strategy only on the basis of pragmatic and objective analysis. Avoid giving or taking tips or market gossip. "Those who tell, don't know; those who know, don't tell."

Aside from short-term swings that professionals consider to be "market noise" dominated by scalpers, prices tend to move in the direction of the dominant force, which is along the path of least resistance. Furthermore, once a major trend starts to develop, it picks up momentum and accelerates along the trend direction.

In a major bull market, as the advance develops, the buying power of the longs, plus the shorts who are covering their losing positions, tends to overpower the sell orders in the market. Likewise, in a major bear market, as the decline develops, the selling power of the shorts, plus the longs who are abandoning their losing positions, tends to overpower the buy orders in the market.

In a bear market, the longer the main bulls cling to their precarious long positions, the harder and farther the market is likely to ultimately fall. The experienced, well-financed professional operators will be in there pressing the market every time it appears vulnerable, or when they sense a buildup of sell stops underneath the market. The same reasoning applies to major bull markets.

Livermore said, "There is only one side of the market, and it is not the bull side or the bear side, but the right side." Follow the real trend of the market; don't permit your market opinion, or your position, which may be against the trend, to influence you to maintain a losing, against-the-trend position. A good maxim to follow is, "The trend is your friend." Remember this when you want to take an against-the-trend position.

Most speculators have a definite bias to the long side of the market. Even when dealing in an obvious bear market, the trader will invariably be long, or be looking for a spot to buy. Instead, he should be short and looking for a spot to sell. The trend of the market should determine your position, not vice versa.

When you put on a position, there is no way to predict how far the move will carry. Therefore, you should follow the premise that each of your positions can result in a "megamove" (moves of at least $6,000 per contract). This attitude will help you avoid any temptation (and there will be many) to capture small scalping profits. There is another old saying, "No one ever goes broke taking profits." That is true, but my response would be, "No one ever gets rich taking small profits." You should try to hold out for the major move, and let your stop orders, which you can set to follow behind the major price move, get you out of the market.

A margin call is a clear signal that your position has gone too far against you. Do not add funds to meet a margin call, as this could be throwing good money after bad. You would be better advised to liquidate all or a portion of your position rather than meet the call. Which positions should be liquidated? Sound strategy suggests that you should keep the best-acting positions and dump the worst-acting ones. Say you are sitting with six positions and you have a profit on four and a loss on two. Close out the two with losses. There is no valid strategy in defending losing positions—better to dump losers and add to the profitable positions.

An extension of the strategy to hold the profitable positions and dump the losers is to buy the strength and sell the weakness. What this means is, when you are putting on a long position, you buy the relatively strongest month; when you are putting on a short, sell the relatively weakest month. For example, if you are going long in an inverted market, you look to buy the front end that is selling at the premium and is the strongest month on the board; if you are going short in an inverted market, you look to sell the back end that is selling at the discount and is the weakest month on the board. In summary, you want to be long the front end and short the back end of an inverted market.

RISK CONTROL

The Scots have an old saying, "Mind your pennies and the pounds will take care of themselves." The corollary to this in futures trading is, "Mind your losses and the profits will take care of themselves."

Clearly, the most important tactic for successful futures trading is to control losses, also known as risk control. If you can control losses and allow profits to run—and that is decidedly difficult to do—you should be a consistent winner.

What we seek is a systematic, objective approach to risk control, which would include the following four steps.

1. Limit your risk on each position. One approach is to equate your risk to the exchange margin for each market—and limit your risk on each position to a given percentage of the market, say, 60 percent (see Table 21.1).

Equating acceptable risk to a percentage of margin is a logical strategy. Margins are set by each exchange and are generally related to the volatility and, indirectly, to the risk/profit potential of each market. For example, on the Chicago Board of Trade, margin on a 5,000-bushel contract of corn or wheat is $675, while the margin on a 5,000-bushel contract of soybeans, considered a more volatile and high-flying market, is $1,687. It

TABLE 21.1
Risk Control Guideline

	Initial Margin	60% of Margin	
		Dollars	Cents/Ticks
Corn	$ 675	$ 405	8.25 cents
Soybeans	1,687	1,015	20.50 cents
Wheat	675	405	8.25 cents
Cattle	560	335	84.00 ticks
Gold	1,300	780	8.00 dollars
Silver	1,330	800	16.00 cents
Crude	1,750	1,050	105.00 ticks
Deutsche mark	1,755	1,055	86.00 ticks

Note: The above table lists exchange minimum initial margin requirements as of September 30, 1991.

is, therefore, logical for a trader to accept a risk of 20.50 cents on soybeans versus just 8.25 cents on corn or wheat, because the profit potential on a favorable soybean move is perceived as being considerably larger than it is on either corn or wheat.

Similarly, one should not use more than one-third of the equity in an account to margin positions. Put another way, at least two-thirds of the capital should be held in reserve, as a cushion, in the event that your positions hit some unexpected setbacks. And, if the equity in your account declines, you should seek to reduce positions so as to try to retain this recommended one-third ratio.

2. Diversify your positions. Each year, we witness a number of megamoves. Unfortunately, we cannot possibly predict which markets will produce such huge profits. We can, however, increase our chances of participating in such moves by diversifying into a number of different positions—at least six, and preferably eight, different markets. This will probably mean that you will have to take smaller positions, possibly even some of the minipositions that are traded on the Mid America

Exchange. Also, one should seek to diversify between long and short positions. Being long in six different markets won't be very much fun on days when the entire list is heading south.

3. Avoid overtrading. This admonition pertains both to excessive trading activity and to putting on too large a position in relation to the available capital. You aren't likely to trade successfully if you are overtrading, if you are excessively focused on short-term scalping, and if the first adverse swing will have the margin clerk on the phone with you—again.

4. Cut your losses. First of all, when you put on a position, you should know where your bailout point (stop loss) will be, and you should enter the stop with your broker. Experienced traders who sit in front of an on-line screen and who have the discipline to dump the position when and if it reaches their bailout point may not actually put the stop to the floor. The key word here is discipline, because this tactic should never be used as a substitute for overstaying a market, or for rationalizing any delay in liquidating at the designated stop point.

Assuming your newly liquidated position starts to move against you from the outset, the stop will get you out at a reasonable loss. However, if the market begins to move favorably, what do you do about the stop protection? One interesting strategy is to advance your stop (if long, raise the stop; if short, lower the stop) after each Friday's close, by an amount equal to 50 percent of the week's favorable move. If the market moves against you on any particular week, you should leave the previous week's stop intact. Eventually, the market will reverse and stop you out; but if you have had a favorable run, you will have advanced into a no-loss stop position and, ultimately, a profitable one.

Disappointment and discouragement are two basic human emotions. A serious trader must have the discipline to overcome the blues and to stick with an objective, systematic method of futures investing, while, at the same time, maintaining the self-confidence necessary to plow through the bad days (or weeks or months). This steadfastness is necessary because it is the only way to recoup the losses, with interest, during the next good period. And, no matter how grim things may appear, there will definitely be a "next good period" as long as you stay alive by limiting losses on adverse positions.

CHAPTER 22

SPREADS

In preceding chapters, attention was focused on price relationships between cash and futures. We saw that interpreting these differences and seeking to profit from their variations is a core objective in the dealer business. In this chapter, we wish to consider other ways of trading price differences, methods available to anyone in or out of the relevant trade or industry. We refer to **straddles** and **spreads,** involving the simultaneous purchase of one delivery position versus the sàle of another, based on some reasonable supposition that price differences will change in the desired direction.

Traditionally, the term *straddle* was commonly used in the New York and London markets, while in the Chicago grains trade the term *spread* was more common. However, since the advent of options trading on futures in the early 1980s, the term *straddle* refers to instruments involving option strategies, whereas the term *spread* now refers to strategies involving futures contracts.

The kinship between straddle-or-spread trading and hedge transactions, which will be discussed in chapters 25–27, is obviously close. In fact, a hedge can be viewed as one important member of a family of straddle transactions, keyed to changing price differences. The economic forces that shape each member of the spread are often similar. That is, changes in the price differential between different futures generally arise for the same reasons as do changes in the **basis** (cash versus futures price difference). *The principal sources of change are the "dynamic threesome": quality, time, and place.* In other words, one position or contract may be stronger than another because it calls for delivery of an increasingly scarce or preferred quality, or because it requires delivery at a specific time or place at which need is most pressing.

Our attention in this chapter will be confined to spreads between futures contracts, although the alert reader may easily extend the analysis to spreads between actuals and futures or between different actuals positions.

Spread positions may be classified as follows:

1. Unicommodity spreads
   A. Time differential
      * **Intracommodity spreads:** purchase of one future versus the sale of another future within the same crop year, or where no distinction exists between crop years (as in silver futures).
      * **Intercommodity spreads:** purchase of a future in one crop or calendar year versus the sale of a future in a different year (i.e., the purchase of May wheat versus the sale of September wheat).
   B. Place differential
      * **Domestic spreads between two locations:** purchase or sale of a silver future in New York versus the opposite position in Chicago silver.
      * **International spreads between two locations:** purchase or sale of March sugar in New York versus the opposite position in London sugar.
   C. Quality differential
      * **Price variations between futures markets for the same commodity, arising from different delivery specifications.** For example, the purchase or sale of May Chicago wheat (based on soft red wheat delivery) versus the opposite position in May Kansas City wheat (based on hard winter wheat).
2. Multicommodity spreads
   * **Spreads based on different stages of processing:** purchase or sale (in equivalent quantities) of January soybeans versus the opposite position in January soybean oil and January soybean meal (the joint products of soybean crushing).

- **Spreads between two completely different commodities:** purchase or sale of a Chicago wheat future versus the opposite position in a Chicago soybean future.

It should be clear that the types of spreads defined in the preceding classification need not be mutually exclusive. Overlapping may occur in a variety of ways. For example, when one purchases London cocoa against the sale of a corresponding position in New York, changes in price relationships may occur in response not only to locational factors and to changes in exchange rates but also to differences in delivery specifications. Thus, supply and demand factors may strengthen or weaken a type of coffee commonly delivered in London (robusta) more than they affect a common type of delivery in New York (milds).

PURPOSE OF THE SPREAD

The purpose of a spread is to make a profit by correctly anticipating variations in the relative market strength of the two positions involved, as expressed by a favorable change in the price differential between the two "legs" of the spread.

To illustrate, assume that March wheat is trading at $4.30 and March corn at $2.70. A trader who believes that a wider wheat premium is justified (or will be justified prior to the expiration of the March contracts) may buy March wheat and sell March corn at the prevailing $1.60 per bushel differential. If, sometime later, the March wheat versus March corn differential widens from $1.60 to $1.90 per bushel, the spread can be liquidated at a 30-cent-per-bushel profit, less commission. If, on the other hand, for some reason the differential ultimately narrows to even money (both futures contracts trading at the same price), the position will be closed out at a $1.60 per bushel loss, plus commission.

It should be emphasized that the spread trader is not concerned with the absolute price change in either March wheat or March corn. He is solely concerned with the relative price fluctuation between the two futures, that is, with changes in the differential between the two legs.

WHEN TO SPREAD

The trader's objective is to successfully predict the direction in which price differences will change, and to select those spread opportunities that seem likely to undergo the projected difference changes. It will probably be helpful, in this connection, to review case histories that cast light on the more important types of spreads. Before proceeding with this survey, however, a bit more may be said about what a spread is, what it is not, and what its possible advantages are as compared with a position involving a net long or short commitment.

Clearly, if we are to favor being long one contract and short another, we must have reason to suppose that the forces affecting the two differ. It is perhaps slightly less obvious that these forces should not differ totally, for if the separation is complete, we have two distinct outright trades and not a spread at all.

To buy wheat and sell silver simultaneously has, in general, no significance as a spread—it merely suggests that two unrelated trading positions were simultaneously initiated. On the other hand, the purchase of wheat versus the sale of corn (or vice versa) has true spread significance because, while there are forces tending to make these two markets act differently, they also enjoy a common bond to the livestock feed economy and may (for this reason or for other reasons) be affected by identical forces as well as by totally distinct ones.

Similarly, if one could buy XYZ futures for delivery this season and sell new crop XYZ for delivery sometime next season, the position would only qualify as a spread if the two seasons were linked to some degree by supply carryover or other elements. If XYZ were completely perishable, carryover nonexistent, and the two seasons totally separate, the position (long XYZ in one season, short in another) would, in a true economic sense, constitute two independent positions and not a spread at all.

When does it make sense to consider a spread in lieu of an outright long or short position in a particular market? Sometimes it is suggested that there is less risk in a spread position. This is not necessarily the case. One should consider risk in relation to profit potential and also to margin required, and these may, at times, be greater in a spread than in an outright long or short position. Where a choice exists between a straddle and an outright position, we must determine on a case basis what the profit-loss ratio seems likely to be. We must, further, take into account any difference in the degree of confidence we place in our estimate.

If we are hunting for the ideal case, our keenest spread preference arises when one leg of the spread seems likely to respond most if the market goes the way we expect, whereas both legs (long and short) seem apt to move together if the market moves contrary to our expectation. In short, our spread preference is at its peak if the spread seems to reduce the profit potential of an outright long or short position far less than it curtails the loss potential in time of error.

So far, we have considered the case in which a spread may be viewed as an alternative to an outright long or short position. The purest form of spread, however, is the one that stands fully on its own, having no alternative of a nonspread variety, and therefore requiring acceptance or rejection solely on its own terms. Purity of this sort is rare. It may exist where one has no knowledge, interest, or desire to predict the behavior of one leg of a spread yet has some confidence in anticipating a change in price differences. Let us say, for instance, that one wishes to speculate on a possible devaluation of the pound sterling and, in order to do so, buys London cocoa and sells New York cocoa. The speculative interest in cocoa price movement itself may be nil. The critical assumption is simply the notion that, if the value of the pound declines vis-à-vis that of the dollar, the sterling price of cocoa in London is apt to rise in response to that monetary event, while the New York price will not. To minimize risk, one would hope to enter such a spread at a price difference that is modest under normal currency conditions. This type of **devaluation spread** has been employed by many speculators in periods when sterling was on the defensive; it brought notable gains when devaluation followed, while exposing traders to modest losses during periods when the pound remained firm.

SELECTING SPREAD POSSIBILITIES

Apart from the possible virtue of simplicity, what canons and procedures might guide us in selecting promising spread possibilities? In general, the following sequence of exploratory steps might be usefully observed by the straddle hunter.

1. *Study a particular commodity situation in depth.* Often the soundest spread ideas evolve out of an appreciation of fundamental or technical forces affecting nearby and distant or new and old crop positions, in a futures market under scrutiny. By all means, use commodity brokers and advisory services to help find spread ideas, but check out the ideas thoroughly yourself.

2. *Review the past behavior of selected spread possibilities.* After deciding that two delivery positions might diverge or converge in the period ahead, study their behavior in comparable past intervals. What has been the typical range of behavior of their price differences? Is this typical behavior likely to recur, based on similarities and differences between the current situation and previous market situations?

3. *Use charts of price differences to help get ideas and to visualize past market behavior.* Plot spread trends with a view toward projecting current price differential formations into probable future trends.

4. *Look for any seasonal regularities in the behavior of the price spread under consideration.* Do not assume that such regularities are invariant. Ask yourself whether similar circumstances apply. Remember, too, that the more unfailing a seasonal pattern seems to be, the more likely that it will be discounted in advance. (In spreads, as in outright position trading, there exists a divine commodity "law" that states that the more popular a "play," the less likely that any profit resides in it.)

5. *Finally, estimate as objectively as possible the risks that seem inherent in the spread.* As in an outright position, evaluate the two key sets of "odds": (1) the chance of failure or success, of being right or wrong on the anticipated direction of change in the price differential, and (2) the estimated magnitude of gain if correct, versus the possible loss if wrong.

THE LOOM OF CARRYING CHARGES

When a spread is concerned primarily with differentials over time, an especially relevant consideration is the magnitude of the premiums or discounts that exist in forward positions.

As noted previously, a market in which distant futures are at premiums over spot and nearby values is commonly termed a premium (contango) market. On the other hand, a market in which forward futures (distants) are at discounts is described as inverted.

It is of considerable importance that in a so-called inverted market there is no set limit to the premium that may prevail on nearby deliveries. On the other hand, in a premium market, the premium of successive delivery months is limited more or less strictly by the magnitude of carrying charges.

Why does this limit exist? Because when a distant delivery trades at anything over a carrying charge premium to a nearby, it immediately becomes profitable for some eagle-eye dealer to buy the near position and to sell the distant one. Having done so, our alert dealer can (if need be) take delivery on the nearby position when it matures, and later retender (redeliver) on the distant (short) position with all his carrying costs paid and with a sure profit on any slight margin above carrying costs.

A premium market is essentially one in which a large supply (i.e., of newly harvested crop) must be carried over a particular period. When this large supply is "looking for holders," there is a tendency for nearby futures to decline relative to distant futures, until the distant futures are at premiums that pay full (or close to full) carrying charges. At this point, trade people are in a position to carry any surplus above immediate requirements. They can purchase the spot commodity and hedge-sell futures at a sufficiently high premium to return their carrying costs (on the actual commodity).

Thus, the activity of the hedger becomes critical in determining the carrying charge relationship between contract months. The short hedger, who is selling futures against his long actuals position, will generally sell that future which best reimburses his carrying costs. If December and March wheat sell at the same price, the hedger does not benefit from carrying the wheat from December to March. He is therefore apt to place his sell-hedges in the December future. Typically, this causes December to decline in price relative to March and reestablishes a more normal price relationship. If, on the other hand, March sells over December by more than the cost of carrying wheat for three months, the hedger may find the sale of March much more enticing. In effect, he is paid a bonus over cost for holding wheat an extra three months. Or, if he markets the wheat sooner, he enjoys a very favorable basis against which to sell his cash wheat.

Although there is a tendency toward full carrying charges when spot supplies are burdensome, spreads will often fall short of that theoretical price differential. One reason is the large incentive that the speculator has to buy spot or nearbys and sell futures at close to carrying-charge differences. Under this circumstance, there is small risk in the spread, since there is very slight scope for the forward contract to widen its premium above the spot or nearby. As discussed earlier, carrying charges tend to establish a limit, albeit an imperfect one, on forward premiums. That is why buying a nearby and selling a distant future at around full carrying costs is a highly popular low-risk spread.

A qualification of the low risk exists when varying interest costs constitute the predominant carrying cost factor; carrying charges themselves may then fluctuate rather widely not only with the price level but also with variations in interest rates.

The actions of the larger commercial firms represent, at times, a major influence over changes in price differentials of nearby futures positions. If, in the period shortly before a future expires, trade interests note that nearby futures are selling at less than full carrying cost discounts to distant futures, they may sell (short) the spot month and purchase a forward future. They can then deliver actuals from their inventory position, with the intention of standing for delivery against their long futures position. In effect, this type of transaction enables a firm to maintain ownership of a commodity during the spread interval (via a long position in futures), without paying the full costs of carrying the commodity.

A trade firm engaging in this transaction will not necessarily wait until its long futures position becomes current in order to take delivery of the actual commodity. Let us assume that the firm has tendered delivery against the short leg of its spread and that other trade firms have done the same. As a consequence of this action, speculators holding long positions in the spot future are faced with heavy deliveries of actual commodities and, if these speculators are not in a position to accept delivery (which they are usually not), they must liquidate (sell) their long positions in the spot month.[1] This concentrated selling of the spot month sometimes depresses that future relative to distant futures. If this occurs, commercial interests may begin to advantageously undo their spreads. That is, they may find it profitable to repurchase contracts sold in the spot month and liquidate their long positions in the deferred months at favorable price differentials. The transaction is completed when they take delivery against their newly assumed long positions (in the spot month), thus restoring their basic inventory position to that which existed prior to the entire transaction.

These transactions are extremely important. They hold the key to the weakness that often occurs in the spot month in carrying-charge markets. They also explain the heavy deliveries that frequently appear on the first delivery day of an expiring contract. This is the time when the speculator may pay the penalty for being long the spot month. Of course, in situations in which a shortage arises, this downward price adjustment in the spot position need not occur; in fact, prices may advance relative to deferred futures. Thus, ever-changing circumstances may account for divergent finales in successive expiring spot months.

With this background in mind, it is now appropriate to examine some of the principal spreads presented in our classifications.

PRINCIPAL SPREADS

Intracommodity Spread—Low-Risk Variety

Let us look more closely at the speculator's "favorite" spread—a position in which one is long a nearby and short a distant future at as close to a carrying-charge premium as possible. By way of example, we may consider the varying fate of the November

---

[1]In practice, speculators liquidating long positions in the spot month frequently reinstate these positions in more deferred futures, thereby maintaining their long futures commitments. Despite this "shifting forward" of positions, there may be a tendency for the spot month to weaken relative to deferred positions.

soybean contract versus a later delivery month, say, January. Let us recall, in this connection, that soybeans are harvested in late September, in October, and most voluminously in November. Usually there are enough new-crop soybeans harvested by November 1 to make deliveries on the Chicago Board of Trade and also to take care of November crushing requirements. However, rainy weather in September and October can delay the harvest, prompting supply limitations in November. As a general rule, therefore, November soybeans do not sell at a full carrying-charge discount to January beans until it is evident that supplies will be ample in November. This may seem clear during the summer if the supply carried over from the previous harvest is large. However, if there appears to be scant carryover, then the situation can remain in doubt until the expiration of trading in November beans. On rare occasions, November beans may trade at a premium to January because of an unexpected weather-induced scarcity.

Historically, normal carrying charges between November and January soybeans should be about 10 cents per bushel. In late October, if November beans are selling 6 cents under January, an elevator operator with newly harvested beans might sell November and buy January. The operator is likely to deliver beans on November 1, thus closing out his short position. The weight of deliveries may well cause November to decline to 9 cents under January. The elevator operator may then buy November and sell January, closing out his long position in January. His position is now long November, and he takes delivery on this position. He thus retains his original position long actual beans, but he has at the same time made a gross profit of 3 cents per bushel from his spread.

Assume that in late October a speculator anticipates an inversion in spread differences. If he buys November and sells January, his risk is limited by carrying charges and by the hedger's willingness to keep them in line. Under ordinary circumstances, the speculator may lose 8 to 10 cents, plus commission. On the other hand, if a shortage develops and November climbs to 20 or 25 cents over January, the speculator's profit could be substantial.

As suggested earlier, the carrying-charge spread can limit risk. However, its gains, though sometimes appreciable, are apt to be infrequent. Led by an "invisible hand," futures markets tend to balance profit and loss potentialities as weighted by their relative frequency of occurrence.

Intercommodity Spread—High-Risk Variety

Where the risks are high, the rewards are apt to be commensurate. When a speculator takes a spread position involving a short in the nearby position versus a long in the distant, the potential risk has no set limit. In other words, while carrying charges limit premiums on distant contracts, there is no comparable restraint on the discount to which a far-off month can decline. Thus, a short nearby versus long distant position is a high-risk spread, except to the degree that the prudent speculator limits his possible equity loss with a protective stop. For most traders, we strongly urge such stop-loss protection.

An interesting example in this connection is a copper spread that many technicians were recommending in September 1988, just as copper prices were beginning to accelerate toward their historic peak, in excess of $1.64/lb, established in December 1988. In September 1988, copper prices had retraced about 60 percent of the previous sharp decline that occurred between January and March of that year. Many technicians, convinced that copper prices were finishing a secondary rally in an emerging bear market, were advising clients to establish outright short positions in December 1988 copper at the 101.00 level. Stops were to be placed at 111.60, for a risk of 10.6 cents, or $2,650 per contract.

More conservative, technically minded traders, however, opted for a short December/long May spread at a nearby differential of about 13 cents premium to the May contract (see Figure 22.1). If prices had declined—as was hoped—the nearby December contract would have fallen faster and with more vigor than the deferred May contract, thereby narrowing the spread to between zero and 2 cents, and possibly into negative territory, to reinstate a normal carrying-charge market. Such a scenario would result in a substantial profit to those who were positioned either outright short or in a bear spread. Conversely, in the event prices continued to climb, the outright shorts certainly would have had some serious problems; however, the bear

FIGURE 22.1

Copper: Intercommodity Spread (December 1988 and May 1989 COMEX)

spreaders were "protected" by their long May position. By design, as long as the December contract did not climb in greater increments than the May contract, rising prices would not present a problem because the original 13-cent spread would not materially widen.

But it did. Within eight weeks, December copper prices rocketed by 45 cents/lb while the May contract rallied by only 26 cents, which widened the spread from 13 to 32 cents—a historically high premium of December copper over May. Unfortunately, the false security of the spread kept most participants in the position far too long—until it became nearly unbearable to watch the bear spread widen day after day in a bullish market environment. Although the spread relationship narrowed considerably after the December contract expired, the trade nonetheless was ill-timed and poorly managed.

We may draw an important lesson from this experience. A spread is not necessarily safer than an outright market position, and can result in significant losses if no predetermined stop is identified and used.

In all cases, however, the spread has meaning only if both legs are related in terms of price. If the front month position is governed by economic forces that are completely distinct from those shaping the deferred months, then the spread is largely mythical. In effect, it is equivalent to two separate outright positions.

When the front month future is volatile, and the deferred month future inert, the principal lure of a spread as an alternative to an outright position is the lower margin it affords the trader. In the case of grains, the old crop versus new crop spread has other winning applications.

As an example, consider a wheat situation in which nearby supplies are ample, so that old crop futures are selling below new crop months. Assume that the possibility exists that some dramatic event could tighten up the old crop position. However, the event that might evoke this change (i.e., a massive wheat shipment to China or the former Soviet Union) is problematical. An outright long position in old crop wheat may seem quite vulnerable, given a continued situation of oversupply. The spread—long old crop and short new crop—may then be an appropriate play. Any developing supply tightness would cause the spread to be profitable, while, failing such tightness, straddle differences may change little so the risk may be small.

Clearly, the two-season (intercommodity) spread is a time spread in which a key event, a new harvest, occurs during the spread interval. This event abruptly changes the supply situation. It signals an end to a period of depletion of old crop carry-over and production, and may in time transform the statistical position.

The concept of an intercommodity spread is applicable not only to crops grown in the ground. Pig crops, for example, move in phases rather like field crops. There are into-storage periods and out-of-storage periods. The start of a large marketing season is akin to the harvest of a crop, with expanded supplies becoming available. Frequently, August pork bellies sell at large premiums to the following February, since marketings during the late fall and winter (after expiration of the August future) are heavy.

Location Spread

A spread based on location differences is distinct from but kindred to **arbitrage,** another member of the great family of price-difference-oriented trades. As commonly defined, arbitrage is the purchase and sale of an identical article in two different locations. Examples of arbitrage include the purchase of British pounds in Zurich versus the sale of pounds at the same time in Paris and the purchase of General Motors stock on the Pacific Coast Exchange versus its sale on the New York Stock Exchange. The hallmark of this sort of transaction is its comparative safety. Typically, the arbitrageur is prepared to accept delivery in one location (if that becomes necessary), cover all costs, and redeliver in another location, at some predetermined price differential.

Unfortunately, this type of ideal arbitrage situation is a rare phenomenon. First, there usually is not an identical article in both locations. Although the same commodity may be traded, delivery specifications usually differ in the two locations. A commodity grade or type delivered in one market may not be tenderable in the other. Even if it is, the cost involved in shipment (from London to New York, for example) may make this procedure uneconomical unless differences are unusually wide. Buying futures in London and selling futures in the same commodity in New York (or vice versa) is, of course, a common operation. But it is not arbitrage in the sense we have defined it. The London delivery may not be exactly identical to the New York delivery, and the purchase of one versus the sale of another does not guarantee a profit based on acceptance of a tender and subsequent redelivery.

To explore the ideal case, we might assume a situation in which an identical commodity is traded in London and New York. Differences in supply and demand conditions may tend to foster price disparities between the two markets. However, as long as it is possible to freely ship the commodity in question from London to New York or vice versa, price disparities are limited by transport costs and affected (in this international case) by currency rates of exchange and tariffs, if applicable.

When the commodity originates in a third country (i.e., Ghana cocoa), the transport factor also involves the comparative cost of shipping from that source to each of the market areas. To the extent that transportation costs are primary, discrepancies in price differences tend to be corrected quickly. Big firms with the most advanced communications technology are operating constantly to take advantage of any price differences that are out of line. These firms are often members of exchanges in both locales and can operate profitably on narrower margins than can public traders.

In practice, international spreads in cocoa, coffee, and sugar between New York and London are also affected by factors that concern the supply and demand of each commodity in the given locale. This impact may be particularly significant in the spot month. In mid-1985, the nearby coffee position in New York moved to a substantial, and unusual, 90 cent/lb premium to the nearby delivery position in London (the usual premium of New York Coffee is 38–42 cents/lb). The premium reflected quality problems and a shortage of mild Central and South American coffees in exchange warehouses in the United States. Meanwhile, in London, which trades robusta coffees mainly from Brazil and Africa, there were relatively abundant supplies of less-than-desirable grades.

In the long run, these price differences will be resolved. As the premium of New York to London widens, origin countries will sell additional amounts of coffee to relieve the short supply situation. On the other hand, until additional mild coffees enter the export market, many importers will opt for a short period for the less expensive London robustas, which will increase the price of London coffee in the process. Eventually, the spread will narrow to a more normal differential between the two locales.

As noted earlier, changes in currency parities can be of vital importance in international spread transactions. For example, during the first quarter of 1991, the British pound fell by 20 percent. Because the price of cocoa, coffee, and sugar did not change appreciably in dollar terms, the British price in pound sterling expressed the "devaluation" almost entirely, increasing by nearly 20 percent. A long position in London profited accordingly, while a short position in London showed a corresponding loss. Roughly speaking, each 100 sterling worth of the commodity became worth 120 sterling.

Clearly, the trader who expects a currency to strengthen or weaken has the option of going long or short in the foreign exchange market itself. He should not enter an international commodity spread unless it has added appeal on noncurrency grounds. Summarizing, in terms of commodity dealing, an interesting "play" to consider under these circumstances involves taking a long position in a commodity in the country with a relatively weak currency and a short position in the country whose currency seems strong.

Spreads Based on Differences in Delivery Grade

Quite often, the difference between two futures markets is primarily a matter of deliverable grades or differentials specified on the respective contracts. The greater this disparity, the more analogous the position is to a spread in two wholly distinct commodities.

If one has reason to suppose that Brazilian cocoa (commonly delivered in New York) will be harvested in abundance this year, while Ghana cocoa (often tendered in London) will be in short supply, then there is *prima facie* reason for considering the purchase of London cocoa versus the sale of New York cocoa.[2] Similarly, if it appears that soft red wheat production will be low and hard wheat production more ample, one may favor purchases of Chicago wheat (based on soft red) versus sales of Kansas City wheat (hard wheat).

Multicommodity Spreads

As was suggested earlier, all sensible spreads involve some logical relation between the different delivery positions involved. In general, two commodities may be spread candidates if: (1) they are, to some degree, substitutes for each other (i.e., corn and oats); (2) they complement each other's use or are coproducts (i.e., crude oil and heating oil); or (3) one commodity is another form of the other (i.e., feeder cattle and live cattle).

Two exchange-traded commodities that are to some degree substitutable are corn and oats. Both are used primarily as animal feeds, and their food value per pound is almost identical. Corn weighs about twice as much per bushel; hence there may be a price disparity of about 2:1. Spread positions involving two bushels or contracts of oats for every one of corn are commonly taken. The incentive to spread may lie in a relatively short supply or surplus in one or the other grain.

Corn and oats are not always substitutable, though. True, an animal can eat either, and gain weight. However, animals do not respond well to abrupt changes in diet, and farmers do not react quickly to minor changes in price differences. Their animals are on a feed formula that they are reluctant to change unless the economic factors become extremely persuasive. Therefore, the exact 2:1 ratio between corn and oats prices does not exist often; nor is the prevailing price ratio necessarily stable.

A most interesting and popular spread is wheat versus corn, notwithstanding the major difference in their use patterns.

---

[2] In an international spread of this kind, one must also consider whether the possibility of a change in currency values exists and whether it supports or discourages the intended trade.

Wheat is typically priced well above corn and is used primarily for human consumption, with very little going into animal feed. However, wheat is superior to corn as a feed if the two are priced evenly. If wheat in Chicago is only 10 cents per bushel over corn, there will be many rural areas where, owing to dislocations or abnormal transportation cost, the two will sell at parity. Therefore, some wheat will go into feed channels. However, the incentive may not develop at every rural area. Furthermore (as noted earlier), farmers are reluctant to alter the diets of their animals in the short run to achieve modest savings. However, a low wheat/corn price difference early in the season can encourage feeders to substitute wheat for corn; this will induce the price of wheat to rise relative to the price of corn. In this instance a spread (long March wheat versus short March corn) may be reasonable because of the significant and dependable relationship between the two commodities. The spread will be profitable if farmers make appreciable substitution and if no extraneous factors affecting either wheat or corn enter the picture. (A disturbing influence might be the cancellation of a large export order by China for Canadian wheat, or a drought in the month of July in the corn belt.)

The wheat–corn relationship (purchase wheat/sell corn) is probably the most popular intermarket spread. Between 1975 and 1991, the spread relationship between the December contracts was as narrow as 5 cents per bushel in 1977 and as wide as 225 cents per bushel in early 1980. If there is a norm for the differential between wheat and corn, it is probably around 90–100 cents per bushel.

The spread trader waits for the differential to move to a level that appears to be extreme by historical standards—either because it is too narrow (40 cents or lower) or because it is too wide (120 cents or higher). Typically, the trader uses anticipated seasonal factors to enter the spread, such as around July 4, right after the wheat marketing period and crop year come to an end. Theoretically, wheat should be bought in early July when supplies are the most plentiful, while at the same time, corn should be sold because prices are being bid up, perhaps for reasons of hot weather. At that time, theoretically, the wheat–corn spread should be at its narrowest price differential and should widen into the winter months (see Figure 22.2).

FIGURE 22.2
December 1988 Wheat–Corn Spread

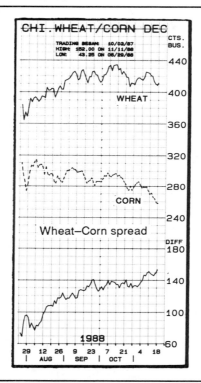

The historical band can be used as a general guideline, but the professional trader of the wheat–corn spread must combine knowledge of the fundamentals of both the current and the expected wheat and corn crops, the pertinent weather factors, foreign crop developments, export sales, and foreign currency changes, as well as the respective technical and chart considerations. Any one of the above-mentioned factors can influence the eventual direction of the spread.

Processor's Spread

A common type of spread involves a single commodity at different stages of processing. For example, soybeans are crushed to

364 Section 6 Tactics of Trading

yield meal and oil. When futures contracts exist for two stages of processing, there is a vehicle for traders to interpret price difference.

The most popular processor's spread is one between soybeans and its products, soybean meal and soybean oil.[3] It is a useful spread for a variety of reasons. In the United States, nearly all harvested soybeans are crushed. The value of by-products other than meal and oil is negligible.

Essentially, this spread entails a long position in products (meal and oil) and a short in beans when it appears the processing margin will widen, and, conversely, a short position in products (jointly) and long beans when a narrowing of the conversion spread is indicated.

The **board conversion** (processing margin) is the premium of meal and oil jointly over beans as computed from prevailing prices on the Chicago Board of Trade. The formula is often used to compare the difference which approximately reflects the meal and oil content of a bushel of beans. The oil price is multiplied by 11, since there are 11 pounds of oil in each bushel. The meal price, quoted in dollars per ton, is first divided by 2,000 to convert it to a per-pound basis; it is then multiplied by 48 since there are 48 pounds of meal in each bushel of beans. The total is then multiplied by 100, since the result is desired in cents rather than in dollars.

A combination of these steps calls for the dollar price of meal to be multiplied by 2.4. For example, if meal sells at $240 per ton, it is equal to about $5.76 per bushel—and if oil is at 25 cents per pound, it is worth $2.75 per bushel. If we combine the two we get a price of $8.51. We then measure this joint product value against the price of soybeans for the same delivery month, and see if there is a minus or a plus conversion difference.

Let us say we are comparing March products and March beans and find that the board conversion is 30 cents. We study past charts of this spread's behavior and find that March products have usually varied from 20 cents under March beans to 50

---

[3]One bushel of soybeans, weighing approximately 60 pounds, is crushed into 48 pounds of soybean meal and 11 pounds of soybean oil.

cents over, with some recurrent tendency (not very consistent) for this difference to widen in the last few months of the life of the March contract.

What will happen this year? The most important single consideration is the size of crushing capacity. If it is very large, then product margins over beans may remain small. On the other hand, if there is reason to anticipate heavy demand for products relative to crushing capacity, product margins can be very wide.

One of the most extraordinary changes in the soybean conversion spreads occurred in 1987 when the premium of cash products over cash beans soared from 29 cents in March 1987 to 132 cents in December. In this instance, the profit on a low margin and relatively low-risk spread matched what one might hope for on an outright position in futures. In this case, the spread widened to a unique degree because the demand for soybean products soared to a level that strained existing processing capacity.

At times, product demand may be especially keen for either meal or oil. Typically, demand for feed meal is most intense during the winter, particularly when weather conditions are unusually severe. Soybean meal is therefore highly dependent on livestock and poultry numbers, whereas oil requirements are especially sensitive to variations in supplies of competitive fats and oils. Beans themselves can come into temporary scarcity during late summer and fall. Shortages around harvest time can be brought about by a holding policy on the part of farmers, by a delayed harvest, or by an extra-large export movement.

As the analyst often notes with some incredulity, the board conversion between beans and products is sometimes very small. On such occasions, the products appear to be worth less than the beans. Is this so? And if it is, how do processors stay solvent? There are several explanations. First of all, beans delivered to a Chicago elevator cost appreciably more than they do on a farm in central Illinois or Iowa, while the crusher buys from the lower-priced farm source. Second, the crusher obtains the small by-product value mentioned earlier. Third, he is able to sell some meal at premium prices, because of higher protein content. And, finally, the processor is often able to use futures to reduce his bean cost or to improve his effective margin. For example, when "board margin" is high, the processor may sell product futures against his bean purchases to, in effect, lock in the higher profit margin.

For any trader initiating a conversion or processor's spread, it is desirable that the dollar amount of the products should about equal the dollar amount of beans. This is achieved minimally when one buys (or sells) one contract of beans versus the sale of one contract each of meal and oil. A more exact ratio entails 10 contracts of soybeans versus 9 contracts of oil and 12 contracts of meal.

OTHER SPREAD PLAYS: FINANCIAL FUTURES SPREADS

During the past decade or so, after the deregulation of the financial markets in the early 1980s and because of increasing volatility in interest rates and foreign exchange rates, spreads between financial futures instruments have grown very popular. Typically, these spreads involve purchasing one currency future or debt instrument while simultaneously selling a different foreign currency or debt instrument—usually on the same exchange—to capture a significant expansion or contraction of the differential. Whether the spread differential moves in the desired direction depends largely on perceptions about the underlying fundamentals of the governments and economies involved or, in the case of interest rate spreads, changing perceptions about the future shape and height of the respective yield curves.

A classic example of a radical shift in the relationship between two foreign currencies occurred in 1989 (see Figure 22.3). For that entire year, prices of Japanese yen futures lost value vis-à-vis the German Deutsche mark (in other words, the mark gained value relative to the yen). In terms of the differential between futures contracts traded on the Chicago Mercantile Exchange, between February 1989 and April 1990, the Japanese yen (nearest futures contract) declined from a 2,500-point premium to a 370 premium to the German mark (nearest futures).

During that period of time, the currency exchange rates and differentials were being impacted by the sudden overthrow of

FIGURE 22.3
Foreign Currency Spread (Weekly Yen–Deutsche Mark [nearest futures])

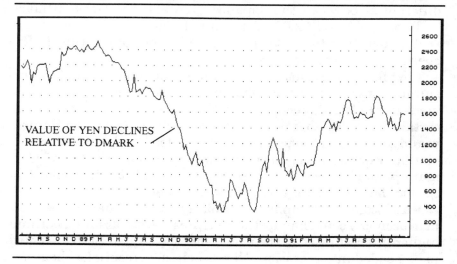

communism in eastern Europe. Although the fall of communism and the prospect of a united Germany for the first time since the end of World War II was considered a positive development for Europe in general (and Germany in particular), some knowledgeable analysts and traders suspected unification would prove to be an extremely expensive undertaking by the German government. For the markets, that meant the German government would need to raise huge amounts of capital to finance its commitment to assimilate the "new Germany." As a result, German interest rates would have to climb to attract "working" capital from the international marketplace and to control inflation, both of which would be considered by-products of such a huge, long-term undertaking. The prospect of relatively high nominal and real (inflation-adjusted) interest rates in Germany relative to potential investment returns elsewhere around the globe attracted buyers to the Deutsche mark throughout 1989 (the Berlin Wall fell in December 1989).

To a trader who is a student of international affairs and who felt compelled to capitalize on the extraordinary events unfolding in Germany, the logical "play" was to purchase German marks and simultaneously sell Japanese yen—a non-European currency whose government was far removed from the historical changes occurring on the Continent. Figure 22.3 shows that the differential between the Japanese yen and the German mark "collapsed" by over 2,000 futures ticks during a 12-month period, amounting to a $25,000 gain per Chicago Mercantile Exchange (CME) spread.

While the description of the then-fundamentals and the resultant contraction in the yen–mark differential may seem obvious in hindsight, keep in mind that, at that time, nothing was certain from day to day. Initially, no one believed communism would self-destruct, especially without bloodshed and armed revolution. Furthermore, no one knew what impact the "new" Germany would have on prospects for "Europe 1992," the timeframe set for the removal of tariffs from member countries of the European Economic Community. Finally, no one knew if the German economy could handle the dual pressures of assimilation and higher interest rates at the same time the United States seemed to be headed into recession. Nevertheless, perceptions about the value of the German mark in relation to the world's other major currencies had changed significantly, which argued for a climb in the value of the mark. For any trader or investor who established spread positions at that time, constant monitoring of the pertinent fundamentals was absolutely essential. Furthermore, because foreign currencies trade virtually around the clock on a spot or cash basis, the spread player who establishes a position in futures on the CME must make certain his clearing firm has access to a competent overnight trading desk that can provide service around the clock on an "exchange for physical" basis and alert him to sudden changes in the currency relationships at any time, even in the middle of the night if need be.

Despite the uncertainties and inherent risks involved in taking such a spread position, differentials between currencies, or **cross-rates,** have become very popular trading vehicles for both individuals and institutions. As long as the trader understands the relationship between the two legs and analyzes the situation with respect to stop-losses and objectives, currency spreads can be included in one's trading repertoire.

Finally, apart from the fundamental and technical reasons for entering a currency spread differential, the trader must remember to enter an equal dollar amount of both currencies in each leg of the spread. In our example, the CME contract for marks contains 125,000 marks, while the yen contract contains 12,500,000 yen. To arrive at the dollar value of each contract, multiply the number of marks by the spot dollar/Deutsche mark exchange rate (i.e., 125,000 DM × $ 0.5882/DM = $73,529.40 per contract of marks; and 12,500,000 JY × $0.0077/yen = $96,250.00 per contract of yen). In the case of the yen–mark spread, to ensure that each leg is of equal value, professional traders would have to buy 1.3 contracts of marks for every contract of yen sold. In other words, although each tick on the CME for both the mark and the yen equals $12.50, on a spread basis, for each tick to have equal dollar-weighting between the two currencies, a professional trader would have to buy 13 contracts of marks and sell 10 contracts of yen. Amateur traders, or traders with limited equity, can still take advantage of the spread strategy in small "odd-lot quantities" on a one-on-one basis, but their returns will not be maximized.

Another popular spread trade that relates two contracts with exactly the same dollar-weighted point values is commonly referred to by its acronym, NOB. To establish an NOB spread, a trader would buy Treasury note futures and simultaneously sell Treasury bond futures on the Chicago Board of Trade (hence, NOtes − Bonds = NOB). The underlying instrument of both contracts is an IOU issued by the United States that has a face value of $100,000 at time of maturity and a yield of 8 percent. The difference is that the note reaches maturity in 10 years or less, while the bond is not callable for at least 15 years.

The NOB trader seeks to take advantage of a price disparity between an intermediate-term debt instrument and a long-term debt instrument. To put it another way, ideally, the buyer of the NOB spread seeks to profit from a decline in interest rates that is more pronounced on the shorter end of the yield curve than on the longer end.

For an example, take a look at Figure 22.4, which is a weekly price chart of the spread between Treasury notes and Treasury bonds between March 1988 and October 1991. If you ignore all the action after January 1990, what you are left with is a declining spread relationship; that is, prices of notes were declining relative to the price of bonds. In terms of interest rates, the contraction of the spread represented a relative in-

FIGURE 22.4
Weekly Treasury Note–Treasury Bond Spread (nearest futures)

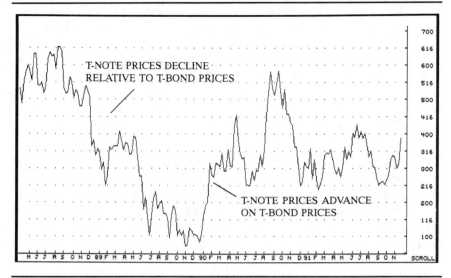

crease in shorter-term interest rates compared with a flat or declining trend in long-term interest rates. When short-term rates rise and long-term rates decline or remain stable, the yield curve (the chart representation of the entire spectrum of yields from three-month to 30-year debt paper) is considered inverted, which many economists argue is a precursor of recession.

Back in late 1989, for an economist, analyst, or businessperson who believed that the U.S. economy was headed for a downturn and therefore into a more normalized yield curve environment (declining short-term interest rates), a logical way to take advantage of such a significant change of course would have been to buy the NOB spread (buy T-notes and sell T-bonds).

As it turned out, for nine months in 1990, the spread increased in value from less than 100 ticks (each tick represents 1/32, or $31.25 per contract) to nearly 600 ticks, or about $15,625 per NOB spread). In terms of the spread, the widening of the differential between notes and bonds reflected a shift by the Federal Reserve toward acceleration of an increasingly accommodative monetary policy, which had the effect of bringing down shorter-term interest rates in relation to long-term interest rates. The financial markets responded to the Fed's actions by flowing money into short-term debt maturities while exerting a fair amount of caution about the inflation-sensitive longer-term debt issues.

Although the near-vertical move in the NOB spread was extremely profitable (for those who bought the spread), we must caution against thinking that this, or any type of spread trade, is easy. Keep in mind that a spread trade like the NOB rests on certain assumptions one must make about the direction of many variable factors such as economic growth, interest rates, inflation, and perhaps even exchange rates. It is a dynamic process every step of the way, subject to sudden changes that could upset the underlying assumptions that were present when the spread relationship was entered.

CONCLUSION

In conclusion, to spread is to play one kind of futures game. To be a winner, one must play this game objectively, not impulsively, and with a full understanding of the rules. Often, the simple, straightforward approach is best. Now and then, a specialized type of spread procedure may be justified.

Some people enter spreads by putting on legs at different times. In this way, they combine an outright position with a spread. This may make sense if it is originally planned in this manner. Sometimes, however, a spread is initiated with the notion of hedging a losing outright position. This is done to prevent a margin call or to avoid the unpleasant necessity of taking a loss. Such a tactic is usually unsound. It will not revoke the loss—it will only initiate a new position. In general, a spread should be chosen on its own merit, or not at all.

A converse tactic may be still more imprudent. Some traders, having erred in their choice of a spread and having established a "paper loss," will lift one leg rather than liquidate both simultaneously and accept the loss. Here they are creating an outright position and a new risk. They are not erasing a loss. The appropriate question to ask is: Would I enter this spread or outright position on its own merits if I were not faced with a previous losing commitment?

CHAPTER 23

FUTURES OPTIONS: AN INTRODUCTION

In futures, as in securities trading, a prime consideration in any speculative undertaking is the magnitude of risk involved. The successful speculator seeks to establish, with every market commitment, an acceptable and predetermined risk allowance. Any method of trading that limits risk while permitting relatively large profit merits close attention.

Experienced futures traders recognize that, over time, the longer-term position trader is more apt to be successful than the short-term "in and out" speculator. However, a major problem facing the position trader is that even when he is correct in his basic market position, he may be whipsawed out of the market by adverse, short-term fluctuations. The advent and development of options on futures enables the investor to initiate and maintain a position, survive the whipsaws, and still realize profit potential, all with limited loss exposure.

Organized, exchange-based option trading was introduced in the United States in 1973 with the creation of the Chicago Board of Options Exchange (CBOE), a stock-based organization. The success of the CBOE and the public's embrace of the "new" options market, in addition to the fact that a significant portion of the commodity option business from the United States was being done on London exchanges (cocoa, coffee, sugar, copper, tin, zinc, lead, and silver were traded in London in the 1960s and 1970s, prior to the inauguration of options trading in the United States), helped secure CFTC approval for exchange-traded options on futures in September 1981. Less than one year later, options on futures in T-bonds, sugar, and gold began trading on their respective exchanges. By late 1984, futures options were available in virtually all major markets: currencies, grains, precious metals, and financial futures (including stock indices).

In the past several years, as the volatility and volume of the futures markets have expanded and intensified, growth of options trading has been tremendous. For example, volume of options traded on T-bond futures was 27.3 million contracts in 1990, compared with 11.9 million contracts in 1985; volume of crude oil options hit 5.3 million in 1990, compared with 3.2 million in 1987 (the first complete year options on crude oil were traded).

WHAT IS AN OPTION ON A FUTURES CONTRACT?

There are two basic classes of options: calls and puts.

- A **call option** gives the holder the right to "call" (or buy) a specified futures contract at a specific price any time prior to the expiration of the option.
- A **put option** gives the holder the right to "put" (or sell) a specified futures contract at a specified price any time prior to the expiration of the option.

Obligations of the Option Buyer and Seller

The option buyer pays for the put or call in full at the time of purchase and has no other expense, obligation, or risk unless or until he exercises the option, which will require him to post initial margin on either a long (call) or short (put) futures position.

The option seller receives the premium paid for the option but must post the necessary margin to carry the position until exercise or expiration.

What the Option Buyer and Seller Hope to Achieve

The buyer has to pay for the option at the time of purchase. The goal of the call buyer is to see the futures price climb to at least a predetermined level by a set date so he can recover his initial investment in addition to realizing a profit. The put buyer, on the other hand, wishes to see the futures price drop.

Conversely, the seller's objective is to see the futures price move in the opposite direction (or stay flat), which will enable him to retain the entire premium he was paid for taking the risk of selling the option.

THE ELEMENTS OF PUT AND CALL OPTIONS

The Strike Price

The strike price is the price at which the holder of a call option can call (buy) his futures contract, or the price at which the holder of a put option can put (sell) his futures contract upon exercise. On exchange-traded options, the exchange determines the strike price and other contract terms.

The Premium

The option premium (also known as the time premium) is the sum of money (price) that the buyer pays for the privilege of owning the option, or the money the seller receives for undertaking the risks associated with writing the option. The price of an option, or the premium, is generally governed by the life span of the option, the volatility of the underlying future, and the proximity of the underlying future price to the strike price. For example, the price of a call option on November soybeans that is 25 cents/bu above the strike price with four weeks to go will be considerably less than the price of a call option on November soybeans that is 5 cents/bu above the strike price with three months until expiration. The nearness of the strike price to the price of the underlying future, coupled with the relatively long period prior to expiration in a commodity that is known for its volatile daily trading ranges, enables the seller to demand more money to undertake the perceived risk.

The Expiration Date

This is the date at a specified and predetermined time that the holder's right to exercise the option (receive a futures position) expires. In addition, it is the date by which the seller of the option is obligated to deliver a futures position. Any option that is at the specified time, or in the money (and can be exercised), is considered abandoned (worthless).

Out-of-the-Money and In-the-Money Options

"Out of the money" and "in the money" describe the relationship between the underlying futures price and the strike price of an option. For example, the owner of a $420 strike call option on June gold at the same time that June gold futures are trading at $403/ounce holds an out-of-the-money gold call. The holder of a $420 strike June gold call with June futures trading at $432/ounce is $12 in the money, or above his strike price.

Intrinsic Value of the Option

The intrinsic value of an option is the value of a call or put that is in the money, minus the premium. Suppose, in our example, that the call option on June gold with a $420 strike price is at $16/ounce (or $1,600 per 100-ounce contract) while June gold futures are trading at $432/ounce. The call is in the money and has intrinsic value of $12, or $1,200 per 100-ounce contract. The $400 additional charge to buy the option is the premium attached by the seller, based on a model that incorporates various determining factors, including time until expiration and volatility, among others. As time runs out on the life of the option, or as the option's price climbs further into the money, the premium diminishes steadily to zero.

Time Decay

For the serious futures speculator, understanding time decay is imperative to successful options trading. Actively traded exchange options have a limited life span of (usually) three to six months. From the minute an options contract is consummated, the time clock is ticking away, reducing the life span of the instrument and, hence, its value.

Time decay is, more often than not, the enemy of the option buyer, for without movement of the underlying future toward the strike price, or into the money, the price of the option will diminish naturally, until it is worthless.

On the other hand, time decay is the ally of the option seller, who hopes the underlying future trades listlessly, or in the opposite direction of the strike price, which, by definition, will undermine the value of the option. In such a case, the seller then gets to pocket the money, or the entire premium he received for the option.

Volatility

Although options volatility can be a complex mathematical subject, for our purposes we need to keep in mind that *the greater the volatility of the underlying futures contract, the greater the premium component of the option price.* Typically, options of foreign currency futures, for example, tend to have a high volatility component largely because IMM foreign exchange contracts have no daily trading limits and because the currencies are susceptible to wild price swings precipitated by the release of economic data and unexpected events in international politics. If Swiss franc futures traverse a range of 50 to 75 ticks a day, which brings the futures within target distance of three strike prices in two days, then the volatility component of the options price certainly will reflect that condition.

HOW TO USE OPTIONS

Now that we have defined the option, the main differences between buyer and seller, and the elements of the option, let's explore the mechanics and basic strategies of options on futures by going through some realistic situations. (These situations are fictitious and serve only to illustrate a point. Prices and certain events have been created solely for the purpose of this text.)

Situation 1

Market outlook for gold: bullish
Trader's goal: defined risk, long-side speculation
Strategy: buy call options

On the morning of March 17, 1993, Mr. E hears from his broker that the producer price index data released by the Labor Department showed an unexpected surge in wholesale price of 1.0 percent for February. In deference to his chart work, which showed a minor basing pattern in gold, coupled with the five-month climb in oil prices, Mr. E believes that the data is the "tip of the iceberg" and that inflation will accelerate in the months ahead. This could be bullish for precious metals. However, he has two concerns that make him extremely cautious about buying gold: (1) despite the minor base pattern, prices are still in a powerful 10-month down trend, and (2) the Federal Reserve could continue to tighten interest rates in subsequent weeks, possibly dissuading investment in gold.

Nonetheless, Mr. E is undeterred. From his technical studies and his business sense, he concludes that if he can define his risk to $3,000 then he will enter the long side of the gold market near the $400/ounce level looking for an upmove of $40/ounce (or $4,000 per contract) within three months. To implement the strategy, he could establish five long futures positions, margined at $2,000 each. Under this plan, although he allocates $10,000 for margin purposes, his exposure could be considerably more than $3,000 if prices decline significantly (i.e., more than $6.00 per ounce per contract). Even if Mr. E places stop loss orders $6.00 per contract below his entry price, this does not preclude a larger loss that might result from a gap-down opening one morning well beneath the level of his stop. Based on Mr. E's game plan, this unlikely, but very real, additional risk is unacceptable.

Mr. E could cut his risk somewhat by establishing a four-contract futures position instead of five contracts. However, even if he risks $750 per contract on his four units (as opposed to risking $600 per contract on five units), and even if he places stop loss orders well below the market, he is still not guaranteed that losses would be kept to $3,000 or less. In fact, he has no assurance that he will not lose his entire $10,000, or all the money in his futures account.

Opting for a safer alternative, Mr. E chooses to buy $10,000 worth of in-the-money gold call options. With the October contract trading at $411 per ounce, he pays $1,700 per call (or $8,500 total) for five $410 strike call options that will expire in seven months. After he pays for the options and the commission, he has defined his cost and his maximum risk exposure ($8,500 plus commission). Furthermore, if the value of his options falls to $5,500, Mr. E will close out the position with a $3,000 loss.

At this point, Mr. E knows his cost, his risk, and his stop loss level. What about his break-even point? Since he paid $17 per option, at expiration, the option price must be at least $17 in the money (above the strike price). For that to happen, the price of the underlying October gold contract must be trading at or above $427 per ounce. If October gold is trading between $410 and $427 per ounce at the time of expiration, then his options will have intrinsic value and he can recover part of his initial outlay. But, should his original fears be realized, and gold prices fall because of rising interest rates, Mr. E will liquidate the position if the value of his options falls below $5,500.

On the other hand, if his analysis proves accurate, and gold futures prices rise by $40 per ounce to $451 within the next six to seven months, then Mr. E will realize a gain of no less than $24 ($2,400) per option contract (excluding commissions), or three times what he intended to risk on the position.

The best outcome for Mr. E would be for gold prices to rally sharply to $450 within 8 to 10 weeks of his purchase. In such a scenario, the price of his options would far exceed $40 per call largely because of the relatively long time until expiration (five months), the high volatility, and the high demand for the options themselves. It is conceivable that, under those circumstances, Mr. E would realize a net gain of $30 to $35 per option at that time (excluding commissions).

Mr. E's commitment to the gold market was straightforward; his outlook was bullish—at least for the next several months—and he was willing to bet on it, but with a predefined and limited cost.

Situation 2

Market outlook for gold: bearish
Trader's goal: defined risk, short-side speculation
Strategy: buy put options

In our example using Mr. E, had he concluded from his analysis that the inflationary news was a short-lived phenomenon (rather than pervasively bullish), and that gold prices would probably fall after a brief rally, then his strategy would have been just the opposite, to buy near- or slightly in-the-money put options that had a time period of six to seven months until expiration. In terms of execution and market dynamics, the trade is similar to the purchase of call options. Mr. E purchases his puts, pays for them in full, and pays the commission, thereby establishing his total cost for the trade. Furthermore, his break-even point and return on investment would be dependent upon how much and how fast gold futures prices declined in the subsequent weeks or months.

Situation 3

Market outlook for crude oil: moderately bullish
Trader's goal: limited risk, long-side speculation
Strategy: buy at-the-money calls, sell far-out-of-the-money calls

Concurrent with his guarded outlook for higher gold prices, Mr. E believes that OPEC really plans to honor the proposed production cutbacks agreed upon at the last meeting and that, despite a 60 percent climb in four months, oil prices are headed still higher. Mr. E's goal, however, is to participate on the long side of the crude oil market without subjecting himself to the volatile swings inherent in a market that has rallied $8.00/bbl in a relatively short period of time.

Mr. E decides to employ an option strategy known as a **bull call spread** that enables him to participate in a further advance of $2.00–$3.00/bbl in crude during the next three months. With

July crude trading at \$21.50/bbl, Mr. E purchases five slightly out-of-the-money July \$22.00 crude oil calls at 66 cents (\$660 per call) each, which expire in the second week of June 1992. His total cost (before commissions) is \$3,300. Currently, the July crude oil future—the underlying instrument—is trading at \$21.50/bbl. If this were the extent of his trade—long call options—Mr. E would have to see July crude trade at or above \$22.66 by expiration for him to break even (before commissions), a \$1.16 upmove on top of a four-month climb of \$8.00/bbl. What are the chances of that happening?

Mr. E considers the chances to be pretty good. What bothers him, however, is the time frame. If crude oil prices embark on a corrective period of four weeks, and July prices decline by just 80 cents per barrel, then his call option position will be nearly \$2.00 from break-even, a real long shot and a waste of money (in that the options will expire worthless).

To mitigate against such losses but to participate in a further surge in oil prices (should one occur) in addition to his purchase of call options, Mr. E sells five far-out-of-the-money July \$24.00 calls for 20 cents each. By selling or writing the options, Mr. E receives \$1,000 of premium into his futures account, which helps to offset the cost of the \$22.00 calls (\$3,300). Mr. E has spent \$3,300 for the near-the-money July \$22.00 calls but has received \$1,000 (before commissions) for the sale of the July \$24.00 calls, for a debit spread of \$2,300. In other words, if his bullish analysis is totally wrong, then Mr. E stands to lose only \$2,300 (net of transaction costs) and not the entire investment of \$3,300. Why? As we commented at the outset of Situation 3, Mr. E is moderately bullish about crude oil. If prices move higher within the prescribed time frame (by the second week of June), Mr. E can benefit from a climb all the way up to the \$24.00 level before the far-out-of-the-money calls begin to reflect intrinsic value. In the subsequent six weeks, a rally in July crude oil to \$2,380 would increase the value of his \$22.00 calls significantly because the options now are in the money by \$1.80, and because some additional "premium" charge would be attached to the selling price of the option, given the relatively long period of time remaining until expiration. It would not be unusual for Mr. E's $22.00 crude calls to be worth $2.30 per option ($1.80 of intrinsic value and 50 cents of time premium).

Meanwhile, the price of $24.00 July crude calls that Mr. E sold has climbed from 20 cents each to 57 cents each. He is losing 37 cents, or $370 per option, on the $24.00 calls, but he is making $1.64, or $1,640 per option, on the $22.00 calls. Mr. E has an unrealized profit of $1,270 per call spread. At this point in time, Mr. E has several alternatives:

1. He can hold both sides of the call spread until expiration, at which time he hopes the $22.00 calls will expire well in the money, and the $24.00 calls expire worthless. In this case, Mr. E would realize all the premium from selling the far-out-of-the-money calls, as well as the intrinsic value of the in-the-money calls.

2. He can exit both sides of the spread. Mr. E could sell the $22.00 calls and take the $1,640 profit per long call option and, at the same time, buy back the $24.00 calls and take a loss of $370 on the short call position. In this scenario, Mr. E would realize a profit and have no further exposure to the market.

3. He can buy back the $24.00 calls and hold the $22.00 calls. This strategy would be useful only if Mr. E continues to be very bullish even after a climb of $1.50/bbl, which pretty much satisfied his original analysis. If Mr. E buys back the far-out-of-the-money calls and takes a small loss, then he is speculating with the $22.00 calls. It is conceivable that crude prices could plummet, which would eat away at his unrealized profit of $1,640 per call, compounding the loss he took by covering the far-out-of-the-money calls and generally destroying his overall option spread strategy.

4. He can sell the $22.00 calls and hold the $24.00 calls, which would be the most dangerous strategy. Although, by selling the profitable $22.00 calls, Mr. E would be taking a hefty profit, under this arrangement he would leave himself short the $24.00 calls, hoping that July crude prices did not continue to rise. If, for some unexpected reason, crude prices rocketed past $24.00 after Mr. E relinquished his $22.00 calls, then he would be at unlimited risk—that is, short calls in a powerfully rising market—the worst and most dangerous situation of all and a far cry from his original intent to limit his risk. Keep in mind that by holding a short call option position, Mr. E is obligated contractually to deliver a long futures position to the account of the holder of the long call option position at expiration (if July crude oil is trading at or above $24.00). In this example, the $24 calls closed 50 cents in the money at option expiration. The holder of the long call position then exercises his option, which means Mr. E is required to deliver a long July crude oil futures contract at a price of $24.00. Upon doing so, Mr. E receives in his account a short futures position, which represents the other side of the exercised option transaction. This means that Mr. E finds himself short July crude oil at $24.00 in a rising market (at option expiration, July futures closed at $24.50).

In this example, Mr. E turned a bull call option spread position with defined risk into a futures position with unlimited risk, largely because he mismanaged the trade and removed one leg of the trade before the other, which left him exposed on the short side of the market. To extricate himself from the dangerous situation, Mr. E should have bought back his short option position prior to expiration to avoid the exercise process and the assumption of a dangerous, unprotected short position. Now that the options have been exercised, the most prudent course of action would be for him to buy back his short futures position and to cut his losses immediately.

A **bear call spread** is the inverse of the bull call spread, which enables one to participate in a declining market using a conservative strategy. The mechanics and risk/reward considerations are identical.

Situation 4

Market outlook for sugar: turning bullish
Trader's goal: long-side speculation with "insurance"
Strategy: buy futures; buy at-the-money put

Essentially, this strategy combines options with futures. It treats the option portion of the strategy as a partial insurance policy and protects the long futures trader against a price collapse or a resumption of the bear trend. By doing so, the trader views the option premium he must pay (the cost of the insurance policy) as expendable and hopes, naturally, that his long futures position more than compensates for the deterioration of the long put position.

Let's return to Mr. E, whose technical work signaled a possible intermediate-term bottom in sugar prices in July 1992. Mr. E decides that picking an intermediate-term bottom in sugar—a market that virtually collapsed after the near-vertical climb in prices during the drought-strickened summer of 1988—could be a hazardous exercise and should be treated with particular care, since he intends to establish a long position in a bear-trending market. With that in mind, Mr. E decides to employ a moderately conservative hedge strategy whereby he purchases an at-the-money October 7.50 cent sugar put for 70 points ($905.00) and, at the same time, enters the long side of March futures at 822. Mr. E intends to hold the put option until he gets confirmed intermediate-term buy signals on sugar, at which time he will sell the put (at a relatively small loss) and remain long the futures with a "trailing" stop loss order.

Conversely, if his analysis proves inaccurate, Mr. E intends to stop himself out of the futures if prices move against him by 72 ticks, and remain long the put option, which will help make back some of the loss he incurred on the futures side of the trade.

As it turned out, March sugar prices began climbing shortly after Mr. E established his hedged long futures position. In fact, on July 28, he received an important buy signal in March sugar, which prompted him to sell his put position at 46 ticks ($515.20) for a loss of 24 ticks, or $268.80 (before commissions) on the trade. Meanwhile, his long futures position, which he established at 822, was now trading at 882, or 60 ticks above his entry price. At this point, Mr. E was just long futures, with a trailing stop loss order beneath his entry price, in a market that was building momentum on the upside. His insurance policy against an adverse price move had satisfied its intended purpose.

This strategy is very different from the others discussed because it combines options with futures and employs the option only as a hedge or as protection at an important turning point in the market.

There are many other strategies that can be devised using options and futures together or using options by themselves. We have reviewed only the basic elements of some widely used option strategies.

Certainly, careers and fortunes have been, and will continue to be, made from options analysis and trading. Those who wish to pursue a more sophisticated study of options should consult the Bibliography.

COMMERCIAL INTERESTS AND THE FUTURES MARKET

CHAPTER 24

FUTURES AS A VERSATILE MARKETING MEDIUM

Our glimpse at the history of futures markets (chapter 1) emphasized that futures originated, basically, in response to an urgent and spontaneous need for a hedging medium—a marketing device for laying off unwanted price risks. This particular use of futures markets is examined in detail in this and ensuing chapters. As a prelude to these hedging chapters, however, let us broaden our focus to include the more universal possibilities of futures, for futures exchange has evolved into a highly versatile pricing and marketing medium offering diverse options and opportunities to both trade and industry.

Quite often, the organized futures exchange of our time is remarkably close to being an ideal market. It is a free and open market, standardized according to contract and trading regulations, and providing virtually complete protection against default of either buyer or seller. Typically, the prices registered in futures trading become the preferred barometer, providing, at any given moment, the most accurate value indicator available for every delivery month of the commodity in question.

The science of economics, in its purest sense, is concerned with the logic of choice. And the modern futures market, with its diverse possibilities, is always ready to broaden the range of sensible and potentially profitable choices available to those who deal in commodities and financial futures.

FUTURES AS AN ALTERNATIVE MARKET

Imagine, for example, that you are a copper user contemplating the forward purchase of 100 tons of copper wire or bar. Let us assume that you consider the prevailing price attractive; you are willing to buy now to take advantage of this price, although you fully realize that copper prices could go up or down prior to the delivery date. What are your available options? You might deal in the **cash market** by buying a forward delivery commitment of actual copper from your regular refiner source. Alternatively, you might purchase similar coverage in the **futures market** by buying eight copper futures contracts (each futures contract contains 25,000 pounds of copper).

The economics of choice is relatively clear. If the actual copper offered by your refiner is inexpensive relative to copper futures, or if the refiner is in a position to offer you the benefit of any price reduction prior to the physical delivery of the copper, then you might well buy this actual copper (it is assumed here that facilities exist for the proper storage, handling, and financing of the copper). If, on the other hand, after a careful study of cash/futures price differences, you conclude that futures are a less expensive source of actual copper than the cash market (i.e., forward premiums on futures total less than the costs of carrying actuals, such as interest on capital storage charges, handling fees, etc.), then you may elect to establish **long coverage** (a buying hedge) on the exchange.

In general, taking the latter option (the buying hedge in futures) means that you have temporarily substituted a futures contract for an actuals commitment. This transaction is referred to as a **temporary substitute** because you will, more than likely, ultimately sell out your long futures hedge position, simultaneously replacing it with the requisite actuals copper purchased from your regular supply source. If you are able to effect this "switch" at a time when the price of the actuals position has declined relative to the price of futures (remember, you are seeking to buy the actuals and sell the futures), then your use of futures has proved profitable and advantageous.

It should be noted that hedging does not eliminate risks. Rather, by establishing a position in futures opposite to that committed in the cash market, hedging substitutes a **basis risk** for the ever-present (with net, nonhedged positions) speculative price risk. We may observe that, from the trade hedger's point of view, the basis risk is generally more tenable than is an outright price risk.

The following hypothetical example should clarify this discussion. Let us assume that, on March 1, a manufacturer of electrical motors determines that he will need a particular type and quantity of actual copper for fabrication around July 1. Assume further that as of March 1 his required actual copper is priced at 1.60 cents per pound, while the copper future (appropriate for his hedging purposes) is priced at 1.35 cents per pound. The manufacturer has, on March 1, the following three options available:

1. He can do nothing until July 1, when he will purchase from his regular supplier the required type and quantity of actual copper.
2. He can buy the specific type and quantity of actual copper, carrying it in inventory until July 1, when it will be used in fabrication.
3. He can buy a long hedge in copper futures, maintaining this hedged position until July 1, when he can switch it into actuals.

Option 1 is deemed too risky. Here the manufacturer would have to assume an outright speculative price risk, with the potential loss should the copper market advance in price being far out of proportion to the anticipated profits on the manufactured items.

Option 2 is considered. However, the manufacturer's analysis of the copper market indicates the likelihood of a decrease in the basis, the premium of spot copper over futures. Accordingly, option 3 is selected.

Let us assume that the manufacturer's market forecast proves to be correct and that, as of July 1, the following prices existed:

Spot copper:	1.43 cents per pound
Future copper:	1.27 cents per pound

Thus, in ultimately switching, on July 1, out of the long futures hedge and into the actuals copper position, the manufacturer would have incurred a loss of 8.00 cents per pound; however, the actual copper had declined by 17.00 cents per pound. Thus, option 3 would have, in fact, yielded a profit of 9.00 cents per pound. (In this illustration we overlook commission and other costs).

The selection of copper in the previous example was arbitrary and illustrative. Whatever (exchange-traded) commodity or financial future one's business entails, there exists an ever-present choice: take a market position in actuals or take one in futures. That choice is reversible whenever changing price relationships render the switch advisable. If and when it appears timely to do so, one can readily liquidate a futures commitment and replace it with a position in actuals or, perhaps with somewhat less facility, switch an actuals position into futures.

For the alert trade firm the futures market affords an alternative facility in which to buy or sell. This alternative may be entirely in lieu of a corresponding position in actuals (i.e., you can sell futures short and fulfill the contract by making delivery, or you can buy futures and then take delivery). More typically, a futures contract may be taken as a temporary substitute for a merchandising contract in actuals, either because the futures position offers a margin of price advantage or because an actuals delivery position covering specific requirements may not be immediately available.

IS IT A HEDGE OR A SPECULATION?

The temporary substitute position referred to earlier may be initiated to offset an existing net long or short position in actuals. If so, it is usual to classify the futures transaction as a **hedge.** On the other hand, the futures position may be initiated as a preferred way to establish the price for a particular transaction, whether on a forward purchase or a sale. In that case, the transaction may be essentially speculative, or it may be partially protective and partially speculative.[1]

Thus, in the above copper illustration, the initial purchase, whether it was effected in actuals or in futures, may have been made simply in the expectation of a price advance. Or, it may have been undertaken as a means of establishing the hedger's input cost against a relatively predictable output price. In this second case, we may assume that the copper user confidently expects to sell a copper-containing product at some time in the future, at a given price. On that assumption, he might prudently decide to buy forward-delivery copper against his anticipated future requirements if and when the copper is available at a particular price.

Is this hedging? It perhaps falls short of meeting the formal requirements of a two-sided hedge operation because one side (the forward sale of product) has not yet been consummated. Yet, in essential concept, the copper user is utilizing a kind of "buy-hedge." His purchase has a clearly protective function; he reasonably expects that copper prices (and hence the manufactured cost of the finished product) will rise, and yet, because of competitive pressures within his industry, he cannot raise his selling prices to compensate for the increased costs.

We begin to appreciate the diverse possibilities of futures use available to industry and trade: it helps to price goods, reduce costs, eliminate unwanted price risks, and accept preferred risks in a selected manner. The outline in Table 24.1 may help to suggest the full range of commercial applications of futures.

In a broad economic sense, futures provide trade and industry with an alternative market in which to buy or sell, a market that is as flexible and adaptable as it is dependable. Thus, in addition to providing value as a hedging facility, futures

- Provide a dependable pricing medium to substitute for an ordinary merchandising contract.

---

[1]In reality, hardly any hedge transactions are completely protective or completely speculative. There exists an element of each on every hedge transaction, with the emphasis on each trade dependent on the market approach and viewpoint of the hedger.

TABLE 24.1
Commercial Uses of Futures Markets

Type of Use	Nature of Operation	Example
Hedging	*Buy hedge:* the purchase of futures against a forward sale of actuals.	A silverware manufacturer books orders for his product at a set price for delivery in six months. He may buy an equivalent silver futures position as a hedge, prior to actually purchasing the spot silver from a bullion dealer. When he ultimately does buy his actual silver, he will simultaneously sell out his long futures hedge position.
	Sell hedge: the sale of futures against the ownership of actuals.	The operator of a country grain elevator buys soybeans from local farmers at harvest time. To protect himself against loss due to price decline in the period before he is able to sell these soybeans, the operator hedges by selling (short) Chicago soybean futures. When he ultimately sells his cash soybeans, he will simultaneously cover his short futures position.
Quasi-hedging or price setting	*Buy versus fixed selling price:* Buy futures to cover input requirements for a product whose selling price is fixed or relatively stable.	A bottler who uses sugar as an ingredient in the manufacture of a soft drink buys forward delivery domestic sugar futures when it affords him a reasonable cost-price basis for the sugar.
	Sell versus fixed cost: Sell futures when it affords an attractive selling basis relative to fixed or relatively stable costs.	A farmer who sees that corn prices have risen sharply sells new crop futures short, even before he plants his seed. This assures him an acceptable price basis on the corresponding portion of his forthcoming new crop.
		A lumber manufacturer sells lumber futures short, at wide premiums over actuals. He calculates that the existing selling basis provides a substantial "cushion" against foreseeable changes in his raw material costs.

Fixing the basis	
Buy on the basis: Establish an acceptable premium or discount for the purchase of a specified grade of actuals.	A chocolate manufacturer buys Ghana cocoa for July delivery, at $155 per ton over the July future. When he considers the price opportune, the manufacturer will purchase July futures, thus fixing his cost basis for Ghana cocoa at the price of the July future plus $155 per ton.
Sell on the basis: Establish an acceptable premium or discount for the sale of a specified grade of actuals.	A cocoa dealer sells a manufacturer actual cocoa for July delivery at $200 per ton above the July future, believing that sometime prior to July he will be able to purchase the Ghana cocoa for less than $200 per ton over December.
Adjusting inventory according to a particular view of the market (speculating)	
Expanding coverage.	A foreign sugar user adds to his coverage in world sugar futures on a scale-down basis when the price is below 10 cents per pound.
Reducing coverage.	A chocolate manufacturer who built up his cocoa bean inventory when prices were low sells futures against this inventory when the market advances above $1,500 per ton, in effect reducing his net coverage.

393

- Provide a flexible medium for carrying inventory, which may be used to either expand or reduce coverage.
- Enable a producer to sell his product whenever the price appears sufficiently attractive (including the sale of a product before it actually exists; i.e., a farmer selling new crop grain futures).
- Enable a user to readily cover forward requirements at a price deemed attractive relative to his selling price.
- Provide a speculative medium in which a properly margined individual or firm can readily take market positions or liquidate positions, in accordance with their market views.

CHAPTER 25

HEDGING FOR INSURANCE AND PROFIT

INTRODUCTION TO HEDGING

We have noted that futures are a versatile marketing medium, offering useful pricing options to both trade and industry. Notwithstanding this diverse capability, futures have come into being and continue to exist, to a large extent, to provide hedging facilities for commercial interests. Experience has demonstrated that, as the need for hedging in a particular commodity decreases, activity in that futures market wanes. Thus, government activities that restrict price fluctuations have often resulted in reduced hedging and dwindling futures trading.

A taste of the theory and practice of hedging has been given in earlier chapters (especially in chapter 1 concerning the history of futures markets). From this and other sources, the reader has no doubt formed an impression of the essential nature of hedging. As a simple definition, we may say that *to hedge is to take a position in futures opposite of that which one has assumed in actuals*. This kind of offset transaction reduces or, under ideal circumstances, eliminates the price risks that arise either from being long actuals (carrying unsold inventory) or from being short actuals (making forward sales without already owning the cash commodity).

Starting from this basic concept, the notion has arisen that hedging is undertaken simply with an eye to minimizing risk, to securing a form of insurance against the hazards of price fluctuation. In reality, hedging—as practiced by people in the commodity business—involves considerably more than risk avoidance. The hedge is a spread in which one is simultaneously long and short different cash and futures positions in the same commodity. In a hedged position (as in a spread) one's salient concern is the direction of change in price differences. The question is, will one's position in actuals advance or decline more than the opposite position in futures? *The hedger has not eliminated risk; he has substituted for the extensive and often unpredictable price risk of an outright long or short position the more acceptable risk of variation in price difference between actuals and a given futures position.* As we shall see later in this chapter, it is the hedger's knowledge of price differences in his commodity that makes this hedging difference a sensible businessman's risk, highly preferable to the risk of speculative loss on an outright position. In fact, for many trade and industry people who deal in actual commodities, speculation in the outright long or short sense may be totally avoidable. On the other hand, speculation in price differences may be viewed as a reasonable part of their business operation and an important element in their pursuit of profits.

Our study of hedging in this chapter has two main facets. First, we consider the nature of risk in commodity ownership and the role of hedging in reducing this risk. Second, we focus on the way in which hedging seeks to enhance opportunities for profit in the commodity business.

THE NEED FOR HEDGING

As a first approximation, it is useful to think of hedging simply as risk avoidance. To understand the need for it, one must appreciate the nature of the risks involved in owning or dealing in commodities. One must study the commodity business and the activities of commercial interests that are among its principal participants.

It is, of course, basic that ownership of goods involves a variety of risks. Financial loss may arise from such hazards as fire or flood damage, deterioration, or theft. The businessman, understandably, contracts to transfer as many of his risks as possible to other parties who, for a financial consideration, undertake to assume them. Some forms of risk transference utilized by businessmen include commercial insurance (protection against loss caused by fire, flood, etc.); commercial bonding (protection against loss due to dishonesty on the part of employees); and sale of accounts receivable (protection against loss due to delay or nonpayment of accounts receivable).

There exists one substantial risk, however, for which no commercial insurance is available, the risk of adverse price change. Prices of agricultural and industrial commodities are constantly fluctuating. Those who deal in commodities are subject to losses due to a decline in the price of a commodity owned and not yet sold, or an advance in the price of a commodity sold ahead for future delivery but not yet owned. For this particular kind of risk, the extraordinary "insurance medium" that has evolved is the futures market.

To appreciate its significance, consider the character of the leading commercial interests that use futures. These firms may be country elevator operators (in the grain trade), shippers (whose function is to move the commodity from one terminal to another), terminal warehousemen, exporters, processors, or the very large merchants whose activities span all or most of these functions. Typically, these businesses operate in an extremely competitive environment, where a small price increment might mean the difference between a profitable or an unprofitable piece of business.

Because the commodity business is so highly competitive, commodity prices are usually more volatile than prices in large "follow the leader" manufacturing industries. In the case of industrial raw materials, severe price fluctuations may arise from mine strikes or other shutdowns, or from cyclic variations in demand. In the case of agricultural produce, drastic and largely unpredictable price changes often occur as a result of capricious weather and crop developments. The consequences of such price disturbances may be extremely damaging to large and small dealers alike.

Let us assume, for example, that a grain elevator operator is carrying an inventory position of 30 million bushels of grain (some of the larger grain elevator firms have in excess of 60 million bushels of storage space). This operator, like others in the industry, handles large quantities of grain at relatively low profit margins and, at times, owns substantial inventory both in transit and in store. A price fluctuation of just 1 cent per bushel on a 30 million bushel position would represent a total inventory value change of $300,000; and grain prices invariably fluctuate by more than 1 cent (per bushel) on any given day. The elevator operator must hedge his unsold inventory position—he just could not manage his business assuming such enormous price risks.

The tendency for commodity prices to fluctuate widely is enhanced because supply and demand for most commodities is typically inelastic. That is, price change has little effect on the size of production (especially in the short run) and also relatively little impact on consumption. Accordingly, if supplies are short in any one season, it may take a considerable price advance to curb consumption enough to restore the supply and demand balance.

Another characteristic of the commodity market that presents problems for the trade is the seasonality of crop production and marketing. It would be easier to synchronize purchases and sales, thus minimizing price risks, if production occurred more or less uniformly during the year. But nature wills it otherwise. Typically, marketing pressure is most intense over a period of two or three months; in this brief period millions of bushels of grain, hundreds of thousands of tons of cocoa, and millions of bales of cotton move into the market. While supplies come in bunches, demand is spaced more evenly throughout the year. For the most part, industry buyers are not in the business of storing commodities, and their warehouse space is usually limited. Normally, it is the dealers who will be heavily long actuals; that is, their purchases will far exceed the quantities they are immediately able to sell. In the absence of a hedging medium and in the face of considerable price uncertainties, dealers might be reluctant to buy much more than they could immediately handle. Yet, to not stock up during the harvest run—whether a hedging market exists or not—is to run the risk of being undersupplied later in quantity or quality, and perhaps of forfeiting business to a more enterprising competitor. Besides, profit margins are apt to be very narrow, and the only way a dealer can earn a respectable return on his investment is by conducting large-volume operations. Yet, as we have seen, a large unhedged inventory position exposes the dealer to the possibility of a disastrous price decline.

Dealers may, at other times, be faced with a different kind of price risk. Late in the season, with inventories at relatively low levels and with both domestic and foreign buyers placing orders for new crop deliveries, the volume of goods sold ahead will, at times, exceed stocks on hand, leaving the dealers short actuals. They have sold for forward shipment at stipulated prices more of the commodity than they actually own. In this case, dealers now run the risk of a price rise between the time of their forward sale and the time that they "cover" this sale through a corresponding purchase. The dealer can, at his option, cover his short actuals position by buying spot or shipment positions in the cash market, or by going long futures contracts. The choice he makes—whether to purchase actuals or "hedge buy" in futures—will depend on the relationship between cash and futures prices (other factors being equal, he will select the least costly of the two alternatives).

Whether the merchant is long or short actuals, it is clear that he would have no need of futures if he could immediately consummate an equal and opposite cash transaction on acceptable terms. He must often wait before he can attractively sell his long or cover his short actuals position; in this interim, it is prudent for him to avoid price risk by offsetting his position in futures. *In nearly all cases, hedging is the use of a futures contract as a temporary substitute for a merchandising contract.*

In addition to reducing or eliminating speculative risks due to price fluctuations, hedging offers another major advantage to the trade firm—it facilitates large-scale financing of inventory positions. Financial institutions will lend a greater percentage of inventory value if the goods have been properly hedged. In fact, some banks require that inventory be hedged as a condition of their providing major financing. In addition, the ability to finance inventory enables a trade firm to utilize its own funds for other constructive operating and capital purposes.

We have examined how price risk comes into being. Let us consider now how it can be reduced or eliminated through hedging in each of the two types of situations discussed—a situation in which one owns unsold actuals and a situation in which actuals have been sold ahead but cover against this sale has not been purchased.

TYPES OF HEDGE TRANSACTIONS

There are two basic types of hedge transactions: (1) the **selling hedge,** where *the hedger is short futures* versus a long cash (actuals) position, and (2) the **buying hedge,** where *the hedger is long futures* versus a short cash (actuals) position.

The Selling Hedge

Assume that a dealer in Chicago has bought 50,000 bushels of corn from an elevator operator. There are no offsetting sales on his books for this particular purchase, so the dealer is long the cash commodity (he owns the physical inventory). If the market declines between the time of this purchase and the time he negotiates a sale, the dealer stands to lose considerably more than the profit he anticipated from a successful transaction. To eliminate this price risk (or, at least, to greatly reduce it) the dealer sells, as a hedge, an equivalent amount of corn futures on the Chicago Board of Trade. It should be noted that when the dealer sells the futures contracts, he does not necessarily contemplate meeting the contractual obligation by delivering the actual grain. Typically, he regards futures not as a delivery outlet but as a marketing medium as well as a means of protection in the event of an adverse price change. His premise is that any price decline in his actuals will be reflected commensurately in his futures position.[1] Once he finds a customer for his grain and consummates a sale, he will buy back his short futures position.

---

[1]This simplified illustration depicts the hedger as hoping merely to "break even" on the entire transaction. In reality, however, the hedger seeks to profit on his hedge through a favorable change in price differences.

TABLE 25.1
The Selling Hedge

	Cash Transactions	Futures Transactions
September 15	Buys 50,000 bushels corn @ 2.36	Sells 50,000 bushels May corn @ 2.57
January 15	Sells 50,000 bushels corn @ 2.31	Buys 50,000 bushels May corn @ 2.51
	Loss: $.05 per bushel	Profit: $.06 per bushel
Result: a gross profit of $.01 per bushel before commissions and costs.		

Having sold his actuals, he no longer needs the protection of a short hedge position in futures.

The sequence of purchases and sales is summarized in Table 25.1.

In the table we have assumed that, after the dealer had bought and hedged his corn, the market declined. As a consequence, he lost 5 cents per bushel on the actuals portion of the hedge transaction. However, the short futures position brought him a 6-cents-per-bushel profit, offsetting the loss in the cash account. Had the market instead advanced in price, the profit on the long cash position would have equaled or, hopefully, exceeded the resultant loss on the short futures position.

The Buying Hedge

Let us now consider the risk that prices may rise after a dealer has made forward sales commitments but before he owns the actual commodity. The dealer, in this case, is said to be **short actuals.** To protect himself from the risk of a price rise, he will initiate a buy-hedge in futures. That is, he will go long futures versus his short actuals position. If cash prices advance, he will be obliged to pay more for the actual commodity than the price at which he sold to his customer. But the loss incurred on this cash account should be offset by a gain in the long futures position, which presumably will also have advanced in price. Let us note again that, although the futures contract, if held to maturity, calls for and indeed compels accepting delivery of the

TABLE 25.2
The Buying Hedge

	Cash Transactions	Futures Transactions
February 15	Sells 30,000 troy ounces silver bullion @ $6.00	Buys six contracts September silver @ 6.37¢
July 15	Buys 30,000 troy ounces silver bullion @ $6.31	Sells six contracts September silver @ 6.68¢
	Loss: 31¢ per ounce	*Profit:* 31¢ per ounce
	Result: break even, before commissions and costs	

actual commodity, *a hedge purchase of futures is rarely undertaken with an eye to accepting delivery.* The purpose, rather, is to obtain protection in the event cash prices advance. Ordinarily, once the dealer has purchased the cash commodity needed to fill his forward sales contract, he will liquidate his long futures position.

An example of the buying hedge is given in Table 25.2. In this example, the market advanced 31 cents per ounce after the dealer committed himself to ship silver. However, this loss was offset by an equal profit on the long futures position.

PRICE VARIATIONS BETWEEN THE CASH AND FUTURES MARKETS: THE BASIS

So far, our hedging examples have been based on the simplifying assumption that cash and futures prices move together in parallel fashion. In reality, significant, although usually modest, price variations do occur between these two markets. To a hedger, these price variations are of crucial importance. In fact, *hedging is typically undertaken to profitably exploit changes in cash versus futures price differences, rather than to simply ensure protection against an overall price change.*

The price spread between a cash commodity and a related future is called the **basis** (or cash basis). The basis expresses the premium or discount (stated in points or cents) at which a cash commodity of specified grade and location sells versus a particular future. For example, it might be said that the basis for No. 2 yellow soybeans at country terminals in southern Illinois is 5 cents under November futures. This simply means that No. 2 yellow cash soybeans at this location are selling at a 5-cent discount to the November future.

From the standpoint of the hedger, the basis is probably the most often used and most important technical term in the entire commodity lexicon.

Merchandising Profits and Risks and the Basis

Hedging eliminates major speculative risks stemming from price changes. However, hedging introduces another, perhaps more complex, risk—the possibility that cash (actuals) prices will not move in parallel with futures prices. This risk is referred to as the **basis risk.**

Suppose, for example, that in June a dealer buys a particular grade of cash soybeans at a point in central Illinois (a major producing region) for $5.47 per bushel. The July future is then selling at $5.53 in Chicago. The dealer decides to hedge his cash purchase by selling July futures. Let us assume the market subsequently declines, with the cash price dropping to $5.32 and the futures price to $5.43. At that point, the short futures position shows a gain of 10 cents; however, the cash position shows a loss of 15 cents. If the dealer were to sell his cash beans and lift his hedge (cover his short futures position), the combined result would be a 5-cent loss. This is a considerably smaller loss than he would have suffered had he bought beans and not hedged. Expressed in basis terms, we would say that the hedge was put on when the basis was 6 cents under and taken off when the basis was 11 cents under. In practice, if such a worsening of the basis had occurred, the dealer might have deferred selling his cash beans until the basis had improved. Or, he might have considered tendering his cash beans against his futures position when it became spot.

Let us see what this tells us about the source of merchant profits. Dealing in commodities must seem a provocatively difficult business. To take a large, unhedged cash position is obviously dangerous; however, it is quite difficult to synchronize cash purchases and sales, let alone to mesh them profitably. Buying cash commodities and selling futures as a hedge provides protection against major speculative price losses. However, hedging can seldom be done at a wide enough spread to assure profitable delivery on futures. Short of such delivery, there is an ever-present basis risk, the risk of the basis moving adversely between the time the hedge is put on and the time it is lifted.

Of course, it is also possible to profit on basis changes, and this understandably is the objective of the hedger. Suppose that in the previous example, when the cash price dropped to $5.32, futures had declined to $5.33. Again, there would be a 15-cent loss in the cash position, but in this case the short position in futures would have yielded a 20-cent profit. The combined result of the cash/futures transactions—the initiating and lifting of the hedge—would be a gross profit of 5 cents per bushel. Again, expressed in basis terms, we would say the hedge was initiated when the basis was 6 cents under (as in the previous example) and taken off when the basis was 1 cent under.

As we observed at the outset of this discussion, in any highly competitive undertaking there can be no profit without a commensurate risk. In order to operate effectively, the responsible merchant must reduce or eliminate the risks associated with outright price speculation. He can then direct his efforts toward analyzing and projecting basis trends, where his specialized knowledge of cash market conditions provides him with a considerable market advantage. Commodity trade firms are, in reality, speculating at all times, but on the basis, not on outright trading. Basis risks are unhedgeable and constitute an acceptable and, in fact, desirable element in cash market operations.

The Nature and Causes of Basis Changes

To further understand the tactics of the dealer-hedger, we must learn more about the nature and causes of basis variations.

Because most futures contracts provide for physical delivery, the ultimate convergence of price with that of the cash commodity, on contract terms, is assured. However, a futures market does enjoy a certain independence from the influence of cash prices even in its own terminal market. This independence is conferred upon it because physical delivery is not permitted until the last month of each contract's life. Prior to this date, futures may be much more responsive than cash to the changing expectations of speculative elements. Sometimes, speculative buying will strengthen futures relative to cash; at other times, speculative selling will cause futures to weaken relative to cash. One way or another, speculative activity contributes to the mutability of cash versus futures price spreads. Apart from speculative influences, the basis reflects a combination of three related factors: location, grade, and time element. A futures market is tied to a specific locality (a particular terminal market). The prices of future deliveries will therefore differ from location to location, depending on shipping cost differences and variations in supply and demand between terminals. The price of wheat in the East or at the Gulf will be at a premium to Chicago and, hence, to Chicago futures prices, because of the freight differential between these regions and Chicago. The precise amount of this premium, however, will vary depending upon the particular supply and demand conditions. For example, if demand from interior mills in the central states is strong while European export interest is relatively weak, the premium will be smaller than if the reverse were true.

The basis also expresses the price difference between the so-called basis grade (the grade or grades deliverable against the futures contract at contract price) and other grades of the same commodity. Price differences between grades reflect their relative abundance or scarcity. For example, a short wheat crop may produce an unusually high percentage of high-protein wheat. Although wheat prices may rise sharply, the premium of the high-protein to the so-called ordinary wheat (deliverable against futures at par) may narrow.

Finally, the basis will tend to reflect the time discount or premium of the cash price to a specific future. In a carrying-charge market, the cash price in the deliverable position will be at a discount to all but an about-to-expire futures delivery; in an inverted market the cash price will be at a premium to all but the about-to-expire future. In the first instance, the basis will be quoted as the number of points under a particular future, in the latter as the number of points over a future.

Consider the example on p. 403. The dealer bought cash beans at a location in central Illinois in June at $5.47 when the nearby July future was selling at $5.53. We would say, in this case, that the basis for No. 2 yellow soybeans was 6 cents under July. Since these cash soybeans represent the basis grade, the cash discount reflects one of two influences, or both, location and time discount. It is impossible to separate the two influences and to determine how much of the discount is attributable to one and how much to the other. All one can say confidently is that the cash price will not appreciably decline below a level that fully reflects both freight and carrying costs. If it did, spreading interests would find it profitable to buy cash beans and sell futures short. They would ultimately liquidate the position by delivering the cash soybeans against their short futures position. Because of competition for such opportunities, it is rare that the price discount of cash to futures is ever sufficient to permit a so-called perfect (riskless) hedge. There are invariably some large commercial operators who are willing to go long the basis (buy actuals versus sell futures) when futures are selling at less than a full carrying and freight premium to cash.

Anticipating Changes in the Basis

The most reliable and predictable change in the basis results from the gradual disappearance of the time premium (in a carrying-charge market) or discount (in an inverse market) of a future relative to the cash commodity, as the future approaches expiration. The dealer who purchases grain in Chicago (in a deliverable position) and sells futures at carrying-charge premiums is assured that he will earn carrying charges for his efforts as the basis gradually strengthens (cash advances in price relative to futures).

We have emphasized that speculative activity may have an important influence on basis variations, particularly in a high open interest situation. In a declining market, liquidation of long positions can, for a time, cause the futures market to assume an identity of its own, declining relative to the cash price, thus causing the basis to strengthen. The opposite situation may arise if speculative trading activity turns overwhelmingly bullish. In this situation, speculative buying may strengthen futures relative to cash, thus weakening the basis.

Strength may develop in an out-of-position locality relative to the terminal location where the futures market is located. For example, there have been occasions when corn prices in Pennsylvania, New York, and other eastern areas have been strong (based largely on export demand), while prices in the Midwest were relatively weak. If a cash commodity gains strength vis-à-vis futures in such so-called out-of-position locations, then cash prices in these locations will rise relative to futures (i.e., the eastern cash basis will strengthen). The limit of this price disparity will be the transportation differential. When it becomes feasible to profitably ship grain from the futures terminal to the out-of-position location, the basis will stabilize.

As general conditions change from abundance to scarcity and vice versa, the price relationship between cash and futures (as well as between different futures) will change. When there are large supplies on hand, the price structure will tend toward carrying charges and the extent of carrying charges will depend on the degree of abundance. If and when spot supplies tighten, buyers must look harder for immediate coverage, and nearbys begin to attract buying support, which they had previously lacked. If cash demand really becomes aggressive, the cash price may even move to premiums over nearby futures. Gradually, the entire futures market may become inverted, with discounts on each successive future. Under these conditions, the basis, by definition, is strengthening, though more for some grades than for others. Conversely, when scarcity is relieved, nearby premiums will gradually disappear. For domestic crops, a return to normalcy generally means a return to a situation in which adequate supplies are carried throughout the year. Carrying charges will then tend to reappear, and the cash basis for all grades will weaken, with the basis for some grades reacting more than for others.

Basis Trading

In the previous example, a cash commodity was bought and a futures contract sold, establishing a short hedge. This transaction may be referred to as being **long the basis** (i.e., long cash versus short futures). Such a hedge will be initiated if the dealer expects the basis to strengthen (i.e., he expects the cash price to gain relative to futures). If the cash price had been initially at a discount to futures, a strengthening basis means that the discount will narrow (as was the case in the previous example) or disappear. If, on the other hand, the cash price had been at a premium to futures, a strengthening basis implies that the cash premium will increase.

In the long hedge (as noted previously), a dealer sells cash forward and hedges this (short) actuals position by buying futures. This long hedge entails being **short the basis,** that is, short actuals versus long futures. For the hedger to profit, futures must strengthen relative to cash, which means that the basis must weaken.

One predictive generalization concerning basis changes is that cash and futures prices must ultimately converge, on contract terms, as each future approaches expiration. Therefore, if cash is priced at a discount to futures, the basis must ultimately strengthen (on contract terms). Conversely, with cash selling at premiums, the basis must ultimately weaken (again, on contract terms). The term *ultimately,* however, should be emphasized because—even in deliverable position—it is temporarily possible for cash and futures prices to diverge.

At locations remote from the futures terminal—the so-called out-of-position areas—there may be no predictable means of forecasting basis changes, even to the expiration of a future. For example, the cash basis of wheat in New York may widen or narrow rather independently of the cash basis of Chicago wheat, within the limits established by time and cost of shipping cash wheat between the two markets.

In his role as hedger, the dealer is not primarily concerned with the absolute level of prices or with the overall trend of the market. His vital interest is in relative price movements or, more specifically, the strength or weakness of cash prices relative to futures. Above all, the hedger thinks in basis terms. If he expects cash prices at a specific location to strengthen relative to a given future, he will go long the basis by buying the cash commodity and putting on a short hedge. If, on the other hand, he foresees a weakening in the basis for some grade in a particular location (i.e., he anticipates a cash decline relative to futures), he may go short the basis by selling cash ahead and buying futures.

When properly executed, hedging offers the trade firm the flexibility of several operating alternatives. The astute hedger enjoys the option of deciding when and how to close out all or just a portion of his hedge position. Depending upon relative prices and conditions underlying both cash and futures, he may deal with his sell hedge in the following ways:

1. Delivering his long actuals position against his short futures position.
2. Selling his actuals in the cash market and simultaneously covering his short futures position.
3. Rolling over his hedge position; that is, while holding his long actuals position, he covers his short futures position, maintaining the hedge by simultaneously selling a different future.

Perhaps the first decision the trade firm must make is how to deal with an existing inventory position in actuals, whether to hedge, in which market, and in which future. The following observations may be useful:

The Premium Market

Here the selling hedge is generally most effective. The higher the premiums on successive futures, the closer they will be to full carrying costs. As futures premiums approach full carrying costs, it becomes progressively more profitable for a trade firm to buy actuals for its inventory position and hedge-sell in futures. Under such circumstances, the hedger stands to gain on the inevitable strengthening of the basis as each future approaches expiration.

The Inverted Market

In an inverted market, the buying hedge is generally most effective. Depending on the extent of price inversion, dealers will find it profitable to sell their actuals position in the cash market and hedge-buy in futures to replenish their inventory. While it may not be feasible for a trade firm to completely deplete its inventory, the astute dealer will maintain stocks at the absolute minimum level, depending on his buy-hedges as the source of needed actuals.

Which Market?

In the event that more than one futures market exists for a given commodity (i.e., sugar and cocoa are traded both in New York and London, and wheat is traded in Chicago, Minneapolis, and Kansas City), the hedger must determine in which futures market to hedge. In general, he will find it advantageous to hedge in that futures market which most closely corresponds to his particular grade and type of actuals.

Which Future?

The hedger must also decide in which futures month to place his hedges. This determination will depend, to a great extent, on the purpose of the hedge. If it is a carrying-cost hedge, he will select that deferred future offering him the highest relative premium. Here, the dealer's intimate knowledge of carrying-cost structure will prove invaluable. If, on the other hand, the hedge is intended as a short-term operational hedge, he may find it advantageous to place his hedges in a nearby future, as it probably bears the closest price relationship to his actuals, offering the maximum risk protection.

Lifting Hedges

When lifting hedges, if an actuals position is sold to a trade firm, which itself must hedge in futures, the (short) hedge position may be simultaneously transferred. This type of exchange of futures is quite common in the commodity trade. The exchange may be effected by the floor broker outside of the trading ring, hence the name "ex-pit transaction."

Clearly, hedging is not the elementary, mechanical process portrayed in our simple risk-avoidance model or in certain popular introductions to hedging. There, the dealer is seen as one who takes a position in actuals and immediately eliminates his risks by hedging. In practice, the dealer's emphasis is twofold: (1) to substitute a basis risk for a speculative price risk and (2) to profit through a correct analysis and projection of basis changes and the timely execution of these hedge transactions.

HEDGING: PITFALLS AND PROPRIETIES

In general, hedging is a subtle and sophisticated operation that requires considerable expertise. Properly managed, hedging can help to protect profits or, indeed, make it possible for farmers, merchants, or processors to operate profitably. It is equally true, of course, that mismanaged hedging can undermine an otherwise sound business. Thus, a few words of caution may be in order.

It is especially important that a hedge be a hedge, and not a cover for a speculative position. In some instances, when markets have seemed intriguing, individual businessmen have allowed themselves to dress speculative intentions in the reassuring cloak of the hedge. An oft-quoted example is the so-called Texas hedge. This refers to the case in which some cattlemen—inspired by a period of consistent price advance—got into the habit of buying futures regularly, as a kind of cover in anticipation of a price rise. Since they already owned the actual cattle, they had, in effect, "doubled up" on the long side by buying futures. To be sure, their gains would multiply if prices moved up, but so would their losses, given any marked price decline. This speculative trading approach is plainly inconsistent with sound, prudent business management. In short, speculation should be undertaken on its own merits and not obscured under the veil of hedging.

The route to successful hedging has been outlined, to a large extent, in this chapter. The hedger's guiding star is a thorough knowledge of the price relationship between a particular commodity and its related futures market. The road map can handily be a chart showing changes in this price basis or simply picturing simultaneous variations in the relevant cash and futures markets.

HEDGING RECAP

General Observations

- Futures markets exist largely as a medium to facilitate hedging. If and when the need for hedging in a particular commodity wanes, trading in that futures market is likely to wane, too.
- The hedge is an offset transaction. It is a long or short position in futures equal and opposite to that assumed in actuals.
- In general, hedging involves the temporary use of a futures position as a substitute for a merchandising contract. Although the futures contract provides for ultimate delivery or acceptance of actuals, hedge transactions in futures are not necessarily undertaken with the objective of making or accepting delivery. In most cases, the merchant will "even up" his actuals position in the cash market, simultaneously closing out his futures position with an offsetting futures trade.
- The basis is probably the most important aspect of hedging to the trade firm. It can be defined as the price spread between a specific cash commodity and a related future.

Specific Observations

Especially for the newly initiated, it may be helpful to keep several precepts in mind as a starting point for successful hedging:

- Above all, know your own basis situation thoroughly. Keep full records of price relationships between the cash grades in which you deal and the various delivery positions in futures.

- Aided by your basis records, establish high and low ranges in which action may be warranted—either to initiate hedge positions or to unwind established positions.
- Take advantage of any consistent seasonal basis variations.
- The sell-hedge is most effective in a premium market. The buy-hedge is most effective in an inverse market.
- The very best hedge is, of course, one in which a profit is "locked in." For example, at times it has been possible to buy cash silver and hedge-sell futures at premiums that more than pay full carrying charges.
- Avoid hedging when you are not clear concerning the basis, and when the contract traded in futures is not related in a fairly determinate way to the respective actuals. Shun the Texas hedge, of course.
- Finally, remember that there is no substitute for an intimate knowledge of both the commodity in question and the factors that ultimately govern changing cash versus futures price relationships.

CHAPTER 26

PROGRAM TRADING WITH STOCK INDEX FUTURES

Joanne M. Hill
Vice President
Goldman Sachs
Dawn Diorio
Vice President
Paine Webber, Inc.

The year 1982 marked two important financial developments—the beginning of a major bull market in equities and the successful introduction of futures contracts on stock indices. The equity futures contract based on the Value Line stock index began trading on February 24, 1982, at the Kansas City Board of Trade. Soon to follow, in April of that year, were futures contracts on the Standard & Poor's 500 index, traded at the Chicago Mercantile Exchange. Futures contracts on the NYSE composite index commenced trading in September of 1983 at the New York Futures Exchange, a unit of the NYSE. Futures on the Major Market Index (MMI) began trading in July of 1984 at the Chicago Board of Trade. This future is based on an index similar in construction to the Dow Jones Industrial Average.

The S&P 500 futures contract traded at the Chicago Mercantile Exchange has been by far the most successful of the three equity contracts, with volume running four to five times that of the NYSE and MMI futures and greatly in excess of that of the Value Line futures. All four index futures represent unique index portfolios in terms of coverage and weighting, although the S&P 500 and the NYSE index futures exhibit a great deal of similarity in their price movement. This chapter is devoted to a presentation of the most important features of stock index futures and the indices on which they are based. An overview of the uses and users of stock index futures markets is also included.

The development of stock index futures markets has been particularly significant because it represents an integration of equity and futures trading. The development has been very painful at times, though, as participants in both markets have seen changes occur as index futures have grown in use. This integration has important implications for both branches of the investment business. Brokerage firms and investment banks have been quick to incorporate equity futures into their market operations. Along with the floor traders at the exchange, they are the most active participants in the markets, using index futures to hedge their inventories, create customized equity index products, and conduct arbitrage with their own investment capital. They have helped to bring to the stock index futures markets the liquidity and pricing efficiency that is so essential to the success of a contract. Now that the stock index futures market has proven itself as a permanent part of the investment scene, other financial institutions and individuals involved in equity management—such as pension funds, money managers, insurance companies, and private investors—have developed applications of stock index futures that fit into their own investment strategies and objectives. Many existing and potential applications of stock index futures are covered in this chapter.

STOCK INDICES: THE UNDERLYING PORTFOLIO

Composition

Stock market indices are designed to reflect overall movements in well-defined portfolios of equity securities. The performance of an equity index is important because it represents the performance of a broadly diversified stock portfolio and gives insight into the returns of a typical stock that meets the features of the index. The performance of indices is also important as a benchmark against which the results of alternative investment strategies can be judged. To be viewed as successful, an investment strategy must demonstrate risk-adjusted performance in excess of a market index over time. Investors who wish to perform in line with the equity market as a whole can try to structure portfolios equivalent to stock indices, usually at a lower cost than managing a portfolio of stocks individually selected for their profit potential. Most of the large mutual fund companies now offer open-end funds managed to track widely followed stock indices. These funds have lower management fees than other actively managed mutual fund products.

Stock indices differ from one another with respect to the range of stocks covered, stock weighting, and index computation. Among the most widely followed indices are the Dow Jones Industrial Average in the United States and the Nikkei 225 in Japan. The Dow consists of the stocks of only 30 large U.S. companies, weighted by their relative prices and added together (a divisor is used to incorporate the impact of stock splits). The Nikkei 225 is another price-weighted index reflecting a long history of movement in the Japanese stock market.

The range of stocks covered in different indices can vary considerably. As already mentioned, the Dow Jones Industrial Average contains only 30 stocks; the Value Line and NYSE indices contain over 1,500 different issues. Indices differ in composition because of the need to measure the price movements of segments of the overall equity market. These segments range from narrow to broad. Even though returns on indices are often highly correlated over time, relative index performance can vary sharply over short periods, such as a month or a quarter. Table 26.1 and Figure 26.1 show the performance of selected equity indices in recent years and through September 30, 1991.

The weighting of stocks in an index is a very important factor in determining index value. Most stock indices are either equal-weighted or market-value-weighted. The most common weighting scheme is market value weighting, used in both the S&P 500 and NYSE indices. The prices of each issue included are weighted by the number of shares outstanding divided by the aggregate number of shares outstanding of all stocks in the index. This means that the changes in the index reflect changes

TABLE 26.1
Performance of Global Stock Indices

	1991*	1990	1989
S&P 500	17.46%	−6.56%	27.25%
NYSE	18.20%	−7.44%	24.79%
S&P 100	17.26%	−5.74%	24.82%
MMI	16.30%	−0.20%	29.70%
DJIA	14.55%	−4.34%	26.96%
Value Line	31.80%	−16.76%	18.18%
Nikkei 225	0.28%	−38.72%	29.04%
FT-SE 100	22.31%	−11.52%	35.11%
DAX 30	14.93%	−21.90%	34.83%
CAC 40	23.93%	−24.03%	27.14%

*Through September 30.

FIGURE 26.1
Performance of Selected Stock Market Indices (January 1976–August 1991)

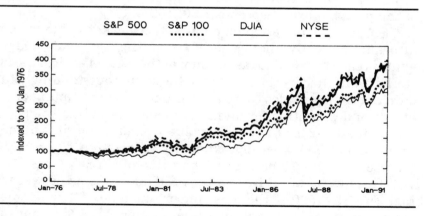

in the aggregate equity value of the stocks included in that index. In addition, stock splits do not affect the value of market-value-weighted indices. Also, mergers and divestitures should not have an impact as long as all of the old and new companies are included before and after the corporate restructuring.

Finally, the method of averaging influences the index value. Most market-value-weighted indices represent arithmetic averages. The Major Market Index and the Dow Jones Industrial Average are arithmetic averages of stock prices (adjusted for stock splits). Another averaging technique is the use of a geometric mean or the square root of the product of the individual stock prices, returns, or value relatives. This method of index construction was used originally for the Value Line index.

The S&P 500 is the key index in terms of institutional investment management. Introduced in the 1930s, this index is broad in its coverage and weights stocks by aggregate market value. It includes most of the largest industrial service, utility, and transportation companies in the United States. Percentage increases in the index represent equivalent percentage increases in the aggregate market value of the stocks included. Companies such as IBM, AT&T, Exxon, and General Motors have large weights in the index compared with small capitalization companies. Table 26.2 shows the 20 largest stocks in the S&P 500 in terms of weighting. Note the impact of market weighting in that these 20 issues, which represent only 4 percent of the stocks covered, had a combined weight of 31 percent of the portfolio as of September 30, 1991.

Since stock prices change daily, the market value weights also automatically change over time. The aggregate market value is easy to calculate as the sum of the price of each of the 500 stocks multiplied by the number of the shares outstanding. Standard & Poor's provides current information on the timing of dividends and weighting for all the stocks in the index. The NYSE composite index is also market-value-weighted, but it is broader than the S&P 500, with approximately 1,700 issues. The S&P 500 represents about 71 percent of the value of NYSE stocks.

The success of futures on the S&P 500 index is not surprising. The S&P 500 is the most important index for investment managers of institutional investment funds. The Dow Jones Industrial Average is the index given more attention by the media. However, because of the narrow coverage of the Dow Jones Industrial Average of only 30 blue-chip companies, this index is too narrow to serve as an indicator of the performance of the overall equity market.

The Value Line index is based on an equal-weighted return average of the approximately 1,500 stocks covered by the Value

TABLE 26.2

Top 20 Stocks in S&P 500 by Capitalization (as of August 31, 1991)

Rank	Ticker	Name	Price	% Weight
1	XON	Exxon Corp.	$ 58.25	2.74
2	MO	Philip Morris Co. Inc.	74.13	2.59
3	GE	General Electric Co.	74.88	2.46
4	WMT	Walmart Stores, Inc.	50.63	2.17
5	IBM	International Business Machines	96.88	2.09
6	MRK	Merck & Co., Inc.	126.88	1.85
7	BMY	Bristol Myers-Squibb	87.00	1.72
8	KO	Coca Cola Co.	65.75	1.66
9	RD	Royal Dutch Pete Co.	81.13	1.64
10	T	American Telephone & Telegraph Co.	39.00	1.62
11	DD	Du Pont E. I. De Nemours	48.25	1.22
12	JNJ	Johnson & Johnson	92.88	1.17
13	PG	Procter & Gamble Co.	83.50	1.09
14	MOB	Mobil Corp.	68.38	1.03
15	AN	Amoco Corp.	52.88	1.00
16	GTE	GTE Corp.	30.00	0.99
17	PEP	Pepsico Inc.	32.38	0.97
18	CHV	Chevron Corp.	71.75	0.95
19	LLY	Lilly Eli & Co.	84.00	0.93
20	BLS	Bellsouth Corp.	48.88	0.88
		Combined weight		**30.77**

Line Investment Services. Compared with the other indices on which futures are traded, the equal weighting of the Value Line index results in a relatively larger weighting for the returns of smaller capitalization companies. In March 1988, the method of calculating the index was changed from a geometric to an arithmetic average. The change in the averaging technique was made for a number of reasons, the primary one being the mathematical nature of a geometric average to always underperform an arithmetic average.

The Major Market is a price-weighted index of 20 blue-chip stocks. It was first constructed as a basis for an index option that was introduced in September 1983 by the American Stock Exchange. This exchange entered an agreement with the Chicago Board of Trade to permit the CBOT to use the index as a basis for

TABLE 26.3
Dow Jones Industrial Average (as of September 30, 1991)

Rank	Ticker	Dow Jones	% Weight
1	ALD	Allied Signal Inc.	2.15
2	AA	Aluminum Co. America	3.79
3	AXP	American Express	1.52
4	T	American Telephone & Telegraph	2.22
5	BS	Bethlehem Steel Co.	1.00
6	BA	Boeing Co.	3.01
7	CAT	Caterpillar Tractors	2.65
8	CHV	Chevron Corp.	4.36
9	KO	Coca Cola Co.	3.82
10	DIS	Disney Walt Products	6.76
11	DD	Du Pont E. I. De Nemours	2.68
12	EK	Eastman Kodak Co.	2.53
13	XON	Exxon Corp.	3.53
14	GE	General Electric Co.	4.11
15	GM	General Motors Corp.	2.22
16	GT	Goodyear Tire & Rubber	2.60
17	IBM	International Business Machines	6.14
18	IP	International Paper	4.04
19	MCD	McDonalds Corp.	2.08
20	MRK	Merck & Co. Inc.	7.72
21	MMM	Minn. Mining & Manufacturing Co.	5.34
22	JPM	Morgan J. P. & Co. Inc.	3.52
23	MO	Philip Morris Cos. Inc.	4.28
24	PG	Procter & Gamble	5.03
25	S	Sears Roebuck & Co.	2.28
26	TX	Texaco Inc.	3.73
27	UK	Union Carbide Corp.	1.20
28	UTX	United Technologies	2.67
29	WX	Westinghouse Electric	1.32
30	Z	Woolworth Corp.	1.71

a financial futures contract. The index is constructed by adding the prices of the component stocks and dividing the sum by a number that reflects stock splits, deletions, and additions. Seventeen of the 20 stocks in the MMI are also in the Dow Jones Industrial Average. The total capitalization of the two indices based on prices as of the end of July 1991 is very close, implying that the average stock in the MMI is actually larger than that of the average in the Dow Jones. Because the index is so narrowly based, arbitrageurs can easily and cheaply construct cash market positions of the stocks included.

Major Market Index (as of September 30, 1991)

Ticker	MMI*	% Weight
AXP	American Express	1.99
T	American Telephone & Telegraph	2.92
CHV	Chevron Corp.	5.71
KO	Coca Cola Co.	5.01
DOW	**Dow Chemical Co.**	**4.06**
DD	Du Pont E. I. De Nemours	3.51
EK	Eastman Kodak Co.	3.31
XON	Exxon Corp.	4.63
GE	General Electric Co.	5.39
GM	General Motors Corp.	2.91
IBM	International Business Machines	8.06
IP	International Paper	5.30
JNJ	**Johnson & Johnson**	**6.87**
MCD	McDonalds Corp.	2.72
MRK	Merck & Co. Inc.	10.12
MMM	Minn. Mining & Manufacturing	7.01
MOB	**Mobil Corp.**	**5.30**
MO	Philip Morris Cos. Inc.	5.61
PG	Procter & Gamble	6.60
S	Sears Roebuck & Co.	2.99

*MMI stocks that are boldfaced are not in the Dow.

The stocks included in the MMI and DJIA as of September 1991 are listed in Table 26.3. The correlations between the indices on which futures are traded is of importance in seeing the extent to which they move together over time. As with most broad-based equity indices, the daily percentage price changes of these particular indices are highly correlated with one another, as shown in Table 26.4. The degree to which they move together can be quite variable within short periods. It is not uncommon for indices like the DJIA and the NYSE to show differences in return of 1 percent or more in any given month.

TABLE 26.4

Correlation Table of Selected Stock Indices (January 1986 to October 1991 [based on daily % changes])

	S&P 500	*NYSE*	*Dow*	*S&P 100*	*MMI*
S&P 500					
NYSE	0.997				
Dow	0.976	0.973			
S&P 100	0.985	0.977	0.977		
MMI	0.959	0.951	0.981	0.973	
Value Line	0.877	0.901	0.847	0.836	0.807

Foreign Stock Indices

Futures contracts are also available on a broad range of indices of stocks traded on foreign exchanges. The most actively traded of these foreign index futures cover Japanese stocks—the Nikkei 225 and Topix indices—as well as British, French, and German issues. The latter include the FT-SE 100 (U.K.), CAC40 (France), and DAX 30 (Germany). Index futures are also available on Canadian stocks (TSE 35), Australian stocks (All Ordinaries index), and Hong Kong issues (Hang Seng index). In general, these indices are weighted by price (Nikkei 225) or market capitalization similar to the indices of the U.S. market and contain the most actively traded stocks on the local exchange.

An equity index future traded on a non-U.S. exchange must receive approval from the CFTC before a futures brokerage firm can accept an order from a U.S. investor for transacting in that index. Such approval is given in a so-called no-action letter by the CFTC. As of September 1991, the index futures traded on foreign exchanges that are open to trading to U.S. investors include the FT-SE 100 in the U.K., the TSE 35 in Canada, the Nikkei 225 contract on the Singapore exchange (SIMEX), and the All Ordinaries in Australia. Access to the Nikkei 225 and Topix Japanese stock indices can also be obtained via futures contracts traded in Chicago at the Mercantile Exchange and the Board of Trade. A summary of the specifications of foreign index futures contracts is provided in the next section of this chapter.

Index-Based Investing and Program Trading

Stock index futures have been controversial because they have played a "chicken and egg" role in terms of the growth of index-based investing and program trading over the last 10 years. During this period, both large and small investors have become aware of the benefits of passively managed portfolios constructed to track a broad spectrum of the equity marketplace. Although indexed portfolios do not provide the high returns of portfolios selected to find the top-performing stocks in the marketplace, they are much cheaper and easier to manage and do not bear the risk of selecting stocks that end up significantly underperforming the equity market averages.

Pension funds and other institutional investors often judge the performance of their money managers relative to a benchmark index. The returns of this benchmark index should represent returns of an unmanaged or naive investment strategy. This strategy can best be applied to those stocks in the equity market that have sufficient volume to facilitate trading by holders of large pools of funds. If a "managed" stock portfolio does not consistently perform over long periods above such an index (on a risk-adjusted basis), one may choose the alternative of directly investing the funds in a portfolio closely resembling an index. This type of portfolio is often called an **index fund** and is designed to mirror the performance of an index. Holdings are rebalanced periodically to mirror index weights. As of 1991, approximately $250 billion was invested in U.S. index funds. Most of the large mutual fund providers offer an index fund portfolio.

INDEX FUTURES CONTRACTS AND TRADING OVERVIEW

Futures on stock indices represent a contractual obligation to have sufficient funds on deposit at delivery to buy or sell the stocks in the index at a predetermined price. This price is the value of the futures contract when the futures position was initiated. The value of stock futures contracts is a multiple of their quoted price. The contract value for most index futures is 500 times the quoted price.

A sample of price quotations for the futures and their underlying indices is shown in Table 26.5. The minimum trading increment is .05 point or $25 (.05 × 500). Unlike most other futures contracts, stock index futures settle in cash rather than in delivery of the stocks in the index underlying the futures contract. Cash settlement is carried out by transferring funds into or out of the contract holder's margin account in an amount based on the settlement price of the contract. Cash settlement is used because of the logistical problems of buying the component stocks in the index in exactly the right amounts to carry out physical delivery.

Stock index futures have a specific termination time and date at which the final settlement price is set and the futures cease trading. For S&P 500 futures, the final index settlement value is based on the opening prices of stock on the expiration day. For other U.S. futures contracts, the time is 4 P.M. (EST) of the last trading day of the contract, and the final settlement price is therefore tied to the closing value of the index on the last trading day. All of the stock index futures (except the MMI futures) terminate in the March, June, September, December cycle.

TABLE 26.5
Price Quotations on Futures (S&P 500 Index)

FUTURES

S&P 500 INDEX (CME) 500 times index

	Open	High	Low	Settle	Chg	High	Low	Open Interest
Dec	386.20	387.45	383.60	385.30	− 1.00	401.50	316.50	142,989
Mr92	388.50	389.65	386.00	387.60	− .95	404.00	374.70	4,650
June	391.65	391.65	388.30	389.70	− 1.05	407.00	379.00	773

Est vol 45,623; vol Thur 51,482; open int 148,445, +1,291.
Indx prelim High 386.13; Low 382.97; Close 384.19 −.88

NIKKEI 225 Stock Average (CME)−$5 times NSA

	Open	High	Low	Settle	Chg	High	Low	Open Interest
Dec	25310.	25320.	25175.	25185.	− 55.0	28900.	22380.	11,539
Mr92	25775.	25775.	25670.	25670.	− 60.0	26725.	23000.	322

Est vol 1,005; vol Thur 572; open int 11,861, +128.
The index: High 24973.58; Low 24819.86; Close 24906.43 − 42.83

NYSE COMPOSITE INDEX (NYFE) 500 times index

	Open	High	Low	Settle	Chg	High	Low	Open Interest
Dec	213.05	213.65	211.55	212.45	− .60	219.70	175.50	4,382
Mr92	213.50	214.35	212.95	213.45	− .65	220.35	207.60	763
June	214.60	214.60	214.60	214.60	− .65	219.00	208.90	166

Est vol 5,148; vol Thur 4,826; open int 5,321, −75.
The index: High 212.71; Low 211.24; Close 211.82 −.50

MAJOR MKT INDEX (CBT) $500 times index

	Open	High	Low	Settle	Chg	High	Low	Open Interest
Nov	320.00	321.50	317.65	319.15	− 1.35	326.05	315.20	3,349
Dec	320.55	321.80	318.40	319.70	− 1.35	326.90	315.75	219

Est vol 1,500; vol Thur 1,121; open int 3,584, +168.
The index: High 321.49; Low 318.22; Close 319.25 −1.09

Cash settlement can be carried out easily because the losses or gains on the futures position have been marked-to-market daily in the variation margin account. This process ensures that funds exist at settlement in the variation margin account in an amount representing the difference between the price paid for the future and the settlement price. If the settlement price is above the price at which the futures contract was established, funds that have been marked-to-market by the futures sellers will be credited to those with long futures positions. If the settlement price is below the purchase price, funds in the marked-to-market account are credited to those who have sold futures contracts at prices in excess of the settlement price.

For example, assume a December 1991 S&P 500 futures contract was purchased in October 1991 at a price of 391.65. Assume that on the last trading day, the price of the future is 393.65. The profit of 2 points, or $1,000 (500 × 2), would be the balance in the marked-to-market account. These funds would have been made available from debits to the variation margin accounts of investors who had sold this contract at prices below 393.65 or investors who had bought at prices above 391.65.

The four U.S. stock index futures contracts currently available cover four different broad market indices and are each traded on different futures exchanges. Futures on the S&P 500 index are the most actively traded equity futures contracts, with daily volume in the range of 50,000–60,000 contracts (as of June 1991) representing roughly $9–10 billion in underlying market value. This can be compared with the $6.2 billion in value of a 180-million-share day on the NYSE, assuming an average share price of $33.50. S&P 500 futures are traded on the floor of the Chicago Mercantile Exchange. Initial hedge margin on this contract is $9,000, or 4.6 percent of contract value at a futures price of 390 and underlying contract value of $190,000.

The NYSE index futures contract calls for delivery of a market-weighted portfolio of all stocks listed on the NYSE. At the end of September 1991, the December NYSE futures were selling for around 214.50 points, or a value of $107,250. Thus, one NYSE futures contract typically represents just under 55 percent of the value of an S&P 500 futures contract. The initial hedge margin deposit is accordingly smaller than that of the

S&P 500 futures—$4,000 versus $9,000. At a contract value of $107,250, this margin represents 4 percent of contract value. The NYSE futures contract is traded at the New York Futures Exchange (NYFE) and is the only stock futures contract traded in direct physical and organizational proximity to a stock exchange.

Value Line index futures are traded at the Kansas City Board of Trade. These futures were the first equity futures contracts to trade, but their volume was quickly overshadowed by the S&P 500 and NYSE futures when they were introduced. At a price of 320 points, one contract represents $160,000 of underlying equity value. The initial hedge margin is $5,000, or 3 percent of contract value. Also, the equal weighting of stocks in the index makes the underlying index and the derivative futures contract more sensitive to the movement of small capitalization stocks.

The Major Market Index futures trade at levels of volume and open interest roughly equal to the NYSE futures. The MMI future has been smaller in size than the other index futures, with a contract value of 250 times the level of the index, or approximately $157,000, as of the end of June 1991. Recently, however, its multiplier has been doubled and the index value cut in half to a level that is more in line with other indices. It is also unique in that it commences trading at 9:15 A.M. New York time, 15 minutes before the opening of the equity market. This provides an early signal of the potential opening level of the Dow Jones Industrial Average.

The MMI futures also have different delivery dates and trading units than do the other stock index futures. The contract months include the next three consecutive months, as well as the next month representing the end of a quarterly cycle. For example, at the end of March 1991, the MMI futures had April, May, June, and September delivery contracts trading. This brings their delivery dates in line with the expiration dates of the option contract on the MMI. The units of trading are .05 of an index point, or $25. The initial hedge margin is $7,500, or roughly 4.5 percent of the underlying share value. Contract specifications of U.S. and selected foreign index futures are shown in Tables 26.6, 26.7, and 26.8.

TABLE 26.6
U.S. Stock Index Futures Contract Specifications

Contract	S&P 500	MMI	NYSE	Value Line
Exchange	CME	CBOT	NYFE	KCBT
Start Date	April 1982	August 1985	May 1982	February 1982
Underlying Index	S&P 500	Major Market Index	NYSE Composite	Value Line
Local Trading Time	8:30 - 3:15	8:15 - 3:15	9:30 - 4:15	8:30 - 3:15
Construction	Mkt Cap-500 stocks	Price Wgt-20 stocks	Mkt Cap-1726 stock	Equal-1653 stocks
Months Traded	Mar, Jun, Sep, Dec	Monthly cycle	Mar, Jun, Sep, Dec	Mar, Jun, Sep, Dec
Contract Size	Index * $500	Index * $500	Index * $500	Index * $500
Minimum Price Move	.05 index points or $25	.05 index points of $25	.05 index points or $25	.05 index points or $25
Daily Price Limit	20 points	15 pts above; 10 & 15 pts below	18 points	30 points
Position Limit	5,000 contracts	8,000 contracts	10,000 fut & opts	5,000 contracts
Initial Margin	Spec Init $22,000 Maintenance $9000 Hedge I&M $9,000	Spec Init $21,000 Maintenance $7500 Hedge I&M $7,500	Spec Init $9,000 Maintenance $4000 Hedge I&M $4,000	Spec Init $7,000 Maintenance $5000 Hedge I&M $5,000
Last Trading Day	Thur prior to the 3rd Fri of contract month	3rd Friday of contract month	Thur prior to the 3rd Fri of contract mont	3rd Friday of contract month
Settlement	Cash settled based on opening prices of the component stocks in the index on the 3rd Friday of contract month.	Cash settled at the closing value of XMI on last trading day	Cash settled	Cash settled at the close of trading on last trading day
Symbol	SP	BC	YX	KV
Avg Daily Volume	51,634	3,619	6,448	250

From an institutional perspective, a synthetic index portfolio can be created with a long position in an index future combined with the holding of a money market instrument. The gains and losses on the futures position should mimic those of an index portfolio. Futures pay no dividends; however, the net of the interest earned on the money market portfolio and the dividends foregone by holding the future are reflected in the futures price. The total returns of the two positions (index portfolio and futures plus money market position) are equivalent when futures trade at their "fair value." As noted earlier, in the instances when futures trade cheap, the returns of the futures

TABLE 26.7
Selected International Stock Index Futures Contract Specifications

	FT-SE 100	CAC 40	DAX 30	All Ordinaries	Hang Seng	Toronto 35
Exchange	LIFFE	MATIF	DTB	Sydney	Hong Kong	Toronto
Start Date	Nov 1985	Jun 1988	Nov 1990	Mar 1988	Mar 1988	Jan 1988
Underlying Index	FT-SE 100	CAC 40 Index	DAX 30 Index	All Ordinaries	Hang Seng	Toronto 35
Local Trading Time	8:35-4:10	10:00 - 5:00	10:30 - 3:00	9:30-12:30, 2:00-4:10	10:00-12:30, 2:30-3:30	9:15-4:15
Trading Method	Open Outcry	Open Outcry	Computerized	Open Outcry	Open Outcry	Open Outcry
Average Daily Volume	6-7,000 contracts	8-9,000 contracts	4-5,000 contracts	1-2,000 contracts	2-3,000 contracts	200-300 contracts
Construction	Cap-Weighted (100 Stocks)	Cap-Weighted (40 Stocks)	Cap-Weighted (30 Stocks)	Cap-Weighted (307 Stocks)	Cap-Weighted (33 Stocks)	Cap-Weighted (35 Stocks)
Months Traded	Mar, Jun Sep, Dec	3 spot mos plus 1 qrtly exp mo	Mar, Jun, Sep, Dec	Mar, Jun, Sep, Dec	Mar, Jun Sep, Dec	Spot month, 3 concurrent mos
Contract Size	Index*L25	Index * FRF200	DM100 per point	Index * A$100	Index*HK$50	Index*C$500
Minimum Price Move	0.05 = L12.50	0.1 = FRF20	0.5 = DM50	0.1 = A$10	1 = HK$50	0.02 = C$10
Daily Price Limit	None	120 points	None	None	300 points	9 points
Initial Margin Requirements	L4,000	FRF30,000	DM13,500	A$20,000	HK$25,000	C$9,000
Last Trading Day	*Last business day of contract month 10:10-10:30	Last business day of delivery month	Third Thursday of delivery month	Last business day of delivery month	Business day prior to last day of month	Third Thursday of delivery month
Settlement	First business day after last trading day (Cash)	Final index value at 4:00 on LTD for cash settlement in 2 days	Third Friday of delivery month (Cash)	2nd business day following last day of trading (Cash)	Business day following last trading day (Cash)	Opening index value on 3rd Fri of delivery month (Cash)
Symbol	Reuters LIJA FFI:chain .FTSE	Reuters CACF FCH:chain .FCHI	Reuters FDX:chain	Reuters YALL YIX:chain .AORD	Reuters HKFI HSI:chain .HSNI	Telerate: 3151 TXF:chain .TSE35
Eligibility for U.S. Investors	Approved	Pending Review	Not Approved	Approved	Pending Review	Approved

* Users of the FT-SE 100 futures should note that the June 1992 delivery month and all subsequent months, will expire on the 3rd Friday of the contract month.

TABLE 26.8

Specifications of Stock Index Futures Contracts on Japanese Indices

	Nikkei 225	Osaka 50	TOPIX	Osaka Nikkei	CME Nikkei
Exchange	SIMEX	Osaka Stock	Tokyo Stock	Osaka Stock	Chicago Mercantile
Start Date	Sep 1986	Oct 1988	Oct 1988	Oct 1988	Sep 1989
Underlying Index	Nikkei 225	Osaka 50	Tokyo Stock Price	Nikkei 225	Nikkei 225
Local Trading Time	8:00-2:15	9:00-11:00; 1:00-3:15	9:00-11:15; 1:00-3:15	Same as TOPIX	8:00-3:15
Trading Method	Open Outcry	Open Outcry	Computerized	Computer Assisted Individual Auction	Open Outcry
Average Daily Volume	2-3,000 contracts	2-3 contracts	7-8,000 contracts	90-100,000 contracts	1-2,000 contracts
Construction	Price Weighted (225 Stocks)	Price Weighted (50 Stocks)	Cap-Weighted (1,117 Stocks)	Price Weighted (225 Stocks)	Price Weighted
Months Traded	Spot Month, Mar, Jun, Sep, Dec	Mar, Jun, Sep, Dec	Mar, Jun, Sep, Dec	Mar, Jun. Sep, Dec	Mar, Jun. Sep, Dec
Contract Size	Index*Y500	Index * Y50,000	Index * Y10,000	Index * Y1,000	Index * $5
Minimum Price Move	5 points	0.5Y	1 point	10 points or Y10,000	5 points or $25
Daily Price Limit	Approx 10% of previous settlement	Approx 3% of previous settlement	Approx 3% of previous settlement	Approx 3% of previous settlement	0-20,000 = 1000 pts 20,005-30,000 = 1500 pts
Initial Margin Requirements	Y1,000,000	9% of contract value (Y6 million minimum)	9% of contract value (Y6 million minimum)	9% of contract value (Y6 million minimum)	Spec: I = $18000 M = $12000 Hedge I&M = $12,000
Last Trading	3rd Wednesday of delivery month	6 business days prior to settlement	3 business days prior to settlement	1st business day prior to 2nd Fri. of contract month	1st business day prior to 2nd Fri. of contract month
Settlement	3rd Wed of delivery month (CASH)	15th day of delivery month (cash or 50 stocks)	2nd Thursday of delivery month (CASH)	4th business day following last trading day (CASH)	Opening quote on the 2nd Friday of contract month
Symbol	Reuters NSKE	Reuters OQOA	Reuters TPXA; JTi:chain .TOPX	Reuters OQOG JNi:chain .NIKI	Reuters NK:chain
Eligibility for U.S. Investors	Approved	Pending Review	Pending Review	Pending Review	Approved

position and money market portfolio should be in excess of what could be earned on a portfolio consisting of the underlying stocks.

On a typical day, the volume of index value traded in U.S. futures markets is about 174 percent of the dollar volume of the NYSE, or $6.2 billion versus $10.75 billion in index futures for the first six months of 1991. Figure 26.2 shows the dollar amount of NYSE volume versus total index futures volume from 1982 through June 1991. Figure 26.3 breaks down the total index futures volume amount by contract. The S&P 500 futures contract represents approximately 88 percent of total futures volume traded as of June 1991. Since program trades are only 10 percent of NYSE volume, the index futures markets see a flow of "synthetic" portfolio trades some 12 times that of the NYSE in a trading session. An S&P 500 futures contract represents $165,000 of stock value at an S&P 500 level of 345 with a commission less than 10 percent of the stock commission on a comparable-size portfolio trade executed on SuperDOT (an express order-entry system). Therefore, in terms of both cost and liquidity, the index futures markets have a considerable com-

FIGURE 26.2
NYSE versus Total Index Futures Dollar Volume Daily Average (1982–June 1991)

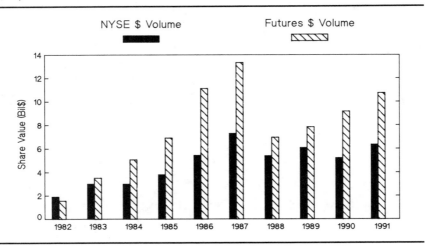

FIGURE 26.3
Index Futures Dollar Volume (by Contract, 1982–June 1991)

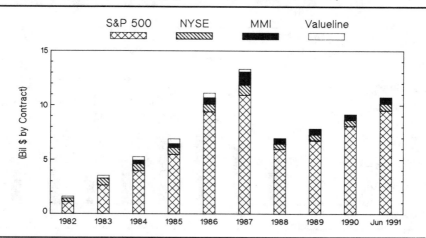

petitive edge as a means of adjusting overall exposure to the equity market.

Futures trading is conducted via open outcry in a trading arena of competitive market makers who each own their own seat. Between one-third and one-half of the volume is represented by intraday trading by these market makers, a feature very different from the typical stock exchange. Open interest reflects positions open at the end of any trading session and thus is a measure of institutional and retail customer use as opposed to trade facilitation by market makers. The chart in Figure 26.4 shows the average open interest and volume in S&P 500 futures over the last several years. The growth in open interest shows the increasing use of index futures as a surrogate for long and short S&P 500 portfolio positions.

For asset allocation adjustments and initiation of short-term synthetic positions in the equity market, futures offer the ease of execution with a single trade instead of trades in a list of stocks, much lower execution costs, and leverage when desired. Futures do have some operational disadvantages, however. Because they have a regulatory structure separate from equities, futures trading requires that a separate account be opened and funds associated with futures trading be segregated from those

FIGURE 26.4
S&P 500 Futures Open Interest versus Volume (Average, 1982–May 1991)

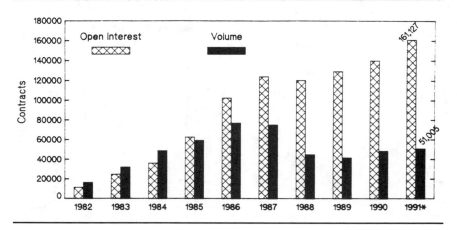

used for stock executions. In addition, futures gains are passed daily from losers to winners, placing more cash flow requirements on futures traders than on stock traders for whom gains and losses are unrealized until the position is closed. Futures also represent only standardized baskets and expire periodically. As a contract approaches expiration, the portfolio manager must decide to switch back into stocks (or cash) when the position expires or roll forward to the next contract. The pricing of the roll or calendar spread can work for or against the trader, and it introduces some risk and reward opportunity to the synthetic index trade with futures.

INDEX FUTURES PRICING, TRADING COSTS, AND INDEX ARBITRAGE

As with other futures or forward contracts, the prices at which stock index futures trade are based first and foremost on the cost and benefits of acquiring a similar position in the underlying cash market. In the case of an index future, this position could be achieved by buying an index portfolio on an equity exchange. Let us look at the case where an investor purchases the equivalent of 500 units of an S&P 500 index portfolio directly, expecting to hold the position for a period of three months. This investor would pay the dollar amount at which the index is trading and receive the dividend earned until expiration. The trading cost of index would include commission and market impact.

$$\text{Index} \times 500 = \text{I}$$

$$\text{Dividend Yield} \times \text{Index} \times 500 = \text{DI}$$

$$\text{Trading Cost} = \text{TI}$$

On the other hand, an investor gaining similar exposure in the S&P 500 via futures would have the amount of the index investment times 500 available to invest in 90-day Treasury bills, some of which could be posted as initial margin; but this investor would not receive any dividends.

$$\text{T-bill Yield} \times \text{Index} \times 500 = \text{YI}$$

$$\text{Trading Cost} = \text{TF}$$

Therefore, the amount one would be willing to contract for an index future would be equal to the amount paid for a comparable stock market position plus any net benefits from holding the futures contract, such as interest or savings in trading cost in excess of dividend income.

$$\text{Index Futures Value} = \underset{(1)}{\text{I}} + \underset{(2)}{(\text{YI} - \text{DI})} + \underset{(3)}{(\text{TI} - \text{TF})}$$

In this equation, the first term (1) represents the value of the underlying index; the second term (2) represents the net carry or difference between interest income and dividend yield on the dollar amount of the index; and the third term (3) represents the difference in trading cost of the index versus the future. Because this last term varies among investors depending upon the size of the transaction, it is often omitted when discussing the "fair value" of a futures contract. It should be noted that different investors also have different benchmark yields on money market instruments when assessing the fair value of an index future because not all of them invest the amount in excess of the initial margin deposit in Treasury bills; some use Eurodollar CDs, money market funds, or commercial paper, which have higher yields than Treasury bills but are of only slightly greater risk. Investors using these alternative cash-equivalent investments would assign a slightly higher value or price to an index future.

One popular index futures strategy is the so-called **index arbitrage.** This is a method for capitalizing on short-term situations in which the above pricing formula does not hold; that is, futures can be bought at prices below their fair value or sold at prices above fair value. These situations occur primarily because the speed with which the index futures market adjusts to new information is often faster than that of the underlying stock markets, or because different supply and demand situations occur in one market versus another. For example, a technically motivated trader who follows trends may choose to buy on a particular day in the futures market, creating upward pressure on the index futures price there. At the same time, a value-driven fundamental trader may be selling a large portfolio of blue-chip stocks on the NYSE, creating supply pressure there. It is very possible that the index futures price can, in this circumstance, move above the value indicated by the equation above. The index arbitrageur would then step in to buy an index portfolio of stock on the NYSE, creating demand there to meet some of the supply, and sell the "overvalued" index futures on the futures exchange, creating supply there to help meet the demand from the technically based trader. Through this arbitrage process, index futures prices would fall relative to the stock prices making up the index, bringing the index and futures values back into line.

In general, index arbitrage takes only a short time, minutes or hours at the longest, to make both the stock and futures markets adequately reflect information and supply and demand conditions. Figure 26.5 shows the mispricing of the S&P 500 future in S&P index points over the period June 1983 through June 1991 using closing prices. The thick solid lines indicating buy and sell levels reflect the net trading costs of conducting arbitrage. When the mispricing moves outside these bands, arbitrage returns cover their execution costs. Since 1988, the incidences of persistent mispricing have been few and very short-lived. This has helped the index futures markets to reestablish

FIGURE 26.5
T-Bill Mispricing of S&P 500 Nearby Futures Basis (June 1983–June 1991)

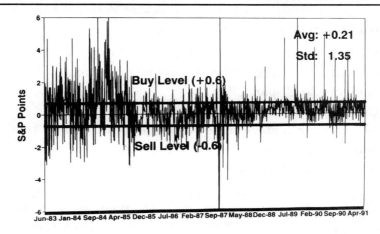

	Futures Volume ($ Bil)					
	S&P 500	**NYSE**	**MMI**	**Valueline**	**Total Fut**	**NYSE**
Avg 1985-89	7.71	0.67	0.61	0.24	9.24	5.61
1990	8.09	0.56	0.49	0.02	9.16	5.22
Jan - Jun 1991	9.52	0.65	0.54	0.04	10.75	6.17

	Futures Volume as a Percent of Total				Total Futures as a
	S&P 500	**NYSE**	**MMI**	**Valueline**	**% of NYSE Volume**
Avg 1985-89	83.4%	7.3%	6.6%	2.6%	164.6%
1990	88.3%	6.2%	5.4%	0.2%	175.5%
Jan - Jun 1991	88.6%	6.0%	5.0%	0.3%	174.2%

the volume and open interest that they lost during the crash, attracting investors who use the market to implement a broad-based index exposure (long or short) at a "fair" price given the underlying index.

INDEX FUTURES STRATEGIES

A wide range of strategies is possible with stock index futures. The groups to whom the market offers the most attractive possibilities are investors and financial institutions with a broad capital base and with exposure to equity securities, either as investors, dealers, or underwriters. Some of the applications of stock index futures are listed below and described in greater detail in the remainder of this chapter. These include

Shifting asset mixes or equity market exposure
Creating synthetic index fund/equitizing cash
Hedging stock portfolios
Capitalizing on stock selection
Investing in a stock index with reduced currency risk
Enhancing returns on cash equivalents
Speculating on stock market moves

Basically, stock index futures provide a means of adjusting, acquiring, or eliminating exposure to the fluctuations in value of the overall stock market. The futures can be an extremely flexible risk management tool because of their liquidity and low transaction costs. Futures can also serve as short-term substitutes for position in the stock index itself. Stock index futures strategies may be preferable to other means of adjusting equity exposure because of cheaper transaction costs, attractive prices available on the futures contract, ease of adjusting positions (liquidity), the difficulty of moving funds quickly and on a large scale into and out of particular stocks, or for leveraging a stock portfolio. In some situations, investing "passively" in equities via stock index funds or index futures may be more cost-effective than purchasing the expertise to acquire particular undervalued stocks.

Shifting Asset Mixes or Equity Market Exposure

At the overall fund, or macro, level, portfolio trading and index derivatives are most widely used for adjusting the asset mix to changing performance expectations for asset classes or country exposures. For example, a shift from bonds to stocks can be accomplished with Treasury-bond and stock index futures or with portfolio trades, thereby increasing the amount held in stock index funds, and selling a portion of a bond index fund or the liquid Treasury securities. Another common application would be the use of a portfolio trade involving the sale of a stock basket constructed to replicate a Japanese market index such as the Nikkei 225 and the purchase of a U.K. stock index portfolio. Index trading is also used to maintain target asset weights as relative changes in asset class values cause aggregate stock and bond holdings to drift away from target levels.

The choice between using stock portfolio trading or derivative securities for accomplishing asset class shifts depends on several factors. Tactical or active asset allocation, which attempts to exploit short-term pricing opportunities across markets, is most cost-effectively implemented with futures. Strategic asset shifts, which are expected to be in place for a year or more, often make sense to implement in the underlying market with a portfolio trade, thus avoiding the cost of rollovers of futures positions every quarter. Futures have the advantage of enabling an *overlay* process for the asset mix management to be used in conjunction with the stock, bond, and cash management. Each process can then be handled by a different party, performance measurement can be separated, and the more expensive stock trading can be confined to turnover motivated by stock-specific considerations.

Creating Synthetic Index Fund Portfolios or Equitizing Cash

Futures can be used to create a portfolio or a portion of a portfolio that has cash flow characteristics similar to those of an index fund portfolio. Individual or institutional investors may wish to hold a portfolio that provides returns very similar to those of a particular market index. These investors may find it expensive to acquire a portfolio as broadly diversified as the NYSE or S&P 500, but may wish to derive the diversification advantages of such a portfolio. They may, in addition, have temporary cash positions that they need to quickly invest in the equity market. For example, mutual funds may receive dividends or cash inflows that they want to put to work quickly in a diversified equity position.

Managing index fund portfolios involves considerable oversight in terms of maintaining the correct weights as prices change and reinvesting any dividends that are received. Index futures can provide a means of cheaper access to such a portfolio. The commissions associated with stock index futures are only a fraction of those for acquiring the stock themselves.

A synthetic index strategy involves purchasing stock index futures with a contract value equal to the desired value of the index fund or dollars to be invested in equities. Funds not used for margin purposes are invested in very low-risk, liquid, short-term securities such as Treasury bills or Eurodollars. The portfolio manager can also be selective in choosing a time to purchase the stock index futures. When the futures are undervalued compared with the cash value of the index and dividends on the index, the manager can possibly lock in a return exceeding the index for the period to expiration of the future. This incremental return is based on the percentage that the contract is undervalued when it is purchased, the percentage (if any) it is overvalued when sold, and the commission savings on the futures relative to acquiring the index itself. If the portfolio manager wishes to switch the futures position into specific stocks, this can be accomplished easily by selling the futures and buying the stocks in the exchange or OTC market.

Hedging Stock Portfolios

The distinction between using stock futures to adjust equity exposure and hedging stock market risk with stock futures is not clear-cut. Hedging has been used to describe a defensive strategy in which one wishes to insulate a portfolio (or position) from adverse market movements. An adjustment of equity exposure, alternatively, could be motivated by a desire to capitalize on a positive market movement, to insulate oneself from stock market declines, or to modify the **beta,** or market risk, of a portfolio.

The objective of hedging with stock index futures would be to reduce or eliminate the sensitivity of an equity portfolio to changes in the value of the underlying index. The sale of stock futures against a stock portfolio creates a hedged position with returns similar to what would be earned on short-term, fixed-income securities. Returns of a fully hedged position may differ from those of a short-term, risk-free security. The returns of the portfolio of stock can differ from those of the index and the futures. If a stock index futures hedge is executed at futures prices above their theoretical value, the hedger might actually be able to earn a return in excess of what could be earned on a cash-equivalent security. With the sale of futures, the hedger will have to meet variation margin requirements during the time the short futures position is open.

Consider a portfolio manager who has an equity position with a beta of 1.3 (i.e., the portfolio is expected to increase or decrease in value by 1.3 percent for each 1 percent market move). This manager anticipates a near-term flat or downward trend in the market. One possible strategy would be to reduce the beta by switching funds into cash-equivalent securities, such as Treasury bills, or into low-beta stocks. Both of these options would constitute major reallocation decisions within the portfolio, would be expensive in terms of transaction costs to implement, and would be cumbersome to reverse should the manager be wrong in his or her outlook.

A much more flexible option would be to sell stock index futures contracts. Stock index futures would be sold representing a market value equal to the market value of the portfolio times its beta. To the extent that the futures contracts move in tandem with the market index, the profits on the short position in futures should offset losses in the stocks in the portfolio associated with the overall market move.

In a particular hedging application often called portfolio insurance, an investor sells a specific quantity of futures, in part based on a desired floor value for his or her portfolio. As the index declines closer to the floor, the amount of the hedge is increased by selling more futures contracts.

Stock index futures are also used by brokers and dealers in hedging their stock inventories. These institutions hold positions in stocks for short periods as a result of their trading operations. Depending on their customers' activities, they may be net long or net short stock issues at any given point in time. Their portfolios, in fact, include changes similar to those occurring in the portfolios of money management firms and individuals. When institutions are buying stocks in large quantities, brokers and dealers find themselves with net short positions in equities.

The ability to hedge market-making activity should ultimately benefit investors who would be more inclined to carry inventories that they can easily hedge and be able to charge their customers a lower-risk premium for their trading services. The stock futures market is a very handy tool for these trading firms, because the liquidity of the market is usually sufficient to absorb the very large trades necessary to hedge their positions.

Capitalizing on Stock Selection

Certain investors may feel that they can profit most by purchasing stocks that are undervalued with respect to company-specific characteristics rather than making a judgment call on the overall stock market. These investors may not wish to subject their portfolio to the risk of overall stock market movements. The strategy being employed has the objective of profiting from favorable movements in prices of the stocks selected because of events uniquely favorable to these stocks.

As discussed, short positions in stock futures added to a portfolio will reduce or eliminate the market-related component of the portfolio's return and risk, and leave the return and risk component associated with the company-specific features of the stocks in the portfolio. Thus, with futures, an investor can more easily separate the overall market- and nonmarket-related returns and risk of a portfolio, thereby adjusting the portfolio's exposure to these different types of risk as appropriate. **Alpha** is a term used to describe returns above those consistent with the market risk (beta) exposure of a portfolio of stocks. A fully hedged portfolio would be managed to maximize the alpha return for a given level of stock-specific or nonmarket risk. Investment managers who wish to specialize in stock selection and sell this service can do so more easily with stock index futures.

Investing in a Stock Index with Reduced Currency Risk

Another application of stock index futures is uniquely suited to investors outside of the United States who are attracted to the U.S. stock market but who wish to insulate themselves from the risk of changes in the value of the dollar relative to their own currency. Consider the case of a Swiss investor who thinks that U.S. stocks are cheap but the dollar overvalued. If stocks appreciate but the dollar falls, capital gains from investment in U.S. equities may be reduced by currency losses.

This investor may wish to assume a position in the U.S. stock market with only a small dollar risk exposure by purchasing stock index futures contracts instead of U.S. stocks. Less than 10 percent of the value of the stock index futures would be required for margin purposes in the form of Treasury bills. The rest can be deposited in a Swiss bank account earning the Swiss short-term interest rate and be protected from exchange rate shifts. In a sense, this strategy is a close substitute for an S&P 500 index fund denominated in Swiss francs. A variation of this strategy would be to purchase the U.S. stocks via S&P 500 or NYSE futures and then deposit the contract value not needed for margin in the currency that the investor thinks is most undervalued. This gives an international investor the opportunity to profit on currency selection and market selection simultaneously. Foreign index futures could be used by U.S. investors in a similar fashion. For example, an investor wishing to buy Japanese stocks but avoid the yen/dollar exchange risk could do so by buying a Nikkei 225 future at the CME and depositing the contract value (in excess of initial margin) in a dollar-based money market fund.

Enhancing Returns on Cash Equivalents

Another application of stock index futures is in the cash portion of the portfolio where stock portfolios hedged with stock index futures are held when they offer returns in excess of benchmark money market rates. Stock index futures at times become rich or overvalued such that an arbitrage trade between the equity and futures market can improve the returns on the cash segment of the portfolio. This strategy is most suitable to investors who already have some of their funds in indexed equity portfolios. A position in a stock index hedged with futures should provide the short-term interest rate in effect until expiration of the futures contract, taking into account the specific transaction and financing costs of the underlying stock index or bond position, as noted above. Short-term supply and demand pressures specific to one market (futures or stock/bond) can send intermarket pricing relationships to levels where implementation of a hedged position can improve returns.

Speculating on Stock Market Moves

A large amount of stock index futures trading is done by investors on the floor (locals) and off the floor who are not necessarily using the futures market as a cheap and liquid alternative to the cash equity market. They are buying and selling futures as a leverage equity trading vehicle based on an opinion about the direction of stock prices and the relative value of futures in the short run. Some of these traders are called **sentiment traders,** and all are called **speculators.** Their presence in the market is critical to providing liquidity.

Stock index futures provide a means to participate in the movements of the equity market as a whole using a high degree of leverage. Since a deposit of approximately 10 percent is required to purchase or sell a stock futures contract, one can take on a considerable amount of market risk via index futures and reap the reward of being correct in a forecast of the stock market direction. For example, the S&P 500 provided a return of almost 20 percent between December 1990 and August 1991. A September 1991 S&P 500 futures contract could have been purchased with a $9,000 margin deposit in December 1990. This contract would have appreciated from 100 to 120 points and earned a $10,000 (20 × 500) profit on a $10,000 investment with a 100 percent return. The risk, however, of the use of such extreme leverage is significant. A 20 percent drop in the market would have required the deposit of that same $10,000 in a mark-to-market account as the losses in the market occurred. Also, even with the 20 percent appreciation in contract value, a market correction of 5 percent during the period would have required a deposit of roughly $9,000 in variation margin at some time during the December–August period.

A wide range of speculative strategies are possible with stock index futures. In addition to an outright short or long position, one can create spreads between stock futures expiring in different contract months, between stock and bond or stock and bill futures, and between stock futures on different indices. The basic notion associated with spread strategies is that the investor has an opinion about where the spread should be and either buys or sells the spread depending on whether he or she expects it to widen or narrow. For example, a spread benefiting from appreciation of smaller capitalized stocks versus large cap issues could be implemented by selling MMI futures and buying NYSE futures, in amounts equating the dollar value of each position. This spread should widen and provide profits regardless of the direction the index moves, as long as the more broadly based NYSE index outperforms the MMI index.

SUMMARY

The success of fixed-income futures contracts encouraged the creation of futures contracts on various stock indices. Stock index futures are dissimilar to many other futures contracts in that the equity index futures call for *cash* settlement on the expiration date rather than delivery of specific securities. Since their introduction in 1982, stock index futures have become an established means of managing the market risk of stock inventories of the brokerage firms. They have also become widely used in portfolios of institutional and individual investors and as arbitrage trading vehicles. The liquidity and low trading cost of these markets make them most suitable for adjusting or creating synthetic equity market exposure hedging against short-term equity price declines, and capitalizing on short-term relative moves of indices representing broad-based components of the equity markets. Many traders conduct arbitrage between stock index futures and the stocks themselves, adding liquidity to both markets.

CHAPTER 27

CASE HISTORIES OF TRADE HEDGING

We have discussed the need for hedging, the diverse objectives of trade hedgers, the principles of sound and proper hedging, and the various types of hedges. We have noted that hedging does not eliminate risk entirely, nor does it assure profitable operations. While the hedger may profit, he may also lose—either because of an error or miscalculation in his operating estimates or because of an adverse change in his basis.

We now examine hedging from a more pragmatic point of view, utilizing four specific examples of trade hedging involving various futures. We shall follow the mechanics in these diverse examples, referring back to the principles and tactics discussed and illustrating the importance of both astute basis trading and a proper sense of market timing.

ABC CHOCOLATE COMPANY

The ABC Chocolate Company, located in Philadelphia, manufactures a diverse line of chocolate products, including chocolate candies and beverages, cocoa powder, baking chocolate, and candy coatings. The company sells its products directly to food processors, candy manufacturers, and large grocery chains.

ABC is, of course, in business to earn a profit from the efficient manufacture of its products. The company has neither the capital nor the inclination to speculate on cocoa price fluctuations. ABC would have little need to hedge in the futures market if all orders from customers were for nearby delivery, and if all

444

grades and origins of cocoa beans required in the manufacturing process were available at dependable price differentials. Unfortunately, these two conditions are rarely present. In their absence, ABC finds that the hedging facilities provided by the New York Coffee, Sugar, and Cocoa Exchange provide an essential supplement to its regular business operations.

Let us assume that, in January, one of ABC's major customers requests a quotation on one million pounds of X brand milk chocolate, for delivery during the fourth quarter of the current year. This order would require approximately 285 metric tons of cocoa beans. ABC does not currently own these beans but anticipates being able to purchase its entire requirements in the cash market by mid-June.

The problem facing ABC is that it must quote the customer a price, in January, for delivery of the finished order some 10 months hence (and some 5 months prior to its purchase of the actual cocoa beans required to produce the order). ABC does this by calculating its costs, based on a price for cocoa beans equivalent to December cocoa futures plus its estimate of the premium required to exchange its futures position for the actual cocoa beans at the appropriate time.

With the December future currently quoted at around $1,100 per metric ton on the New York Coffee, Sugar, and Cocoa Exchange, ABC estimates that it will be able to buy 285 metric tons of the precise blend of beans needed at a premium of approximately $220 per metric ton over futures. It therefore "costs" its cocoa beans at $1,320 per metric ton, then adds the cost of other materials required in the production of X brand milk chocolate and the operating costs involved. After estimating his manufacturing costs, and then adding a margin for profit adjusted to competitive conditions, ABC's sales manager can now quote a price to his customer.

Upon receipt of the customer's order, ABC buys 28 contracts of December cocoa at $1,100 per metric ton on the New York Coffee, Sugar, and Cocoa Exchange. In this way, ABC's short actuals position (actual cocoa sold ahead in the form of chocolate for future delivery) has been hedged through the purchase of 28 contracts of futures, and ABC has relieved itself of concern over fluctuations in the price of cocoa beans. The only significant factor now is the basis (differential between cash and future prices) in effect at the time that ABC goes into the market to buy its cash beans. As long as this basis does not exceed $220 per metric ton, the hedge has been successful.

This hedging operation did not guarantee a profit, because ABC's cost estimates could have erred or the basis change could have proved adverse. However, the hedge operation substituted basis risk for the much more substantial outright price risk, which would have been incurred had the firm sold chocolate without covering its bean requirements in the cash market.

Table 27.1 lists the actual details of ABC's hedge operations.

Summarizing this hedge operation, ABC sustained a $17,640 loss on its cash transaction and a profit of $19,150 on the futures transaction, for a net $1,870 profit on the overall hedge. In basis terms, the hedge was initiated at a difference of $220 per metric ton and closed out at $206 per metric ton, for a gross profit of $14 per metric ton, amounting to $3990. Needless to say, the basis in a hedge operation is subject to fluctuation, and the

TABLE 27.1
ABC Chocolate Hedge Operation

	Cash Market	Futures Market
January	ABC sells one million pounds of X brand milk chocolate based on a bean cost of $1,320 per metric ton (285 metric tons of cocoa beans).	ABC buys 28 contracts (285 metric tons) of December cocoa at $1,100 per metric ton.
	Total price $376,200	**Total cost $313,500**
June	Buys 285 metric tons of cocoa beans at an average cost of $1,383 per metric ton.	Sells 28 contracts of December cocoa at $1,777 per metric ton.
	Loss on cash operation $17,640	*Profit on futures operation $19,510* (gross profit of $21,560 less commission of $2,050).

hedger will either turn a profit or incur a loss, depending on his skill (and good fortune) in anticipating and trading basis changes.

AMALGAMATED COPPER CORPORATION

The Amalgamated Copper Corporation (ACC) operates copper smelting and refining plants in New Jersey and Virginia. ACC's business consists largely of buying scrap copper from dealers throughout the country and fabricating it into industrial products, mostly in the form of electrolytic wire and bar. Most of ACC's orders come from manufactures of consumer and industrial electrical appliances.

Each 200 tons of copper scrap produces approximately 175 tons of finished copper products at a cost of about 10 cents per fabricated pound. The typical processing period from scrap to finished product spans approximately 30 days. ACC, like most other industrial operators, seeks to profit from the efficient fabrication of its products, while eliminating—or at least minimizing—the speculative risks of adverse copper price changes. The firm's policy of balancing scrap purchases with sales of finished products cannot always be attained; accordingly, ACC, as a routine part of its operations, hedges its net long or short actuals position in the futures market.

On a given day, ACC buys 275 tons of copper scrap at an average price of 88 cents per pound. The sales department has orders in hand for 53 tons of finished products, requiring approximately 60 tons of scrap copper. Of the remaining 215 tons held unsold, ACC decides to hedge 200 tons, being willing to hold a net 15-ton long position, based on the firm's bullish view of the market. The hedging operation, involving the 200 tons of scrap copper, is described in Table 27.2.

In this illustration, a loss in the cash operation has been more than offset by a profit on the short hedge position in futures. Once again, it should be noted that there is no assurance that a net profit will result. However, the hedger may have good prospects of emerging profitably if his positions in cash and futures are initiated advantageously.

TABLE 27.2
Amalgamated Copper Hedge Operation

	Cash Market	Futures Market
May	ACC holds 200 tons of copper scrap valued at 88¢ per pound.	ACC sells 16 contracts (200 tons) of December copper at 109¢ per pound.
	Cost $352,000	**Total value $436,000**
	Fabricates 200 tons of copper products at a cost of 10¢ per pound.	
	Fabrication cost $40,000	
	Total cost of fabricated copper $392,000	
August	Sells 200 tons of fabricated copper at 92¢ per pound.	Buys 16 contracts of December copper at 101¢ per pound.
	Total receipts $368,000	**Total cost $404,000**
	Loss on cash operation $24,000	Net profit on futures operation $31,760 (gross profit of $32,000 less commission of $240)

AZK INTERNATIONAL MOTORWORKS COMPANY

The AZK International Motorworks Company, a U.S. automobile importer, receives an order in November from Upscale Car Rental for a fleet of 16 German luxury cars. Delivery is specified for March, in advance of the summer driving season.

AZK contacts the German car manufacturer, who quotes a price of 1.8 million Deutsche marks (equal to $900,000 based on the then-existing exchange rate of 2.00 marks to the dollar) for the entire order. AZK's dollar cost per car comes to $56,250. AZK then quotes Upscale a price of $62,500 per car, or $1 million total, and Upscale accepts the quote. AZK stands to make

$100,000 profit on the transaction, barring any dollar devaluation during the ensuring four months.

The principals of AZK know that the dollar versus Deutsche mark exchange rate, currently at 2.00, is unlikely to remain constant during the four-month life of the contract, and that even a small adverse rate fluctuation could considerably reduce their profit. They know that, upon taking delivery of the cars, if the dollar exchanges for more than 2.00 marks their profit will be increased by the profit on exchange; if the dollar converts to less than 2.00 marks, they stand to lose some portion, or possibly all, of their $100,000 "built-in" profit.

AZK opts to "lock in" its $100,000 profit, rather than speculate on the currency exchange, by establishing a hedge in the futures market. Table 27.3 lists the details of that hedge.

Because the dollar weakened against the mark during the four months of the contract, AZK lost $25,450 on the cash side of the transaction. However, it had a profit of $24,768 on the long futures position, for a net loss of $682 on the hedging transaction. This loss is perfectly acceptable, representing less than 1 percent of the anticipated $100,000 profit on the entire deal. The bottom line is that AZK made a profit of $99,318 ($100,000 minus $682). Needless to say, without the futures hedge, AZK would have lost at least 25 percent of its anticipated profit.

GENERAL FARM CORPORATION

General Farm Corporation (GFC) owns and operates farms and livestock herds throughout Illinois and Indiana, with corn accounting for three-quarters of its total grain output. The corn is planted around mid-May and reaches maturity in late August. Harvest commences about October 15, just after the first hard frost, and nears completion by the middle of November. Nearly 80 percent of GFC's corn crop is consumed as livestock feed on the same farms where it is grown, while the balance is sold in the marketplace as "cash crop."

Let us assume that, during the first week of November, GFC's management decides to store 300,000 bushels of its newly harvested corn in bins located on its farms. The company intends

TABLE 27.3
AZK Motorworks Hedge Operation

	Cash Market	Futures Market
November	AZK contracts with a German car manufacturer to take delivery of 16 luxury cars at DM 112,500 ($56,250) per car based on the existing rate of 2.00 marks per dollar. **Total commitment** $900,000	AZK buys 16 contracts (DM 125,000 per contract) at 51.00, for a total of DM 2 billion.
March	Takes delivery of 16 cars and converts $900,000 in marks at an exchange rate of DM 1.945 per dollar. **Proceeds of conversion** DM 1,750,500 *Loss on cash transaction* DM 49,500, or $25,450 (at an exchange rate of DM 1.945 per dollar)	Sells 16 contracts of March Deutsche marks at 52.25, for a profit of 125 ticks equal to $1,563 per contract. *Profit on the 16-contract futures position* $24,768 (gross profit of 25,008 less commission of $240)

to sell this corn in the marketplace later in the season. The corn is to be hedged on the Chicago Board of Trade, with the dual objective of avoiding the speculative risk of loss due to a possible decline in corn prices and utilizing the futures market as a means of earning carrying costs plus a profit on the stored corn.

GFC's hedging manager, studying the then-prevailing cash versus futures price situation (the basis), notes that corn in his local cash market is selling at 14½ cents under the Chicago December future, and at approximately 23½ cents under the May future. From past experience, as well as on the basis of charts and other technical studies, the hedging manager recognizes that the cash basis tends to be at its widest point during the height of the harvest movement, narrowing later in the season as cash marketings start to fall off. As a matter of fact, cash corn prices at country points usually approach the price of Chicago futures by late spring or early summer.

Anticipating that the 300,000 bushels of cash corn may not be sold until sometime in the spring, the hedging manager elects to place his short hedges in the May future, with the cash basis then 23½ cents off (discount to) May. The hedge operation would be handled as shown in Table 27.4.

In this instance, the combined cash–futures operation grossed GFC 20½ cents more per bushel than would have been obtained by simply selling the 300,000 bushels in November. From this gross profit, one must deduct commissions and carrying costs incurred during the November-to-May period. Measured in terms of the changing basis, the hedge sale of futures was initiated, with cash 23½ cents off (discount to) May, and closed out at 3 cents off; hence a profit of 20½ cents per bushel. This type of hedge, based on the consistent seasonal tendency of the cash corn basis to narrow from harvest time to late spring, represents one of the most popular and successful producer hedge operations.

It should be clear that the incentive to initiate such a hedge operation depends largely on the existence of what is judged to

TABLE 27.4
General Farm Hedge Operation

	Cash Market	Futures Market
November	GFC holds 300,000 bushels of corn currently valued at $2.27 per bushel (23½¢ under May).	GFC sells 300,000 bushels of May corn at $2.50½ per bushel.
May	Sells 300,000 bushels of corn at $2.43½ per bushel (3¢ under May).	Buys 300,000 bushels of May corn at $2.46½ per bushel.
	Profit on cash operation 16½¢ per bushel (less cost of carrying corn)	Profit on futures operation 4¢ per bushel (less $90.00 total commission)

be an attractive basis at harvest time. If this basis happened to be, rather unusually, 3 cents in November rather than 23½ cents, GFC might have deemed it wiser to avoid basis uncertainties and commission costs, and sell its corn at once in the cash market.

THE PHILOSOPHY OF A BILLION-DOLLAR FUND MANAGER

CHAPTER 28

LARRY HITE ON
TRADING STRATEGY

Larry Hite
Founder and Managing Director,
Mint Investment Management.

In my early days in the commodity business, when I first started *O.J.* trading for myself, I had an orange juice spread that wasn't quite working out the way I had planned. I called my broker and instructed him to get me out at a spread of two cents. He told me he could get me out at three. I told him that it said two cents on my screen and I wanted to get out at two; he said that though it might say two I couldn't do two on the floor.

I wanted to wait for two. For the next few days it said three on the screen, so I finally said I would pay three, but by then my broker was telling me it would cost me four.

This went on for two weeks. Had I gone with the original three, I would have lost about $2,000. In the end, I lost about $25,000.

And therein I learned some valuable lessons: your first loss *lessons* is your best loss, and you can only take what the market gives *1.* you. Anything else is dangerous fantasy. *2.*

Not long thereafter, my partner and I were bartering office space from a group of people who were trading stock options. They got a piece of our business for letting us have the office space. Their firm had a young analyst who was supposedly a genius (he didn't tell anybody that he was using astrology to determine his trading decisions, however).

One day, the head of the group next door called me into the office and told me that this kid had put them in the hole for

455

$100,000 on the stock option spread and wanted to know how I would handle it. I explained to them that from my way of thinking, one's first loss is one's best loss, and that if it were my money, I would bail out, lick my wounds, and go on to the next trading decision.

The guy running the firm was a very good salesman, not really a trader at all. He thanked me for my opinion and dismissed me. A few weeks later, I found out that they had stayed with the coffee trade, which managed to come back and provide them with a bit of a profit after all.

I told my partner that we should look for another office because we were sharing space with a guy who, having found himself in the middle of a mine field, closed his eyes, walked forward, and got through. He then believed that the way you go through a mine field is by shutting your eyes and walking forward. Seldom do I say that I'm really sure about something, but I knew that this was not going to work. This guy was going to blow himself up, and we should not be attached to him in any way.

As it turned out, nine months later the guy next door got himself into another mine field, called a neutral spread, and, in the end, blew himself up. He blew out all the capital in the firm. He closed his eyes, and boom, he was financially obliterated. Initially, he didn't learn the right lesson, because he made money doing the wrong thing despite a very dangerous situation. The second time, he wasn't so lucky.

It was at that point in my career that I realized I would not let that happen to me. I would not put myself, my firm, or my family in a position of losing everything on one trade, or even a few trades. In my judgment, nothing is worth that fate. I set out to make money in the futures market with one rule set in stone: know your equity and do not risk very much of it on any one trading situation. As long as I have money to play the game, I can play. And my experience concludes that you can't win unless you bet—but if you lose all your chips, you can't play. If I can't play, I definitely can't win.

Very early in my career, another experience made a lasting impression on me. I was considered to be a pretty good technician at this time, and was working as a broker for a big commission house that employed some well-known technical analysts. In fact, in 1968, one guy turned $20,000 into $1 million, which is like $5 million today.

One night I was working late, and the head of the firm and his chief technical analyst called me in to settle an argument. They were looking at a chart, and they wanted to know whether I thought the formation was a reverse head and shoulders bottom formation or some other kind of pattern that would break on the down side.

At that moment I said to myself, "Here I am, in an office with the head of the firm, a guy I really admire, and his chief technical analyst. They are two phenomenally educated guys asking a kid who has been in the business for less than two years to interpret squiggles on a page." One thing I knew was that it didn't look very scientific. There had to be a better way; something was not quite right. It wasn't that the charts weren't right, it was the idea of leaving so much of one's decision making to the interpretation of squiggles on a page.

That was a turning point in my career. I knew then that you have to have a clear, precise, fact-based methodology. Like a number. You can't argue with me that the number 6 is 6. There can be no interpretation, no disputing this fact. And that's how I knew I should conduct my trading.

I began to devote my resources to developing a nonemotional, risk-averse quantitative approach to the markets. Price data was subjected to rigorous computer testing to determine if there were recurrent statistical "events." If so, then the events were subjected to further testing using strict risk parameters to determine if such a disciplined methodology could be consistently profitable. I don't see markets, I see probabilities, risk, and rewards.

I discovered that, yes, I could risk a very small part of the farm and make above-average returns with reasonable consistency. Yes, I could totally avoid any interpretations of the chart patterns or underlying supply and demand factors that impact a particular market, and my returns would not suffer. And, yes, I could diversify into many markets, remain extremely disciplined, and still show an appealing return on investment.

I considered my strategy to be a real accomplishment because it was a trading plan that suited my personality *and* my wallet—

discipline, quantitative and profitable. I have developed a set of mathematically proven rules that have worked for me. (However, without an excellent statistician, Dr. Peter Matthews, and a great scientist and programmer, Michael Delman, I could not have done it, because without statistics and science, it's just so much conjecture.)

THE GOOD BETS BUSINESS

I consider myself to be in the good bets business. That is, through the use of a computer, we search for good bets and try to play only good bets. If the bet does not meet our standards, we throw it out, even if it is something that someone else might jump at. It is analogous to actuarial work. Essentially, what I did was to take a highly charged, exhilarating profession and turn it into an actuarial process—something that would appeal to anyone who finds accounting too exciting. I de-emotionalized markets and trading and reduced them to a probability study.

If you take 100,000 40-year-old middle-class executives and insure their lives, you know with certainty that some of them are going to die soon. That is a calculated bet. On the other hand, if you had to insure any particular individual's life, you wouldn't have the same bet. For all you know, that individual is engaged in self-destructive behavior that an insurance company wouldn't know about. It would be lovely to think that one could make the specific individual bet with great certainty. (That kind of bet used to thrill my partner, who is a statistician. Deep in his heart, he would love to be able to make this bet. But he got rich making statistical bets, not individual bets.)

ZEN AND THE ART OF TRADING

For me, this is a very Zen-like business, and your most valuable tool is yourself. There is a Japanese book about sword fighting whose premise is this: when you get into a sword fight, immediately assume that you're dead so you won't have to worry about getting killed. Then all you have to worry about is making the appropriate move.

Once you figure out the right action, assemble the means to implement it correctly, and then proceed. That is what a good trader does. He or she sets out a program either through the use of a computer (which often is used as little more than a counting machine) or through some other method to achieve a designated objective. In my case, I thought de-emotionalizing the markets was the right way to approach the idea of consistent returns. If that is not exciting enough for some people in the business, then so be it. I don't trade for excitement, I trade for profits. (So far, I have had both.)

It is important to realize that the futures markets will occasionally experience shocks or aberrations, such as the Soviet coup attempt in August 1991, but they do not affect the overall game plan. One's discipline should not be changed. If you are not willing, if you are not "de-geared" enough to take that shot, you have no business trading. That is not to say that it is not painful to lose money on a blind-sided hit, but, within the bounds of what I'm supposed to do, I have built in those tolerances.

It's like getting hit in football. I have a friend who was a pretty good tight end in his younger days, but he quit. He told me that he loved catching the ball and running with it but that he hated getting hit. He just did not like some 240-pound guy smashing him with his helmet or his elbow. It seemed to me that my friend was right to quit, because if you're going to play football, you had better expect to get hit, sometimes so hard that you get hurt. It goes with the territory.

It is the same with futures markets. The sooner you realize that these markets experience shocks, like the coup, and that you're going to get hit every once in a while, the better off you'll be as a trader.

It boils down to a de-emotionalized, risk management game for both the big trader and the small speculator. Although we are sometimes involved in as many as 50 markets at once, we have set a risk parameter, or stop level, in every one of those 50 markets. Beyond that, we use a percentage draw-down, which relates risk on each position to total equity. That is, we limit the risk on each position in our portfolio to 1 percent of the account's total equity, based on closing prices. Any time the loss on any position, as of the close, equals 1 percent (or more) of total equity, we liquidate that position the following morning.

MANAGING MONEY, LARGE OR SMALL

There is not much difference in the way I would manage the money for a multimillion-dollar fund and the way I would do so for the individual trader who has, say, $50,000 at his disposal. Although the $50,000 trader cannot diversify horizontally across the markets, he might diversify in a linear way. For example, he can take a series of 10 trades in the same market, and use tight stops on each one so that he does not lose more than $500 on any one trade. Or, he might diversify into four or five markets, but place stops on his entire position that would not cause a cumulative loss of more than about 5 percent on a total equity of $50,000.

But remember, even the guy who has $50,000 to invest must make good bets derived from his methodology. For me, that means that based on my definition of a good bet, in the statistical, quantifiable sense, I go into a market to risk part of my $50,000 only if I like the odds a lot. I don't see a particular market, like grains, metals, or currency. All I see is a good or bad bet. For someone else who has $50,000, his method might be studying chart patterns. Even though chart pattern interpretation is not my style, someone else might be able to de-emotionalize the charts to concentrate on finding a handful of patterns that he can identify with profitable trading opportunities in the past. In that case, once he finds the pattern, he puts on the trade. Based on his methodology, that is his good bet.

Regardless of the methodology, once the good bet trade is found, the downside risk is determined and the worst-case scenario is calculated. If all the variables of the trade fit one's pocketbook, then at that point the trade plan is set. After the trade is entered, the calculations are refigured prior to the start of every trading session. In that way, if the trade is profitable, the stops will be adjusted and the worst-case scenario recalculated to reflect the increase in equity.

In my judgment, at that point, you are on the right track. You have a system for selecting the good bets. More important, you have a money management discipline in place. That's the whole game. It's the way you manage the money.

Many people have systems that work, but it's the way they manage the money that determines the performance. It's not what you know about markets or commodities, because you probably don't know enough. It's not about what the underlying value is, because there is no intrinsic value in commodities. A commodity has a quotational value—it is worth what someone is willing to pay for it. It is unlike a security, which has two values—its quotational value and the intrinsic worth or earning power of the underlying business. Therefore, the commodity game is largely a question of how you manage your money.

For me, this game is not about being the greatest trader that ever lived. I view it as having a methodology that works for me. My partners and I have a method that works very well for us. We know where it goes; it's good, and we have proven it statistically, as we have scientists who have proven our methodology to our satisfaction and can live with it. We don't care what anyone else in the world does because we don't know their facts or even if their facts are, in fact, facts. People can make money for the wrong reasons, but that is not a consistent way to get good outcomes.

We try to do the best job we can with the broadest possible mix of assets. We don't do only futures, we do currencies, we do stocks, because that's the best way to handle money—on a risk-adjusted basis.

This is going to sound wildly impractical, but I just don't think about how my clients feel. I don't even look at the market during the day. My job is to figure out what is statistically right, then do it. That is the best protection for my client.

APPENDIX

Cattle (live)

Where Traded	Chicago Mercantile Exchange
Trading Hours (NY Time)	10:05 A.M. to 2:00 P.M.
Contract Size	40,000 pounds
How Price Is Quoted	Cents per pound
Minimum Fluctuation	
Per Pound	.025 cent
Per Contract	$10
Value 1-Cent Move	$400
Maximum Trading Limit from Previous Close	1.50 cents (equals $600)

Cocoa

Where Traded	New York Coffee, Sugar, and Cocoa Exchange
Trading Hours (NY Time)	9:30 A.M. to 2:15 P.M.
Contract Size	10 metric tons
How Price Is Quoted	Dollars per metric ton
Minimum Fluctuation	
Per Ton	$1
Per Contract	$10
Value $1.00 Move	$10
Maximum Trading Limit from Previous Close	$88 (equals $880)

Coffee

Where Traded	New York Coffee, Sugar, and Cocoa Exchange
Trading Hours (NY Time)	9:15 A.M. to 1:58 P.M.
Contract Size	37,500 pounds
How Price Is Quoted	Cents per pound
Minimum Fluctuation	
Per Pound	.05 cent
Per Contract	$18.75
Value 1-Cent Move	$375
Maximum Trading Limit from Previous Close	6.00 cents (equals $2,250)

Copper

Where Traded	New York Commodity Exchange (COMEX)
Trading Hours (NY Time)	9:25 A.M. to 2:00 P.M.
Contract Size	25,000 pounds
How Price Is Quoted	Cents per pound
Minimum Fluctuation	
Per Pound	.05 cent
Per Contract	$12.50
Value 1-Cent Move	$250
Maximum Trading Limit from Previous Close	None

Corn

Where Traded	Chicago Board of Trade
Trading Hours (NY Time)	10:30 A.M. to 2:15 P.M.
Contract Size	5,000 bushels
How Price Is Quoted	Cents per bushel
Minimum Fluctuation	
Per Bushel	.25 cent
Per Contract	$12.50
Value 1-Cent Move	$50
Maximum Trading Limit from Previous Close	10 cents (equals $500)

Cotton

Where Traded	New York Cotton Exchange
Trading Hours (NY Time)	10:30 A.M. to 2:40 P.M.
Contract Size	50,000 pounds
How Price Is Quoted	Cents per pound
Minimum Fluctuation	
Per Pound	.01 cent
Per Contract	$5
Value 1-Cent Move	$500
Maximum Trading Limit from Previous Close	2 cents (equals $1,000)

Crude Oil

Where Traded	New York Mercantile Exchange
Trading Hours (NY Time)	9:45 A.M. to 3:10 P.M.
Contract Size	1,000 barrels
How Price Is Quoted	Dollars per barrel
Minimum Fluctuation	
Per Barrel	1 cent
Per Contract	$10
Value 1-Cent Move	$1,000
Maximum Trading Limit from Previous Close	$1 per barrel (equals $1,000)

U.S. Dollar Index

Where Traded	New York Cotton Exchange
Trading Hours (NY Time)	8:20 A.M. to 3:00 P.M.
Contract Size	$500 × Index
How Price Is Quoted	Dollars
Minimum Fluctuation	
Per .01 point	$5
Value 100-Point Move	$500
Maximum Trading Limit from Previous Close	200 points (equals $1,000)

British Pound

Where Traded	IMM Division, Chicago Mercantile Exchange
Trading Hours (NY Time)	8:20 A.M. to 3:00 P.M.
Contract Size	62,500 pounds sterling
How Price Is Quoted	U.S. dollars
Minimum Fluctuation Per .05	2 points ($.0002 per pound sterling)
Value 100-Point Move	$625
Maximum Trading Limit from Previous Close	None

Canadian Dollar

Where Traded	IMM Division, Chicago Mercantile Exchange
Trading Hours (NY Time)	8:20 A.M. to 3:00 P.M.
Contract Size	100,000 Canadian dollars
How Price Is Quoted	U.S. dollars
Minimum Fluctuation Per 1 Point	$10
Value 100-Point Move	$1,000
Maximum Trading Limit from Previous Close	None

Swiss Franc

Where Traded	IMM Division, Chicago Mercantile Exchange
Trading Hours (NY Time)	8:20 A.M. to 3:00 P.M.
Contract Size	125,000 Swiss francs
How Price Is Quoted	U.S. dollars
Minimum Fluctuation Per .01	$12.50
Value 100-Point Move	$1,250
Maximum Trading Limit from Previous Close	None

Deutsche Mark

Where Traded	IMM Division, Chicago Mercantile Exchange
Trading Hours (NY Time)	8:20 A.M. to 3:00 P.M.
Contract Size	125,000 Deutsche marks
How Price Is Quoted	U.S. dollars
Minimum Fluctuation Per .01	$12.50
Value 100-Point Move	$1,250
Maximum Trading Limit from Previous Close	None

Japanese Yen

Where Traded	IMM Division, Chicago Mercantile Exchange
Trading Hours (NY Time)	8:20 A.M. to 3:00 P.M.
Contract Size	12,500,000 yen
How Price Is Quoted	U.S. cents
Minimum Fluctuation Per .0001	$12.50
Value 100-Point Move	$1,250
Maximum Trading Limit from Previous Close	None

Gold (NY)

Where Traded	New York Commodity Exchange (COMEX)
Trading Hours (NY Time)	8:20 A.M. to 2:30 P.M.
Contract Size	100 troy ounces
How Price Is Quoted	Dollars per troy ounce
Minimum Fluctuation Per Ounce Per Contract	10 cents $10
Value $1.00 Move	$100
Maximum Trading Limit from Previous Close	None

Heating Oil

Where Traded	New York Mercantile Exchange
Trading Hours (NY Time)	9:50 A.M. to 3:10 P.M.
Contract Size	42,000 gallons
How Price Is Quoted	Cents per gallon
Minimum Fluctuation	
Per Gallon	.01 cent
Per Contract	$4.20
Value 1-Cent Move	$420
Maximum Trading Limit from Previous Close	2 cents

Hogs (live)

Where Traded	Chicago Mercantile Exchange
Trading Hours (NY Time)	10:10 A.M. to 2:00 P.M.
Contract Size	40,000 pounds
How Price Is Quoted	Cents per pound
Minimum Fluctuation	
Per Pound	.025 cent
Per Contract	$10
Value 1-Cent Move	$400
Maximum Trading Limit from Previous Close	1.50 cents

Lumber

Where Traded	Chicago Mercantile Exchange
Trading Hours (NY Time)	10:00 A.M. to 2:05 P.M.
Contract Size	160,000 board feet
How Price Is Quoted	Dollars per 1,000 board feet
Minimum Fluctuation	
Per 1,000 Board Feet	10 cents
Per Contract	$16
Value $1.00 Move	$160
Maximum Trading Limit from Previous Close	$5

Platinum

Where Traded	New York Mercantile Exchange
Trading Hours (NY Time)	8:20 A.M. to 2:30 P.M.
Contract Size	50 troy ounces
How Price Is Quoted	Dollars per troy ounce
Minimum Fluctuation	
Per Ounce	10 cents
Per Contract	$5
Value $1.00 Move	$50
Maximum Trading Limit from Previous Close	$25

Pork Bellies

Where Traded	Chicago Mercantile Exchange
Trading Hours (NY Time)	10:10 A.M. to 2:00 P.M.
Contract Size	40,000 pounds
How Price Is Quoted	Cents per pound
Minimum Fluctuation	
Per Pound	.025 cent
Per Contract	$10
Value 1-Cent Move	$400
Maximum Trading Limit from Previous Close	2 cents

NYSE Composite Index

Where Traded	New York Futures Exchange
Trading Hours (NY Time)	9:30 A.M. to 4:15 P.M.
Contract Size	$500 × Index
How Price Is Quoted	Index
Minimum Fluctuation	
Per .05 Point	$25
Value 100-Point Move	$500
Maximum Trading Limit from Previous Close	There is a limit of 3 points in either direction for the first 3 minutes of trading, a 7-point decline limit during the first 30 minutes, a 12-point decline limit in any one hour, and a total limit of 18 points in either direction.

S&P 500 Index

Where Traded	Index and Option Market Division of the Chicago Mercantile Exchange
Trading Hours (NY Time)	9:30 A.M. to 4:15 P.M.
Contract Size	$500 × Index
How Price Is Quoted	Index
Minimum Fluctuation Per .05 Point	$25
Value 100-Point Move	$500
Maximum Trading Limit from Previous Close	There is a 5-point limit up or down during the first 3 minutes of trading, a 12-point decline limit during the first 30 minutes, a 20-point decline limit in any one hour, and a total limit of 30 points in either direction.

Silver (NY)

Where Traded	New York Commodity Exchange (COMEX)
Trading Hours (NY Time)	8:25 A.M. to 2:25 P.M.
Contract Size	5,000 troy ounces
How Price Is Quoted	Cents per troy ounce

Minimum Fluctuation
    Per Ounce
    Per Contract
	.5 cent
	$25

Value 1-Cent Move	$50
Maximum Trading Limit from Previous Close	None

Soybeans

Where Traded	Chicago Board of Trade
Trading Hours (NY Time)	10:30 A.M. to 2:15 P.M.
Contract Size	5,000 bushels
How Price Is Quoted	Cents per bushel

Minimum Fluctuation
    Per Bushel
    Per Contract
	.25 cent
	$12.50

Value 1-Cent Move	$50
Maximum Trading Limit from Previous Close	30 cents

Soybean Meal

Where Traded	Chicago Board of Trade
Trading Hours (NY Time)	10:30 A.M. to 2:15 P.M.
Contract Size	100 short tons
How Price Is Quoted	Dollars per ton
Minimum Fluctuation	
Per Ton	10 cents
Per Contract	$10
Value $1.00 Move	$100
Maximum Trading Limit from Previous Close	$10.00 (equals $1,000)

Soybean Oil

Where Traded	Chicago Board of Trade
Trading Hours (NY Time)	10:30 A.M. to 2:15 P.M.
Contract Size	60,000 pounds
How Price Is Quoted	Cents per pound
Minimum Fluctuation	
Per Pound	.01 cent
Per Contract	$6
Value 1-Cent Move	$600
Maximum Trading Limit from Previous Close	1 cent (equals $600)

Sugar No. 11 (world)

Where Traded	New York Coffee, Sugar, and Cocoa Exchange
Trading Hours (NY Time)	10:00 A.M. to 1:43 P.M.
Contract Size	112,000 pounds
How Price Is Quoted	Cents per pound
Minimum Fluctuation	
Per Pound	.01 cent
Per Contract	$11.20
Value 1-Cent Move	$1,120
Maximum Trading Limit from Previous Close	.50 cent ($560)

Wheat (Chicago)

Where Traded	Chicago Board of Trade
Trading Hours (NY Time)	10:30 A.M. to 2:15 P.M.
Contract Size	5,000 bushels
How Price Is Quoted	Cents per bushel
Minimum Fluctuation	
Per Bushel	.25 cent
Per Contract	$12.50
Value 1-Cent Move	$50
Maximum Trading Limit from Previous Close	20 cents (equals $1,000)

Eurodollars

Where Traded	IMM Division of the Chicago Mercantile Exchange
Trading Hours (NY Time)	8:20 A.M. to 3:00 P.M.
Contract Size	$1,000,000
How Price Is Quoted	Terms of the IMM index
Minimum Fluctuation	
Per .01 Point	$25
Value 100-Point Move	$2,500
Maximum Trading Limit from Previous Close	None

T-Bills

Where Traded	IMM Division of the Chicago Mercantile Exchange
Trading Hours (NY Time)	8:20 A.M. to 3:00 P.M.
Contract Size	$1,000,000
How Price Is Quoted	Points of 100%
Minimum Fluctuation	
Per .01 Point	$25
Value 100-Point Move	$2,500
Maximum Trading Limit from Previous Close	None

T-Bonds

Where Traded	Chicago Board of Trade
Trading Hours (NY Time)	7:00 P.M. to 10:30 P.M./ 8:20 A.M. to 3:00 P.M.
Contract Size	$100,000
How Price Is Quoted	Points/32nd of 100%
Minimum Fluctuation Per 1/32 Point	$31.25
Value 100-Point Move (32/32)	$1,000
Maximum Trading Limit from Previous Close	96/32 (equals $3,000)

Value Line Index

Where Traded	Kansas City Board of Trade
Trading Hours (NY Time)	9:15 A.M. to 4:15 P.M.
Contract Size	$500 × Index
How Price Is Quoted	Index
Minimum Fluctuation Per .05 Point	$25
Value 100-Point Move	$500
Maximum Trading Limit from Previous Close	20 points

Major Market Index

Where Traded	Chicago Board of Trade
Trading Hours (NY Time)	9:15 A.M. to 4:15 P.M.
Contract Size	$500 × Index
How Price Is Quoted	Index
Minimum Fluctuation Per .05 Point	$25
Value 100-Point Move	$500
Maximum Trading Limit from Previous Close	20 points

BIBLIOGRAPHY

Ackerman, Kenneth D. *The Gold Ring: Jim Fisk, Jay Gould and Black Friday 1869.* New York: Dodd, Mead & Company, 1988.

Ainsworth, Ralph M. *Profitable Grain Trading.* Greenville, S.C.: Traders Press, 1933.

Allen, R. C. *How To Use the 4-Day, 9-Day and 18-Day Moving Averages to Earn Larger Profits from Commodities.* Greenville, S.C.: Traders Press (no date).

Angell, George. *Winning in the Commodities Market.* Garden City, N.Y.: Doubleday & Company, 1979.

Ansbacher, Max G. *The New Options Market.* 2nd ed. New York: Walker and Company, 1975.

Apel, Gerald. "The Moving Average Convergence-Divergence Method." Great Neck, N.Y.: Signalert Corporation, 1979.

Babcock, Bruce. *The Business One Irwin Guide to Trading Systems.* Homewood, Ill.: Business One Irwin, 1989.

Belveal, L. Dee. *Charting Commodity Market Price Behavior.* Homewood, Ill.: Dow Jones-Irwin, 1985.

_____ . *Speculation in Commodity Contracts and Options.* Homewood, Ill.: Business One Irwin, 1986.

Bernstein, Jacob. *Short-Term Trading in Futures: A Manual of Systems, Strategies and Techniques.* Chicago: Probus Publishing, 1987.

_____ . *The Handbook of Commodity Cycles: A Window on Time.* New York: John Wiley & Sons, 1982.

Bollenbacher, George M., with Samuel P. Peluso. *The Professional's Guide to the U.S. Government Securities Markets.* New York: New York Institute of Finance, 1988.

Brown, Brendan, and Charles Geisst. *Financial Futures Markets.* New York: St. Martin's Press, 1983.

Clasing, Henry K., Jr. *Dow Jones-Irwin Guide to Put and Call Options.* Homewood, Ill.: Dow Jones-Irwin, 1978.

Conticommodity Research Department. *Seasonality in Agricultural Futures Markets.* Chicago: Conticommodity Services, Inc., 1983.

Dobson, Edward. *The Trading Rule that Can Make You Rich.* Greenville, S.C.: Traders Press, 1979, 1985.

Edwards, Robert D., and John Magee. *Technical Analysis of Stock Trends.* 5th ed. Massachusetts: John Magee, 1967.

Fabozzi, Frank J. *The Handbook of Fixed-Income Options: Pricing, Strategies and Applications.* Chicago: Probus Publishing, 1989.

Figlewski, Stephen, et al. *Financial Options: From Theory to Practice.* Homewood, Ill.: Business One Irwin, 1990.

Frost, A. J., and Robert Prechter. *Elliott Wave Principle.* Gainesville, Ga.: New Classics Library, 1978, 1983.

Futures: The magazine of commodities and options. Cedar Falls, Iowa: Oster Communications, Inc.

Gann, W. D. *How to Make Profits in Commodities.* Washington, D.C.: Lambert-Gann Publishing, 1942.

Gart, Alan. *Handbook of the Money and Capital Markets.* New York: Quorum Books, 1988.

Gold, Gerald. *Modern Commodity Futures Trading.* New York: Commodity Research Bureau, 1959, 1990.

Hardy, C. Colburn. *Trader's Guide to Technical Analysis.* Greenville, S.C.: Traders Press, 1984.

Herbst, Anthony F. *Commodity Futures: Markets, Methods of Analysis, and Management of Risk.* New York: John Wiley & Sons, 1986.

Hieronymus, Thomas A. *Economics of Futures Trading.* New York: Commodity Research Bureau, 1971.

Jones, Paul Tudor, II. *The Trader: Paul Tudor Jones.* New York: Glyn-Net, 1987. Video.

Kaufman, Perry J. *Handbook of Futures Options: Commodity, Financial, Stock Index, and Options.* New York: John Wiley & Sons, 1984.

Keltner, Chester W. *How to Make Money in Commodities.* Missouri: The Keltner Statistical Service, 1960.

Kroll, Stanley. *Kroll on Futures Trading Strategy.* Homewood, Ill.: Dow Jones-Irwin, 1988.

_____. *The Professional Commodity Trader.* Greenville, S.C.: Traders Press, 1974.

Labuszewski, John W., and Jeanne Cairns Sinquefield. *Inside the Commodity Options Market.* New York: John Wiley & Sons, 1985.

Labuszewski, John W., and John E. Nyhoff. *Trading Financial Futures: Markets, Methods, Strategies, and Tactics.* New York: John Wiley & Sons, 1988.

———. *Trading Options on Futures.* New York: John Wiley & Sons, 1988.

LeBeau, Charles, and David W. Lucas. *Technical Traders' Guide to Computer Analysis of the Futures Market.* Homewood, Ill.: Business One Irwin, 1992.

Lefevre, Edwin. *Reminiscences of a Stock Operator.* Greenville, S.C.: Traders Press, 1923, 1985.

Little, Jeffrey B. *Stock Options.* New York: Chelsea House Publishers, 1988.

Lofton, Todd, ed. Compiled by Chicago Mercantile Exchange. *Trading Tactics.* Chicago: Chicago Mercantile Exchange, 1986.

Longstreet, Roy W. *Viewpoints of a Commodity Trader.* New York: Frederick Fell, 1968.

Luskin, Donald L. *Index Options and Futures: The Complete Guide.* New York: John Wiley & Sons, 1987.

McLaren, William. *Gann Made Easy: How to Trade Using the Methods of W. D. Gann.* Overland Park, Kans.: Gann Theory Publishing, 1986.

Metz, Tim. *Black Monday.* New York: William Morrow and Company, 1988.

Murphy, John J. *Intermarket Technical Analysis: Trading Strategies for the Global Stock, Bond, Commodity and Currency Market.* New York: John Wiley & Sons, 1991.

———. *Technical Analysis of the Futures Markets.* New York: New York Institute of Finance, 1986.

Natenberg, Sheldon. *Option Volatility and Pricing Strategies.* Chicago: Probus Publishing, 1988.

Nison, Steve. *Japanese Candlestick Charting Techniques.* New York: New York Institute of Finance, 1991.

Options Institute, The Educational Division Chicago Board of Options Exchange, ed. *Options: Essential Concepts and Trading Strategies.* Homewood, Ill.: Business One Irwin, 1990.

Pacelli, Albert. *The Speculator's Edge: Strategies for Profit in the Futures Markets.* New York: John Wiley & Sons, 1989.

Paris, Alexander. *A Complete Guide to Trading Profits.* Greenville, S.C.: Traders Press, 1970.

Pring, Martin J. *Technical Analysis Explained.* 3rd ed. New York: McGraw-Hill, 1991.

Schonberg, James S. *The Grain Trade: How It Works.* New York: Exposition Press, 1956.

Schwager, Jack D. *A Complete Guide to the Futures Markets: Fundamental Analysis, Technical Analysis, Trading, Spreads, & Options.* New York: John Wiley & Sons, 1984.

_____ . *Market Wizards: Interviews With Top Traders.* New York: Harper & Row, 1989.

Scott, David L. *Wall Street Words: Financial Literacy for a Changing Market.* Boston: Houghton Mifflin, 1988.

Sklarew, Arthur. *Techniques of a Professional Commodity Chartist.* New York: Commodity Research Bureau, 1980.

Sloane, Leonard. *The Anatomy of the Floor.* New York: Doubleday & Company, 1980.

Smith, Charles W. *The Mind of the Market.* New Jersey: Rowman and Littlefield, 1981.

Smith, Courtney. *Commodity Spreads: Analysis, Selection and Trading Techniques.* Greenville, S.C.: Traders Press, 1988.

_____ . *Options Strategies: Profit-Making Techniques for Stock, Stock Index and Commodity Options.* New York: John Wiley & Sons, 1987.

Sobel, Robert. *The Last Bull Market: Wall Street in the 1960s.* New York: W. W. Norton & Company, 1980.

_____ . *The Money Manias: Tales of Entrepreneurs and Investors During the Eras of Great Speculation in America, 1770–1970.* New York: Weybright and Talley, 1973.

Sun-tzu. James Clavell, ed. *The Art of War.* New York: Dell Publishing, 1983.

Tamarkin, Bob. *The New Gatsbys: Fortunes and Misfortunes of Commodity Traders.* New York: William Morrow and Company, 1985.

Teweles, Richard J., Charles V. Harlow, and Herbert L. Stone. *The Commodity Futures Game: Who Wins? Who Loses? Why?* New York: McGraw-Hill, 1974.

Thomas, Dana L. *The Plungers and the Peacocks.* New York: William Morrow and Company, 1989.

Train, John. *The Money Masters.* New York: Penguin Books, 1980.

Van Peebles, Melvin. *Bold Money: A New Way to Play the Options Market.* New York: Warner Books, 1986.

Walmsley, Julian. *The Foreign Exchange Handbook: A User's Guide.* New York: John Wiley & Sons, 1983.

Wilder, J. Welles, Jr. *New Concepts in Technical Trading Systems.* McLeansville, N.C.: Trend Research, 1978.

INDEX

Also available from BUSINESS ONE IRWIN . . .

TECHNICAL TRADERS GUIDE TO COMPUTER ANALYSIS OF THE FUTURES MARKET
Charles LeBeau and David W. Lucas

Here's everything you need to develop and test profitable futures trading systems. A hands-on, how-to book from page one, this step-by-step guide shows you how to create your own personalized trading system so you can detect if something has gone wrong *before* major losses occur.
(223 pages, 8 1/2 x 11)
ISBN: 1-55623-468-6

THE HANDBOOK OF ECONOMIC CYCLES
Jake Bernstein's Comprehensive Guide to Repetitive Price Patterns in Stocks, Futures, and Financials
Jake Bernstein

Discover how to uncover lucrative seasonal trends in virtually all stock and commodity markets as well as the overall economy. This veritable "catalog of cycles" gives you 150 charts and graphs you can use to improve your trading strategy. (304 pages, 8 1/2 x 11)
ISBN: 1-55623-294-2

CLASSICS I AND II
An Investor's Anthology and Another Investor's Anthology
Edited by Charles D. Ellis with James R. Vertin

The definitive writing on investment practice and theory from the industry's leading thinkers. You'll find answers to all of your investment challenges, market movements, and business in general from professionals including: Babson; Buffet; Graham; Price, Jr.; Samuelson; and many others. (759 and 480 pages respectively)
ISBN: Classics I 1-55623-098-2
Classics II 1-55623-358-2